Arabic Culture and Society

Edited by Hazza Abu Rabia and Maha Darawsha

Central Connecticut State University

cognella®
academic publishing

Bassim Hamadeh, CEO and Publisher
Michael Simpson, Vice President of Acquisitions
Jamie Giganti, Managing Editor
Jess Busch, Senior Graphic Designer
John Remington, Acquisitions Editor
Brian Fahey, Licensing Associate

Copyright © 2014 by Cognella, Inc. All rights reserved. No part of this publication may be reprinted, reproduced, transmitted, or utilized in any form or by any electronic, mechanical, or other means, now known or hereafter invented, including photocopying, microfilming, and recording, or in any information retrieval system without the written permission of Cognella, Inc.

First published in the United States of America in 2014 by Cognella, Inc.

Trademark Notice: Product or corporate names may be trademarks or registered trademarks, and are used only for identification and explanation without intent to infringe.

Cover image: Copyright © 2012 by Depositphotos / Anna Omelchenko

Printed in the United States of America

ISBN: 978-1-62661-099-6 (pbk) / 978-1-62661-100-9 (br)

www.cognella.com   800-200-3908

Contents

Part I

Early Islam in the Arab World

1

Arabia Before Islam

by Abdul Hameed Siddiqui

T he following is an excerpt from Abdul Hameed Siddiqui's book, *The Life of Muhammad* (peace and blessings be upon him).

Physical Features of Arabia

Between the Red Sea and the Persian Gulf lies a continent, arid and well nigh waterless, save where an occasional flood lends to the scene the freshness and charm of an oasis. Most of it is an uninviting place, unfriendly too, from the physical point of view. For miles around there appears to be no end to barren hills, no end to the glittering, blazing desert; no respite from the fiery heat except for the few green places which abound in palm and water and provide rest to the wandering tribes of the Arabs. The streams are few and seldom reach the sea. Most of them come to existence only when swelled by occasional rains and disappear in the sandy plains.

The peninsula was divided by the ancient geographers into "Arabia Petraea," "Arabia Felix," and "Arabia Dersta." "Arabia Petraea" corresponded to the present Hijaz and eastern part of Najd; "Arabia Felix" to Yemen and Hadramaut, and "Arabia Deserta" comprised the rest of the country. In the north lies the hilly

Abdul Hameed Siddiqui, "Arabia Before Islam," *The Life of Muhammad*, pp. 1–38. Copyright © 1999 by Islamic Publications (Pvt.) Ltd. Reprinted with permission.

tract, once inhabited by the Edomites and Midianites of the Hebrew Testament. Then comes Hijaz proper which extends along the Red Sea between Syria in the north and Yemen in the south. In this part are situated the famous cities of Mecca, Medina and Jeddah and is traversed by hills extending from the isthmus of Suez to the Indian Ocean.

There were but a few points at which, in ancient times, Arabia touched the outer world. The northern region, stretching from Syria to Euphrates, was occupied, in the second century, by some of those tribes which had, according to native tradition, about that time immigrated from the south and of whom we frequently hear in the later annals of the Roman Empire. To the west, in the Syrian Desert with their capital at Palmyra, was the dynasty of the Ghassanides; and to the east on the banks of the Euphrates, the kingdom of Hira: the former, as a rule, adhered to the Roman, the latter to the Persian Empire.[1]

The ancient records of Arab history eloquently speak of the fact that it was but the farther outskirts of the peninsula which came into contact with the civilized world. "The rest of Arabia was absolutely unknown; and, excepting through the medium of countrymen engaged in merchandise, or settled on the confines of Syria, the Arabs themselves had but little knowledge of anything beyond their own deserts."[2]

Within the bounds of the country, the city of Mecca occupied a prominent position. It was but a small town, nestling in a plain amid arid, volcanic rocks, some fifty miles away from the shores of the Red Sea, from which the ground rises gradually towards the great table land of inner Arabia. As a commercial center and as a sanctuary of great holiness, the Ka'bah attracted innumerable people from all parts of Arabia every year.

The control of the Ka'bah had been the chief object of ambition for the Arab tribes on account of the great influence its directors exercised over the whole of Arabia. There had been, therefore, constant struggle to secure the eminent position of the custodianship of the "House of Allah".

As far as history reveals, we find that the Ishmaelites remained the guardians of the Ka'bah for a long time. Afterwards it passed on to the Jurhamites and then to the Amalekites. Later on, the Ishmaelites and the Jurhamites united their forces to expel the common foe, i.e., the Amalekites, from Mecca and having succeeded in doing so; the Jurhamites finally became the guardians of the Ka'bah.

Banu Bakr and Banu Khuza'ah envied this privilege of the guardianship of Ka'bah and united their forces and fought against the Jurhamites, dispossessing them of the charge of the Ka'bah and taking its control in their own hands. After this Qusayy conspired with Bani Kin'anah, defeated Banu Bakr and Banu Khuza'ah and established their own authority over Mecca and the Ka'bah.

Thus the control of the Ka'bah and Mecca was restored to the Qurayshites after the lapse of about four hundred years.

Next, the guardianship of the Ka'bah passed first to 'Abd al-Dar and then to his sons and grandsons. To cite Muir:

The house of 'Abd al-Dar originally possessed all the public offices; but in the struggle with Hashim they were stripped of several important dignities, their influence had departed, and they were now fallen into a subordinate and insignificant position. The offices retained by them were still, undoubtedly, valuable; but divided among separate members of the family, the benefit of combination was lost; and there was not steady and united effort to improve their advantages towards the acquisition of social influence and political power. The virtual lordship of Mecca, on the other hand, was now with the descendants of 'Abd Menaf. Among these, again, two parties had arisen—the families, namely, of his sons Hashim and 'Abd Shams. The grand offices of giving food and water to the pilgrims secured to the house of Hashim, a commanding and permanent influence under the able management of Muttalib, and now of 'Abd al-Muttalib who, like his father Hashim, was regarded as the chief of the Sheikhs of Mecca.[3]

Thus at the time of Muhammad's birth this honour was enjoyed by his family, and his grandfather was the venerable chief of the theocratic commonwealth which was constituted round the Ka'bah. According to P. De Lacy Johnstone:

> Medina, according to Arab tradition, was originally settled by the Amalekites, but these gave way in very early time to Jewish invaders, driven from their own land (probably) by the national disasters wrought by Nebuchadnezzar and later conquerors. Prominent among them were the Nazir, Quraiza, and Qainuqaa tribes. About 300 A.D., the Aus and Khazraj tribes, of Azdite stock, struck back south from their kindred in Ghassan, and at first lived on good terms with Jews who had hospitably welcomed them. But when they grew in numbers and felt their power, they, about the end of the fifth century, rose against their Jewish partners, in the Government, massacred the chiefs, seized the best of their lands, and reduced the tribes to subjection. The treachery and massacre was avenged by Abu Karib, a prince, who slew the leaders, and devastated the cultivated lands, but had then to retire. Thereafter followed twenty years of strife between the rival clans; a truce for half a century, then renewed war, ending after a terrible battle at Buath in 616 A.D. (where the strength of Jews divided between the contending tribes, and desert allies joined in the fray) in triumph of the Khazraj, whose chief, Abdullah ibn Ubai, was about to be raised to the kingship of Medina, when the exile from Mecca changed the fortunes of the city.[4]

Before the recent gush of oil and the gold that it has brought, the Arabs were living a life of extreme poverty. Their soil was poor; and constant tilling enabled them to wring only a precarious subsistence. They earned their livelihood either by rearing camels, horses, cattle, and sheep, pitching their tents within certain limits, where water and pasturage were most abundant, or they were engaged in the transport of merchandise along the trading routes through the desert.

Notes

1. William Muir, *The Life of Muhammad*, (1912) p. lxxx.
2. Ibid., p. xciii.
3. William Muir, op. cit., p. ciii.
4. P. De Lacy Johnstone, *Muhammad and His Power* (New York 1901), pp. 35, 36.

The Arab Character

They were no doubt poor, yet they took life lightheartedly. They were in fact free from all the inner tensions and stresses which are so peculiar to our times. Men of strong passions were they, fiery of temper, ardent in love and bitter in hate, delighting in war, in the chase, and the banquet, not sparing the wine-cup at the feast, but of unmatched forbearance for cold, thirst and hunger when need arose. They were generous in their tongues, and eloquent in their utterances. They could be easily touched by every form of poetry, in praise of themselves, their kindred and their friends, or bitter shafts of blame and satire against their foes.

Writing, of course, there was little or none; the literature of the desert was preserved 'living on the lips of men and graven on the tablets of their hearts'; the perfect warrior was also the famous poet, and the name of many a poetess adorns the Arab bead-roll of glory:

The staple of their poetry is, however, largely a description of the joys of battle, the struggle for mastery, and the perils of the long, dark journeyings through the waste; the noble horse and camel, the keen flashing sword in the battle, the deadly lance and arrow; the swift, sudden storms that sweep over mountain and plain, driving the goats and wild antelopes in panic fear to their fastness, while the lightning flashes and thunder roars, and the rain-torrents hurry down the stony watercourses—these are the themes of their songs. And prefaced to nearly every one of t longer poems is a wail of lament over the ashes of a long-deserted encampment, once the home of a beloved maiden, a tearful note of human sorrow to attune the heart of softened melancholy. One type, one theme, is strangely absent from it all,—the devotional. Praise or prayer is seldom heard, though wild and terrible oaths are not wanting. The old Arab was, above all things, self-centered, self-reliant, confident that the cunning of his own strong right hand could conquer fate. His worship did not greatly pervade his life or his thoughts. The warrior would take the arrows of divination, but if the answer squared not with this desire, he could hurl them back wrathfully and scornfully in the face of his idol.[1]

We reproduce here some of the snatches of songs which would give a very clear idea to the readers about the sensuous delight of the Arab, his pleasures and pains, and his metaphysical beliefs:

He is a young boy of charming countenance;
He looks promising and is growing with the perfection of Harith
Age and youth blended together.
They are best of men,
What of their fine great ancestors
They are the best drunkards. [2]
When she flashes across the eyes of old hermit,
He who lies on the peaks of hill,
He too is enchanted by her beauty,
Lends ears to her and comes out of his hut.
Were not a human being, you would
Have been a full moon. [3]

There are innumerable verses of pre-Islamic Arabic poetry which are indicative of the fact that despite love for sensuous pleasures, the Arabs were very brave and had the courage to meet all kinds of situation manfully:

Roast flesh, the glow of fiery wine,
To speed on camel fleet and sure.
As thy soul lists to urge her on
Through all the hollow's breadth and length.
White women, statue-like, that trail
Rich robes of price with golden hem,
Wealth, easy lot, of no dread of ill,

To hear the lutes complaining string,
These are life's joys. For man is set
The prey of Time, and Time is change.
Life strait or large, great store or nought
All's one to time, all men to deaths.[4]

Now follow part of the dirge which a brave chief sang for himself when, before his death, he faced the foes that had overwhelmed him:

Upbraid me not, yet twain: enough is the shame for me,
To be as I am, no gain upbraiding to you or me.
Know ye not that in reproach is little that profits men?
It was not my wont to blame my brother when I was free.
Mulaika, my wife, knows well that time when I stood forth
A lion to lead men or face those that rushed on me.
Yea, many a slaughtered beast I gave to the gamers, oft
I journeyed along where none would venture to share my way;
And of times I slew, to feast fellows, the beast I rode,
And of times I rent my robe in twain for two singing girls.
And when 'neath the stress of spears our steeds plunged and broke and backed,
Yet mine were the fingers deft then turned from our line their steel.
And hosts like the locusts swarm have swept upon me alone,
And my hand it was that stemmed and gathered in one their spears.
Now am I as though I ne'er had mounted a noble steed,
Or called to my horsemen charge! Gain space for our men to breathe,
Or brought for a wealth of gold the full skin of wine or cried
To true hearts at play-Heap high the blaze at our beacon fire![5]

These verses which have been taken from Hamasah, speak eloquently of the ideal of Arab virtue which can be expressed in terms of muruwwah, (manliness) and ird (honour). "It is not mere chance," observes Reynold A. Nicholson, "that Abu Tammam's famous anthology is called the Hamasah, i.e., 'Fortitude', from the famous anthology is caleed the Hamasah, i.e., 'Fortitude', from the title of its first chapter, which occupies nearly half the book. Hamasah denote the virtues most highly prized by the Arabs—bravery in battle, patience in misfortune, persistence in revenge, protection of the weak and defiance of the strong; the will, as Tennyson has said, "To strive, to seek, to find, and not to yield".

As types of the ideal Arab hero we may take Shanfara of Azd and his comrade in foray, Ta'abbata Sharr. Both were brigands, outlaws, swift runners, and excellent poets:

Of the former it is said that he was captured when a child from his tribe by the Banu Salaman, and brought up among them; he did not learn his origin until he had grown up, when he vowed vengeance against his captors, and returned to his own tribe. His oath was that he would slay a hundred men of Salaman; he slew ninety-eight, when an ambush of his enemies succeeded in taking him prisoner. In the struggle one of his hands was hewn off by a sword stroke, and, taking it in the other, he flung it in the face of a man of Salaman and killed him, thus making ninety-nine. Then he was overpowered and slain, with one still wanting to make, up his number. As his skull lay bleaching on the ground, a man of enemies passed by that way and kicked it with his foot; a splinter of bone entered his foot, the wound mortified, and he died, thus completing the hundred.[6]

The following passage is translated from Shanfara's splendid ode named Lamiyyatu'l Arab in which he describes his own heroic character and the hardships of a predatory life:

And somewhere the noble find a refuge afar from scathe,
The outlaw a lonely spot where no kin with hatred burn.
Oh, never a prudent man, night-faring in hope or fear,
Hard pressed on the face of earth, but still he had room to turn.
To me now, in your default, are comrades a wolf untired,
A sleek leopard, and a fell hyena with shaggy mane:
True, comrades: they ne'er let out the secret in trust with them,
Nor basely foresake their friend because that he brought them bane![7]

The Arabs were also fully conscious of the blessings of unity and they always exhorted their clans to stand together:

Woe be upon you that you are scattered
Whereas the others are united.
The princes of Persia rally together to attack you
They care not the defence of forts,
They are marching upon you armed to the teeth.
They will inflict disgrace upon you,
Gird up your loins and fall upon them.
The one who can stun others finds safety
Select your chief one who is courageous and brave
Who is not indulgent and can admirably stand the
Onslaughts of hardships
One who is experienced
Who knows how to serve and be served
Strong and formidable
Mature of age, neither old nor weak.[8]

These verses describe the rudiments of Arabian virtues of courage, hardness and strength. "Arab courage is like that of the ancient Greeks, dependent upon excitement and vanishing quickly before depression and delay."[9] Hence the Arab hero is defiant and boastful, as he appears, e.g., in the Mu'allaqa of 'Amr b. Kulthum.[10]

A study of the poetry of the pre-Islamic Arabs will reveal that the Arabs were generally cheerful; but whenever they thought of old age, their cheerfulness at once gave place to despondency. An old poet, Harith B. Ka'b, while lamenting over his youth, sings the dirge:

I consumed my youth bit by bit and it was no more:
I wasted hundreds of months

I have seen with my eyes the passing of three generations.
They were gone; gone for ever
Alas, I have grown old, one:
Who can neither eat to his heart's content
Nor walk easily; a victim to the helplessness,
I spend my sleepless night in counting starts,[11]
Nabighah also sings with great pathos:
The man longs to live longer,
But the long life is painful for him;
He is deprived of the cheerfulness of his countenance,
And the cup of life is filled with grief,
The age betrays him terribly
And he finds little joy in life.[12]

Generosity and hospitality were also greatly cherished in the desert and are still prominent virtues of the Arab. A large heap of ashes and bones outside the tent was a mark of high excellence in a chief, for it meant that he had entertained many guests. "The Bedouin ideal of generosity and hospitality is personified in Hatim of Tay of whom many anecdotes are told."[13]

Hatim was himself a poet. The following lines are addressed to Muawiyah, his wife:

O, daughter of 'Abdullah and Malik and him who wore
The two robes of Yemen stuff—the hero that rode the roan.
When thou has prepared two meals, entreat to partake thereof.
A guest—I am not the man to eat, like a churl, alone:
Some traveller; thro' the night, or house-neighbour for in sooth.
I fear the reproachful talk of men after I a am gone.
The guests' slave am I, 'tis true, as long as he bides with me,
Although in my nature also no trait of the slave is shown.[14]
The Arab's generosity consists in ungrudging assistance to people who seek it:
He is generous and gives unhesitatingly
And bears all the oppressions boldly.[15]
This generosity was shown not only to the human beings, but even the animals and the beasts:
I traversed many a valley on the camel-back
Valleys where even the bravest would die,
There we heard the voices of the owl
As the bells rang in the darkness of night,
There emerge before us the tops of the hills
Near our hearth there came a wolf;
I threw bone at him and I showed no niggardliness to my companion;
The wolf turned back moving its joyful head
And looked to be a brave warrior coming back
Proudly with his booty.[16]

Another aspect of the Arab's life which deserves mention is the Bedouin's deep-rooted emotional attachment to his clan. Family, or perhaps tribal pride, was one of the strongest passions with him.

"All the virtues," remarks Professor Nicholson, "which enter into the Arabian conception of honour were regarded not as personal qualities inherent or acquired, but as hereditary possessions which a man derived from his ancestors, and held in trust that he might transmit them untarnished to his descendants. It is the desire to uphold and emulate the fame of his forbears rather than the hope of winning immortality for himself, that causes the Arab 'to say the say and do the deeds of the noble.' ... Ancestral renown (*hasab*) is sometimes likened to a strong castle built by sires for their sons, or to a lofty mountain which defies attack. The poets are full of boasting (*mafakhir*) and revilings (*mathalib*) in which they loudly proclaim the nobility of their own ancestors, and try to blacken those of their enemy without any regard to decorum."[17]

The doctrine of unity of blood as the principle that bound Arabs into a social unity was formed under a system of mother kinship, "the introduction of male-kinship was a kind of social revolution which modified society to its very roots."[18]

"Previously house and children belonged to the mothers; succession was through mothers and the husband came to wife, not the wife to the husband."[19] Whatever might have been the nature of kinship, one thing emerges clearly that kinship among the Arabs means a share in the common blood which is taken to flow in the veins of every member of a tribe, in one word, it was the tribal bond which knit men of the same group together and gave them common duties and responsibilities from which no member of the group could withdraw. This bond was a source of great pride for them.

The tribal constitution was a democracy guided by its chief men, who derived their authority from noble blood, noble character, wealth, wisdom, and experience. As a Bedouin poet has said in a homely language:

A folk that hath no chiefs must soon decay,
And chiefs it hath not when the vulgar sway.
Only with poles the tent is reared at last,
And poles it hath not save the pegs hold fast.
But when the pegs and poles are once combined,
Then stands accomplished that which was designed.[20]

The enthusiasm with which the tribes' men have been urged to stand united and elect as their leader one who is wise, sagacious and brave, can be seen from the following verses:

Nothing can be achieved without the leader,
The leadership of the ignorant is not leadership,
The maters are set aright by the consent of the wise men.
Or fall in the hands of mischief-mongers.[21]

An Arab was no doubt wedded to his tribe and was deeply attached to his leaders but was not prepared to give up his individuality and follow them blindly. Every many ruled himself, and was free to rebuke presumption in others. If you are our Lord (i.e., if you act discreetly as Sayyid should) you will lord over us, but if you are prey to pride, go and be proud (i.e., we will have nothing to do with you).

The tribal solidarity was sometimes extended to a kind of confederacy amongst the various tribes. This alliance of the tribes was "brought through either *hilf* (confederacy, mutual oaths) or *jiwar* (the formal granting of protection). For many purposes the *hilf* and the jiwar, the 'confederates' and the 'client' were treated as members of the tribe in order to maintain it in existence.

While the tribe or confederation of tribes was the highest political unit, there was also a realization of the fact that the Arabs were in some sense a unity. This unity was based on common language (though with variation of dialect), a common poetical tradition, some common conventions and ideas, and a common descent. Language was possibly the original basis of the distinction between Arabs and 'foreigners'—'Arab' and 'Ajam'.[22]

The Arabs had a keen sense of their being distinct from the other peoples and showing their superiority to them but there is not gainsaying the fact that it was the tribal solidarity which formed the bedrock of their unity and governed the actions of the best people. One should not, however, lose sight of the fact that even this solidarity was never absolute. An Arab is an individualist to the marrow of his bone and never accepts the position of an automaton which could work ungrudgingly at the gesture of his master.

Loyalty and fidelity were also the important virtues [of the Arabs]. Ideally a man ought to be ready to spring to the aid of a fellow tribesman whenever he called for help; he should act at once without waiting to inquire into the merits of the case.[23]

If the Arab was, as we have seen, faithful to his tribe and its leader and was prepared to risk his all for the sake of its honour, 'he had in the same degree an intense and deadly feeling of hatred towards his enemies. He who did not strike back, when struck, was regarded as a coward.'[24]

Humble him who humbles thee, close tho' be your kindredship;
If thou canst not humble him, wait till he is in thy grip.
Friend him while thou must; strike hard when thou hast
Him on the hip.[25]

The obligation of revenge lay heavy on the conscience of the pagan Arabs:

Vengeance, with them, was almost a physical necessity, which if it be not obeyed, will deprive its subject of sleep, of appetite, of health. It was a tormenting thirst which nothing could quench except blood, a disease of honour which might be described as madness, although it rarely prevented the sufferer from going to work with coolness and circumspection.[26]

The were in fact obliged to exercise their arms frequently, by reason of independence of their tribes, whose frequent jarrings made wars almost continued; and they chiefly ended their disputes with the help of the sword.

"The whole law of the old Arabs really resolves itself into a law of war—blood-feud, blood-wit and booty are the points on which everything turns."[27] The true Arab feeling is expressed in verses like these:

With the sword will I wash my shame away,
Let God's doom bring on me what it may.[28]

We may sum up the Arab character by saying that the pagan Arab "is a cynical materialist with a keenly logical outlook, a strong sense of his own dignity, and a consuming avarice. His mind has no room for romance, still less for sentiment; he has very little inclination for religion and takes but slight heed of anything which cannot be measured in practical values. His sense of personal dignity cannot be measured in practical values. His sense of personal dignity is so strong that he is naturally in revolt against every form of authority. On the other hand he is loyal and obedient to the ancient traditions of his tribe; the duties of hospitality, alliance in war, of friendship, and such like, are faithfully performed on the lines of recognized precedent, he keeps punctiliously the letter of the law, that is to say, of the unwritten law of his own tribal custom, but owns no obligation outside the strict letter."[29]

The Arabs had developed no great art of their own except eloquence and perfect skill in their own tongue. "If the Greek gloried primarily in his statues and architecture, the Arabian found in his ode (*qasidah*) and the Hebrew in his psalm, a finer mode of self-expression. The beauty of man, declares and Arabic adage, 'lies in the eloquence of his tongue.'

"Wisdom," in a late saying, "has alighted on three things: the brains of the Franks, the hands of the Chinese and the tongue of the Arabs. Eloquence, i.e., ability to express oneself forcefully and elegantly in both prose and poetry, together with archery and horsemanship were considered in the Jahileyah period the basic attributes of the perfect man (al-Kamil).[30] Their orations were of two sorts, metrical and prosaic, the one being compared to pearls strung, and the other to loose ones.

Poetry was esteemed more than prose. It was indeed a great accomplishment with them, and a proof of ingenious extraction, to be able to express themselves in verse with ease, and elegance on any extraordinary occurrence; and even in their common discourse they made frequent applications to celebrated passages of their famous poets. In their poems were preserved the distinction of descendants, the rights of tribes, and their achievements, the memory of great actions, and the propriety of their language.

Notes

1. P. De Lacy Johnstone, *Muhammad and his Power* (New York 1901), pp. 35, 36.

2. Ibn Qutaybah, al-Shi'r wa'al-Shu'ara', ed. Ahmad Muhammad Shakir, Cairo (1367 H). Vol. 1, p. 109.

3. Ibid., p. 114.

4. Charles James Lyall, Translations from *Ancient Arabian Poetry*, (Edinburgh 1885), p. 64.

5. Charles James Lyall, op. ct., p. 64.

6. *A Literary History of the Arabs* (Cambridge 1933), p. 79.

7. Reynold A. Nicholson, op cit, pp. 79–80. English translation of the *Lamiyya* by G. Hughes (London 1896), quoted in ibid., p. 80.

8. Ibn Qutaybah, op. cit., pp., 153–154.

9. Mahaffy: *Social Life in Greece*, quoted by Nicholson, op.cit., p. 82.

10. Nicholson, Ibid., p. 52.

11. Ibn Qutaybah, p. 52.

12. Ibid., p. 111.

13. Nicholson, op. cit., p. 85.

14. Hamasah, 729, quoted ibid, p. 87.

15. Ibn Qutaybah, p. 84.

16. Ibid., p. 164.

17. Nicholson, op. cit., p. 100.

18. W. Robertson Smith, *Kinship and Marriage in Early Arabia*, (2nd Edition London 1903), p. 182.

19. Ibid., p. 172.

20. Nicholson, op. cit., p. 83.

21. Ibn Qutaybah, p. 145.

22. W. Montgomery Watt, *Muhammad At Mecca* (Oxford 1960), pp. 17–18.

23. W. Montgomery Watt, op. cit., p. 21.

24. Nicholson, op. cit., p. 92.

25. Hamasah, p. 321 quoted by Nicholson, op. cit., p. 93.

26. Nicholson, op. cit., p. 93.

27. W. Robertson Smith, *Kinship and Marriage in Early Arabia*, p. 55.

28. Hamasah, quoted by Prof. Nicholson, op. cit., p. 93.

29. De Lacy O'Leary, *Arabia Before Muhammad*, pp. 20–21.

30. Philip K. Hitti, *History of Arabs*, pp. 90–91.

Social Life of the Arabs

To keep up an emulation among their poets, the tribes of Arabia held once a year, a general assembly, at 'Ukaz a place between Nakhlah and Ta'if. This fair, however, revived the scenes of Rome's greatest glory in gaiety and licentiousness. Warriors of all tribes, sworn blood enemies for generations, sat in open-air cafes and taverns. Wine goblets were filled and emptied with alarming rapidity. Amidst this merrymaking the poets recited their poetical compositions, contending and vying with each other for the coveted first honour. A poet made a name for himself here or nowhere.

Drinking had in fact become a second nature with the Arabs. Wine and woman go together, and as a result of licentious drinking, fornication was very rampant. The caravans which radiated from Mecca with native merchandise to the Byzantine Empire, Syria, Persia, and India, returned therefrom with all luxurious habits and vices and imported slave girls from Syria and Iraq who afforded vast opportunities of sensual pleasures to the rich with their dancing and singing and all corruption which usually goes with them. We reproduce below some of the verses which would give an idea of the immoral life which the Arabs of pre-Islamic period were habituated to lead:

> Either evening or morning will bid farewell,
> To thee, so do thou resolve to what state thou wilt resort.
> Verily the engagement with fondling woman from under the curtain
> (having) lovely eye (with) languor in it —
> who are profusely anointed with musk[1] and whom fine apparel, easy
> life and silk (garments) lend charms, like the marble statues in the
> niches or like the egg (ostrich) in the garden whose flowers are
> blooming —
> Does not become thee now and thou hast grown sober-minded and
> The sign of hoariness has appeared in thy temple.
> Turning white of the black (hair) is amongst the warnings of Evil[2]
> And is there, after it, any warning for the living?[3]

This relish for sensual pleasures had made the Arabs profligate voluptuaries. The members of the tribe, including male and female, young and old often met together in order to enjoy drinking, dancing and gambling. Those who shunned such evil practices were considered mean, stingy and unsociable:

> And when I die, marry not one who is humble, weak or who does

Not gamble, and avoids people.

This is the will left by a husband to his widow. A poet of that time describes the pleasures of these parties:

So, come, let us greet our band of drinkers aglow with wine
And wash from our hearts sour speech of wisdom with cups abrim
And cut short the ills of life with laughter and joy![4]

The old Arab poetry has so many tales to narrate of the drinking orgies of the people of Arabia before the advent of Islam. Their parties were in fact wine-bubbling springs converted into a sort of gambling-den. The Arab found solace in wine and felt proud on drinking it:

Sometime in wine was my solace. Good wine I drank of it,
Suaging the heat of the evening paying in white money
Quaffing in goblets of saffron, pale-streaked with ivory
Hard at my hand their companion, the flask to the left of me.
Truly this bidding squandered half my inheritance;
Yet was my honour a wide word. No man had wounded it.[5]

Decency and modesty had been swept away from the society by these drinking revelries, so common and so frequent, and by the absence of any social discipline; the heathen Arabs had little regard for the sanctity of matrimonial relations. They took pride in flouting them and describing publicly their adulterous adventures. Imra al-Qays, for instance, brazenly states:

Many a fair one like thee, though not like thee virgin,
Have I visited by night,
And many a lovely mother have I diverted from the care of her
Yearning in fact adorned with amulets,
When the suckling behind her cried
She turned round to him with half her body,
But half of it, pressed beneath my embrace, was not turned from me.[6]

There was in fact no notion of conjugal fidelity among most of the Arab tribes. "In old Arabia, the husband was so indifferent to his wife's fidelity, that he might send her to cohabit with another man to get himself a goodly seed.[7] There was no stain of illegitimacy attached to the child of a harlot.

The custom of polyandry, *i.e.*, a custom of marriage under which a woman receives more than one man as her husband was very common in Arabia. The oldest and most direct evidence is that of Strabo which throws a good deal of light on the family life of the pagan Arabs:[8]

Brothers have precedence over children, the kinship also and other offices of authority are filled by members of the stock in order of seniority. All the kindred have their property in common, the eldest being lord; all have one wife and it is first come first served, the man who enters to her leaving at the door the stick which it is usual for everyone to carry; but the night she spends with the eldest. Hence all are brothers of all (within the stock) they have also conjugal intercourse with mothers; and adulterer is punished with death; and adulterer means a man of another stock. [9]

Under such conditions when a woman is considered to be the property of the whole tribe and she has no right to withhold her favours from any of the kinsfolk, "the idea of unchastity could not exist; their children were all full tribesmen, because the mother was a tribeswoman, and there was no distinction between legitimate and illegitimate offspring in our sense of the word."[10] Individual fatherhood is a comparatively modern notion which is fully defined and enunciated by Islam. The pagan Arabs "were in fact reckoned to the stock of their mother's lords before they were one man's children."[11]

Social life in Arabia is paradoxical and presents a gloomy picture of striking contrast. The Arabs, on the one hand, were generous and hospitable even to the point of fault, and took pride in entertaining liberally not only human beings, but also animals and beasts. On the other hand, the impending fear of poverty weighed so heavily upon them that they buried their female children alive, lest they should be impoverished by providing for them. In the same way, they had, on the one hand, little or no regard for chastity and would proudly narrate obscene accounts of their immoral exploits. On the other hand there had sprung up in them an utterly false sense of honour that impelled them to the practice of female infanticide, the underlying idea being that womenfolk, particularly daughters, were objects of disgrace.

The famous commentator Zamakhshari in his note on Sura Al-Takwir, verse 8, gives an account of how female infants were buried alive in the graves:

When the girl attained the age of six, the husband said to the wife: 'perfume her and embellish her with ornaments.' He would then carry the female babe to the relatives of his wife and set forth to the wilderness. There a pit was dug. The child was made to stand by it. The father said, 'Fix your eyes on it' and then pushed her from behind so that she fell in the pit where the unfortunate soul wept bitterly in a state of utter helplessness. The ditch was covered with clay and then levelled to the ground.[12]

It was said proverbially, "The despatch of a daughter is a kindness," and "the burial of the daughters is a noble deed."[13] Perhaps the most touching lines in Arabian poetry are those in which a father, oppressed by the thoughts of poverty and disgrace, wishes that his daughter may die before his very eyes and thus spared the pangs of hunger and indignation:

> But for Umayma's sake I ne'er had grieved to want nor braved
> Night's blackest horror to bring home the morsel that she carved,
> Nor my desire is length of days because I know too well
> The orphan girl's hard lot, with kin unkind enforced to dwell,
> I dread that some day poverty will overtake my child,
> And shame befall her when exposed to every passion wild,
> She wishes me to live, but I must wish her dead, woe, me;
> Death is the noblest wooer a helpless maid can see,
> I fear an uncle may be harsh, a brother be unkind
> When I would never speak a word that rankled in her mind.[14]

As to the extent to which child murder was practised as late as the time of the Prophet, we have some evidence in the fact that Sa'sa'a claimed to have saved a hundred and eight daughters.[15]

It is recorded that when Muhammad (peace be upon him) conquered Mecca and received the homage of the women in the most advanced centre of Arabian civilization, he still deemed it necessary formally to demand from them a promise not to commit child murder.[16]

It was due to the teachings of Islam that this custom of female infanticide, so prevalent amongst the Arabs and so many other nations of the world, came to an end. Mark with what force the Qur'an condemns this inhuman practice:

Surely lost are they who slay their offspring foolishly and without knowledge and have forbidden that which Allah had provided for them; a fabrication against Allah. Surely they have strayed and have not become guided ones. (6:141)

And slay not your offspring for fear of want. We it is Who provide for you and them. (6:152)

And slay not your offspring for fear of want. We provide for them and for yourselves. Verily their slaying is a great crime. (17:33)

And when the girl buried alive shall be asked for what sin she was slain. (81:8)

The weaker sex was in fact an unwelcome figure for the Arabs. The news of the birth of a daughter was received with a terrible shock in the family and the whole clan was rocked with anger. The Holy Qur'an has in its own eloquent style drawn a vivid picture of this sad event:

They attribute daughters unto God—far be it from Him! And for themselves they desire them not. When a female child is announced to one of them, his face darkens wrathfully with shame; he hides himself from his people, because of the bad news he has had! Shall he retain it on (sufferance and contempt) or bury it in the dust? And what an evil (choice) they decided on. (16:59–61)

Not only were the female infants buried alive, but those who were spared led a life of unspeakable misery and wretchedness. They were a sort of marketable commodity which could be sold in the open market to the highest bidder. At the time they were transferred to the custody of the husband their position was still worsened. Marriage for them was a kind of bondage and the marital rights of the husband were a kind of overlordship, and he was free to treat and dispose of his property as he liked. There is a very instructive passage as to the position of married women, which commences by quoting two lines spoken by a woman of the Banu Amir ibn Sa'sa'a married among the Tay:

Never let sister praise brothers of hers; never let daughter
Bewail a father's death,
For they have brought her where she is no longer a free woman
And they have banished her to the farthest ends of the earth.

The contract of marriage entitled the husband to a certain property right which was absolutely his to enjoy, or to transfer at his will. Indeed this right could even be inherited by his heir. It is recorded that in pagan Arabia, widows were inherited by the heirs of the deceased as goods and chattels. It was generally the eldest son who had the strongest claim to lay upon them. But in the cases, where there were no sons, the widows were passed on to the brother of the deceased or to his nephews.[17] Sometime a sheet of cloth was cast on them in order to secure their property rights.[18] The heirs in such cases either took them as their own wives or married them to the other people by getting a good price for them or kept them in confinement unless they redeemed themselves by paying off handsomely. It is this evil practice which has been condemned in the Holy Qur'an in the following verse:

O ye who believe. It is not allowed unto you that ye may heir the woman forcibly.[19] (iv: 19)

Females were allowed no share in the inheritance of their husbands, parents and other relatives. "So far as the widow of the deceased is concerned, this is almost self-evident; she could not inherit because she was herself not indeed absolutely, but qua wife, part of her husband's estate, whose freedom and hand were at the disposal of the heirs".

There was no check on the number of wives that a man could take. One could marry as many women as he liked and dismiss them according to his own sweet will. No restriction was imposed upon man's lust. The pregnant woman was turned out of her husband's house without any claim and was taken by others under agreement with her former husband.

Notes

1. It was apparently considered a sign of luxury that ointments were applied in excess.
2. viz., death
3. Abi B. Zaid al-Ibadi (480 A.D.), *Early Arabic Odes* by Dr. S.M. Husain (Dacca) 1938, pp. 172–73.
4. Charles James Lyall, op. cit., p. 72.
5. *The Seven Golden Odes of Pagan Arabia*, translated by Anne Blunt (London MDCCIII).
6. Diwan Imr- al-Qays edited by Muhammad Abul Fazl Ibrahim, (Cairo, 1958), p. 12.
7. W. Robertson Smith, op. cit., p. 116.
8. Ibid., p. 128.
9. Quoted by W. Robertson Smith, op. cit., p. 133.
10. Ibid., pp. 139–40.
11. W. Robertson Smith, op. cit., p. 147.
12. *Al-Kashshaf*, Ed., Mustafa Hussain Ahmad, Cairo, iv. p. 708.
13. Freytag, *Arabum Proverbia*. Vol. 1 p. 229, quoted by Prof. Nicholson, in his *A Literary History of the Arabs*, p. 91
14. *Hamasah*, p. 150: Prof. Nicholson writes: Although these verses are not pre-Islamic and belong in fact to a comparatively later period of Islam, they are sufficiently pagan in feeling to be cited in this connection (p. 92.).
15. W. Roberston Smith, op. cit., p. 282.
16. Ibn al-Athir (Bulaq ed.), II p. 105.
17. Quoted by Ibn Jarir Tabari in his famous *Tafseer* on the authority of Muhammad b. 'Ammar, edited by Muhammad Shakir and Ahmad Shakir, Cairo, Vol. viii, p. 107.
18. *Ibid*, p. 107.
19. "Forcibly" is a mere statement of fact, not a condition precedent. The parctice of taking widows in heritage was actually carried on against their will. There is no suggestion here that the would become any more the lawful, if the widows submitted to it willingly. (A Commentary of the Holy Qur'an [English] by Maulana 'Abdul Majid Daryabadi, Vol. I p. 152).

Economic Life

On examining closely the literature of *Sirah* and *Hadith* one can form a clear idea of the economic life of pre-Islamic Arabia. It should, however, be borne in mind that while it is convenient to speak of "Arabia", we are mainly concerned only with one region of it—the areas surrounding Mecca and Medina, Hijaz in the wider sense and the adjoining steppe-land of Najd.

The nomads who formed an overwhelming majority of Arab population depended upon stock-breeding, especially the breeding of the camel for their sustenance. Agriculture was practised in the oasis and certain favoured spots high up in the mountains. "The chief crop at the oasis was date, while in the mountains, as at al-Ta'if cereals were important. Yathrib (later known as Medina) was a large and flourishing oasis in the time of Muhammad (peace be upon him). There were several Jewish agricultural colonies such as Khaybar. At Mecca, on the other hand, no agriculture at all was possible. The Yemen or Arabia Felix, was a fertile agricultural country where artificial irrigation had been practised from early times."[1]

Mecca, Muhammad's home for half a century, as we have observed earlier was not fit for agriculture: "The town that had grown up around the well of Zamzam and the sanctuary of Ka'bah, was advantageously placed "at the extreme ends of the Asia of the whites and the Africa of the blacks, near a breach in the chain of the Sana, close to a junction of roads leading from Babylonia and Syria to the plateaus of the Yemen, to the shores of the Indian Ocean and the Red Sea.[2]

To Mecca, therefore, the nomad came for the goods brought from the four points of the compass by caravans. Originally the Meccans themselves were probably only middlemen and retailers and not the importers and entrepreneurs who organised caravans. But by the end of the sixth century A.D. they had gained control of most of the trade from Yemen to Syria—an important route by which the West got Indian luxury goods as well as South Arabian frankincense.[3]

Various charges were levied upon the traders who passed through the route of Mecca; for example, tithes were paid for entering the city, a special tax for securing permits to stay there, and a departure tax while leaving the town. In short, foreign merchants were entangled in a very intricate fiscal system, whether they settled in Mecca, or only passed through it, especially those who did not obtain the *jiwar* or guarantee of a local clan or notability.[4]

Mecca may rightly be called a merchant republic. The financial operations of considerable complexity were carried on in the city. The nobility of Mecca in Muhammad's time besides the religious heads, and Sheikhs of clans, comprised of "financiers, skillful in the manipulation of credit, shrewd in their speculations, and interested in any potentialities of lucrative investment from Aden to Gaza or Damascus. In the financial net that they had woven not merely were all of the inhabitants of Mecca caught, but many notables of the surrounding tribes also. The Quran appeared not in the atmosphere of the desert, but in that of high finance.[5]

The women shared these commercial instincts: Abu Jahl's mother ran a perfumery business. The activities of *tadjjra Khadijah* are well-known. Hinda the wife of Abu Sufyan, sold her merchandise among the Kalbis of Syria.[6]

Riba in all its ugliness formed the backbone of the pre-Islamic financial and economic system. The usual method adopted for lending and then of its repayment was highly exploitative. The money-lenders lent money to the people on heavy rates of interest, and when the money borrowed was not paid at the stipulated time, it was doubled and then trebled at the expiry of the third year. This is how it was enhanced with the passage of time.[7]

In case when the debtor failed to pay loans along with the amounts of interest the creditor sometimes took possession of the borrower's wife and children.

Speculation too was rampant, on the rates of exchange, the load of a caravan which one tried to buy up, the yield of the harvests and of the flocks and lastly the provisioning of the town. Fictitious associations were formed and sales were made on which loans were borrowed.[8]

The other important town, which was commercially the rival of Mecca is known as Ta'if, the capital of an important tribe Thaqif. It had an advantage over Mecca, that, along with its business activities, it had fertile lands. "The surrounding valleys supplied its export trade with ample materials, particularly easy to market in a region so unfavoured by nature as the Hijaz; wine, wheat and wood. Its bracing climate, its fruits, its grapes, the famous Zahib suggested this city to belong to Syria rather than to the bare landscapes of western Arabia.

"Ta'if was also an industrial town and leather was manufactured in its tanneries, which were so numerous, as we are told, as to render the air around foul. At the entrance and exit to the sea of the sands, Ta'if offered the ships of the desert provisions in the varied produce of the soil and loads in the products of its industry.

"There was a kind of *entente cordiale* between Mecca and Ta'if, an entente cemented by matrimonial alliances between Quraysh and Ahlaf. Many Meccans lived in Ta'if and has estates there.[9]

The way in which Median is favoured by nature forms a striking contrast to Mecca. Its noteworthy feature is richness in water unusual in Arabia. The soil is of salty sand, lime and loamy clay and is everywhere fertile, particularly in the South. It was, therefore, called the city of farmers. The people of Medina were highly skilled cultivators and efficient in the methods of transplantation. There is a tradition in the Sahih of al-Bukhari, narrated on the authority of Abu Huraira, which sheds a good deal of light on the occupations of the people of Mecca and Medina during the time of the Holy Prophet. He observes: "My brethren muhajirin (after their migration to Medina) were occupied in buying and selling goods in the market, whereas my brethren Ansar remained busy in cultivation and gardening."[10] The Jews of Medina were, however, interested in trade and industry besides cultivation.

Notes

1. W. Montgomery Watt, *Muhammad at Mecca*, p. 2.
2. *Encyclopeaedia of Islam*, Vol. III, Article "Mecca" (1936).
3. W. Montgomery Watt, op. cit., p. 3.
4. *Encyclopeaedia of Islam*, Vol. III, Article "Mecca" (1936).
5. W. Montgomery Watt, op. cit., p. 4.
6. *Encyclopeaedia of Islam*, Vol. III, Article "Mecca".
7. *Tafsir Tabari*, Vol. IV, p. 55, in connection with *Sura* 3: *A'yat* 130.
8. *Encyclopeaedia of Islam*, Vol. III, Article "Mecca".
9. *Encyclopeaedia of Islam*, Article, "Ta'if".
10. Bukhari, *Kitab al-Muzara'*

Religion of the Pre-Islamic Arabs

No history of pre-Islamic Arabia would be complete without an account of the religion of the Arabs. Unfortunately the material which we possess does not enable us to form a complete and vivid picture of the religion of the ancient Arabs. Whatever we know about it comes to us through isolated statements of Greek writers and from Greek or Semitic inscriptions, poetical compilations of the old poets, the few anecdotes and traditions embedded in the later Islamic literature. Some information may also be gathered from polemical allusions in the Qur'an. Much credit goes to a few early Muslim scholars who laboriously collected and handed down to posterity, in a systematic form, information on heathen mythology and ritual. Among these scholars a specially prominent place must be assigned to Hisham al-Kalbi, usually known as Ibn al-Kalbi (819–920 C.E.), the author of Kitab al-Asnam (The Book of Idols).

Judged by the scanty evidence available, it suffices to show that Muhammad's (may the peace of Allah be upon him) contemporaries and the generations immediately preceding them, had little of any religion.

To spiritual impulses he (the pagan Arab) was lukewarm, even indifferent. His conformity to religious practice followed tribal inertia and was dictated by his conservative respect for tradition. Nowhere do we find an illustration of genuine devotion to a heathen deity. A story told about Imru 'al-Qays illustrates this point. Having set out to avenge the murder of his father he stopped at the temple of dhual-Khalasah to consult the oracle by means of drawing arrows. Upon drawing 'abandon' thrice, he hurled the broken arrows at the idol exclaiming, "Accursed One! Had it been thy father who was murdered thou wouldst not have forbidden my avenging him."[1]

The Arabs were undoubtedly indifferent towards religion, but that should not lead any one to conclude that they had no notion of religion whatsoever. They had had an idea of an All-Supreme power controlling the Universe, His Wrath and Favour, the life after death and the angels. But all these ideas had been adulterated with idolatry—that yearning of the baser self in a man for a visible object of devotion, something that the eye can see and the hands can touch, which finally develops into the worship of the creature more than that of the Creator. That the Arabs had a concept of an All-Powerful Lord can be illustrated from so many verses. Nabigha, for instance, says:

I took an oath and left no margin of doubt for who else can support man, besides Allah.[2]

Zahir b. Abi. Salma in his well-known couplet affirms his faith in the day of judgement:

The deeds are recorded in the scroll to be presented on
The day of judgement;
Vengeance can be taken in this world too;[3]

The Holy Qur'an eloquently testifies the fact that the unbelievers and polytheists of Arabia did not deny the existence of a Supreme Power, nor did they deny the fact that Allah is the Sole Creator of the heavens and the earth; or that the whole mechanism of nature is operated in accordance with His Command, that He pours down the rain, drives the winds, controls the sun, the moon, the earth and everything else. Says the Qur'an:

And if you ask them, Who created the heavens and the earth and constrained the sun and the moon (to their appointed task) they would say: Allah. How, then, are they turned away? (29:61)

And if thou were to ask them, Who causeth water to come down from the sky, and wherewith reviveth the earth after its death? they would verily say: Allah. (29:63)

And if you ask them Who created them they will surely say: Allah. How then are they turned away? (43:87)

And if you should ask them, Who created the heavens and the earth? they would most certainly say: The Mighty, the Knowing One has created them. (43:9)

These verses make it abundantly clear that the Arabs of pre-Islamic period believed in the existence of one Great Deity, but at the same time they entertained the notion that the All-Powerful Lord delegated His powers to some of His sacred personalities and objects—both animate and inanimate—who serve as the media through which the worshipper could come in contact with Him and thus earn His pleasure. It was under this misconception that they worshipped the idols of saintly persons, heavenly bodies and stones which were sometimes regarded not as divinities, but as the incarnations of Divine Being.

We have seen earlier that the Arabs had deep-rooted love for the tribe to which they belonged. This belief in the greatness and excellence of their tribe led them to carve a deity of their own and they sang hymns in its praise in order to win its favour. The tribe called Kalb worshipped *Wadd*, the Hudhayl worshipped *Suwa*.

The tribe of Madh'hij as well as the people of Quraysh worshipped *Yaghuth*, the Khaywan worshipped *Ya'uq*. The last-named idol was placed in their village called Khaywan at a distance of two nights' journey towards Mecca. Similarly the tribe of Himyar adopted *Nasr* as their god and worshipped it in a place called *Balkha*. The Himyar had also another temple (*bayt*) in San'a. It was called Ri'am, the people venerated it and offered sacrifices to it.[4]

The most ancient of all these idols was Manah. The Arabs named their children after them as *'Abd Manah* and *Zayd Manah*. Manah was erected on the seashore in the vicinity of Mushallal in Qudayd, between Medina and Mecca. All the Arabs used to venerate her and offer sacrifices to her. The Aus and the Khazraj were her most faithful devotees.[5]

Another goddess which was ardently worshipped by the Arabs was known as al-Lat. "She was a cubic rock beside which a certain Jew used to prepare his barley porridge (*Sawiq*). Her custody was in the hands of Banu Attab Ibn Malik of the Thaqif who had raised an edifice over her. She was venerated by the Quraysh and almost all the tribes of Arabia and they named their children after her, e.g., Zayd al-Lat and Taym al-Lat. The Arabs worshipped her till the tribe of Thaqif embraced Islam. It was on this occasion that Muhammad (may the peace of Allah be upon him) sent al-Mughirah ibn Shu'bah to destroy this idol. It is recorded that when al-Lat was demolished, Shaddad ibn 'Arid-al-Jushmai gave in verse a grim note of warning to the tribe of Thaqif:

> Come not for help to al-Lat, Allah has doomed her to destruction.
> How can you be helped by one who is not victorious,
> Verily, that which, when set on fire, resisted not the flames.
> Nor saved her stones, inglorious and worthless.
> Hence when the Prophet will arrive in your place,
> Not one of her devotees shall be left at the time of his departures.[6]

Still another goddess who was venerated by the Arabs is known as *al-Uzza*. She was introduced to the people by a person known as Zalim ibn As'ad. Her idol was erected in a valley in Nakhlat al-Shamiya called Hurad alongside al-Ghumyayr to the right of the road from Mecca to Iraq about Dhat-Iraq and nine miles from al-bustan. A grand superstructure was raised around it where the people would sit and receive oracular communication. It was a common practice with the Arabs to name their children after this goddess. The Quraysh were sent to circumambulate the Ka'bah and sing hymns for these goddesses whom they called 'the daughters of Allah':[7]

> By al-Lat and al-Uzza, and Manah,
> The third idols beside, verily they are the most exalted females.
> Whose intercession is to be sought after.

The Holy Qur'an has vehemently repudiated such foolish ideas and said in unequivocal terms:

Have ye seen Lat and Uzza and another? The third (goddess) Manah? What? For you the male sex and for Him, the female? Behold, such would be indeed a division most unfair.

These are nothing but names which ye have devised, ye and your fathers—for which God had sent down no authority (whatever). They followed nothing but fancy and what their own souls desire. Even though there has already come to them guidance from the Lord. (53: 19–23).

The Quraysh also had several idols in and around the Ka'bah. The greatest of these was *Hubal*. It was carved out of red agate, in the form of a man with the right hand broken off. It stood inside the Ka'bah.

Beside him stood ritual arrows used for divination by the soothsayer (*Kahin*) who drew lots. On one of these arrows the word *Sarih* was inscribed and on the other was written the word *Mulsaq*, which means 'consociated alien'. Whenever the legitimacy of a newborn babe was questioned the Arabs would shuffle the arrows and then throw them. If the arrow shoed the word pure, it was finally decided that the child was legitimate. If, unfortunately, the arrow bearing the word '*Mulsaq*' was drawn, the child was condemned as illegitimate. There were also some other arrows which could help the Arabs in the divination concerning marriage, death or the success or failure of the intending journey.[8]

The idol of *Hubal* was widely venerated by the Arabs, especially by the people of Mecca. It was the same idol which Abu Sufyan ibn Harb addressed when he emerged victorious after the battle of Uhud saying: "*Hubal*! be though exalted (i.e. may thy religion triumph)." At this the Prophet replied: "Allah is more Exalted, and more Majestic."[9]

Among other idols *Usaf* and *Na'ilah* are well-known. One of them stood close to the Ka'bah, while the other was placed by the side of the Zamzam. Later, both of them were set together near the sacred fountain and the Arabs offered sacrifices to both of them. Ibn al-Kalbi writes:

The Arabs were passionately devoted to the idols and worshipped them with fervour. Some of them erected a temple around which they centered their worship, whereas the others adopted venerated idols. A person who was devoid of means to build the temple for himself or carve an idol to worship it, would fix a stone in front of the sacred House or any other temple according to his desire and then circumambulate it in the same manner in which he would circumambulate around the Ka'bah.[10]

They were so deeply attached to them that when any one amongst them intended to go on a journey, his last act before saying goodbye to the house, would be to touch the idol in the hope of an auspicious journey, and when he returned home the first act that he would perform was to touch it again with reverence in gratitude for a propitious return.[11]

The Arabs called these stones to which they shoed veneration as *ansab*. Whenever these stones resembled a living form they called them idols (*Asnam*) and graven images (*awthan*). The act of circumambulating them was called circumrotation (*dawr*).[12]

The Arabs were, however, fully conscious of excellence and superiority of Ka'bah to which they turned their steps for pilgrimage and visitation. The worship of the stones during their travels meant to perpetuate the religious ceremonies which they had performed at Ka'bah because of their immense devotion to it.

This practice originated in the custom of men carrying a stone from the sacred enclosures of Mecca when they set out on a journey, out of reverence for the Ka'bah and withersoever they went they set it up and made circumambulations round about it as is made around the Ka'bah till at the last they adored every goodly stone they saw, forgot their religion, and substituted the faith of Ibrahim and Isma'il with the worship of the images and the idols.

It will not be out of place to mention briefly some of the practices at the Ka'bah. Amongst these practices, it is interesting to note that some came down from the time of Ibrahim and Isma'il such as the veneration of the House and its circumambulation, the pilgrimage, the vigil (*al-Wukuf*) on 'Arafah and al-Muzdalifah, sacrificing she-camels and raising the voice in the acclamation of the name of the Lord (*tahlil*) but the Meccans had polluted all sacred performances with idolatrous practices, for example, whenever they raised their voices in *tahlil*[13] they would declare their implicit faith in the unity of the Lord through the *talbiyah*, but it was not unity pure and simple. It was alloyed with the association of their gods with Him. Thus their *talbiyah* was expressed in these words:

Here we are, O Lord! Here we are! There is no associate for Thee except one who is thine. Thou has full supremacy over him and over everything that he possesses.[14]

The Arabs, both men and women, circumambulated the Ka'bah in a state of nudity with their hands—clapping, shouting and singing[15] and it was thought to be an act of highest piety. The argument which they advanced to justify such an indecent act was that it was unfair on their part to perform this sacred ceremony in those very clothes in which they had committed sins. They vehemently stressed this point by saying: "We will not circumambulate with the dress in which we perpetrated crimes. We will not worship Allah in the attire in which we committed heinous acts. We will not circumambulate in attire in which we disobeyed our Lord.[16]

The history of pre-Islamic Arabia brings into light the fact that the Arabs, besides the worship of idols, worshipped the heavenly bodies, trees and dead heroes of their tribes. "The Sun (*Shams*) construed as feminine, was honoured by the several Arabian tribes with a sanctuary and an idol. The name *'Abd Shams* is found in many parts of the country. In the North we meet with the name *Amr-I-Shams*, "man of the Sun". For the worship of the rising sun, we have the evidence of *Abd-al-Sharq* "servant of the Raising one."[17] The heavenly bodies, especially worshipped were Canopus (*Suhail*), Sirius (*al-Sh'ira*), Aldebaran in Taurus with the planets Mercury (*Utarid*), Venus (*al-Zuhra*) Jupiter (*al-Mushtri*) and Sale states that the temple at Mecca was said to have been consecrated to Saturn (*Zuhal*).[18]

The Arabs' devotion to the Sun, Moon and other heavenly bodies is unquestionable; but it is wrong to infer from this that the religion of the Arabs or even of the Semites entirely rested upon the worship of the heavenly bodies. This theory is not supported by facts. The Arabs had so many deities which cannot be explained as astral powers.[19] There were not a few deities which were supposed to possess animal forms, e.g., *Ya'uq* represented by a horse and *Nasr* thought to have the figure of a vulture (*Nasr*). *Yauq* is said to have been god of the Hamdan or of the Morad or of both tribes.[20] "*Nasr*, the vulture-god is said to have been an idol of Himyarites."[21]

Some of the Arabian deities seem to be personifications of abstract ideas, but they appear to have been conceived in a thoroughly concrete fashion. In particular, it is to be noticed that the Arabs, form a very early period, believed in the existence of certain supernatural powers which shaped their destiny. Thus, for instance time in the abstract form was popularly imagined to be the cause of all earthly misery. The Holy Qur'an also refers to this wrong belief of the Meccans:

"And they say: what is there but life in this world? We shall die and we live, and nothing but time can destroy us. But of that they have no knowledge. They merely conjecture." (45:24)

The Arab poets had also been alluding to the action of Time (*dahr, Zaman*) which brings sorrows and adversities. Then there is a fate which determines course of life and irresistibly drives them to their destined ends. No one can change the pattern wrought by fate and no action, howsoever concentrated, can alter that which is unalterable. There is, however, one other expression, *Maniyah,* which often appears in poetry and throws a good deal of light on the fatalist views of the Arabs. The Meccans believed that he universe had been created by the Lord, but after bringing it into existence He had retired to the position of a silent spectator and now it was the driving force of time and fate which was moving it to its destined end and bringing into being new events and episodes of life.[22]

In addition to these deities the pagan Arabs looked upon their priests with the same reverence as they had for their gods. In this class figured high the care-takers of temples and other sanctuaries. The priest or temple-guard (the Arabic word is *Sadin*), was, like the Nordic Code, a venerable man who was regarded as the owner of the sacred precinct. As a rule this privilege of ownership and direction belonged to a clan whose chief was the actual priest, but any member of the tribe could carry out the priestly functions, which, in addition to the guarding of the sacred grove, building of the idols, and the treasury where the *votine* gifts were stored, consisted of the practice of casting lots to determine the will of God, or to obtain His advice concerning important undertakings. The Priest also served as an intermediary between the mortal and his Master.

Besides priesthood, there was a certain guild of seers whose members received their esoteric knowledge from spirit. *Kahins*, as they were called, were supposed to possess the power of foretelling the coming events and of performing other superhuman feats. Anyone who was eager to known what the future had in store for him would go in their presence with presents of food and animals. Sacrifices were offered at their feet and *Kahin* would then lend his ear to a mysterious "voice from the heaven" known as the "oracle" and communicate it to the person concerned.[23]

The pagan Arabs included the poet also in the category of those mysterious beings who are endowed with supernatural knowledge, "a wizard in league with spirits (*Jinn*) or satans (*Shayatin*) and dependent on them the magical powers which he displayed … the pagan *Sha'ir* is the oracle of his tribe, their guide in peace and their champion in war. It was to him they turned for counsel when they sought new pastures; only at his word would they pitch or strike their 'house of hair'.[24]

Not only the idols, the stars and the saints, were worshipped in Arabia, but the demons and jinn also were venerated in every section of their society. "These jinn differed from the gods not so much in their natures as in their relation to man. The gods are, on the whole friendly; the *jinn*, hostile. The latter are, of course, personifications of the fantastic notions of the terrors of the desert and its wild animal life. To the gods belong the regions frequented by man, to the jinn belong the unknown and untrodden parts of the wilderness."[25]

The Arabs also adored the graves of their forefathers and sought assistance from the departed souls in the hour of distress. They believed that the souls of the dead person had the power to incarnate itself in different bodies, both human and non-human.

The belief in signs as betokening future events, was, of course, found no less among the Arabs than among other peoples. Some birds were regarded as auspicious, other as ominous. The animals that crossed a man's path and the direction in which they moved alike conveyed a meaning. Many of these signs were such as everyone could understand; others were intelligible only to persons especially trained. One peculiar art consisted in scaring birds and drawing omens from their flight; this operation was known as *Zajr*.[26]

The pages of history reveal the fact that fire was also worshipped in Arabia as a symbol of divine power. This practice seems to have penetrated in the Arab lands from their neighboring country Persia, where it had been rooted deeply. The Magian religion was popular particularly with the tribe of Tamim.

The Jews who fled in great numbers into Arabia from the fearful destruction of their country by the Romans made proselytes of several tribes, those of Kinanah, al Harith Ibn Ka'bah, and Kindah in particular, and in time became very powerful, and possessed of several towns and fortresses. "But the Jewish religion was not unknown to the Arabs at least about a century before. Abu Qarib Asad who was the king of Yemen introduced Judaism among the idolatrous Himyarites."[27]

Christianity had likewise made a little progress amongst the Arabs before the advent of Muhammad (may the peace of Allah be upon him). How this religion was actually introduced into this land is uncertain, but the persecutions and disorders which took place in the Eastern Church soon after the beginning of the third century, obliged great number of Christians to seek shelter in that country of liberty. "The principal tribes that embraced Christianity were Himyar, Ghassan, Rabi'a, Tagh'ab, Bahra, Tunukh, part of the Tay and Khud'a, the inhabitants of Najran, and the Arabs of Hira. As to the two last, it may be observed that those of Najran became Christian in the time of Dhu Nuwas"[28]

Christianity as a religion could not, however, succeed in making a permanent hold in Arabia and could not supersede idolatry. The Christian anchorites, dwelling in their solitary cells in the country aided in gaining scattered converts amongst the Arabs. This failure of the Christian monks in spreading the Gospel among the people of Arabia may be attributed to the fact that by the time of its penetration into Arabia, it had ceased to be a living force. It was a mere hotchpotch of dogmas and transcendental hopes having no relationship with the practical life. Its promoters, the clergymen, had degenerated themselves into a class of selfseekers:

The clergy by drawing the abstrusest niceties into controversy, and dividing and subdividing about them into endless schisms and contentions, they had so destroyed that peace, love and charity from among them which the Gospel was given to promote, and instead thereof continually provoked each other to that malice, rancour, and every evil work, that they had lost the whole substance of their religion, while they thus eagerly contended for their own imaginations concerning it, and in a manner quite drove Christianity out of the world by those very controversies in which they disputed with each other about it. In those dark ages it was that most of those superstitions and corruptions we now just abhor in the Church of Rome were not only broached but established, which gave great advantages to the propagation of Muhammadanism. The worship of the saints and images, in particular, was then arrived at such a scandalous pitch that it even surpassed whatever is now practised amongst the Romanists.[29]

Such were the real religious conditions of the Arabs before Muhammad (may the peace of Allah be upon him). "Causes are sometimes conjured up", observes Muir, "to account for results produced by an agent apparently inadequate to effect them. Muhammad arose, and forthwith the Arabs were aroused to a new and a spiritual faith; hence the conclusion that Arabia was fermenting of the change and prepared to adopt it. To us, calmly reviewing the past, pre-Islamic history belies the assumption. After five centuries of Christian evangelisation, we can point to but a sprinkling here and there of Christian converts, the Bani Harith of Nairan; the Bani Hanifa of Yemena; some of the Bani Tay at Tayma; and hardly any more. Judaism, vastly more powerful, had exhibited spasmodic efforts at proselytism; but, as an active and converting agent, the Jewish faith was no longer operative. In fact, viewed in a religious aspect, the surface of Arabia had been now and then gently rippled by the feeble efforts of Christianity, the sterner influences of Judaism had been occasionally visible in a deeper and more troubled current; but the tide of indigenous idolatry and Ishmaelite superstition setting strongly from every quarter towards the Ka'bah gave ample evidence that the faith and worship of Mecca held the Arab mind in a rigorous and undisputed thraldom."[30]

Notes

1. Phillip K. Hitti, *History of the Arabs* (London, 1951), p. 96

2. Ibn Qutayba, *al-Sh'r-wa'asl-Shu'ara*, p. 110.

3. *Ibid.*, p. 88

4. Hisham Ibn Al-Kalbi, Kitab al-Asnam, edited by Ahmad Zaki Pasha. (Cairo, 1927), pp. 9–14.

5. *Ibid.*, p. 14.

6. Hisham Ibn Al-Kalbi, op. cit., p. 17.

7. *Ibid*, pp. 26–28.

8. Hisham Al-Ibn Kalbi, op. cit., p. 28.

9. *Ibid.*

10. Hisham Ibn Al-Kalbi, op. cit., p. 33.

11. *Ibid.*

12. *Ibid.*, p. 33

13. The formula of the *tahlil* is—*La-ilaha illa-Allah* (There is no god but Allah).

14. Ibn Kathir, *al-Bidaya, wa'al-Nihaya* (Cairo, 1932), Vol. II, 188.

15. This seems to be implied in the Qur'anic reference to the pagan Meccan: *Their prayers at the House are nothing else than whistling through the fingers, and clapping of hands." (8:35).*

16. Dr. Jawad Ali: *Tarikh al-Arab Qabl al-Islam*, Matba'al-Ilm al-Iraqi (1955), Vol. V, p. 225.

17. *Encyclopaedia of Religion and Ethics*, Article "Ancient Arab", Vol. 1, p. 661.

18. J.W.H. Stobbart, *Islam and its Founder*, p. 32.

19. *Encyclopaedia of Religion and Ethics*, Article "Ancient Arab"

20. W. Robertson Smith: *Kinship and Marriage in Early Arabia*, p. 208.

21. *Ibid*, p. 209.

22. Sayyid Mahmud Shakir al-Alusi: *Bulugh al-Irb-fi Ahwal al 'Arab* (Cairo), Vol. II, pp. 220–21.

23. Dr. Jawad Ali: *Tarikh al-Arab*, Vol. V, p. 177.

24. Nicholson: *A Literary History of the Arabs*, pp. 72–73.

25. Hitti, *History of the Arabs*, p. 98.

26. Jawad Ali: *Tarikh al-Arab*, Vol. V, p. 40.

27. *Encyclopaedia of Religion and Ethics*, Vol. I, p. 667 "Arabs, Ancient", (N.Y., 1908).

28. E.M. Wherry, *A Commentary of the Qur'an*, (London, 1882).

29. E.M. Wherry, *A Commentary of the Qur'an*, (London, 1882), Vol. I, pp. 61–62.

30. William Muir, *Life of Muhammad* p. lxxxv.

2

Brief History of Islam

by Ismail Nawwab, Peter Speers, and Paul Hoye

The Prophet of Islam

In or about the year 570 the child who would be named Muhammad and who would become the Prophet of one of the world's great religions, Islam, was born into a family belonging to a clan of Quraish, the ruling tribe of Mecca, a city in the Hijaz region of northwestern Arabia.

Originally the site of the Kaabah, a shrine of ancient origins, Mecca had, with the decline of southern Arabia, become an important center of sixth-century trade with such powers as the Sassanians, Byzantines, and Ethiopians. As a result, the city was dominated by powerful merchant families, among whom the men of Quraish were preeminent.

Muhammad's father, "Abd Allah ibn" Abd al-Muttalib, died before the boy was born; his mother, Aminah, died when he was six. The orphan was consigned to the care of his grandfather, the head of the clan of Hashim. After the death of his grandfather, Muhammad was raised by his uncle, Abu Talib. As was customary, the child Muhammad was sent to live for a year or two with a Bedouin family. This custom, followed until recently by noble families of Mecca, Medina, Taif, and other towns of the Hijaz, had important implications for Muhammad. In addition to enduring the hardships of desert life, he acquired a taste for the rich language so loved by the Arabs, whose speech was their proudest art, and also learned the patience

Ismail Nawwab, Peter Speers, and Paul Hoye, from *Saudi Aramco and Its World: Arabia and the Middle East*. Copyright © 1968 by Aramco Services Company. Reprinted with permission.

and forbearance of the herdsmen, whose life of solitude he first shared, and then came to understand and appreciate.

About the year 590, Muhammad, then in his twenties, entered the service of a merchant widow named Khadijah as her factor, actively engaged with trading caravans to the north. Sometime later he married her, and had two sons, neither of whom survived, and four daughters by her.

In his forties, he began to retire to meditate in a cave on Mount Hira, just outside Mecca, where the first of the great events of Islam took place. One day, as he was sitting in the cave, he heard a voice, later identified as that of the Angel Gabriel, which ordered him to:

"Recite: In the name of thy Lord who created, Created man from a clot of blood." (Quran 96:1–2)

Three times Muhammad pleaded his inability to do so, but each time the command was repeated. Finally, Muhammad recited the words of what are now the first five verses of the 96th chapter of the Quran—words which proclaim God to be the Creator of man and the Source of all knowledge.

At first Muhammad divulged his experience only to his wife and his immediate circle. But, as more revelations enjoined him to proclaim the oneness of God universally, his following grew, at first among the poor and the slaves, but later, also among the most prominent men of Mecca. The revelations he received at this time, and those he did later, are all incorporated in the Quran, the Scripture of Islam.

Not everyone accepted God's message transmitted through Muhammad. Even in his own clan, there were those who rejected his teachings, and many merchants actively opposed the message. The opposition, however, merely served to sharpen Muhammad's sense of mission, and his understanding of exactly how Islam differed from paganism. The belief in the Oneness of God was paramount in Islam; from this all else follows. The verses of the Quran stress God's uniqueness, warn those who deny it of impending punishment, and proclaim His unbounded compassion to those who submit to His will. They affirm the Last Judgment, when God, the Judge, will weigh in the balance the faith and works of each man, rewarding the faithful and punishing the transgressor. Because the Quran rejected polytheism and emphasized man's moral responsibility, in powerful images, it presented a grave challenge to the worldly Meccans.

The Hijrah

After Muhammad had preached publicly for more than a decade, the opposition to him reached such a high pitch that, fearful for their safety, he sent some of his adherents to Ethiopia. There, the Christian ruler extended protection to them, the memory of which has been cherished by Muslims ever since. But in Mecca the persecution worsened. Muhammad's followers were harassed, abused, and even tortured. At last, seventy of Muhammad's followers set off by his orders to the northern town of Yathrib, in the hope of establishing a new stage of the Islamic movement. This city which was later to be renamed Medina ("The City"). Later, in the early fall of 622, he, with his closest friend, Abu Bakr al-Siddeeq, set off to join the emigrants. This event coincided with the leaders in Mecca plotting, to kill him.

In Mecca, the plotters arrived at Muhammad's home to find that his cousin, 'Ali, had taken his place in bed. Enraged, the Meccans set a price on Muhammad's head and set off in pursuit. Muhammad and Abu Bakr, however, had taken refuge in a cave, where they hid from their pursuers. By the protection of God, the Meccans passed by the cave without noticing it, and Muhammad and Abu Bakr proceeded to Medina. There, they were joyously welcomed by a throng of Medinans, as well as the Meccans who had gone ahead to prepare the way.

This was the Hijrah—anglicized as Hegira—usually, but inaccurately, translated as "Flight"—from which the Muslim era is dated. In fact, the Hijrah was not a flight, but a carefully planned migration that marks not only a break in history—the beginning of the Islamic era, and the Islamic calendar start from this date—but also, for Muhammad and the Muslims, a new way of life. Henceforth, the organizational principle of the community was not to be mere blood kinship, but the greater brotherhood of all Muslims. The men who accompanied Muhammad on the Hijrah were called the Muhajiroon—"those that made the Hijrah" or the "Emigrants"—while those in Medina who became Muslims were called the Ansar, or "Helpers or Supporters."

Muhammad was well acquainted with the situation in Medina. Earlier, before the Hijrah, various of its inhabitants came to Mecca to offer the annual pilgrimage, and as the Prophet would take this opportunity to call visiting pilgrims to Islam, the group who came from Medina heard his call and accepted Islam. They also invited Muhammad to settle in Medina. After the Hijrah, Muhammad's exceptional qualities so impressed the Medinans that the rival tribes and their allies temporarily closed ranks as, on March 15, 624, Muhammad and his supporters moved against the pagans of Mecca.

The first battle, which took place near Badr, now a small town southwest of Medina, had several important effects. In the first place, the Muslim forces, outnumbered three to one, routed the Meccans. Secondly, the discipline displayed by the Muslims brought home to the Meccans, perhaps for the first time, the abilities of the man they had driven from their city. Thirdly, one of the allied tribes which had pledged support to the Muslims in the Battle of Badr, but had then proved lukewarm when the fighting started, was expelled from Medina one month after the battle. Those who claimed to be allies of the Muslims, but tacitly opposed them, were thus served warning: membership in the community imposed the obligation of total support.

A year later the Meccans struck back. Assembling an army of three thousand men, they met the Muslims at Uhud, a ridge outside Medina. After initial successes, the Muslims were driven back and the Prophet himself was wounded. As the Muslims were not completely defeated, the Meccans, with an army of ten thousand, attacked Medina again two years later but with quite different results. At the Battle of the Trench, also known as the Battle of the Confederates, the Muslims scored a signal victory by introducing a new form of defense. On the side of Medina from which attack was expected, they dug a trench too deep for the Meccan cavalry to clear without exposing itself to the archers posted behind earthworks on the Medina side. After an inconclusive siege, the Meccans were forced to retire. Thereafter Medina was entirely in the hands of the Muslims.

The Conquest of Mecca

The Constitution of Medina—under which the clans accepting Muhammad as the Prophet of God formed an alliance, or federation—dates from this period. It showed that the political consciousness of the Muslim community had reached an important point; its members defined themselves as a community separate from all others. The Constitution also defined the role of non-Muslims in the community. Jews, for example, were part of the community; they were dhimmis, that is, protected people, as long as they conformed to its laws. This established a precedent for the treatment of subject peoples during the later conquests. Christians and Jews, upon payment of a nominal tax, were allowed religious freedom and, while maintaining their status as non-Muslims, were associate members of the Muslim state. This status did not apply to polytheists, who could not be tolerated within a community that worshipped the One God.

Ibn Ishaq, one of the earliest biographers of the Prophet, says it was at about this time that Muhammad sent letters to the rulers of the earth—the King of Persia, the Emperor of Byzantium, the Negus of Abyssinia, and the Governor of Egypt among others—inviting them to submit to Islam. Nothing more fully illustrates the confidence of the small community, as its military power, despite the battle of the Trench, was still negligible. But its confidence was not misplaced. Muhammad so effectively built up a series of alliances among the tribes that, by 628, he and fifteen hundred followers were able to demand access to the Kaaba. This was a milestone in the history of the Muslims. Just a short time before, Muhammad left the city of his birth to establish an Islamic state in Medina. Now he was being treated by his former enemies as a leader in his own right. A year later, in 629, he reentered and, in effect, conquered Mecca, without bloodshed and in a spirit of tolerance, which established an ideal for future conquests. He also destroyed the idols in the Kaabah, to put an end forever to pagan practices there. At the same time 'Amr ibn al-'As, the future conqueror of Egypt, and Khalid ibn al-Walid, the future "Sword of God," accepted Islam, and swore allegiance to Muhammad. Their conversion was especially noteworthy because these men had been among Muhammad's bitterest opponents only a short time before.

In one sense Muhammad's return to Mecca was the climax of his mission. At the age of 63, in 632, just three years later, he was suddenly taken ill and on June 8 of that year, with his third wife Aisha in attendance, the Messenger of God "died with the heat of noon."

The death of Muhammad was a profound loss. To his followers this simple man from Mecca was far more than a beloved friend, far more than a gifted administrator, far more than the revered leader who had forged a new state from clusters of warring tribes. Muhammad was also the exemplar of the teachings he had brought them from God: the teachings of the Quran, which, for centuries, have guided the thought and action, the faith and conduct, of innumerable men and women, and which ushered in a distinctive era in the history of mankind. His death, nevertheless, had little effect on the dynamic society he had created in Arabia, and no effect at all on his central mission: to transmit the Quran to the world. As Abu Bakr put it: "Whoever worshipped Muhammad, let him know that Muhammad is dead, but whoever worshipped God, let him know that God lives and dies not."

The Caliphate: 632–661 CE

The Caliphate of Abu Bakr and Umar

With the death of Muhammad, the Muslim community was faced with the problem of succession. Who would be its leader? There were four persons obviously marked for leadership: Abu Bakr al-Siddeeq, who had not only accompanied Muhammad to Medina ten years before, but had been appointed to take the place of the Prophet as leader of public prayer during Muhammad's last illness; Umar ibn al-Khattab, an able and trusted Companion of the Prophet; Uthman ibn 'Affan, a respected early convert; and 'Ali ibn Abi Talib, Muhammad's cousin and son-in-law. There piousness and ability to govern the affairs of the Islamic nation was uniformly par excellence. At a meeting held to decide the new leadership, Umar grasped Abu Bakr's hand and gave his allegiance to him, the traditional sign of recognition of a new leader. By dusk, everyone concurred, and Abu Bakr had been recognized as the khaleefah of Muhammad. Khaleefah—anglicized as caliph—is a word meaning "successor", but also suggesting what his historical role would be: to govern according to the Quran and the practice of the Prophet.

Abu Bakr's caliphate was short, but important. An exemplary leader, he lived simply, assiduously fulfilled his religious obligations, and was accessible and sympathetic to his people. But he also stood firm when some tribes, who had only nominally accepted Islam, renounced it in the wake of the Prophet's death. In what was a major accomplishment, Abu Bakr swiftly disciplined them. Later, he consolidated the support of the tribes within the Arabian Peninsula and subsequently funneled their energies against the powerful empires of the East: the Sassanians in Persia and the Byzantines in Syria, Palestine, and Egypt. In short, he demonstrated the viability of the Muslim state.

The second caliph, Umar—appointed by Abu Bakr—continued to demonstrate that viability. Adopting the title Ameer al-Mumineen, or Commander of the Believers, Umar extended Islam's temporal rule over Syria, Egypt, Iraq, and Persia in what, from a purely military standpoint, were astonishing victories. Within four years after the death of the Prophet, the Muslim state had extended its sway over all of Syria and had, at a famous battle fought during a sandstorm near the River Yarmuk, blunted the power of the Byzantines—whose ruler, Heraclius, had shortly before refused the call to accept Islam.

Even more astonishingly, the Muslim state administered the conquered territories with a tolerance almost unheard of in that age. At Damascus, for example, the Muslim leader, Khalid ibn al-Walid, signed a treaty which read as follows:

This is what Khalid ibn al-Walid would grant to the inhabitants of Damascus if he enters therein: he promises to give them security for their lives, property and churches. Their city wall shall not be demolished; neither shall any Muslim be quartered in their houses. Thereunto we give them the pact of God and the protection of His Prophet, the caliphs and the believers. So long as they pay the poll tax, nothing but good shall befall them.

This tolerance was typical of Islam. A year after Yarmook, Umar, in the military camp of al-Jabiyah on the Golan Heights, received word that the Byzantines were ready to surrender Jerusalem. Consequently, he rode there to accept the surrender in person. According to one account, he entered the city alone and clad in a simple cloak, astounding a populace accustomed to the sumptuous garb and court ceremonials of the Byzantines and Persians. He astounded them still further when he set their fears at rest by negotiating a generous treaty in which he told them: "In the name of God … you have complete security for your churches, which shall not be occupied by the Muslims or destroyed."

This policy was to prove successful everywhere. In Syria, for example, many Christians who had been involved in bitter theological disputes with Byzantine authorities—and persecuted for it—welcomed the coming of Islam as an end to tyranny. And in Egypt, which Amr ibn al-As took from the Byzantines after a daring march across the Sinai Peninsula, the Coptic Christians not only welcomed the Arabs, but enthusiastically assisted them.

This pattern was repeated throughout the Byzantine Empire. Conflict among Greek Orthodox, Syrian Monophysites, Copts, and Nestorian Christians contributed to the failure of the Byzantines—always regarded as intruders—to develop popular support, while the tolerance which Muslims showed toward Christians and Jews removed the primary cause for opposing them.

Umar adopted this attitude in administrative matters as well. Although he assigned Muslim governors to the new provinces, existing Byzantine and Persian administrations were retained wherever possible. For fifty years, in fact, Greek remained the chancery language of Syria, Egypt, and Palestine, while Pahlavi, the chancery language of the Sassanians, continued to be used in Mesopotamia and Persia.

Umar, who served as caliph for ten years, ended his rule with a significant victory over the Persian Empire. The struggle with the Sassanid realm had opened in 687 at al-Qadisiyah, near Ctesiphon in Iraq, where Muslim cavalry had successfully coped with elephants used by the Persians as a kind of primitive tank. Now with the Battle of Nihavand, called the "Conquest of Conquests," Umar sealed the fate of Persia; henceforth it was to be one of the most important provinces in the Muslim Empire.

His caliphate was a high point in early Islamic history. He was noted for his justice, social ideals, administration, and statesmanship. His innovations left an all enduring imprint on social welfare, taxation, and the financial and administrative fabric of the growing empire.

The Caliphate of Uthman ibn Affan

Umar ibn Al-Khattab, the second caliph of Islam, was stabbed by a Persian slave Abu Lu'lu'ah, a Persian Magian, while leading the Fajr Prayer. As Umar was lying on his death bed, the people around him asked him to appoint a successor. Umar appointed a committee of six people to choose the next caliph from among themselves.

This committee comprised Ali ibn Abi Talib, Uthman ibn Affan, Abdur-Rahman ibn Awf, Sad ibn Abi Waqqas, Az-Zubayr ibn Al-Awam, and Talhah ibn Ubayd Allah, who were among the most eminent Companions of the Prophet, may God send His praises upon him, and who had received in their lifetime the tidings of Paradise.

The instructions of Umar were that the Election Committee should choose the successor within three days, and he should assume office on the fourth day. As two days passed by without a decision, the members felt anxious that the time was running out fast, and still no solution to the problem appeared to be in sight. Abdur-Rahman ibn Awf offered to forgo his own claim if others agreed to abide by his decision. All agreed to let Abdur-Rahman choose the new caliph. He interviewed each nominee and went about Medinah asking the people for their choice. He finally selected Uthman as the new caliph, as the majority of the people chose him.

Uthman led a simple life even after becoming the leader of the Islamic state. It would have been easy for a successful businessman such as him to lead a luxurious life, but he never aimed at leading such in this world. His only aim was to taste the pleasure of the hereafter, as he knew that this world is a test and temporary. Uthman's generosity continued after he became caliph.

The caliphs were paid for their services from the treasury, but Uthman never took any salary for his service to Islam. Not only this, he also developed a custom to free slaves every Friday, look after widows and orphans, and give unlimited charity. His patience and endurance were among the characteristics that made him a successful leader.

Uthman achieved much during his reign. He pushed forward with the pacification of Persia, continued to defend the Muslim state against the Byzantines, added what is now Libya to the empire, and subjugated most of Armenia. Uthman also, through his cousin Mu'awiyah ibn Abi Sufyan, the governor of Syria, established an Arab navy which fought a series of important engagements with the Byzantines.

Of much greater importance to Islam, however, was Uthman's compilation of the text of the Quran as revealed to the Prophet. Realizing that the original message from God might be inadvertently distorted by textual variants, he appointed a committee to collect the canonical verses and destroy the variant recensions. The result was the text that is accepted to this day throughout the Muslim world.

During his caliphate, Uthman faced much of hostility from new, nominal Muslims in newly Islamic lands, who started to accuse him of not following the example Prophet and the preceding caliphs in matters concerning governance. However, the Companions of the Prophet always defended him. These accusations never changed him. He remained persistent to be a merciful governor. Even during the time when his foes attacked him, he did not use the treasury funds to shield his house or himself. As envisaged by Prophet Muhammad, Uthman's enemies relentlessly made his governing difficult by constantly opposing and accusing him. His opponents finally plotted against him, surrounded his house, and encouraged people to kill him.

Many of his advisors asked him to stop the assault but he did not, until he was killed while reciting the Quran exactly as the Prophet had predicted. Uthman died as a martyr.

Anas ibn Malik narrated the following:

"The Prophet once climbed the mountain of Uhud with Abu Bakr, Umar, and Uthman. The mountain shook with them. The Prophet said (to the mountain), 'Be firm, O Uhud! For on you there is a Prophet, an early truthful supporter of mine, and two martyrs.'" (Saheeh al-Bukhari)

The Fourth Caliph: Ali ibn Abi Talib

Ali's Election

After Uthman's martyrdom, the office of the caliphate remained unfilled for two or three days. Many people insisted that Ali should take up the office, but he was embarrassed by the fact that the people who pressed him hardest were the rebels, and he therefore declined at first. When the notable Companions of the Prophet (peace be on him) urged him, however, he finally agreed.

Ali's Life

Ali bin Abi Talib was the first cousin of the Prophet (peace be on him). More than that, he had grown up in the Prophet's own household, later married his youngest daughter, Fatima, and remained in closest association with him for nearly thirty years.

Ali was ten years old when the Divine Message came to Muhammad (peace be on him). One night he saw the Prophet and his wife Khadijah bowing and prostrating. He asked the Prophet about the meaning of their actions. The Prophet told him that they were praying to God Most High and that Ali too should accept Islam. Ali said that he would first like to ask his father about it. He spent a sleepless night, and in the morning he went to the Prophet and said, "When God created me He did not consult my father, so why should I consult my father in order to serve God?" and he accepted the truth of Muhammad's message.

When the Divine command came, "And warn thy nearest relatives" [26:214], Muhammad (peace be on him) invited his relatives for a meal. After it was finished, he addressed them and asked, "Who will join me in the cause of God?" There was utter silence for a while, and then Ali stood up. "I am the youngest of all present here," he said, "My eyes trouble me because they are sore and my legs are thin and weak, but I

Amatullah Abdullah, "The Caliphate of Uthman ibn Affan," *A Brief History of Islam*. Copyright © 2007 by Amatullah Abdullah.

shall join you and help you in whatever way I can." The assembly broke up in derisive laughter. But during the difficult wars in Mecca, Ali stood by these words and faced all the hardships to which the Muslims were subjected. He slept in the bed of the Prophet when the Quraish planned to murder Muhammad. It was he to whom the Prophet entrusted, when he left Mecca, the valuables which had been given to him for safekeeping, to be returned to their owners.

Apart from the expedition of Tabuk, Ali fought in all the early battles of Islam with great distinction, particularly in the expedition of Khaybar. It is said that in the Battle of Uhud he received more than sixteen wounds.

The Prophet (peace be on him) loved Ali dearly and called him by many fond names. Once the Prophet found him sleeping in the dust. He brushed off Ali's clothes and said fondly, "Wake up, Abu Turab (Father of Dust)." The Prophet also gave him the title of 'Asadullah' ('Lion of God').

Ali's humility, austerity, piety, deep knowledge of the Qur'an and his sagacity gave him great distinction among the Prophet's Companions. Abu Bakr, 'Umar and Uthman consulted him frequently during their caliphates. Many times 'Umar had made him his vice-regent at Medina when he was away. Ali was also a great scholar of Arabic literature and pioneered in the field of grammar and rhetoric. His speeches, sermons and letters served for generations afterward as models of literary expression. Many of his wise and epigrammatic sayings have been preserved. Ali thus had a rich and versatile personality. In spite of these attainments he remained a modest and humble man. Once during his caliphate when he was going about the marketplace, a man stood up in respect and followed him. "Do not do it," said Ali. "Such manners are a temptation for a ruler and a disgrace for the ruled."

Ali and his household lived extremely simple and austere lives. Sometimes they even went hungry themselves because of Ali's great generosity, and none who asked for help was ever turned away from his door. His plain, austere style of living did not change even when he was ruler over a vast domain.

Ali's Caliphate

As mentioned previously, Ali accepted the caliphate very reluctantly. Uthman's murder and the events surrounding it were a symptom, and also became a cause, of civil strife on a large scale. Ali felt that the tragic situation was mainly due to inept governors. He therefore dismissed all the governors who had been appointed by Uthman and appointed new ones. All the governors excepting Muawiya, the governor of Syria, submitted to his orders. Muawiya declined to obey until Uthman's blood was avenged. The Prophet's widow Aisha also took the position that Ali should first bring the murderers to trial. Due to the chaotic conditions during the last days of Uthman it was very difficult to establish the identity of the murderers, and Ali refused to punish anyone whose guilt was not lawfully proved. Thus a battle between the army of Ali and the supporters of Aisha took place. Aisha later realized her error of judgment and never forgave herself for it.

The situation in Hijaz (the part of Arabia in which Mecca and Medina are located) became so troubled that Ali moved his capital to Iraq. Muawiya now openly rebelled against Ali and a fierce battle was fought between their armies. This battle was inconclusive, and Ali had to accept the de facto government of Muawiya in Syria.

However, even though the era of Ali's caliphate was marred by civil strife, he nevertheless introduced a number of reforms, particularly in the levying and collecting of revenues.

It was the fortieth year of Hijra. A fanatical group called Kharijites, consisting of people who had broken away from Ali due to his compromise with Muawiya, claimed that neither Ali, the Caliph, nor Muawiya, the ruler of Syria, nor Amr bin al-Aas, the ruler of Egypt, were worthy of rule. In fact, they went so far as to say that the true caliphate came to an end with 'Umar and that Muslims should live without any ruler over them except God. They vowed to kill all three rulers, and assassins were dispatched in three directions.

The assassins who were deputed to kill Muawiya and Amr did not succeed and were captured and executed, but Ibn-e-Muljim, the assassin who was commissioned to kill Ali, accomplished his task. One morning when Ali was absorbed in prayer in a mosque, Ibn-e-Muljim stabbed him with a poisoned sword. On the 20th of Ramadan, 40 A.H., died the last of the Rightly Guided Caliphs of Islam. May God Most High be pleased with them and grant to them His eternal reward.

With the death of Ali, the first and most notable phase in the history of Muslim peoples came to an end. All through this period it had been the Book of God and the practices of His Messenger—that is, the Qur'an and the Sunnah—which had guided the leaders and the led, set the standards of their moral conduct and inspired their actions. It was the time when the ruler and the ruled, the rich and the poor, the powerful and the weak, were uniformly subject to the Divine Law. It was an epoch of freedom and equality, of God-consciousness and humility, of social justice which recognized no privileges, and of an impartial law which accepted no pressure groups or vested interests.

After Ali, Muawiya assumed the caliphate and thereafter the caliphate became hereditary, passing from one king to another.

·

3

The Qur'an as Scripture

by Abdullah Saeed

'Qur'an' is an Arabic Term Which Means 'recitation' or 'reading'. It comes from the Arabic root *q-r-'*,[1] which is also the root of the first word that the Prophet Muhammad received as revelation, *iqra'*, meaning 'recite' or 'read'. Muhammad's role as a prophet began when he was commanded to 'recite'. Although the Qur'an uses a range of names to refer to itself, the name 'Qur'an' has become the most common one for the holy scripture of Islam. Other names used by the Qur'an to refer to itself include the Revelation (*tanzil*), the Reminder (*dhikr*), the Criterion (*furqan*) and the Scripture (*kitab*). The Qur'an also attributes a number of characteristics to itself such as Noble (as in the commonly cited phrase 'the Noble Qur'an'), Clear, Glorious and Blessed.

There are several Qur'anic verses which indicate that during the time of the Prophet, the Qur'an came to be conceived of as 'scripture', despite the fact that it had not yet been compiled into a written book. As shown above, the Qur'an often refers to itself as the Book or Scripture (*kitab*). For instance, the Qur'an says, 'God has sent down the Scripture and Wisdom to you, and taught you what you did not know';[2] and 'Now We have sent down to you [people] a Scripture to remind you.'[3] In fact, the Qur'an uses *kitab* to refer to itself more than 70 times in various contexts, indicating that the concept of the Qur'an as a book, or scripture, was well established before the Prophet's death.[4] However, it was not until the time of the third caliph of Islam, Uthman ibn Affan (d.35/656), that the Qur'an was compiled as a book. Muslim

Abdullah Saeed, "The Qur'an As Scripture," *The Qur'an*, pp. 38–59. Copyright © 2008 by Taylor & Francis Group LLC. Reprinted with permission.

tradition also holds that it was Abu Bakr, the first caliph, who initially ordered compilation of the Qur'an and Uthman simply relied on the compilation of Abu Bakr.

In this chapter we will discuss:

- the way in which the Qur'an is structured;
- some views of Muslims and certain Western scholars about the compilation of the Qur'an as a written text;
- the evolution of the Qur'anic script;
- Muslim understandings of the Qur'an's inimitability; and
- other important texts in the Islamic tradition.

Structure of the Qur'an

The Qur'an is made up of 114 chapters (*suras*) of varying lengths. Each chapter comprises a number of verses (*ayas*), the length of which also varies significantly. Some verses may consist of several sentences, while others may only be a short phrase or, in some cases, a single word. For example, '*al-Rahman*'[5] (the Lord of Mercy) is the first verse of a chapter by the same name. In Arabic, it is written as one word. By contrast, verse 282 of chapter 2 (the Cow) is longer than many of the shorter chapters of the Qur'an. In English translation, this verse is over 300 words long. It contains a lengthy discussion of commercial transactions and the requirements for writing a contract between the parties involved.

With the exception of the first chapter, *al-Fatiha* (the Opening), the Qur'an is generally organized according to the length of its chapters. The first chapter is in the form of a prayer, which is seven verses long and is recited several times by Muslims in their daily prayers (*salat*). In addition to *al-Fatiha*, a Muslim is expected to recite a few other verses of the Qur'an during prayer. Although not all verses are in the form of prayers—for instance, some are historical, and others are ethical or legal in nature—any part of the Qur'an can be recited during prayer.

Chapter 1 of the Qur'an: al-Fatiha (the Opening)

In the name of God, the Lord of Mercy, the Giver of Mercy! Praise belongs to God, Lord of the Worlds, the Lord of Mercy, the Giver of Mercy, Master of the Day of Judgment. It is You we worship; it is You we ask for help. Guide us to the straight path: the path of those You have blessed, those who incur no anger and who have not gone astray.

Starting with the second chapter, *al-Baqara* (the Cow), which is the longest and comprises 286 verses, the chapters of the Qur'an gradually become shorter. Thus, the shortest chapters, 110, 108 and 103, all appear towards the end of the Qur'an and comprise only three verses each.

Some chapters of the Qur'an

The following table gives an overview of selected chapters of the Qur'an. The first column refers to the position of the chapter in the order according to the standard numbering of the Qur'an. The number of verses is shown, and the location where the chapter was revealed is provided.

No.	Sura name	Translation	Number of verses	Location of revelation
1	*al-Fatiha*	the Opening	7	Mecca
2	*al-Baqara*	the Cow	286	Medina
3	*Al Imran*	the Family of Imran	200	Medina
4	*al-Nisa'*	Women	176	Medina
14	*Ibrahim*	Abraham	52	Mecca
19	*Maryam*	Mary	98	Mecca
24	*al-Nur*	Light	64	Medina
30	*al-Rum*	the Byzantines	60	Mecca
40	*Ghafir*	the Forgiver	85	Mecca
41	*Fussilat*	(Verses) Made Distinct	54	Mecca
42	*al-Shura*	Consultation	53	Mecca
53	*al-Najm*	the Star	62	Mecca
55	*al-Rahman*	the Most Beneficent	78	Medina
67	*al-Mulk*	Sovereignty	30	Mecca
68	*al-Qalam*	the Pen	52	Mecca
71	*Nuh*	Noah	28	Mecca
91	*al-Shams*	the Sun	15	Mecca
92	*al-Layl*	the Night	21	Mecca
113	*al-Falaq*	the Daybreak	5	Mecca
114	*al-Nas*	Humankind	6	Mecca

An example of a short chapter of the Qur'an

97. *Laylat al-Qadr* (the Night of Glory)

This Meccan *sura* celebrates the night when the Qur'an was first revealed.

In the name of God, the Lord of Mercy, the Giver of Mercy
We sent it down on the Night of Glory. What will explain to you what that Night of Glory is? The Night of Glory is better than a thousand months; on that night the angels and the Spirit descend again and again with their Lord's permission on every task; [there is] peace that night until the break of dawn.

Each chapter of the Qur'an has a very short name—in most cases, only one word—which Muslim scholars generally agree was assigned by the Prophet Muhammad under divine instruction. In many cases, this name refers to an issue, event or person found or mentioned in the chapter. 'The Cow' referred to in the name of chapter 2 (*al-Baqara*) appears in connection with a story of the Prophet Moses and the Israelites. This story relates the response of the Israelites to God's command to sacrifice a cow. The name 'Cow' appears to have been chosen because of the significance of the story rather than its length, as the story comprises only seven out of the 286 verses in the chapter.[6] Although this story is not mentioned elsewhere in the chapter, the theme of disobedience to God's commandments, to which the story relates, is touched on repeatedly.

The story of the Cow, from chapter 2: *al-Baqara* (the Cow)

Remember when Moses said to his people, 'God commands you to sacrifice a cow.' They said, 'Are you making fun of us?' He answered, 'God forbid that I should be so ignorant.' They said, 'Call on your Lord for us, to show us what sort of cow it should be.' He answered, 'God says it should neither be too old nor too young, but in between, so do as you are commanded.' They said, 'Call on your Lord for us, to show us what colour it should be.' He answered, 'God says it should be a bright yellow cow, pleasing to the eye.' They said, 'Call on your Lord for us, to show us [exactly] what it is: all cows are more or less alike to us. With God's will, we shall be guided.' He replied, 'It is a perfect and unblemished cow, not trained to till the earth or water the fields.' They said 'Now you have brought the truth,' and so they slaughtered it, though they almost failed to do so. (Qur'an 2:67–73)

At other times, the chapter's name may simply be a prominent word found in the chapter, in some cases the first word of the chapter, which may not be related to a particular narrative. For instance, the title of the thirty-sixth chapter, *Ya'-Sin*, comes from the two Arabic letters *ya'* and *sin*, with which that chapter begins. Several chapters begin with such combinations of letters, which Muslim commentators believe to have a hidden meaning.

Examples of chapters of the Qur'an which begin with combinations of Arabic letters

Twenty-nine chapters of the Qur'an begin with a combination of Arabic letters. The letters are part of the Arabic alphabet, and have no specific meaning by themselves. The following are examples of such chapters:

No.	Sura name	Translation	Beginning letters
2	al-Baqara	the Cow	Alif Lam Mim
3	Al Imran	the Family of Imran	Alif Lam Mim
7	al-A'raf	the Heights	Alif Lam Mim Sad
10	Yunus	Jonah	Alif Lam Ra'
11	Hud	Hud	Alif Lam Ra'
12	Yusuf	Joseph	Alif Lam Ra'
13	al-Ra'd	Thunder	Alif Lam Mim Ra'

14	Ibrahim	Abraham	Alif Lam Ra'
15	al-Hijr	al-Hijr (Stone City)	Alif Lam Ra'
19	Maryam	Mary	Kaf Ha' Ya' Ain Sad
20	Ta Ha	(the Letters) Ta' Ha'	Ta' Ha'
26	al-Shu'ara'	the Poets	Ta' Sin Mim
27	al-Naml	the Ants	Ta' Sin
28	al-Qasas	the Stories	Ta' Sin Mim

Compiling the Qur'an as a Single Text: The Muslim View

Muslims believe that while the Qur'an was being revealed between 610 and 632 CE, the Prophet reportedly instructed his followers to memorize the verses as they were revealed and also to write them down. However, there was not yet an urgent need to compile them into a single book; the Arab society of the time had a strong oral tradition, and many relied on memory and narration to preserve the most important texts of the culture, such as poetry. The Qur'an, although it is not poetry, had some elements of the poetic style and it was considered a text of very high literary quality. Muslim tradition holds that it was the literary beauty of the Qur'an which initially attracted many people to Islam during the time of the Prophet.

In keeping with this oral tradition, the Prophet and the first Muslim community would often recite parts of the revelation both publicly and in private throughout the 22 years of revelation. From the year 620 CE, once the five daily prayers had been made a religious obligation, Qur'anic verses would also be recited regularly during these prayers. Similarly, all the revelations the Prophet had received up to the beginning of the month of Ramadan (the month of fasting) each year would also be recited during that month, helping to preserve the text in the memory of the community.

Although the Qur'an was not compiled as a single volume before the death of the Prophet, Muslim tradition holds that most, if not all, verses had in fact been written down on a variety of different materials by the time of the Prophet's death in 11/632. It is believed that the Prophet left clear instructions as to how the Qur'an should be organized and read as a single text. These instructions are understood to be the basis of the Qur'an's order as it exists today.

Muslim tradition holds that Abu Bakr (r.11–13/632–634), who reigned briefly as the first caliph, instructed Zayd ibn Thabit (d.45/665), one of the Prophet's foremost scribes of the Qur'an, to compile the text of the Qur'an as a single book. Zayd was assisted by a committee made up of other Companions of the Prophet. This instruction was apparently given in response to the deaths in battle of many Muslims who had retained the Qur'an in their memory. If a large number of these Muslims were to die, there was a danger that parts of the Qur'an could be lost, or disputes could emerge about their authenticity. It is reported that the complete, written text, as it was compiled during Abu Bakr's reign, remained with him until his death. The text was then left in the care of the second caliph, Umar ibn al-Khattab (r.13–23/634–644), and then entrusted to Umar's daughter Hafsa (d.45/666), a wife of the Prophet.

While the sources indicate that the texts of the Qur'an had already been gathered together in some form during the time of Abu Bakr, it was the third caliph, Uthman (r.23–35/644–656), who saw the need to establish a standardized text that could be disseminated widely. The need for a standardized text was based on advice received by Uthman that disputes about the Qur'an and its recitations were emerging throughout the newly expanding Muslim caliphate.[7] Thus, Uthman instructed Zayd and several other Companions to use the first collection of the Qur'an, along with other reliable sources, to compile a single authoritative text. Due to the existence of variant readings, Uthman instructed Zayd and his committee to favour the Quraysh dialect of Arabic (of Mecca) in instances where the reading of a particular text was disputed. This was based on the fact that the Prophet himself was from the tribe of Quraysh, and the Qur'an was revealed in this dialect. The Qur'an says: 'We [God] have never sent a messenger who did not use his people's own language to make things clear for them.'[8]

After Zayd had collected the verses of the Qur'an and checked them with other Companions, copies were made of the final text, which were sent to the provincial centres of the caliphate, such as Damascus, Basra and Kufa, in about 24/645. Uthman then instructed his governors to destroy all other texts of the Qur'an circulating in their provinces, and to establish the codex that was sent to them as the single authoritative text of the Qur'an. In so doing, Uthman unified Muslims around a single text. Today, this text, known as 'the Mushaf of Uthman' (the Uthmanic Codex), is the authorittive text of the Qur'an for all Muslims. In the post-Uthmanic period the Qur'an came to be known not only in its oral form (as it existed at the time of the Prophet) but also as a written codex (*mushaf*) or 'closed official corpus'[9] to which nothing could be added.

In discussing the difference between the Qur'an as an idea at the time of the Prophet and as a standardized codex in the post-prophetic period, William Graham, a scholar of Middle Eastern studies, says:

> It is obvious that 'al-Qur'an' in the later, fixed meaning of God's Word as written down in the *masahif* [plural of *mushaf*] is necessarily a post-Uthmatic, or at the very least a post-Muhammadan, usage. Until the codification of what has since served as the *textus receptus*—or at least until active revelation ceased with Muhammad's death—there could have been no use of 'al-Qur'an' to refer to the complete body of 'collected revelations in written form'. This is not to deny that even in the Qur'an there may be hints of a developing notion of the collective revelation in the use of the words *qur'an* and *kitab*, but rather to emphasize the fallacy involved in 'reading back' the later, concretized meaning of these terms into all of their Qur'anic or other traditional-text occurrences.[10]

Although this view is not considered controversial by most Muslims, it should be noted that it is easy to fall into the trap to which Graham refers in this quote; namely that of understanding the words 'Qur'an' and '*kitab*', as they were used during the time of the Prophet, as referring to a completed and written text during the time of the Prophet. For this reason, the use of terminology is important in any debate about the Qur'an. Use of the word '*qur'an*' during the time of the Prophet should be understood as a reference to the ongoing revelations that were being received and were in fact evolving. Only in the post-Uthmanic period can it also be understood as a physical *mushaf* or codified text.

Important dates of the Qur'an according to Muslim tradition	
610:	First verses of the Qur'an revealed.
620:	Five daily prayers are made obligatory and the Prophet experiences his Night Journey to Jerusalem and Ascension to Heaven.
2/624:	Verses revealed which make *zakat* (giving in charity) and fasting in Ramadan compulsory and which change the direction of prayer to Mecca.

3/625:	Verses revealed which prohibit drinking wine.
9/631:	Verses revealed which make Hajj obligatory, and prohibit riba (understood to mean usury or interest).
11/632:	The final Qur'anic revelation occurs, the Prophet Muhammad dies and Abu Bakr becomes the caliph.
11/633:	The first collection of the Qur'an is completed under Abu Bakr.
13/634:	Abu Bakr dies and Umar ibn al-Khattab becomes the caliph; Umar is entrusted with the collected texts of the Qur'an which he later entrusts to his daughter Hafsa.
23/644:	Umar dies and Uthman ibn Affan becomes the caliph.
24/645:	Uthman commissions Zayd and his committee to create an official codex of the Qur'an to be circulated through the Muslim provinces. The Uthmanic Codex is finalized and disseminated throughout the Muslim lands; any variants are destroyed.
35/656:	Uthman dies and Ali ibn Abi Talib (Muhammad's son-in-law) becomes the caliph.

Although the vast majority of Muslims today from both the Sunni and Shi'i[11] streams of Islam accept this codex, some early Shi'a Muslims disputed the traditional account of its compilation. Some early Shi'a believed that Ali ibn Abi Talib, the Prophet's son-in-law and one of the most revered figures in Shi'ism, transcribed the Qur'an as a single text in the days following the death of the Prophet. This text was said to include not only the text of the Qur'an in chronological order, but also commentary and interpretation by the Prophet, as well as the Prophet's clarifications about which verses of the Qur'an had abrogated others, which were to be understood as 'clear' and which were to be seen as 'ambiguous'.[12] Unfortunately, there is no evidence to suggest that any copies of this reported text of Ali are still in existence.

Muslim tradition holds that the codex compiled during the caliphate of Uthman was accurate and uncorrupted, since it was compiled within a short period after the Prophet's death and in the presence of those who had witnessed the revelation.

Although the Uthmanic Codex is considered accurate, there is some question as to whether it includes everything that was revealed to the Prophet. In fact, some argue that the Qur'an itself points to the possibility that some verses might have been excluded during the Prophet's lifetime. For instance, verse 2:106 says: 'Any revelation We cause to be superseded or forgotten, We replace with something better or similar. Do you [Prophet] not know that God has power over everything?'[13] Some Muslim scholars argue, based on this verse, that certain verses may have been 'abrogated' and erased from the Qur'an altogether by God, or by the Prophet on divine instruction. Even if this were the case, Muslim scholars on the whole reject the notion that the compilers of the Qur'an themselves may have discarded any parts of the revealed text. The early exegete Zamakhshari (d.539/1144) summarizes the general Muslim understanding of abrogation as follows, in his interpretation of verse 2:106:

> To abrogate a verse means that God removes (azala) it by putting another in its place. To cause a verse to be abrogated means that God gives the command that it be abrogated; that is, He commands Gabriel to set forth the verse as abrogated by announcing its cancellation. Deferring a verse means that God sets it aside (with the proclamation) and causes it to disappear without

a substitute. To cause a verse to be cast into oblivion means that it no longer is preserved in the heart. The following is the meaning [of the verse 2:106]: Every verse is made to vanish whenever the well-being (*maslaha*) (of the community) requires that it be eliminated—either on the basis of the wording or the virtue of what is right, or on the basis of both of these reasons together, either with or without a substitute.[14]

Thus, from a Muslim perspective, the codex of Uthman represents the historical and authentic codification of the revelation to the Prophet Muhammad. Any texts that God may have caused to be superseded or forgotten, or the variant readings which were omitted in the attempt to unify Muslims on one text by Uthman, are not considered as being an essential part of the codified text. As such, this codification has become the basis of Islamic teachings and practices, and the many developments in understanding and interpretation of the Qur'an throughout history. For many Muslims, to question its authenticity and reliability amounts to questioning Islam itself.

Challenges by Western Scholars of the Qur'an

A number of Western scholars have criticized the traditional Muslim view of the history of the Qur'an. They include Richard Bell, whose ideas were, to some extent, taken up by other scholars, such as Montgomery Watt. Bell questioned the validity of aspects of the traditional Muslim view, arguing that some Muslim sources include contradictory statements about whether it was Abu Bakr, Umar or Uthman who initiated the task of collecting the Qur'an. He also had doubts about the supposed reasons for initiating the collection of the Qur'an, questioning the truth of reports that a large number of those who memorized the Qur'an were killed in battle. He further suggested that if it were true that the first collection of the Qur'an was, in fact, initiated by Abu Bakr, it was obviously not accorded much authority, as Uthman apparently made a fresh collection only a few years later. Bell's view is that any collection made during Abu Bakr's time was probably only partial and unofficial.

While positions such as Bell's do not question Muslim tradition regarding the collection of the Qur'an in its entirety, other Western scholars have attempted to revisit fundamental aspects of this tradition. Many have argued that the Qur'an was an evolving text, the content of which may not have been fixed, in either oral or written form, until well after the Prophet's death. This position clearly contradicts key aspects of Islamic tradition regarding the Qur'an. Some scholars have also argued that much of the Islamic tradition and literature on issues related to the collection of the Qur'an was fabricated during the second century of Islam. The British scholar John Wansbrough was one of the foremost proponents of this approach. His main ideas are found in his work, *Quranic Studies: Sources and Methods of Scriptural Interpretation*, which has influenced numerous scholars in the West.

One of the most controversial aspects of Wansbrough's work was that he approached the Qur'an as a literary work, in the tradition of the Hebrew and Christian scriptures, and regarded it as a purely man-made product. Wansbrough made a number of 'conjectural' proposals, as he called them, among them that Islam could be more accurately defined as a sect which grew out of the Judaeo-Christian tradition during a period of fierce debate between existing Jewish and Christian groups. He suggested that during this time, Arab tribes adapted Judaeo-Christian texts to their own cultures, eventually developing their own 'Islamic' scriptures over the first/seventh and second/eighth centuries.[15] This argument was supported by Wansbrough's assertion that no textual evidence existed regarding the concept of 'Islam', or the collection of the Qur'an as a text, until 150 years after the Prophet's death.[16]

Wansbrough's use of methods of biblical criticism led him to conclude that the Islamic tradition is a 'salvation history'—a term used in biblical studies to describe a theologically and evangelically motivated myth related to a religion's origins that is projected back in time.[17] However, his main aim was not to identify why the Qur'an was compiled. Rather, Wansbrough's focus was on determining how and when the Qur'an came to be accepted and canonized as 'scripture'; something he believed did not occur until the Umayyad caliphate, over 100 years after the Prophet's death.[18]

Wansbrough's work inspired other scholars in the revisionist tradition, such as Michael Cook and Patricia Crone, who attempted to reconstruct the history of the origins of Islam. In *Hagarism: The Making of the Islamic World*,[19] Cook and Crone proposed that Islam was actually a messianic Arab movement allied with Judaism, which attempted to reclaim Syria and the Holy Land from the Byzantine empire. Wansbrough himself was critical of the book's methodological assumptions, and the authors themselves have since moved away from some of their initial theories.

According to a British scholar, Gerald Hawting, Wansbrough was mainly concerned to separate the link typically made between the Qur'an and the life of the Prophet Muhammad, who he believed to be merely an idea created by the Islamic tradition, just as some biblical scholars believe Jesus to be a product of Christianity.[20] Hawting suggests that many scholars do not approach Islam seriously—instead of examining the religion with academic rigour, many refrain from questioning issues such as the origins of the Qur'an, possibly out of a desire not to offend Muslims. In contrast, he argues that Wansbrough took Islam seriously by subjecting the Qur'an to the same critical historical analysis used in the study of Christian and Jewish texts.

However, for many Muslims, the views of scholars like Wansbrough are highly controversial and, indeed, unpalatable. An example of the Muslim response to this scholarship is the work of Muhammad Azami, who, in his work *The History of the Qur'anic Text from Revelation to Compilation*,[21] attempts to defend the historical reliability of the Qur'an. Azami cites traditional Muslim sources in arguing that approximately 65 Companions served as scribes for the Prophet for varying periods, and were reported to have written down entire sections of the Qur'an before the Prophet's death.[22] He also suggests that written documents were, in fact, already part of early Muslim culture, and that many Companions reportedly had their own records of parts of the Qur'an.[23] Azami argues that, based on available records, the only variations of Qur'anic verses known at the time were minor and did not alter the meaning of the texts. For instance, minor variations in vowels sometimes occurred, or there was a shift from the second person to the third person, with little or no impact on meaning.[24]

A criticism of this traditional response is that many of these arguments are circular. While revisionist Western scholars like Wansbrough have questioned the very authenticity of the Qur'an and the traditions concerning its collection and compilation, Azami's counter-arguments are based almost entirely on these traditions and the Qur'an itself. As a scholar of hadith, he seems to rely on an authentication of these traditions, using the traditional approach to hadith criticism, which a number of Western scholars have also rejected.

However, other scholars of the Qur'an, including some Western scholars, have cited debates among Muslim communities from the first/seventh century about the content of the Qur'an as evidence of the Qur'an's early compilation. For example, it is reported that during this time the Kharijis rejected the twelfth chapter of the Qur'an, and that some early Shi'a accused the official compilers of excluding certain verses, which supported their views, from the complete official text.[25] Other scholars, such as John Burton, have also argued that the Prophet himself had 'sanctioned' a complete 'edition' of the Qur'an by the time of his death.[26]

An American scholar, Estelle Whelan, has also criticized aspects of Wansbrough's analysis for assuming that the Qur'an's compilation followed a similar path to that of Hebrew scripture.[27] Whelan refers to evidence of Qur'anic inscriptions at the Dome of the Rock, in Jerusalem, that date from around 65–86/685–705, only half a century after the Prophet's death. Some of the most prominent inscriptions appear to be drawn from Qur'anic verses. While most match the standard Uthmanic Codex, some appear to contain slight modifications, and at one point two verses are conflated.[28]

Whelan argues that the best explanation for the modifications is that they were introduced to allow the inscription to flow as a single text. She comments that although there were 'efforts to establish and preserve a standard version [of the Qur'an] … there has [also] been a tradition of drawing upon and modifying that text for a variety of rhetorical purposes.'[29] This practice was 'dependent upon recognition of the text by the listeners, or readers'.[30] This implies that for creative use of Qur'anic texts to have occurred, they must already have been the 'common property of the community'.[31] Further, had the codex still been undergoing revision at this early stage, it is difficult to believe that the variations in such a prominent inscription would not have influenced the final version.[32]

Other evidence cited by Whelan includes Qur'anic inscriptions from the Prophet's mosque, in Medina, that seem to indicate that the order of at least chapters 91–114 had been established by the end of the first/ seventh century.[33] She also cites evidence from a number of sources about the existence of professional Qur'an copyists in Medina at a similar time, which indicates a demand for copies of an established text.[34] Further discussion of Western scholarship on the Qur'an can be found in Chapter 6.

Evolution of the Script of the Qur'an and its Presentation

The earliest copies of the Qur'an were written in what is referred to as 'Uthmanic orthography' (*al-rasm al-uthmani*). Uthman's committee for the compilation of the Qur'an, led by Zayd, wrote the first complete codex of the Qur'an using this orthography. The original manuscript of the Uthmanic Codex was written in an early Arabic script, known as Hijazi. In its first/seventh-century form, this script did not mark any vowels and it was difficult to differentiate between certain consonants. For example, the Arabic letters *ba'*, *ta'* and *tha'* could only be distinguished from one another based on their context, as the letters themselves were written in exactly the same way. Although this may seem problematic, it is unlikely that these features caused difficulties for the first generation of Muslims, who were predominantly Arabic-speaking and had a reasonable knowledge of the Qur'an.

However, as the number of non-Arabic-speaking Muslims began to grow, reliance on this basic script became increasingly difficult. Consequently, from the end of the first/seventh through to the third/ninth centuries, continual improvements were made to the script in order to facilitate reading of the Qur'an by both Arab and non-Arab Muslims. These changes to the script also came about because of the interest of early caliphs in 'Arabizing' the bureaucracy of the Muslim state, particularly under the Umayyad caliphate. In order to achieve this, it was necessary to develop a more efficient and readable script for use in official documentation and correspondence. As the script was improved, reading of the Qur'an also became easier.

Improvements to the Arabic script included the addition of dots to differentiate between certain consonants with the same basic form, and the addition of short and long vowels.[35] Other improvements specific to the Qur'an included signs to indicate the end of a verse, parts of a sentence where reciters might pause, and parts where they should continue in order to avoid reading a partial section which may convey an incorrect meaning.

Given that Arabic words without vowel markings can be read in a number of different ways, their inclusion helped greatly to guide readers of the Qur'an who were unfamiliar with the text in its oral form, or were not Arabic speakers. Copies of the Qur'an published today contain full vowel markings in order to allow both Arabic and non-Arabic speakers to read the Qur'an with greater ease. Many printed copies also contain recitation marks, as described above. Because vowel and recitation markings are not necessary for comprehension, they are not found in other modern Arabic texts, such as newspapers or books.

Despite all these improvements, the underlying form of the original Uthmanic orthography of the Qur'an has not been altered significantly. This fact reflects the desire of early Muslims to retain the original wording and script of the Qur'an. This desire has persisted until modern times and, in the early twentieth century, attempts to transcribe the Qur'an using scripts such as the Latin alphabet were vigorously opposed by Muslim scholars, who argued that this might lead to distortion of the Qur'anic text.

For ease of reference, modern copies of the Qur'an also include verse numbers. Unlike the numbering of chapters, which is fixed, there is more than one method for numbering the verses, although the actual text remains the same. Hence, the total number of Qur'anic verses may range from 6,212 to 6,250, depending on the system used. The reasons for such differences are varied. Richard Bell and Montgomery Watt have suggested that the 'varying systems of verse-numbering depend to some extent, though not entirely, upon varying judgement as to where the rhyme was intended to fall in particular cases.'[36] In other cases, the reasons for differences are more straightforward. For instance, some Indo-Pakistani systems count the basmala phrase (which reads 'In the name of God, the Lord of Mercy, the Giver of Mercy', and is found at the beginning of every chapter except chapter 9, *al-Tawba*, Repentance) as part of the number of verses. Most other numbering systems around the world only include this phrase as part of the first chapter (the Opening or *al-Fatiha*), while some do not include it at all. Other variations are less predictable, as in one Indian system that divides verse 6:73 into two, while it combines verses 36:34–35 into one.[37]

The Egyptian numbering system, first introduced under King Fu'ad and originally published in 1925,[38] has become the standard used throughout most of the Muslim world today. However, other variations, such as those mentioned above, are still in circulation.[39] One of the better-known variations in the West was devised by the German Orientalist Gustav Flügel in 1834. Flügel is believed to have created his numbering system based on his reading of the rhyming endings of phrases in the Qur'an. However, it does not correlate exactly with any known Muslim tradition. Despite this, his system has served as the basis for many European translations and other works on the Qur'an.[40]

The final method of partitioning the Qur'an to be discussed here is based on the common Muslim practice of reciting the full text of the Qur'an over 30 days during the month of Ramadan. This division involves separating the Qur'an into 30 parts, of roughly equal length, each known as a *juz'* (part). Each *juz'* is named after the first word or phrase that appears in it. The first *juz'* is a slight exception to this rule, as it is named *alif lam mim* after the three-letter beginning of chapter 2, rather than the first chapter with which it begins.

The Nature of the Qur'anic Text: The Idea of Inimitability

For Muslims, the Qur'an is considered the most perfect expression of the Arabic language; a unique piece of writing that is comparable to no other and which, as the Qur'an itself states, can be matched by no human composition.[41] This aspect of the Qur'an, referred to generally as its 'inimitability' (*i'jaz al-qur'an*), has been the subject of major works by Muslim linguists, interpreters of the Qur'an and literary critics.

The idea of the Qur'an's inimitability is supported by a number of Qur'anic verses,[42] which challenged the Prophet Muhammad's opponents in Mecca to produce a literary compilation similar to the Qur'an. These challenges came in response to accusations by the Prophet's opponents that the Qur'an was composed by the Prophet himself rather than God. In one such challenge, the Qur'an states, 'Say: "Even if all human-kind and *jinn*[43] came together to produce something like this Qur'an, they could not produce anything like it, however much they helped each other".'[44] In other places it explicitly challenges people to produce ten chapters like it, saying: 'If they say, "He [Muhammad] has invented it [the Qur'an] himself," say, "Then produce ten invented *suras* like it, and call in whoever you can beside God, if you are truthful".'[45] As the Meccans continually failed to meet this challenge, it was later reduced to producing just one chapter like the Qur'an.[46] According to Muslim tradition, the Qur'an's inimitability is supported by the fact that no Meccan was ever able to meet this challenge, despite their general reputation as masters of Arabic expression.

Another important idea associated with the inimitability of the Qur'an is the belief that the Prophet Muhammad was illiterate, and thus incapable of producing a work as eloquent as the Qur'an by his own efforts. Some suggest that the Prophet's illiteracy is supported by at least two Qur'anic verses,[47] but the meaning of the word translated as 'illiterate' (*ummiy*) was often debated by early Muslims. Although it can mean illiterate, *ummiy* can also be translated as 'gentile', reflecting the fact that the Prophet was an Arab, not a Jew. Some Muslim scholars believed that the Prophet was able to read and write, though not proficiently.[48]

Muslim views regarding the basis for the Qur'an's inimitability vary considerably. Some suggest that the impossibility of producing anything like the Qur'an is because God prevented anyone from doing so. The majority of Muslims, however, believe it is because of the Qur'an's unique style and content. This argument is generally related to the presumably unsurpassable eloquence and unique style of the Qur'an. The content of the Qur'an, particularly its inclusion of historical information about earlier prophets and their communities that would have been impossible for any person of the Prophet's period to know, is also seen as evidence of the Qur'an's inimitability, as is the apparent lack of contradictions found in the text.

In recent years, some Muslims have also approached the Qur'an's inimitability from a mathematical perspective. One view claims that certain permutations of the number 19 can be found in the words and phrases of the Qur'an. For instance, a number of key phrases in the Qur'an are said to contain 19 letters, or appear 19 times, or a multiple thereof.[49] The recurrence of the number 19 and its multiples is said to be evidence of God's handiwork. It is argued that, without access to computers, the Prophet could not have independently composed a work of the Qur'an's significance, while inserting such a numerical pattern into the text.

A number of modern theorists cite scientific 'facts' found in the Qur'an that were not discovered until the modern era as a basis of this inimitability. For example, proponents of this theory claim that the following verse refers to the Big Bang: 'Are the disbelievers not aware that the heavens and the earth used to be joined together and that We ripped them apart, that We made every living thing from water?'[50] This so-called scientific inimitability of the Qur'an has been a source of much debate in the modern period.

These two approaches, the 'mathematical' and 'scientific', are indicative of some of the new ways that Muslims today are attempting to demonstrate the 'truth' of the Qur'an. These approaches have a certain level of popular appeal.

Connection Between the Qur'an and the Traditions of the Prophet

The Qur'an occupies a central place in Islam's textual tradition, but it is not the only source from which Islamic laws, principles and traditions are drawn.

The second most important textual source of Islam is hadith. Hadith refers to the reports by the Prophet's contemporaries about the Prophet's speech and conduct. These hadith were initially narrated informally, before being collected and compiled by hadith scholars. Hadith are considered to be a crucial part of the Islamic textual tradition, as a result of the importance of the relationship between the Qur'an and the normative behaviour of the Prophet (which is referred to as his sunna). As we will see later, the Qur'an itself provides relatively few explicit instructions about how to live as a Muslim, that is, in submission to God. A large number of the Qur'an's ethical teachings are expressed in general terms and were only put into practice by early Muslims after they were given a practical interpretation by the Prophet. Thus, the Prophet is often referred to in Muslim tradition as the 'walking Qur'an', and his sunna, or his ways of doing things, was regarded as a practical commentary on the Qur'an. Adherence to the sunna constitutes the practical element of what it means to be a Muslim. A Muslim's knowledge of the Prophet's sunna comes from the hadith.

There are two components to a hadith: its *matn* or textual content, and its *sanad* or chain of transmission. An important field of study in Islamic scholarship is the analysis of hadith and their chains of transmission. In the first two centuries of Islam a large number of hadith of questionable origin were in circulation. In response to this situation, scholarly efforts were made to collect and evaluate all available hadith according to several criteria. These criteria related either to the reliability of the narrators of hadith, or the internal consistency of their textual content. One of the most important and reliable narrators of hadith was the Prophet's wife, A'isha.

Two of the most important collections of hadith were made in the third/ ninth century by Bukhari (d.256/870) and Muslim ibn Hajjaj (d.261/875). Bukhari's hadith collection, called *Sahih* (meaning 'The Authentic'), is considered by Sunni Muslims to be the most authentic collection. Bukhari is said to have considered over 600,000 hadith circulating during his time. After stringent analysis, only about 7,000 of the 'soundest' narrations were eventually included in his collection. Sunnis also consider the multi-volume hadith collection by Muslim, also called *Sahih*, to be highly accurate. Other, less reliable hadith collections also exist, and Shi'a Muslims also have their own collections of hadith.

Despite the stringency of the hadith collectors' methods, questions still remain about the authenticity of many hadith. In particular, the authenticity of hadith which seem to contradict core Islamic teachings, such as those which support sectarian or misogynistic views, is now being questioned. Some Western scholars, such as Joseph Schacht, have questioned the authenticity of the entire corpus of hadith.[51] Many Muslim scholars today, while rejecting the idea that all hadith are fabrications, have also called for a reexamination of the hadith literature in the light of new methods of textual analysis and criticism.

An example of a hadith related to the Qur'anic injunction to pray is as follows:

> A man entered the mosque and started praying while the Messenger of God was sitting some-where in the mosque. Then (after finishing the prayer) the man came to the Prophet and greeted him. The Prophet said to him, 'Go back and pray, for you have not prayed.' The man went back, and having prayed, he came and greeted the Prophet. The Prophet after returning his greetings said, 'Go back and pray, for you did not pray.' On the third time the man said, '(O Messenger of God!) teach me (how to pray).' The Prophet said, 'When you get up for the prayer, perform the ablution properly and then face the Qibla [direction of prayer] and say "God is the Greatest", and then recite of what you know of the Qur'an, and then bow, and remain in this state till you feel at rest in bowing, and then raise your head and stand straight; and then prostrate till you feel at rest in prostration, and then sit up till you feel at rest while sitting; and then prostrate again till you feel at rest in prostration; and then get up and stand straight, and do all this in all your prayers.'[52]

This hadith provides details about how the Prophet actually prayed. The injunction to pray is repeated several times in the Qur'an, as in the following verse: 'Keep up the prayer, pay the prescribed alms, and bow your head [in worship] with those who bow theirs.'[53] But the Qur'an does not provide any details as to how a Muslim should perform the prayer. These practical details are found in hadith. Hence, the hadith form a critical part of the development of Islamic practice and are also highly relevant to the practice of Qur'anic interpretation.

Summary

Some of the important points we have discussed in this chapter include:

- The word Qur'an means 'recitation' or 'reading'.
- According to Islamic sources, a complete codex of the Qur'an was compiled within 25 years of the Prophet's death.
- Original copies of the Qur'an did not have vowel markings; today copies of the Qur'an often include vowel and other markings to assist with recitation.
- Muslims believe that, as the Word of God, the Qur'an is inimitable, and its style cannot be reproduced by humans.
- Reports of the Prophet's sayings and deeds, known as hadith, are an important component of the Islamic textual tradition.

Recommended Reading

Muhammad Mustafa Al-Azami, *The History of the Qur'anic Text from Revelation to Compilation*, Leicester: UK Islamic Academy, 2003.

- In this book Azami provides insights into the history of the Qur'anic text, with a view to refuting historical and contemporary attacks on the Qur'an. He also assesses a number of alternative Western theories regarding the Qur'an and questions their motivation and accuracy.

Farid Esack, 'Gathering the Qur'an', in *The Qur'an: A Short Introduction*, Oxford: Oneworld, 2001, pages 77–99.

- In this chapter Esack traces the collection and documentation of the Qur'an as a book, from the time of revelation until the period of the third caliph, Uthman.

William Graham, *Beyond the Written Word*, Cambridge: Cambridge University Press, 1993.

- In this book Graham re-examines the concept of 'scripture' by analysing the traditions of oral use and sacred writings of religions around the world. He suggests that there is a need for a new perspective on understanding the words used to describe 'scripture' in the Qur'an, and the way in which scripture has been used by people throughout history.

Daniel A. Madigan, *The Qur'an's Self-Image: Writing and Authority in Islam's Scripture*, Princeton, NJ: Princeton University Press, 2001.

- In this book Madigan explores the ways in which the Qur'an refers to itself. His first chapter in particular, 'The Qur'an as a Book', explores the concept of the Qur'an as a book or scripture. Throughout the book, Madigan makes reference to the Qur'an's own perspective as expressed through a number of Qur'anic verses.

Notes

1. As with other Semitic languages, most words have a root, which consists of three consonants that are then combined with other vowels and letters to produce derivates of the root meaning. The last root consonant of Qur'an—'—represents a glottal stop in Arabic transliteration.
2. Qur'an: 4:113; see also 2:231; 4:105.
3. Qur'an: 21:10.
4. Qur'an: 16:64; 6:155; 6:154–157; 2:176; 3:7; 4:105; 29:47.
5. Qur'an: 55:1.
6. Qur'an: 2:67–73.
7. Caliphate: a system of governance that combines both religious and political rule.
8. Qur'an: 14:4.
9. Mohammed Arkoun, *Rethinking Islam*, trans. Robert D. Lee, Boulder: Westview Press, 1994, p. 37.
10. William Graham, *Beyond the Written Word*, Cambridge: Cambridge University Press, 1993, p. 89.
11. See Chapter 1 for further discussion of religio-political groups in Islam.
12. Ali Abbas (ed.), 'The Quran Compiled by Imam Ali (AS)', *A Shi'ite Encyclopedia*, Chapter 8. Accessed 20 February 2007: www.al-islam. org/encyclopedia/.
13. Qur'an: 2:106.
14. Zamakhshari, *al-Kashshaf*, in Helmut Gatje, *The Qur'an and its Exegesis*, trans. and ed. Alford T. Welch, Oxford: Oneworld, 1997, p. 58.
15. See John Wansbrough, *Qur'anic Studies: Sources and Methods of Scriptural Interpretation*, New York: Prometheus Books, 2004, pp. 78–81.
16. See Wansbrough, *Qur'anic Studies*, pp. 43–50.

17. Toby Lester, 'What is the Qur'an?', *The Atlantic Monthly*, January 1999, vol. 283, no. 1, p. 55.

18. See Wansbrough, *Qur'anic Studies*, p. 202.

19. Cambridge: Cambridge University Press, 1977.

20. Stephen Crittenden, 'John Wansbrough Remembered: Interview with Gerald Hawting', 26 June 2002, ABC, Radio National—The Religion Report. Accessed 20 August 2007: http://www.abc.net.au/rn/talks/8.30/ relrpt/stories/s591483. htm.

21. Muhammad Mustafa Al-Azami, *The History of the Qur'anic Text from Revelation to Compilation*, Leicester: UK Islamic Academy, 2003.

22. Azami, *The History of the Qur'anic Text*, p. 68.

23. Azami, *The History of the Qur'anic Text*, p. 69.

24. Azami, *The History of the Qur'anic Text*, p. 97–105.

25. Farid Esack, *The Qur'an: A Short Introduction*, Oxford: Oneworld, 2001, p. 91. Note—the Kharijis were an early school of Islamic thought that has largely disappeared today; the Shi'i stream of Islam is still in existence today. For more information on these groups see Chapter 11.

26. John Burton, *The Collection of the Qur'an*, Cambridge and New York: Cambridge University Press, 1977, pp. 239–240.

27. Estelle Whelan, 'Forgotten Witness: Evidence for the Early Codification of the Qur'an', *Journal of the American Oriental Society*, vol. 118, no. 1 (Jan–Mar 1998), p. 3.

28. Whelan, 'Forgotten Witness', pp. 4–6.

29. Whelan, 'Forgotten Witness', p. 8.

30. Whelan, 'Forgotten Witness', p. 8.

31. Whelan, 'Forgotten Witness', p. 8.

32. Whelan, 'Forgotten Witness', pp. 5–6.

33. Whelan, 'Forgotten Witness', pp. 8–10.

34. Whelan, 'Forgotten Witness', pp. 10–13.

35. The vowels that were added to the script are still used today. These are 'a', 'i' (pronounced like the English 'ee') and 'u' (pronounced like the English 'oo').

36. Montgomery Watt and Richard Bell, 'The External Form of the Quran', *Introduction to the Quran*, Edinburgh: Edinburgh University Press, 1995, pp. 70–71.

37. 'Different verse numbering systems in the Qur'an'. Accessed 20 February 2007: http://www.answering-islam.de/Main/ Quran/Text/numbers.html.

38. Ahmad von Denffer, 'Introduction to the Qur'an: A Rendition of the Original Work Titled *Ulum al Qur'an*', A.E. Souaiaia (ed.), *Studies in Islam and the Middle East (SIME) Journal*, SIME ePublishing (majalla.org), 2004. Accessed 5 September 2007: http://www.islamworld.net/UUQ/.

39. von Denffer, 'Introduction to the Qur'an'.

40. A. Jeffery and I. Mendelsohn, 'The Orthography of the Samarqand Codex', *Journal of the American Oriental Society*, vol. 63, New Haven: American Oriental Society, 1943, pp. 175–195.

41. See Qur'an: 2:23; 11:13; 10:38.

42. See Qur'an: 2:23; 11:13; 10:38.

43. *Jinn* are imperceptible spirits who, like humans, are capable of both good and evil. They are said to be created from fire.

44. Qur'an: 17:88.

45. Qur'an: 11:13.

46. See Qur'an: 10:38.

47. Qur'an: 7:157; 7:158.

48. For instance, Rashid al-Din Fadl Allah (d.718/1318) argued that it was highly unlikely that 'the best of created beings' would not have known the art of writing (*al-Madjmu'a al-rashidiyya al-sultaniyya*, in E. Geoffroy, 'Ummi', p. 864, P.J. Bearman et al. (eds), *Encyclopaedia of Islam*, vol. 10, Leiden: Brill, 2000, pp. 863–864).

49. Edip Yuksel, *www.19.org*, cited in Dave Thomas, 'Code 19 in the Quran?', *New Mexicans for Science and Reason*. Accessed 18 February 2007: http://www.nmsr.org/code19.htm.

50. Qur'an: 21:30.

51. See Joseph Schacht, *The Origins of Muhammadan Jurisprudence*, Oxford: Oxford University Press, 1950.

52. Bukhari, *Sahih al-Bukhari*, Vol. 8, Book 78 'The Book of Oaths and Vows', Chap. 15, No. 660, narrated by Abu Hurayra, in *The Translation of the Meanings of Sahih Al-Bukhari*, trans. Muhammad Muhsin Khan, Ankara, Turkey: Hilal Yayinlari, 1977, pp. 429–430.

53. Qur'an: 2:43. See also 2:110, 277; 11:114; and 22:78.

4

The Sunna of the Prophet

by Abdullah Saeed

T he most important source of authority for Muslims, after the Qur'an, is the normative behaviour of the Prophet Muhammad (known as Sunna). Sunna is literally 'the trodden path' and originally meant the customary law and practices prevalent in Arabia during the pre-Islamic era. For Muslims, however, it came to represent the normative behaviour of the Prophet. This Sunna is documented in hadith. Originally, the term hadith simply meant 'new' and was used in reference to a story or a report. Later, it came to refer to information about the Prophet Muhammad, such as his sayings and deeds and descriptions of his person, as reported by the Companions.

Before Muhammad ibn Idris al-Shafi'i (d. 204/819), after whom the influential Shafi'i school of law was named, a distinction was often made between Sunna and hadith. The Sunna was seen as the normative behaviour of the Prophet supported by generally agreed-upon practice of the Muslim community which in turn was based on the practice of the Prophet and the earliest Muslims. The focus was on 'normative practice'. This practice may or may not be supported by a particular hadith. What this means is that where there is a particular practice followed by the community and there is also a hadith to support that practice, the reliability of the hadith is strengthened. Similarly, where there is a hadith but no supporting practice, questions could be raised about the reliability of the hadith. A clear distinction therefore needed to be made between 'Sunna' and 'hadith' at the time. However, in the post-Shafi'i period—in large part due to his

Abdullah Saeed, "The Sunna of the Prophet," *Islamic Thought*, pp. 33–42. Copyright © 2006 by Taylor & Francis Group LLC. Reprinted with permission.

arguments—Sunna came to be equated with hadith. For Shafi'i, any authentic hadith was Sunna, whether or not there was a common practice in the community to back that hadith.

In both classical and modern times, however, arguments have been raised against equating the Sunna with the canons of hadith. Groups such as the Kharijis and the Mu'tazilis in the classical period (and certain modernists today) accepted the validity of the Sunna as the normative practice of the Prophet, but objected to the formulation of Sunna in hadith terms.

Anatomy of a Hadith

A hadith has two parts: (1) a chain of transmitters (*isnad*), which lists the names of the authorities who transmitted the particular hadith; and (2) a text (*matn*) which is the content of the hadith.

Chain of transmitters:

> Yahya related to me from Malik from Hisham ibn Urwa from his father from A'isha, the wife of the Prophet [may Allah bless him and grant him peace].

Text:

> … that al-Harith ibn Hisham asked the Messenger of Allah [may Allah bless him and grant him peace], 'How does the revelation come to you?' and the Messenger of Allah [may Allah bless him and grant him peace] said, 'Sometimes it comes to me like the ringing of a bell, and that is the hardest for me, and when it leaves me I remember what has been said. And sometimes the angel appears to me in the likeness of a man and talks to me and I remember what he says.' A'isha added, 'I saw it [revelation] coming down on him on an intensely cold day, and when it had left him his forehead was dripping with sweat.'

Hadith *Qudsi*

While hadith usually refers to traditions reporting the sayings and deeds of the Prophet Muhammad, some hadith belong to a special subset called hadith *qudsi* (sacred hadith). This is where the content of the hadith deals with something that God has said or revealed, but couched in the words of the Prophet. They differ from the verses of the Qur'an, in that the latter are considered the actual words of God, not of the Prophet. A hadith qudsi, for example, cannot be recited in the obligatory prayer in place of verses of the Qur'an. An example of a hadith qudsi is:

> On the authority of Anas [may Allah be pleased with him], who said: I heard the Messenger of Allah [may the blessings and peace of Allah be upon him] say: 'Allah the Almighty said: "O child of Adam, so long as you call upon Me and ask of Me, I shall forgive you for what you have done, and I shall not mind. O child of Adam, were your sins to reach the clouds of the sky and were you then to ask forgiveness of Me, I would forgive you. O child of Adam, were you to come to Me with sins nearly as great as the earth and were you then to face Me, ascribing no partner to Me, I would bring you forgiveness nearly as great as it
> [i.e. the earth]".'

Hadith: the Standard Muslim View

Preservation and Collection

Many Muslims believe that preservation of hadith began during the time of the Prophet. This was not in the form of written documents, but through memorization, a method familiar to the Arabs of the time, whose culture was largely an oral one and through which the common knowledge of the society was preserved. It is generally accepted that transmission of hadith began to occur during the Prophet's time when those of his followers who witnessed a particular instruction conveyed it to others who were not present. Such a practice was to be expected given the importance of the role of the Prophet in the first Muslim community. Among those who were well known for their transmission of a large number of hadith was the Prophet's wife A'isha bint Abu Bakr (d. 58/678), who had the opportunity to observe him most closely. She even criticized other Muslims if she felt they were transmitting hadith incorrectly, and acted as a judge for determining the veracity of a report.

After the death of the Prophet, reports about his judgements, opinions and practice must have played an important role in the decision-making in the first Muslim community, at least in areas where the Prophet had expressed views that were commonly known. During the Prophet's lifetime, many of his followers sought his opinion on a wide variety of matters, following the dictates of the Qur'an: 'Believers … obey the messenger [Muhammad]', and 'You have an excellent example in the messenger of God'. After his passing, it is understandable that his Companions would wish to pass on such information to new Muslims enlarging the Muslim community.

Reports suggest that in transmission of hadith some Companions asked others to provide evidence for the truth of what was being transmitted, but not necessarily on a systematic basis. Several Companions were active in transmitting hadith in their teachings, for example Ubay ibn Ka'b (d. circa 35/656), Abd Allah ibn Mas'ud (d. 32/652), Abd Allah ibn Abbas (d. 68/687), Ali ibn Abi Talib (d. 40/661) and, as previously mentioned, A'isha. Following the Prophet's death, writing down of hadith was not seen as important. It was the Umayyad caliph Umar ibn Abd al-Aziz (d. 101/720) who is credited with being the first to organize the collation and recording of collections of hadith.

As the Prophet's Companions and their successors moved away from Medina and Mecca, spreading out across the ever-widening Muslim caliphate (empire), more and more students of hadith began to emerge and travel in search of hadith knowledge. Furthermore, sectarian strife and the establishment of the first dynastic caliphate (Umayyads in 41/661) gave some urgency to acquiring knowledge from authentic sources. Mecca, Medina, Yemen, Iraq and Syria became major centres of hadith collection and gradually written collections became indispensable. Among the first collections, probably works of a legal character, were those of Ibn Jurayj (d. 157/774), al-Awza'i (d. 159/775), and Sufyan al-Thawri (d. 161/777); however, none is extant. Among the earliest surviving complete texts with a collection of hadith is *Muwatta'* by Malik ibn Anas (d. 179/795), after whom the Maliki school of law was named.

In time, different kinds of hadith compilations emerged, arranged either by subject matter or by transmitter. These are classified into several groups:

- *sahifa*: the earliest type of compilation, being collections of hadith written down by the Prophet's Companions or their Successors
- *rasa'il* or *kutub*: collections dealing with one of eight specific topics (beliefs; laws; piety; etiquette; Qur'an commentary; history; crises; appreciation and denunciation of people and places)

- *musannafs*: large collections arranged into chapters according to subject matter
- *musnads*: technically referring to those collections arranged according to the names of the final Companion in the chain of transmission of a hadith, but also used to refer generally to reliable collations of hadith
- *jami's*: large collections of hadith covering all eight topics (see *rasa'il* above)
- *sunans*: works dealing only with legal hadith.

Naturally, some collections became well respected and more famous than others. Amongst Sunni Muslims, the *Sahih* of Bukhari (d. 256/870) and the *Sahih* of Muslim (d. 261/874) are considered the two most authoritative sources of hadith, although some individual hadith contained therein have been criticized by later scholars. Other important works include collections by Abu Dawud (d. 275/883), Tirmidhi (d. 279/892), Ibn Maja (d. 273/886) and Nasa'i (d. 303/915). The most important *musnad* work is by Ahmad ibn Hanbal (d. 233/847), after whom the Hanbali school of law is named.

Development of Hadith Criticism

When hadith began to be transmitted formally, a system of checking of isnad (chain of transmitters) developed, which provided the basis for determining whether or not a particular hadith was authentic. Some Muslim scholars argue that the beginnings of the isnad system can be traced back as early as the students of the Prophet's Companions. However, a formal system probably did not emerge until the latter half of the first/seventh century or even the early part of the second/eighth century.

Scholars specializing in the discipline of collecting and scrutinizing hadith (known as Traditionists), as well as jurists dealing with religious law, developed certain principles for the criticism of a hadith's chain of transmitters (isnad) and for its text (matn). In assessing the authority of a hadith based on its isnad, traditionists stipulated that its chain must be traced back to the original reporter through a continuous succession of transmitters whose identity, unquestionable character and high moral qualities were established. Also, if the hadith reported an event that occurred in the presence of a large number of people (particularly if it occurred on a regular basis), it was required to have been originally reported by several transmitters. If such a hadith was reported by one Companion alone, it was considered unacceptable by some early authorities. They reasoned it was impossible for an event witnessed by so many of the Prophet's Companions to be reported only by one transmitter.

As hadith and their chains of transmission began to be systematically scrutinized, a 'science of biography' (of those associated with hadith transmission) developed, known as *asma' ar-rijal*. Details of the lives and characters of various transmitters were recorded, which allowed evaluation of their credibility. The following are some of the criteria utilized for this purpose:

- The name, nickname, title, parentage and occupation of each transmitter in the chain of transmission should be known.
- The original transmitter of the hadith should have stated that he heard the hadith directly from the Prophet.
- If a transmitter received his hadith from another transmitter, the two should have lived in the same period and have had the possibility of meeting each other.
- At the time of hearing and transmitting the hadith, the transmitter should have been physically and mentally capable of understanding and remembering it.

- The transmitter should have been known as a pious and virtuous person.
- The transmitter should not have been accused of having lied, given false evidence or committed a crime.
- The transmitter should not have spoken against other reliable people.
- The transmitter's religious beliefs and practices should have been known to be correct (and not heretical).
- The transmitter should not have carried out or practised peculiar religious beliefs of his own.

However, proving the authenticity of a chain of transmission does not necessarily prove the authenticity of the text of the hadith, as the text may be a faithfully memorized and transmitted forgery. Some general principles utilized in criticism of the hadith text include:

- It must not be contrary to the text of the Qur'an, or the basic principles of Islam.
- It must not be contrary to other hadith on the subject which have already been accepted by authorities as authentic and reliable.
- It must not be against dictates of reason and natural laws, and common experience.
- It must not contain statements about disproportionately high rewards or severe punishments for otherwise ordinary deeds of a person.
- If it exalts a particular people, tribe, place or even a chapter of the Qur'an for a specific reason, generally it should be rejected.
- If it contains detailed prophecies of future events with dates, it should be rejected.
- If it contains observations and remarks attributed to the Prophet, but these are not in keeping with what is generally known about him and his views, it should be rejected.

Grading of hadith

Hadith are graded as accepted (*maqbul*) or rejected (*mardud*). Accepted hadith are then graded into 'authentic' (*sahih*) (either by itself, or because of the presence of other similar authentic hadith) or 'agreeable' (*hasan*) (again either by itself or due to the existence of other similar hadith). Defects which affect the grading of an accepted hadith include factors such as a transmitter narrating a hadith as a statement of the Prophet, when most others have ascribed it to one of his Companions, or a transmitter who has a high moral character but lacks literary skills.

Rejected hadith are also sub-divided, and may be rejected owing to a defect in a transmitter, such as if he or she was known to be a liar. Other grounds for rejection are if there is a discontinuity or missing name in the chain of transmission or for other incidental reasons such as a famous hadith purposely being given a different chain of transmission, so that whoever 'possessed' it would be given credit for being able to teach a novel hadith (i.e. a famous hadith but with a new chain).

Shi'i conception of hadith

The Shi'a also believe that the Sunna of the Prophet is a primary source of law. However, they hold that hadith (known among them as *akhbar*) should be transmitted by a member of the family of the Prophet or by his descendent imams who are considered reliable, truthful and honest. For this reason, many of the transmitters of hadith included in Sunni hadith collections may not be acceptable from a Shi'i point of view. While the texts of hadith can be similar between Sunni and Shi'i collections, this may not be the case for their chains of transmission.

Just as Sunni scholars rely on compilations such as the *Sahih* of Bukhari, so too are there Shi'i collections. Several Shi'i scholars collected hadith that are considered reliable from their point of view. These scholars arranged the contents of those source collections into four accessible books that continue to play a pivotal role among Shi'a today. Scholars who compiled these collections are al-Kulayni (d. circa 329/941); Ibn Babawayh (d. circa 381/991); al-Tusi (d. circa 460/1067).

For the Twelver (Imami) Shi'a, there are four main categories of hadith:

- *sahih* (authentic): a hadith whose chain of transmission is unbroken through narrations from just imams of the Imami Shi'a, or followers of the imams who adhere to the Ja'fari school of jurisprudence
- *hasan* (good): a hadith reported by commendable Imamis whose reliability cannot be confirmed. If the chain contains a single reliable non-Imami then the hadith is classified as dependable and if it contains a single weak reporter then the whole hadith is classified as weak
- *muwaththaq* (dependable—also termed *qawi* 'strong'): a hadith considered reliable by classical scholars, although narrated by scholars of a different school of religious law, or even by transmitters belonging to those who opposed the Imamis
- *da'if* (weak): a hadith where one of the reporters is known to be a fabricator, immoral or unreliable, or is unknown.

Modern Critique of Hadith

In the modern period, many Western scholars of hadith have argued that much of the hadith literature should be considered the work of early Muslims and should not be attributed to the Prophet. From their point of view, early Muslims incorporated the practice of the Prophet and of his Companions and Successors, as well as of later jurists and their opinions, and then projected these back on to the Prophet.

Ignaz Goldziher (d. 1921) was a Hungarian Orientalist scholar and student of convert Arminius Vambery (d. 1913). Some believe Goldziher also secretly converted to Islam. Goldziher held that hadith were mostly formulated in the early second/eighth century as a result of sectarian and political rivalries and the need for jurists to defend their legal views. The 'worldly' Umayyads, argued Goldziher, were not really interested in the development of religious literature; instead, pious aphorisms and the magnified heroics of the Prophet's military career were what concerned them. He rejected the assertion that Umar II (d. 101/719), the Umayyad caliph, was the first to sponsor a systematic collection of hadith, and argued that hadith literature followed on from the formulation of Islamic jurisprudence. He pointed to the earliest extant work that includes a collection of hadith, Malik's *Muwatta*, and noted that the various versions of the collection display a concept of Sunna as a community practice supported by reference to hadith but not bound by them. In his view, consideration of the consensus of people of Medina (where the Prophet lived in his final years and where Malik also lived) on a particular issue was such an overriding concern for Malik that he did not hesitate to prefer the 'consensus' over authentic hadith that he included in his collection (*Muwatta*).

According to this view, it was not until the time of Bukhari (d. 256/869) and Muslim (d. 261/875) that strict isnad criticism emerged. However, even for Bukhari—who for his *Sahih* made a skeletal outline of areas of concern, for which he later filled in the necessary traditions—there were not enough traditions of the highest standard to complete his fiqh map. Later compilers found it necessary to relax isnad criticism and rely on lesser-quality hadith in order to find enough to cover every point of Islamic law. Eventually, the status given to the Companions of the Prophet and the Successors meant that it was unbecoming for later Muslims even to question their motives or trustworthiness, thereby allowing the reinstatement of previously rejected material.

Following on from the work of Goldziher, another Orientalist scholar, Joseph Schacht (d. 1969), saw the development of hadith literature (in particular the isnad system) as springing from pressure on jurists to defend their views. He held that the early Islamic period (the first two centuries of Islam) was more complex than Goldziher believed, although the historicity of the early jurists' material was weakened when later jurists formulated hadith chains to justify their conclusions.

To demonstrate this thesis, Schacht developed the 'common link' theory, which was also taken up by another modern Orientalist, Gautier H. A. Juynboll. The common link theory was derived via a process of analysing hadith with similar texts (ostensibly the same prophetic utterance) to draw a map of isnad chains, called an 'isnad bundle'. A common link transmitter is one who passes a particular tradition on to a number of pupils, but who usually only heard it from one immediate authority. Juynboll, like Schacht before him, argued that most hadith have common link transmitters, and thus points of origin in the second/eighth century. Taking a middle position between Muslim and other Western scholars, Juynboll is wary of accepting the authenticity of a hadith (i.e. that it accurately reflects a statement or deed of the Prophet Muhammad), except where a common link transmitter can be found at the Companions level.

There are Muslim scholars today who, while not going as far as Goldziher, Schacht or Juynboll, argue that the traditional Muslim position on hadith is difficult to justify. For example, Fazlur Rahman (d. 1988) held that Western scholars are correct about the development of the Sunna content, but not the Sunna concept itself. For Rahman, the prophetic Sunna was a valid concept from the very beginning of Islam; the problem was that Sunna also came to include the interpretations and agreed practices of the early Muslim communities following the death of the Prophet. The Prophet, from Rahman's point of view, was not primarily a 'pan-legist' (he seldom resorted to acting in a legislative capacity, in his view), but rather was a moral reformer. Rahman argued that the bulk of the hadith corpus is nothing but the Sunna and juristic reasoning of the first generations of Muslims; in other words, the opinions of an individual that over time received the sanction of community consensus (*ijma'*). Such a view of hadith authenticity is generally rejected by mainstream Muslim opinion, for whom hadith refers to the authenticated sayings, deeds and descriptions of the Prophet Muhammad, not of the early generations.

Implications of Hadith Scholarship Today

Although some Muslim scholars have attempted to counter Orientalist claims, the two worlds of scholarship have remained largely isolated and unconnected. Western scholarship does not appear to have had a significant impact on traditional Muslim approaches to the study of hadith. This may be due in part to the condescending tone of early Orientalists (which allowed their claims to be written off as 'anti-Islamic') as well as the failure of Western scholars to grasp adequately the complexities of the traditional methods.

Nevertheless, the implication for hadith scholarship in the 'meeting' of these two worlds is quite significant. A case is the recent experience of the Muslim academic and feminist Amina Wadud, who led a Friday prayer service in 2005, an activity almost always performed by Muslim men only. After publicity about the event held in New York, a number of articles appeared on the internet that drew on interpretation of hadith and points of Islamic jurisprudence to affirm or discredit the legitimacy of female-led prayer.

Nevin Reda, a feminist writer, used a number of arguments to support her thesis that female-led prayer is acceptable in the universe of Islamic interpretation. She pointed to the existence of a hadith in which the Prophet is said to have commanded a woman Umm Waraqa to lead a congregation that included a male assigned to make the call to prayer. It was on this basis that a minority of classical jurists—including the famous Tabari—reportedly allowed women to lead men in prayer, a point that belies the notion that there is consensus on this prohibition (that is, woman leading men in prayer). Reda also referred to Juynboll's method of isnad analysis and rejected the notion that hadith must be accepted as unimpeachable simply because they appear in the classical canons, particularly if they appear to transgress positive Qur'anic teachings on leadership of women.

Zaid Shakir wrote a response to Reda from a traditionalist Sunni perspective, analysing the strengths of the various narrations of the hadith of Umm Waraqa and their legal value for ruling on the permissibility of female-led prayer. He rejected her interpretation of key Arabic terms used in the hadith, as well as Juynboll's thesis about isnad analysis, in order to defend the Maliki, Hanafi, Shafi'i and Hanbali interpretations of prohibition. This case, which received international exposure, shows that modern hadith scholarship is as relevant today as it ever was.

Profile of a hadith scholar

Abu Abd Allah Muhammad ibn Isma'il al-Bukhari, the most famous traditionist in Islamic history, was of Persian origin. He was born in Bukhara in 194/810 and died near Samarqand in 256/869. His father studied under the famous scholars Malik ibn Anas, Hammad ibn Zayd (d. 179/795) and Ibn al-Mubarak (d. 181/797). Bukhari's early education took place at the feet of his mother, with whom he and his brother went in search of knowledge after mastering all the knowledge in his native town of Bukhara. He interrogated more than one thousand scholars of hadith in places such as Balkh, Merv, Nishapur, Hijaz, Egypt and Mesopotamia. The *Sahih* of Bukhari is considered by Sunnis to be the most important textual source after the Qur'an.

Bukhari's objective was to collect only the most authentic traditions of the Prophet and to compile them into a work divided into several parts, taking a portion of each hadith as a heading. Where relevant, he would repeat hadith in different chapters devoted to different subjects. The number of hadith in his book with full isnads totals well over seven thousand; however, without repetition they total about two and a half thousand. His biographers report that Bukhari reduced this number from six hundred thousand hadith by applying his strict criteria.

For an isnad to be ranked authentic and included in his *Sahih*, Bukhari applied strict conditions. The transmitters must be of exemplary character and possess a high literary and academic standard. There must be evidence that the transmitters met one another and that each student learned from each teacher. The difference between the *Sahih* of Bukhari and that of Muslim was on this last point. Muslim accepted that if two transmitters lived in the same locale, it was possible, even if not proved, that they could have learned from each other. Therefore the chain of transmission (for Muslim) was not broken and hadith linked in this manner were acceptable. Bukhari, on the other hand, required positive evidence that the student learned from the teacher and for this reason his *Sahih* tended to gain wider acceptance by later Muslims as the stronger of the two works.

5

The Islamic Calendar, or Hijri Calendar

by Hazza Abu Rabia

The Islamic calendar, Muslim calendar, or Hijri calendar is a lunar calendar consisting of twelve months in a year of 354 or 355 days.

It is used to date events in many Muslim countries (concurrently with the Gregorian calendar), and used by Muslims everywhere to determine the proper days on which to observe the annual fast, to attend pilgrimage, or Hajj, and to celebrate other Islamic holidays and festivals.

The first year was the Islamic year beginning in 622 AD, during which the emigration of the Islamic Prophet Muhammad from Mecca to Medina, known as the Hijra, occurred. Each numbered year is designated either H for Hijra or AH for the Latin *anno Hegirae* (in the year of the Hijra)[1], hence, Muslims typically call their calendar the Hijri calendar.

The current Islamic year is 1434 AH. In the Gregorian calendar, 1434 AH runs from approximately November 14, 2012 (evening) to November 4, 2013 (evening).

---

1 Watt, W. Montgomery. "Hidjra." In P. J. Bearman, Th. Bianquis, C. E. Bosworth, E. van Donzel, and W. P. Heinrichs. *Encyclopaedia of Islam Online.* Brill Academic Publishers. ISSN 1573–3912.

Hazza Abu Rabia / Adapted from "Islamic Calendar" at en.wikipedia.org/CCBY-SA3.0

Hijri Months

Hijri months are named as follows in Arabic:[2]

1. Muḥarram—"forbidden"—so called because battle was set aside (haram) during this month. Muharram includes the Day of Ashura.
2. Ṣafar—"void"—supposedly named because pagan Arabs looted during this month and left the houses empty.
3. Rabīʿ I (Rabīʿ al-Awwal)—"the first spring."
4. Rabīʿ II (Rabīʿ ath-Thānī, or Rabīʿ al-Ākhir)—"the second (or last) spring."
5. Jumādā I (Jumādā al-Ūlā)—"the first month of parched land."—often considered the pre-Islamic "summer."
6. Jumādā II (Jumādā ath-Thāniya, or Jumādā al-Ākhira)—"the second (or last) month of parched land."
7. Rajab—"respect" or "honor." This is another sacred month in which fighting was traditionally forbidden.
8. Shaʿbān—"scattered," marking the time of year when Arab tribes dispersed to find water.
9. Ramaḍān—"scorched." Ramadan is the most venerated month of the Hijri calendar, during which Muslims have to fast from dawn until sunset and honor poor people with something a brother or a sister needs within his or her society.
10. Shawwāl—"raised," as she-camels normally would be in calf at this time of year.
11. Dhū al-Qaʿda—"the one of truce." Dhu al-Qaʾda was another month during which war was banned.
12. Dhū al-Ḥijja—"the one of pilgrimage," referring to the annual Muslim pilgrimage to Mecca, the Hajj.

Pre-Islamic Calendar

Inscriptions of the ancient South Arabian calendars reveal the use of a number of local calendars. At least some of these calendars followed the lunisolar system. For Central Arabia, especially Mecca, there is a lack of epigraphical evidence, but details are found in the writings of Muslim authors of the Abbasid era. Both al-Biruni and al-Masʾudi suggest that the Ancient Arabs used the same month names as the Muslims, though they also record other month names used by the pagan Arabs.[3]

The Islamic tradition is unanimous in stating that Arabs of Tihamah, Hejaz, and Najd distinguished between two types of months, permitted (ḥalāl) and forbidden (ḥarām) months. The forbidden months were four months during which fighting is forbidden, listed as Rajab and the three months around the pilgrimage season, Dhū al-Qiʿda, Dhū al-Ḥijja, and Muḥarram. Information about the forbidden months is also found in the writings of Procopius, where he describes an armistice with the Eastern Arabs of the Lakhmid al-Mundhir, which happened in the summer of 541 AD. However, Muslim historians do not link these months to a particular season. The Quran links the four forbidden months with Nasīʾ, a word that literally means "postponement."[4] According to Muslim tradition, the decision of postponement was

2 B. van Dalen, R. S. Humphreys, A. K. S. Lambton, et al., "Tarikh." In P. J. Bearman, Th. Bianquis, C. E. Bosworth, E. van Donzel, and W. P. Heinrichs. *Encyclopedia of Islam Online*. Brill Academic Publishers. ISSN 1573–3912.

3 F. C. De Blois, "TARĪKH": I.1.iv. "Pre-Islamic and Agricultural Calendars of the Arabian Peninsula." *The Encyclopaedia of Islam*, 2nd edition, X:260.

4 Ibid. X:260.

administered by the tribe of Kinanah,[5] by a man known as the al-Qalammas of Kinanah and his descendants (pl. qalāmisa).[6]

Different interpretations of the concept of Nasī' have been proposed.[7] Some scholars, both Muslim[8] and Western,[9] maintain that the pre-Islamic calendar used in Central Arabia was a purely lunar calendar, similar to the modern Islamic calendar. According to this view, Nasī' is related to the pagan practices of the Meccan Arabs, in which they would alter the distribution of the forbidden months within a given year without implying a calendar manipulation. This interpretation is supported by Arab historians and lexicographers, such as Ibn Hisham, Ibn Manzur, and the corpus of Quranic exegesis.[10] It is also corroborated by an early Sabaic inscription, where a religious ritual was "postponed" (ns''w) because of war. According to the context of this inscription, the verb ns'' has nothing to do with intercalation, but only with moving religious events within the calendar itself. The similarity between the religious concept of this ancient inscription and the Quran suggests that non-calendering postponement is also the Quranic meaning of Nasī'.[11] Thus the *Encyclopaedia of Islam* concludes that the "The Arabic system of [Nasī'] can only have been intended to move the Hajj and the fairs associated with it in the vicinity of Mecca to a suitable season of the year. It was not intended to establish a fixed calendar to be generally observed."[12]

Others concur that it was originally a lunar calendar, but suggest that about two hundred years before the Hijra it was transformed into a lunisolar calendar containing an intercalary month added from time to time to keep the pilgrimage within the season of the year when merchandise was most abundant. This interpretation was first proposed by the medieval Muslim astrologer and astronomer Abu Ma'shar al-Balkhi, and later by al-Biruni,[13] al-Mas'udi, and some Western scholars.[14] This interpretation considers Nasī' to be a synonym for the Arabic word for "intercalation" (kabīsa). It also suggests that every second or third year, the beginning of the year was postponed by one month. The intercalation doubled the month of the pilgrimage; that is, the month of the pilgrimage and the following month were given the same name, postponing the names and the sanctity of all subsequent months in the year by one. The first intercalation doubled the first month Muharram, then three years later the second month Safar was doubled, continuing until the intercalation had passed through all twelve months of the year and returned to Muharram, when it was repeated.

---

5 Moberg. "NASI'." *The Encyclopaedia of Islam,* 2nd edition, VII:977.

6 Abu Ma'shar al-Balkhi (787–886), *Kitab al-Uluf, Journal Asiatique,* series 5, xi (1858) 168+. (French) (Arabic).

7 For an overview of the various theories and a discussion of the problem of "hindsight chronology" in early and pre-Islamic sources, see Maurice A. McPartlan, *The Contribution of Qu'rān and Hadīt to Early Islamic Chronology* (Durham, 1997).

8 Mahmud Effendi (1858), as discussed in Sherrard Beaumont Burnaby, *Elements of the Jewish and Muhammadan Calendars* (London: 1901), pp. 460–470.

9 F. C. De Blois, "TA RĪKH": I.1.iv. "Pre-Islamic and Agricultural Calendars of the Arabian Peninsula." *The Encyclopaedia of Islam,* 2nd edition, X:260

10 Muḥammad al-Khuḍarī Bayk. (1935). *Muḥāḍarāt tārīkh al-Umam al-Islāmiyya 2,* 4th edition. Al-maktaba al-tijāriyya. pp. 59–60

11 F. C. De Blois, "TA RĪKH": I.1.iv. "Pre-Islamic and Agricultural Calendars of the Arabian Peninsula." *The Encyclopaedia of Islam,* 2nd edition, X:260

12 *The Encyclopedia of Islam,* 2nd edition, Index, p. 441.

13 Abu Ma'shar al-Balkhi (787–886), *Kitab al-Uluf, Journal Asiatique,* series 5, xi (1858) 168+. (French) (Arabic)

14 Moberg, "NASI'," *E. J. Brill's First Encyclopaedia of Islam.*

Prohibiting Nasī'

In the tenth year of the Hijra, as documented in the Quran (sura 9:36–37), God revealed the "prohibition of the Nasī'":

> The number of months with Allah has been twelve months by Allah's ordinance since the day He created the heavens and the earth. Of these four are known as forbidden [to fight in]; That is the straight usage, so do not wrong yourselves therein, and fight those who go astray. But know that Allah is with those who restrain themselves.
>
> Verily the transposing (of a prohibited month) is an addition to Unbelief: The Unbelievers are led to wrong thereby: for they make it lawful one year, and forbidden another year, of months forbidden by Allah and make such forbidden ones lawful. The evil of their course seems pleasing to them. But Allah guideth not those who reject Faith. (Quran 9: 36–37; Surat At-Tawba 9:36–37)

The prohibition of Nasī' would presumably have been announced when the intercalated month had returned to its position just before the month of Nasi' began. If Nasī' meant intercalation, the number and the position of the intercalary months between 1 AH and 10 AH are uncertain; Western calendar dates commonly cited for key events in early Islam, such as the Hijra, the Battle of Badr, the Battle of Uhud, and the Battle of the Trench, should be viewed with caution, as they might be in error by one, two, or even three lunar months.

This prohibition was mentioned by Prophet Muhammad during the farewell sermon, which was delivered on 9 Dhu al-Hijja 10 AH (Julian date Friday, March 6, 632 AD) on Mount Arafat during the farewell pilgrimage to Mecca:

> Certainly the Nasi' is an impious addition, which has led the infidels into error. One year they authorize the Nasi', another year they forbid it. They observe the divine precept with respect to the number of the sacred months, but in fact they profane that which God has declared to be inviolable, and sanctify that which God has declared to be profane. Assuredly time, in its revolution, has returned to such as it was at the creation of the heavens and the earth. In the eyes of God the number of the months is twelve. Among these twelve months four are sacred, namely, Rajab, which stands alone, and three others which are consecutive.[15]

The three successive forbidden months mentioned by Prophet Muhammad (months in which battles are forbidden) are Dhu al-Qi'dah, Dhu al-Hijjah, and Muharram, months eleven, twelve, and one. The single forbidden month is Rajab, month seven.

Numbering the Years

In pre-Islamic Arabia, it was customary to identify a year after a major event that took place in it. Thus, according to Islamic tradition, Abraha, governor of Yemen, then a province of the Christian Kingdom of Aksum (Ethiopia), attempted to destroy the Kaaba with an army that included several elephants. The

---

15 Sherrard Beaumont Burnaby, *Elements of the Jewish and Muhammadan Calendars* (London: 1901), p. 370.

raid was unsuccessful, but that year became known as the Year of the Elephant, during which Prophet Muhammad was born (sura al-Fil). Most equate this to the year 570 AD, but a minority use 571 AD.

The first ten years of the Hijra were not numbered, but were named after events in the life of Muhammad, according to Abū Rayḥān al-Bīrūnī:[20]

1. The year of permission.
2. The year of the order of fighting.
3. The year of the trial.
4. The year of congratulation on marriage.
5. The year of the earthquake.
6. The year of inquiring.
7. The year of gaining victory.
8. The year of equality.
9. The year of exemption.

In 638 AD (17 AH), Abu Musa Ashaari, one of the officials of the Caliph Umar in Basrah, complained about the absence of any years on the correspondence he received from Umar, making it difficult for him to determine which instructions were most recent. This report convinced Umar of the need to introduce an era for Muslims. After debating the issue with his counselors, he decided that the first year should include the date of Prophet Muhammad's arrival at Medina (known as Yathrib, before Prophet Muhammad's arrival). Uthman ibn Affan then suggested that the months begin with Muharram, in line with the established custom of the Arabs at that time.[16] The years of the Islamic calendar thus began with the month of Muharram in the year of Muhammad's arrival at the city of Medina, even though the actual emigration took place in Safar and Rabi' I.[17] Because of the Hijra, the calendar was named the Hijra calendar.

The first day of the first month of the Islamic calendar (1 Muharram 1 AH) was Friday, July 16, 622 AD, the equivalent civil tabular date (same daylight period) in the Julian calendar.[18] The Islamic day began at the preceding sunset on the evening of July15. This Julian date (July 16) was determined by medieval Muslim astronomers by projecting back in time their own tabular Islamic calendar, which had alternating thirty- and twenty-nine-day months in each lunar year, plus eleven leap days every thirty years. For example, al-Biruni mentioned this Julian date in the year 1000 AD.[19] Although not used by medieval Muslim astronomers nor modern scholars to determine the Islamic epoch, the thin crescent moon would have also first become visible (assuming clouds did not obscure it) shortly after the preceding sunset on the evening of July 15, one and a half days after the associated dark moon (astronomical new moon) on the morning of July14. 10.[20]

---

16 *Appreciating Islamic History* (Microsoft Word document).
17 Watt, W. Montgomery. "Hidjra." In P. J. Bearman, Th. Bianquis, C. E. Bosworth, E. van Donzel, and W. P. Heinrichs. *Encyclopaedia of Islam Online*. Brill Academic Publishers. ISSN 1573–3912.
18 Sherrard Beaumont Burnaby, *Elements of the Jewish and Muhammadan Calendars* (1901) pp. 373–5, 382–4.
19 al-Biruni, *The Chronology of Ancient Nations,* tr. C. Edward Sachau (1000/1879) 327.
20 *NASA Phases of the Moon,* 601–700.

The First of Muharram

Muharram is the first month of the Islamic calendar. It is one of the four sacred months of the year.[21] Because the Islamic calendar is a lunar calendar, Muharram moves from year to year when compared with the Gregorian calendar.

Muharram is derived from the word *haraam*, meaning "sinful." It is held to be the most sacred of all the months, excluding Ramadan. Some Muslims fast during these days. The tenth day of Muharram is the Day of Ashura, which to Shia Muslims is part of the Mourning of Muharram.

Some Muslims fast during this day, because it is recorded in the hadith that Musa (Moses) and his people obtained a victory over the Egyptian pharaoh on the tenth day of Muharram; accordingly, the Islamic prophet Muhammad asked Muslims to fast on this day that is Ashura and on a day before that, the ninth, so that they are not similar to Jews (because, according to him, Jews used to fast for one day because of the same reason, and many practices recorded in the hadith are specifically performed to avoid any apparent similarity to those of contemporary neighboring Jews and Christians).

Fasting differs among the Muslim groupings; mainstream Shia Muslims stop eating and drinking during sunlight hours and do not eat until late afternoon. Sunni Muslims also fast during Muharram for the first ten days of Muharram, or just the tenth day, or on both the ninth and tenth days, with the exact term depending on the individual. Shia Muslims do so to replicate the sufferings of Hussein ibn Ali on the Day of Ashura.

Timing

The Islamic calendar is a lunar calendar, and months begin when the first crescent of a new moon is sighted. Because the Islamic lunar calendar year is eleven to twelve days shorter than the solar year, Muharram migrates throughout the solar years.

Islamic Events Taking Place During Muharram

1. Muharram: The Islamic New Year.
2. Muharram: Shi'a Muslims begin the Commemoration of Muharram, which marks the anniversary of the Battle of Karbala.
3. Muharram: The death anniversary of Umar ibn al-Khattab, the second Sunni Caliph of the Rashidun Caliphate.
4. Muharram: Hussein ibn Ali enters Karbala and establishes camp. Yazid's forces are present.
5. Muharram: Access to water was banned for Husayn ibn Ali, by Yazid's orders.
6. Muharram: Referred to as the Day of Ashurah (lit. "the tenth")—the day on which Hussein ibn Ali was martyred in the Battle of Karbala. Shia Muslims spend the day in mourning, while the Sunni Muslims fast on this day, commemorating the rescue of the people of Israel by Musa (Moses) from the pharaoh.[22]

---

21 The others are Dhu al-Qi'dah, Dhu al-Hijjah, and Rajab.
22 Sahih Bukhari, 003.031.222–225.

Hazza Abu Rabia / Adapted from "Muharram" at en.wikipedia.org / CC BY-SA 3.0

Many Sufi Muslims fast for the same reason as the Sunnis mentioned above, but also for the martyrs; they pray for them and send upon them peace and blessings.

Mawlid An-Nabī

Mawlid an-nabī is the observance of the birthday of the Islamic prophet Muhammad, which occurs in Rabi' al-awwal, the third month in the Islamic calendar. The term *Mawlid* is also used in some parts of the world, such as Egypt, as a generic term for the birthday celebrations of other historical religious figures, such as Sufi saints.

The basic earliest accounts for the observance of Mawlid can be found in eighth-century Mecca, when the house in which Prophet Muhammad was born was transformed into a place of prayer by Al-Khayzuran (mother of Harun al-Rashid, the fifth and most famous Abbasid caliph),[23] though public celebrations of the birth of Muhammad did not occur until four centuries after his passing away. The oldest Mawlid text is claimed to be from the twelfth century and most likely is of Persian origin.[24]

The early celebrations included elements of Sufic influence, with animal sacrifices and torchlight processions along with public sermons and a feast.[25] The celebrations occurred during the day, in contrast to modern-day observances, with the ruler playing a key role in the ceremonies.[26] Emphasis was given to the Ahl al-Bayt, with presentation of sermons and recitations of the Quran. The event also featured the award of gifts to officials in order to bolster support for the ruling caliph.[27]

Legality

Traditionally, Sufi and Shia scholars have approved celebration of Mawlid-an-Nabi, the exception being some Sunni and Deobandi[28] scholars, who do not.

In the Muslim world, the majority of Islamic scholars are in favor of Mawlid. They consider observing Mawlid necessary or permissible in Islam, and see it as a praiseworthy event and positive development, while the Salafi minority says it is an improper innovation and forbid its celebration. One of the most acceptable leaders of Salafiyyun, Ibn Taymiyya, forbade Mawlid celebration.[29]

---

23 "Mawlid (a.), or Mawlud," *Encyclopedia of Islam.*
24 *The Music of the Arabs,* Touma (1975), p. 148.
25 Schussman, p. 216.
26 Kaptein (1993), p. 30.
27 Ibid, p. 30.
28 *Deobandi* is a term used for a revivalist movement in Sunni Islam (Ahlus-Sunnah wal-Jamaʾah) under the Hanafi School. It is centered primarily in India, Pakistan, Afghanistan, and Bangladesh and has recently spread to the United Kingdom and has a presence in South Africa. The name derives from Deoband, India, where the school Darul Uloom Deoband is situated. The movement was inspired by the spirit of scholar Shah Waliullah (1703–1762), while the foundation of Darul Uloom Deoband was laid on May 30, 1866.
29 "Mawlid, According to the Salafi ʿUlama." www.alifta.org. Retrieved May 19, 2013.

Hazza Abu Rabia / Adapted from "Mawlid An-Nabī" at en.wikipedia.org / CC BY-SA 3.0

Mufti Ali Gomaa, Chief Mufti of the world's oldest and largest Islamic university, Al Azhar in Egypt, Yusuf al-Qaradawi, the primary scholar of the Muslim Brotherhood movement, Muhammad Alawi al-Maliki, Grand Mufti of Cyprus Nazim Al-Haqqani, Habib Ali al-Jifri of Yemen, Syed Shujaat Ali Qadri, Muhammad Ilyas Qadri, the founder of Dawat-e-Islami, Nuh Ha Mim Keller, Grand Mufti of Bosnia Mustafa Cerić, Abdalqadir as-Sufi, Hamza Yusuf, Gibril Haddad, Shaykh Said Afandi al-Chirkawi, Shaykh Hisham Kabbani, Grand Mufti of India Akhtar Raza Khan, Kanthapuram A. P. Aboobacker Musalyar of Markazu Saqafathi Sunniya, and Zaid Shakir all subscribe to Sunni Sufi Islam, and have given their approval for the observance of Mawlid.[30] They suggest that fasting on Mondays is also a way of commemorating Muhammad's birthday.

Scholars and preachers who consider Mawlid to be heresy and forbid its celebration belong to the Wahabi and Deobandi ideologies; they include Abd al-Aziz ibn Abd Allah ibn Baaz, who was the Grand Mufti of Saudi Arabia,[31] Abdul Rahman Al-Sudais, the imam of the Masjid al-Haram in Mecca, Saudi Arabia,[32] Zakir Naik,[33] Bilal Philips[34] of the Wahabi/Salafi movement, and Ebrahim Desai, who subscribes to the Deobandi movement. Although all agree that the birth of Muhammad was the most significant event in Islamic history, they point out that the companions of Prophet Muhammad and the second and third generation of Muslims did not observe this event.

Observances

Mawlid is celebrated in most Muslim countries, and in other countries where Muslims have a presence, such as India, Britain, Russia, and Canada. Saudi Arabia is the only Muslim country where Mawlid is not an official public holiday. Participation in the ritual celebration of popular Islamic holidays is seen as an expression of the Islamic revival.

Where Mawlid is celebrated in a carnival manner, large street processions are held, and homes or mosques are decorated. Charity and food is distributed, and stories about the life of the Prophet Muhammad are narrated with recitation of poetry by children. Scholars and poets celebrate by reciting "Qaṣīda al-Burda Sharif," the famous poem by thirteenth-century Arabic Sufi Busiri.

During Pakistan's Mawlid, known in Urdu as Eid Milad-un-Nabi, a public holiday, celebrations and processions, the national flag is hoisted on all public buildings, and a thirty-one-gun salute in Islamabad, capital of Pakistan, and a twenty-one-gun salute at the provincial capitals are fired at dawn. The public and private buildings are illuminated with fairy lights. The cinemas show religious rather than secular films on the eleventh and twelfth of Rabi-ul-Awwal. Hundreds of thousands of people gather at Minar-e-Pakistan in Lahore between the intervening night of the eleventh and twelfth of Rabi' al-awwal for Mawlid celebrations; this is the world's biggest gathering for Mawlid celebrations. The tradition of year-round celebration of Eid Milad-un-Nabi is also observed. The A Na`at hymns specifically praise the prophet Muhammad. The

---

30 *Shaykh Qardawi Approves of Celebrating Mawlid.* Yusuf Al-Qaradawi.
31 *Reasons for the Forbiddance of Celebrating the Birthday of the Prophet,* by Saalih al-Fawzaan.
32 http://www.docstoc.com/docs/71875801/Following-The-Sunnah-and-Shariah-Ruling-on-Milad-un-Nabi-by-Sheikh-Abdur-Rahman-Sudais.
33 www.youtube.com/watch?v=9nkiu_22Y6c. Watch Dr. Zakir Naik about celebratatorinbbirthdays.
34 Dr. Bilal Phillips, "Celebrating the Mawlid."

practice is popular in South Asia (Pakistan and India), commonly in Urdu and Punjabi languages. People who recite Na`at are known as Naat-Khua'an, or Sana'a-Khua'an.

Among non-Muslim countries, India is noted for its Mawlid festivities. The relics of the Prophet Muhammad are displayed after the morning prayers in the Indian state of Jammu and Kashmir at the Hazratbal Shrine, on the outskirts of Srinagar. Shab-khawani night-long prayers held at the Hazratbal Shrine are attended by thousands.

Laylat al-Qadr

Laylat al-Qadr is variously rendered in English as the Night of Destiny, Night of Power, Night of Value, Night of Decree, or Night of Measures. It is the anniversary of two very important dates in Islam that occurred in the month of Ramadan. It is the anniversary of the night when Muslims believe the first verses of the Quran were revealed to the Islamic Prophet Muhammad.

Revelation to Prophet Muhammad

Laylat al-Qadr is believed to be the night when the Quran was first revealed. Some but not all Muslims believe that revelation of the Quran occurred in two phases, with the first phase being the revelation in its entirety on Laylat al-Qadr to the angel Gabriel (Jibril in Arabic) in the lowest heaven, and then the subsequent verse-by-verse revelation to Muhammad by Gabriel, across twenty-three years. The revelation started in 610 AD at the Hira cave on Mount Nur in Mecca. The first surah that was revealed was Surah Al-Alaq, which is also commonly referred to as Surah Iqra'. During the first revelation the first five verses of this surah, or chapter, were revealed. The first word of the revelation, "Iqra," meaning "read," is significant, as the Prophet Muhammad could not read. The verses spoken by the angel Gabriel were imprinted in the heart of the Prophet Muhammad. The command "read" thus remains a foremost command addressed to every Muslim and this points to the importance of reading, learning, and knowledge in Islam. The pillar of Islam standing on no lesser a theme through propagation of the Quran and the traditions of Prophet Muhammad the religion gained and continues to gain strength. Muslims should worship as much as they can on this night because of its historical significance. It is also believed to be the night when God decides the destiny of everyone.

Sunnah

Muslims often pray extra prayers on this day, particularly the night prayer. They awake, pray, and hope God will give them anything they may desire on this night. Mostly, they perform *tilawat* (reading the Quran).

Those who can afford to devote their time to the remembrance of God stay in the mosque for the final ten days of Ramadan. This worship is called I'tikāf (retreat). They observe a fast during the day and occupy themselves with the remembrance of God, performing voluntary prayers and studying the Quran, day and night, apart from the obligatory prayers, which they perform with the congregation. Food and other

Hazza Abu Rabia / Adapted from "Laylat al-Qadr" at en.wikipedia.org / CC BY-SA 3.0

necessities of life are provided for them during their stay in the mosque. While devoting time to remembering God, Muslims also hope to receive divine favors and blessings connected with Lailat ul-Qadr.

Date

Sunni Islam: Laylat al-Qadr is to be found in the last five odd nights of the third decade of Ramadan. There is no history in the Quran as to when the specific date is. Therefore, in the Sunni communities of all the Islamic countries, the Laylat al-Qadar is found to be on the last nights of Ramadan. Mostly it is on one of the odd nights, that is, the twenty-first (means the night that follows the day number twenty-first, twenty-third, twenty-fifth, twenty-seventh, or twenty-ninth night. Many traditions insist particularly on the night before the twenty-seventh of Ramadan.

Shia Islam: Similarly, Lailatul Qadr' is to be found in the last ten odd nights of Ramadan, but mostly on the nineteenth or twenty-first or twenty-third or twenty-seventh night of Ramadan. The nineteenth, according to the Shia belief, coincides with the night Ali was attacked in the Mihrab while worshipping in the Great Mosque of Kufa, and he died on the twenty-first of Ramadan. Shia Muslims worship and regard these four nights as greatly rewarding.

Many Shia Muslims, who make up the largest minority of Islamic followers—including the Ismailis and especially Dawoodi Bohras—observe Laylat al-Qadr on the night of the twenty-third, in keeping with traditions received through Ali and his wife Fatimah, Muhammad's daughter, and Fatimid Imams. The tradition is also said to have been articulated by Ja'far al-Sadiq and other Shia Imams.

Religious Importance

> We have indeed revealed this (Message) in the Night of Power:
> And what will explain to thee what the night of power is?
> The Night of Power is better than a thousand months.
> Therein come down the angels and the Spirit by Allah's permission, on every errand:
> Peace! … This until the rise of dawn!
>
> —Sura 97 (Al-Qadr), āyāt 1–5

The verses above regard the night as better than one thousand months. The whole month of Ramadan is a period of spiritual training wherein believers devote much of their time to fasting, praying, reciting the Quran, remembering God, and giving charity. However, because of the revealed importance of this night, Muslims strive harder in the last ten days of Ramadan because the Laylat al-Qadr could be one of the odd-numbered days in these last ten (the first, third, fifth, seventh, or ninth). Normally, some Muslims from each community perform i'tikāf in the mosque: they remain in the mosque for the last ten days of the month for prayers and recitation. Women, too, observe i'tikaf. They remain in prayer and meditation mostly, although they are allowed to do the minimum domestic work needed to run the family. When Muhammad observed i'tikaf in a tent, he saw a few tents around his. His wives joined him by pitching tents.

Isra and Mi'raj

The Isra and Mi'raj are the two parts of a Night Journey that, according to Islamic tradition, the prophet of Islam, Muhammad took during a single night around the year 621 AD. It has been described as both a physical and spiritual journey. A brief sketch of the story is in *sura* 17 *Al-Isra* of the Quran, and other details come from the *Hadith*, supplemental writings about the life of Prophet Muhammad. In the journey, Prophet Muhammad travels on the steed Buraq[35] to "the farthest mosque" where he leads other prophets in prayer. He then ascends to Heaven, where he speaks to God, who gives Muhammad instructions to take back to the faithful regarding the details of prayer.

According to traditions, the journey is associated with the *Lailat al Mi'raj* as one of the most significant events in the Islamic calendar.

Islamic Sources

The Night Journey started with the appearance of the Angel Jibreel, who had been bringing Prophet Muhammad the Quranic revelation piecemeal on different occasions. The angel led the Prophet Muhammad to a white, horse-like creature, which was taller than a mule but shorter than a horse, with wings attached at its thighs. This heavenly creature had carried other prophets, including Ibrahim, and was the buraq or spirit horse (heavenly creature). Prophet Muhammad mounted it, and it carried him high onto the sky. The Buraq reached as far as the horizon at each stride.

He arrived at Jerusalem, where he met a company of all the prophets, including Ibrahim, Musa, and Isa. Ibrahim looked like no one else, but also no one did not look like him. Moses was tall, tanned, and slim, with a hooked nose and curly hair. Muhammad was asked to lead them in prayer, and he did.

Three dishes were placed in front of Prophet Muhammad containing wine and milk. The Prophet Muhammad liked to drink milk, so he chose that; Jibreel said to him, after choosing, that if he had chosen wine, the Muslim community would have become disoriented and lost the true path of Allah (God).

When he finished, he mounted the Buraq, and in the company of Jibreel (Gabriel) flew at an unimaginable speed up to the first level of Heaven. The first gate of Heaven was guarded by an angel whose name was Ishmael. This angel was in charge of twelve thousand angels, each of whom was in charge of twelve thousand additional angels, collectively totaling 144,000,001, all commissioned to guard this first gate. Ishmael asked Jibreel if Muhammad was the one sent to deliver God's message to humankind, and Jibreel confirmed this, so Prophet Muhammad was let through with some prayers.

Prophet Muhammad passed through seven heavenly realms. In the First Sky he saw Adam being shown the souls of his descendants, both the good and the bad. In the Second Sky he saw Isa and John, son of Zachariah. In the Third Sky he saw the handsome Joseph, son of Jacob. In the Fourth Sky he saw Idris,

---

35 Al-Burāq "lightning" is a mythological steed, described as a creature from the heavens that transported the prophets. The most commonly told story is how, in the seventh century, Al-Buraq carried the Islamic prophet Muhammad from Mecca to Jerusalem and back during the Isra and Mi'raj, or "Night Journey."

Hazza Abu Rabia / Adapted from "Isra and Mi'raj" at en.wikipedia.org / CC BY-SA 3.0

the prophet from the time before the flood. In the Fifth Sky he saw Moses's older brother, Harun, with his long, white beard. In the Sixth Sky Muhammad met a tall man with a hooked nose, and Gabriel said it was Moses. In the Seventh Sky Muhammad saw an old man in a seat by the gate to Paradise where seventy thousand angels pass through each day but do not return until Judgment Day. Jibreel identified the old man as Ibrahim. Jibreel then took Prophet Muhammad into Paradise, where he spoke to God.

God told Muhammad the importance of regular prayers. On the way back Musa asked how many prayers had been commanded, and Prophet Muhammad said fifty per day. Musa told him to go back to God and get the number cut. God reduced the number to ten per day, but Musa again said this was too many. Muhammad returned, and they were reduced to five times per day. Musa said this was still too many, but Prophet Muhammad told Musa he would be too embarrassed to return to God again. Prophet Muhammad returned to Makkah.

Prophet Muhammad described his journey to followers, but many did not believe he had gone to Jerusalem in one night, had seen the Seven Heavens, and had spoken with God. Some who stopped believing went to Abu Bakr, and Abu Bakr saw Prophet Muhammad, asking him to describe Jerusalem. He did so, and Abu Bakr declared that all the details were accurate, and therefore Prophet Muhammad must have been there.

Quran

Exalted is He who took His Servant by night from al-Masjid al-Haram to al-Masjid al-Aqsa, whose surroundings We have blessed, to show him of Our signs. Indeed, He is the Hearing, the Seeing.

—Quran, *Chapter 17 (Al-Isra), Verse 1*

And [remember, O Muhammad], when We told you, "Indeed, your Lord has encompassed the people." And We did not make the sight which We showed you except as a trial for the people, as was the accursed tree [mentioned] in the Quran. And We threaten them, but it increases them not except in great transgression.

—Quran, *Chapter 17 (Al-Isra), Verse 60*

And he certainly saw him in another descent,
At the Lote-tree of the Utmost Boundary—
Near it is the Garden of Refuge—
When there covered the Lote Tree that which covered [it]
The sight [of the Prophet] did not swerve, nor did it transgress [its limit].
He certainly saw of the greatest signs of his Lord.

—Quran, *Chapter 53 (An-Najm), Verses 13–18*

Ramadan

Ramadan is the ninth month of the Islamic calendar; Muslims worldwide observe this as a month of fasting. This annual observance is regarded as one of the Five Pillars of Islam. The month lasts twenty-nine to thirty days based on the visual sightings of the crescent moon, according to numerous biographical accounts compiled in the hadiths.[36] The word Ramadan comes from the Arabic root *ramiḍa* or *ar-ramaḍ*, which means scorching heat or dryness.[37] Fasting is obligatory for adult Muslims, except those who are ill, traveling, pregnant, breastfeeding, or diabetic or going through menstrual bleeding.

While fasting from dawn until sunset, Muslims refrain from consuming food, drinking liquids, smoking, and engaging in sexual relations; in some interpretations they also refrain from swearing. Food and drink are served daily, before sunrise and after sunset. According to Islam, the *thawab* (rewards) of fasting are many, but in this month they are believed to be multiplied.[38] Fasting for Muslims during Ramadan typically includes the increased offering of *salat* (prayers) and recitation of the Quran.

In the Quran

Chapter 2, Revelation 185 of the Quran states:

> The month of Ramadan is that in which was revealed the Quran; a guidance for mankind, and clear proofs of the guidance, and the criterion (of right and wrong). And whosoever of you is present, let him fast the month, and whosoever of you is sick or on a journey, a number of other days. Allah desires for you ease; He desires not hardship for you; and that you should complete the period, and that you should magnify Allah for having guided you, and that perhaps you may be thankful.
>
> —Quran 2:185

Thus, according to the Quran, Prophet Muhammad first received revelations in the lunar month of Ramadan. Therefore, the month of Ramadan is considered to be the most sacred month of the Islamic calendar, the recording of which began with the Hijra.

Important Dates

The beginning and end of Ramadan are determined by the lunar Islamic calendar.

---

36 Bukhari-Ibn-Ismail, AbdAllah-Muhammad. "Sahih Bukhari—Book 031 (*The Book of Fasting*), Hadith 124." hadithcollection. com. Retrieved July 25, 2013.

37 Muslim-Ibn-Habaj, Abul-Hussain. "Sahih Muslim—Book 006 (*The Book of Fasting*), Hadith 2391." hadithcollection.com. Retrieved July 25, 2013.

38 Bukhari-Ibn-Ismail, AbdAllah-Muhammad. "Sahih Bukhari—Book 031 (*The Book of Fasting*), Hadith 125." hadithcollection. com. Retrieved July 25, 2013.

Hazza Abu Rabia / Adapted from "Ramadan" at en.wikipedia.org / CC BY-SA 3.0

Beginning

Hilāl (the crescent) is typically a day (or more) after the astronomical new moon. Because the new moon marks the beginning of the new month, Muslims can usually safely estimate the beginning of Ramadan. [14] However, to many Muslims, this is not in accordance with authenticated Hadiths stating that visual confirmation per region is recommended. The consistent variations of a day have existed since the time of Prophet Muhammad.

Laylat al-Qadr, or Night of Power

Laylat al-Qadr, which in Arabic means "the night of power" or "the night of decree," is considered the most holy night of the year. This is the night in which Muslims believe the first revelation of the Quran was sent down to Muhammad, stating that this night was "better than one thousand months [of proper worship]," as stated in Chapter 97:3 of the Quran.

Also, generally, Laylat al-Qadr is believed to have occurred on an odd-numbered night during the last ten days of Ramadan, that is, the night of the twenty-first, twenty-third, twenty-fifth, twenty-seventh, or twenty-ninth. The Dawoodi Bohra community believes that the twenty-third night is Laylat al-Qadr.

End

Eid al-Fitr and Eid Prayers

The holiday of *Eid al-Fitr* ("festivity of breaking the fast") marks the end of Ramadan and the beginning of the next lunar month, Shawwal. This first day of the following month is declared after another crescent new moon has been sighted or the completion of thirty days of fasting if no visual sighting is possible because of weather conditions. This first day of Shawwal is called Eid al-Fitr. *Eid al-Fitr* may also be a reference to the festive nature of having endured the month of fasting successfully and returning to the more natural disposition (*fitra*) of being able to eat, drink, and resume intimacy with spouses during the day.

Practices during Ramadan

The predominant practice in Ramadan is fasting from sunrise to sunset. The pre-dawn meal before the fast is called the *suhoor*, while the meal at sunset that breaks the fast is the *iftar*. Considering the high diversity of the global Muslim population, it is impossible to describe typical suhoor or iftar meals.

Muslims also engage in increased prayer and charity during Ramadan.

Fasting, or *Sawm of Ramadan*

Ramadan is a time of spiritual reflection, improvement, and increased devotion and worship. Muslims are expected to put more effort into following the teachings of Islam. The fast (sawm) begins at dawn and ends at sunset. In addition to abstaining from eating and drinking, Muslims also increase restraint, such as abstaining from sexual relations and generally sinful speech and behavior. The act of fasting is said to redirect the heart away from worldly activities, its purpose being to cleanse the soul by freeing it from harmful impurities. Ramadan also teaches Muslims how to better practice self-discipline, self-control, sacrifice, and empathy for those who are less fortunate, thus encouraging actions of generosity and compulsory charity (zakat).

It becomes compulsory for Muslims to start fasting when they reach puberty, so long as they are healthy and sane, and have no disabilities or illnesses. Many children endeavor to complete as many fasts as possible as practice for later life.

Exemptions to fasting are travel, menstruation, severe illness, pregnancy, and breast-feeding. However, many Muslims with medical conditions insist on fasting to satisfy their spiritual needs, although it is not recommended by the hadith. Professionals should closely monitor individuals who decide to persist with fasting. Those who were unable to fast still must make up the days missed later.

Suhoor

Each day before dawn, many Muslims observe a pre-fast meal called suhoor. After stopping a short time before dawn, Muslims begin the first prayer of the day, Fajr. At sunset, families hasten for the fast-breaking meal known as iftar.

Iftar

In the evening, dates are usually the first food to break the fast; according to tradition, Muhammad broke fast with three dates. Following that, Muslims generally adjourn for the Maghrib, or sunset prayer, the fourth of the five daily prayers, after which the main meal is served.

Social gatherings, many times in a buffet style, at iftar are frequent, and traditional dishes are often highlighted, including traditional desserts, especially those made only during Ramadan. Water is usually the beverage of choice, but juice and milk are also consumed. Soft drinks and caffeinated beverages are consumed to a lesser extent.

In the Middle East, the iftar meal consists of water, juices, dates, salads and appetizers, one or more entrees, and various kinds of desserts. Usually, the dessert is the most important part of the meal during iftar. Typical entrees are lamb stewed with wheat berries, lamb kebabs with grilled vegetables, or roast chicken served with chickpea-studded rice pilaf. A rich dessert such as luqaimat, baklava, or kunafeh (a buttery, syrup-sweetened kadaifi noodle pastry filled with cheese) concludes the meal.

Over time, iftar has grown into banquet festivals. This is a time of fellowship with families, friends, and surrounding communities, but may also occupy larger spaces at masjid or banquet halls for one hundred or more diners.

Nightly Prayers, or *Tarawih*

In addition to fasting, Muslims are encouraged to read the entire Quran. Some Muslims perform the recitation of the entire Quran by means of special prayers, called Tarawih. These voluntary prayers are held in the mosques every night of the month, during which a whole section of the Quran (*juz'*, which is one-thirtieth of the Quran) is recited. Therefore, the entire Quran would be completed at the end of the month. Although it is not required to read the whole Quran in the Tarawih prayers, it is commonly practiced.

Cultural Aspects

In some Muslim countries today, lights are strung up in public squares and across city streets to add to the festivities of the month. Lanterns have become symbolic decorations welcoming the month of Ramadan. In a growing number of countries, they are hung on city streets. The tradition of lanterns as a decoration becoming associated with Ramadan is believed to have originated during the Fatimid Caliphate primarily centered in Egypt, where Caliph al-Mu'izz li-Din Allah was greeted by people holding lanterns to celebrate his ruling. From that time lanterns were used to light mosques and houses throughout the capital city of Cairo. Shopping malls, places of business, and people's homes can be seen with stars and crescents, as well as, various lighting effects.

Law and Restrictions

Many countries have laws and policies regarding Ramadan.

The Soviet Union officially suppressed the practice of Ramadan and emphasized work schedules to make its practice difficult.[39] Chinese officials have restricted the practice of Ramadan in Xinjiang through Document 19 and other policies. Government employees are prohibited from fasting.[40] Party officials and students under the age of eighteen are also prohibited from fasting.

Some countries have laws penalizing public eating during Ramadan. Kuwaiti Law Number 44 of 1968 imposes a fine of no more than 100 Kuwaiti dinars, or jail for no more than one month, or both penalties, for those seen eating, drinking, or smoking during Ramadan daytime. In the United Arab Emirates (UAE), eating or drinking during the daytime of Ramadan is considered a minor offense and punishable by up to 240 hours of community service.

In Egypt, alcohol sales are banned during Ramadan.

Some countries have laws that amend work schedules in Ramadan. Under UAE labor law, the maximum working hours are to be six per day and thirty-six per week. Qatar, Oman, Bahrain, and Kuwait have similar laws.

Origins

Origin of the Word Ramadan

Ramadan, as a name for the month, is of Muslim origin. However, prior to Islam's exclusion of intercalary days from its calendar, the name of this month was Nātiq and, because of the intercalary days added, always occurred in the warm season.

It is believed that the first revelation to Prophet Muhammad was sent down during the month of Ramadan. Furthermore, God proclaimed to Prophet Muhammad that fasting for His sake was not a new innovation in monotheism, but rather an obligation practiced by those truly devoted to the oneness of God.

---

39 Minahan, James. (2004). *The Former Soviet Union's Diverse Peoples*. ABC-CLIO, p. 162.
40 Olimat, Muhammad. (2012). *China and the Middle East*. Routledge, p. 32.

Zakat al-Fitr

Zakat al-Fitr is charity given to the poor at the end of the fasting in the Islamic holy month of Ramadan. The word *Fitr* means the same as *Iftar*, breaking a fast, and it comes from the same root word as *Futoor*, which means breakfast.

Classification

Sadaqat al-Fitr is a duty that is wajib (required) of every Muslim, whether male or female, minor or adult, as long as he or she has the means to do so.

According to Islamic tradition (Sunnah), Ibn 'Umar said that Muhammad made *Zakat al-Fitr* compulsory for every slave and free man, male and female, young and old, among the Muslims; one Saa` of dried dates or one Saa` of barley. [Sahih Bukhari—Arabic/English, vol. 2, p. 339, no. 579]

The head of the household may pay the required amount for the other members. Abu Sa'eed al-Khudree said:

> On behalf of our young and old, free men and slaves, we used to take out during Allah's Messenger's (upon whom be God's peace and blessings) lifetime one Sa` of grain, cheese or raisins. [Sahih Muslim—English transl. vol. 2, p. 469, no. 2155]

Significance

The significant role played by *Zakat* in the circulation of wealth within the Islamic society is also played by the *Sadaqat al-Fitr*. However, in the case of *Sadaqat al-Fitr*, each individual is required to calculate how much charity is due from himself and his dependents and go into the community in order to find those who deserve such charity. Thus, *Sadaqat al-Fitr* plays a very important role in the development of the bonds of community. The rich are obliged to come in direct contact with the poor, and the poor are put in contact with the extremely poor. This contact between the various levels of society helps build real bonds of brotherhood and love within the Islamic community and trains those who have to be generous to those who do not have.

Purpose

The main purpose of *Zakat al-Fitr* is to provide the poor with a means with which they can celebrate the festival of breaking the fast (`Eid al-Fitr) along with the rest of the Muslims.

Every Muslim is required to pay *Zakat al-Fitr* at the conclusion of the month of Ramadan as a token of thankfulness to God for having enabled him or her to observe the obligatory fast. Its purpose is as follows:

1. As a levy on the fasting person. This is based on the hadith: the Prophet of Allah said, "The fasting of the month of fasting will be hanging between earth and heavens and it will not be raised up to the Divine Presence without paying the *Zakat al-Fitr*."
2. To purify those who fast from any indecent act or speech and to help the poor and needy.

Hazza Abu Rabia / Adapted from "Zakat al-Fitr" at en.wikipedia.org / CC BY-SA 3.0

The latter view is based upon the hadith from Ibn `Abbas, who related, "The Prophet of Allah enjoined *Zakat al-Fitr* on those who fast to shield them from any indecent act or speech, and for the purpose of providing food for the needy. It is accepted as *Zakah* for the one who pays it before the `Eid prayer, and it is sadaqah for the one who pays it after the prayer." [Abu Dawood—Eng. transl. vol. 2, p. 421, no. 1605—rated Sahih]

Conditions

Zakat al-Fitr is only Wajib for a particular period of time. If one misses the time period without a good reason, he has sinned and cannot make it up. This form of charity becomes obligatory from sunset on the last day of fasting and remains obligatory until the beginning of `Eid Prayer (i.e., shortly after sunrise on the following day). However, it can be paid prior to the above mentioned period, as many of the Sahabah (companions of the Prophet) used to pay *Sadaqah al-Fitr* a couple days before the `Eid.

After the spread of Islam, the jurists permitted its payment from the beginning and middle of Ramadan so as to ensure that the *Zakat al-Fitr* reached its beneficiaries on the day of `Eid. It is particularly emphasized that the distribution be before the `Eid prayers so that the needy who receive are able to use the *fitr* to provide for their dependents on the day of `Eid.

Nafi` reported that the Prophet's companion Ibn `Umar used to give it to those who would accept it, and the people used to give it a day or two before the `Eid. [Bukhari—Arabic/English, Vol. 2, p.339, no. 579]

Ibn `Umar reported that the Prophet ordered that it (*Zakat al-Fitr*) be given before people go to perform the (`Eid) prayers.

One who forgets to pay this *Zakat al-Fitr* on time should do so as soon as possible, even though it will not be counted as *Zakat al-Fitr*.

Rate

The amount of *Zakat* is the same for everyone regardless of their different income brackets. The minimum amount is one *sa`* (four double handfuls) of food, grain, or dried fruit for each member of the family. This calculation is based on Ibn `Umar's report that the Prophet made *Zakat al-Fitr* compulsory and payable by a sa` of dried dates or a *sa`* of barley. Cash equivalent (of the food weight) may also be given if food collection and distribution are unavailable in that particular country.

A companion of Muhammad, Abu Sa`eed al-Khudree, said, "In the Prophet's time, we used to give it (Zakatal-Fitr) as a *sa`* of food, dried dates, barley, raisins, or dried cheese." [Bukhari—Arabic/English vol. 2, p. 340, no. 582] According to the majority of Sunni scholars, One sa' is approximately between 2.6 kilograms and 3 kilograms.

The distribution of Zakat al-Fitr is the same as that of Zakah, and is included within its broader sense. Those who may receive *Zakat al-Fitr* are the eight categories of recipients mentioned in Surat Al-Tawbah [9: 60]. They include the following:

1. The poor
2. The needy
3. Collectors of Zakah
4. Reconciliation of hearts
5. Freeing captives or slaves (*fee al-Riqab*)

6. Debtors
7. In the Way of Allah/Islamic causes (*fee sabeel illah*)
8. The traveler
9. *Zakat al-Fitr* must go to the above-mentioned categories. The Zakat al-mal cannot be used for any other things, either.

Eid al-Fitr

Eid al-Fitr ("festival of breaking of the fast"), also called the Feast of Breaking the Fast and the Lesser Eid, is an important religious holiday celebrated by Muslims worldwide that marks the end of Ramadan, the Islamic holy month of fasting (*sawm*). The religious Eid is a single day, and Muslims are not permitted to fast that day. The holiday celebrates the conclusion of the twenty-nine or thirty days of dawn-to-sunset fasting during the entire month of Ramadan. The day of Eid, therefore, falls on the first day of the month of Shawwal. This is a day when Muslims around the world try to show a common goal of unity. The date for the start of any lunar Hijri month varies based on the observation of new moon by local religious authorities, so the exact day of celebration varies by locality. However, in most countries, it is generally celebrated on the same day as it is in Saudi Arabia.

Eid al-Fitr has a particular Salat (Islamic prayer) consisting of two Rakats (units) and generally offered in an open field or large hall. It may only be performed in congregation (*Jama'at*) and has an additional extra six Takbirs (raising of the hands to the ears while saying "Allāhu Akbar," literally, "God is greater"), three of them in the beginning of the first raka'ah and three of them just before Ruku' in the second raka'ah in the Hanafi school of Sunni Islam. Other Sunni schools usually have twelve Takbirs, seven in the first, and five at the beginning of the second raka'ah. This Eid al-Fitr salat is, depending on which juristic opinion is followed, *Fard* (obligatory), *Mustahabb* (strongly recommended, just short of obligatory), or mandoob (preferable).

Muslims believe that they are commanded by God, as mentioned in the Quran, to continue their fast until the last day of Ramadan and pay the Zakat and fitra before offering the Eid prayers.

History

Before the advent of Islam in Arabia, there is mention of festivals as well as some others among the Arabs. The Israelites had festivals as well, but as is evident from the Old Testament and other scriptures, these festivals related more to commemorating certain days of their history.

Eid al-Fitr was originated by the Prophet Muhammad. It is observed on the first of the month of Shawwal at the end of the month of Ramadan, during which Muslims undergo a period of fasting.

According to certain traditions, these festivals were initiated in Madinah after the migration of Prophet Muhammad from Mecca. Anas reports:

> When the Prophet arrived in Madinah, he found people celebrating two specific days in which they used to entertain themselves with recreation and merriment. He asked them about the nature

Hazza Abu Rabia / Adapted from "Eid al-Fitr" at en.wikipedia.org / CC BY-SA 3.0

of these festivities at which they replied that these days were occasions of fun and recreation. At this, the Prophet remarked that the Almighty has fixed two days [of festivity] instead of these for you which are better than these: Eid al-Fitr and Eid al-Adha.[41]

For Muslims, both the festivals of Eid al-Fitr and Eid al-Adha are occasions of showing gratitude to God and remembering Him, and are an occasion of entertainment. 'Aishah narrates that when on an Eid day her father Abu Bakr stopped young girls from singing, Prophet Muhammad said, "Abu Bakr! [Let them sing!]; every nation has an 'eid and [this day] is our Eid."

General Rituals

Eid al-Fitr is celebrated for one, two, or three days. Common greetings during this holiday are the Arabic greeting 'Eid Mubārak ("Blessed Eid") or 'Eid Sa'īd ("Happy Eid"). In addition, many countries have their own greetings in the local language—in Turkey, for example, a typical saying might be "*Bayramınız kutlu olsun,*" or "May your *Bayram*—Eid—be blessed." Muslims are also encouraged on this day to forgive and forget any differences with others or animosities that may have occurred during the year.

Typically, practicing Muslims wake up early in the morning—always before sunrise—offer Salatul Fajr (the pre-sunrise prayer), and, in keeping with the traditions of the Prophet Muhammad, clean their teeth with a toothbrush, take a shower before prayers, put on new clothes (or the best available), and apply perfume.

It is forbidden to fast on the Day of Eid. It is customary to acknowledge this with a small, sweet breakfast, preferably of the date fruit, before attending a special Eid prayer.

As an obligatory act of charity, money is paid to the poor and the needy (Arabic: *Sadaqat-ul-fitr*) before performing the 'Eid prayer:

- To show happiness
- To give as much charity as is possible
- To pray Fajr in the local Masjid
- To go early for Eid salaat
- To read the takbirat in an open field.
- Go to the Eid prayer on foot.
- Do not speak one word other than words that remember Allah or any Islamic terms before and after Eid Salaat. You can speak once you've left the Masjid, or Mosque, or any other place you were praying.
- Say "*Eid Mubarak*" to other Muslims.
- Muslims recite the following incantation in a low voice while going to the Eid prayer: "*Allāhu Akbar, Allāhu Akbar, Allāhu Akbar. Lā ilāha illà l-Lāh wal-Lāhu akbar, Allahu akbar walil-Lāhi l-ḥamd.*" Recitation ceases when they get to the place of Eid or once the Imam commences activities.
- Muslims are recommended to use separate routes to and from the prayer grounds.

The Eid prayer is performed in congregation in open areas, such as fields, community centers, and so forth, or at mosques. No call to prayer is given for this Eid prayer, and it consists of only two units of prayer with an additional six incantations. The Eid prayer is followed by the sermon and then a supplication asking

---

41 Ahmad ibn Hanbal, Musnad, vol. 4, 141–142 (no. 13210).

for God's forgiveness, mercy, peace, and blessings for all living beings across the world. The sermon also instructs Muslims as to the performance of rituals of Eid, such as the zakat.[13] Listening to the sermon at Eid is not required and is optional, a Sunnah i.e. while the sermon is being delivered. After the prayers, Muslims visit their relatives, friends, and acquaintances or hold large communal celebrations in homes, community centers, or rented halls.

Eid gifts, known as *Eidiey*, are frequently given at Eid to children and immediate relatives.

Islamic Tradition

Eid al-Fitr marks the end of the fasting month of Ramadan. This has to do with the communal aspects of the fast, which expresses many of the basic values of the Muslim community, for example, empathy for the poor, charity, worship, steadfastness, and patience. Fasting is also believed by some scholars to extol fundamental distinctions, lauding the power of the spiritual realm, while acknowledging the subordination of the physical realm. It also teaches a Muslim to stay away from worldly desires and to focus entirely on the Lord and thank Him for His blessings. It is a rejuvenation of the religion, and it creates a stronger bond between the Muslim and his Lord. After the end of Ramadan is a big celebration of Eid.

Eid Practices by Country
Egypt

Eid al-Fitr is a three-day feast and an official holiday in Egypt, with vacations for schools, universities, and government offices. Some stores and restaurants are also closed during Eid.

The Eid day starts with a small snack, followed by Eid prayers in congregation attended by men, women, and children, in which the sermon reminds Egyptians of the virtues and good deeds they should do unto others, even strangers, during Eid and throughout the year.

Afterwards, neighbors, friends, and relatives start greeting one another. The most common greeting is "Eid Mubarak" ("Blessed Eid"). Family visits are considered a must on the first day of the Eid, so they have the other two days to enjoy by going to parks, cinemas, theaters, or the beaches. Some like to go on tours or a Nile cruise, but Sharm El Sheikh is also considered a favorite spot for spending holidays in Egypt.

Children are normally given new clothes to wear throughout the Eid. Also, women (particularly mothers, wives, sisters, and daughters) are commonly given special gifts by their loved ones. It is customary for children to also receive a Eid-ey-yah from their adult relatives. This is a small sum of money that the children receive and is used to spend on all their activities throughout the Eid. Children will wear their new clothes and go out to amusement parks, gardens, or public courtyards based on how much their Eidyah affords. The amusement parks can range from the huge ones on the outskirts of Cairo-Nile; Felucca Nile rides are one common feature of Eid celebration in Egyptian villages, towns, and cities.

The family gatherings involve cooking and eating all kinds of Egyptian food, such as Fata, but the items most associated with Eid al-Fitr are Kahk (singular: Kahka), which are cookies filled with nuts and covered with powdered sugar. Egyptians either bake them at home or buy them in the bakery. Thus, a bakery crowded in the last few days of Ramadan with Kahk buyers is a common scene. TV in Egypt celebrates Eid, too, with a continuous marathon of movies as well as programs featuring live interviews from all over Egypt of both public figures and everyday citizens sharing their Eid celebrations.

For a lot of families from working neighborhoods, the Eid celebration also means small, mobile neighborhood rides, much like a neighborhood carnival. In a lot of neighborhood courtyards, kids also gather around a storyteller, a puppeteer, or a magician mesmerized by Egyptian folktales or by a grownup's sleight of hand. It is also customary for kids to rent decorated bikes to ride around town.

Egyptians like to celebrate with others, so the streets are always crowded during the days and nights of Eid.

Pakistan

In Pakistan on the day of Eid al-Fitr, people wear new clothes to get ready for Eid prayer. People are supposed to give obligatory charity on behalf of each of their family members to the needy or poor before Eid day, or at least before Eid prayer. This will allow everybody to share the joy of Eid and won't feel depressed. There is a three-day national holiday for Eid celebration, while festivities and the greetings tradition usually continue for the whole month. There is also a tradition that has developed in the recent past of people sending Eid greeting cards to distant family members, relatives, and friends.

For Eid prayer, people gather at large open areas, such as sports grounds or parks. After Eid Salat, people meet and greet each other with a traditional hug of friendship. Before going home, people give charity to the needy and the poor, to further make it possible to have everybody be able to enjoy the day. On their way home, people buy sweets, gas balloons for kids, and gifts for the family. At home family members enjoy a special Eid breakfast with various types of sweets and deserts, including traditional desert *sheer korma*, which is made of vermicelli, milk, butter, dry fruits, and dates.

Eid is mainly enjoyed by the kids, as they mostly receive money in cash, called "Eidi," as a gift from every elder in the family and relatives when they visit their places. On Eid day kids are allowed to spend their gift money (Edi) as they want. The media also covers Eid festivities all day and airs various special programs on TV for all age groups.

In the neighborhood lots of mobile food shops, games, and outdoor amusements, such as fairground rides, are enjoyed all day. People visit their elder relatives first, then others and friends and share the joy of the day. Some go to parks, the seaside, or river or lake fronts to enjoy and relax. Families get together in the evening to enjoy Eid dinner and plan how to celebrate the second and third day of Eid.

India

In India the celebrations are similar, having been once a single nation from the days of the Mughal Empire and British Raj share many similarities with regional variations mentioned below. The night before Eid is called Chaand ki Raat, which means "Night of the Moon." Muslims in these countries will often visit bazaars and shopping malls with their families for Eid shopping. Women, especially younger girls, will often apply the traditional *Mehndi*, or henna, on their hands and feet and wear colorful bangles.

The traditional Eid greeting is "*Eid Mubarak*," and it is frequently followed by a formal embrace. Gifts are frequently given—new clothes are part of the tradition—and it is also common for children to be given small sums of money (*Eidi*) by their elders. It is common for children to offer *salam* to parents and adult relatives.

After the Eid prayers, it is common for some families to visit graveyards and pray for the salvation of departed family members. It is also common to visit neighbors, family members, especially senior relatives called *Murubbis*, and to get together to share sweets, snacks, and special meals, including some special dishes that are prepared specifically on Eid. Special celebratory dishes in India, Pakistan, and Bangladesh include *Lachcha* or *sivayyana*, a dish of fine, toasted, sweet vermicelli noodles with milk and dried fruit.

On Eid day before prayers, people distribute a charity locally known as *fitra*. Many people also avail themselves of this opportunity to distribute zakat, an Islamic obligatory alms tax of 2.5 percent of one's annual savings, to the needy. Zakat is often distributed in the form of food and new clothes.

In India, there are many popular places for Muslims to congregate to celebrate Eid at this time, including the Jama Masjid in New Delhi, Mecca Masjid in Hyderabad, and Aishbagh Idgah in Lucknow; in Kolkata there is a prayer held on Red Road. Muslims turn out by the thousands, as there is a lot of excitement surrounding the celebration of this festival. It is common for non-Muslims to visit their Muslim friends and neighbors on Eid to convey their good wishes. Eid is celebrated grandly in the city of Hyderabad, which has a rich Islamic heritage. Hyderabadi haleem, a type of meat stew, is a popular dish during the month of Ramadan; it takes center stage and becomes the main course at Iftar (the breaking of the fast).

Mehndi is the application of henna as a temporary form of skin decoration, commonly applied during Eid al-Fitr.

Saudi Arabia

Eid al-Fitr is celebrated with great pomp in Saudi Arabia. Saudis decorate their homes and prepare sumptuous meals for family and friends.

Eid festivities in Saudi Arabia may vary culturally, depending on the region, but one common thread in all celebrations is of generosity and hospitality. First, it is common Saudi tradition for families to gather at the patriarchal home after the Eid prayers. Before the special Eid meal is served, young children will line up in front of the adult family members, who dispense riyals to the children. Family members will also typically have a time where they will pass out gift bags to the children. These bags are often beautifully decorated and contain candies and toys.

Many shopkeepers will show their generosity at Eid, providing free Eid gifts with each purchase. For example, during Eid, many of the chocolate shops will give each customer who buys a selection of candies a free crystal candy dish with their purchase.

In the spirit of Eid, many Saudis go out of their way to show their kindness and generosity. It is common for even complete strangers to greet one another at random, even by occupants of vehicles waiting at stoplights. Sometimes even toys and gifts will be given to children by complete strangers.

It is also traditional in some areas for Saudi men to go and buy large quantities of rice and other staples and then leave them anonymously at the doors of those who are less fortunate. Also, in some areas in the middle of Saudi Arabia, such as Al Qassim, it's a common tradition that during Eid morning and after the Eid prayer people put large rugs on one of streets of their neighborhood, and each household will prepare a large meal, then these meals will be shared by all neighbors; it's also a common practice that people will swap places to try more than one kind of meal.

Indonesia

Eid is known in Indonesia as Idul Fitri (or more popularly as Lebaran) and is a national holiday. Shopping malls and bazaars are usually filled with people to get things for Lebaran, such as new clothes, shoes, sandals, and even food to serve days ahead of *Idul Fitri*, which creates a distinctive festive atmosphere throughout the country, along with traffic mayhem. Many banks and government and private offices are closed for the duration of the *Lebaran* festivities.

One of the largest temporary human migrations globally is the prevailing custom of the *Lebaran* wherein workers, particularly, return to their home town or city to celebrate with their families and to ask forgiveness from parents, in-laws, and other elders. In 2013 there are around thirty million Indonesians traveling to their hometowns during the *Lebaran* holiday. This is known in Indonesia as *mudik, pulang kampung* (homecoming). It is an annual tradition for people in big cities, such as Greater Jakarta and Surabaya, or elsewhere in Indonesia. The government of Indonesia provides additional transportation to handle the huge amount of travelers. However, the impact is still tremendous, as millions of cars and motorcycles jam the roads and highways, causing kilometers of traffic jams each year.

The night before Idul Fitri is called *takbiran*; it is filled with the sounds of many muezzin chanting the takbir in the mosques or musallahs, and people usually fill the street and also chant the takbir. In many parts of Indonesia, especially in the rural areas, *pelita* (oil lamps, similar to tiki torches) are lit up and placed outside and around homes. Also, during *takbiran* people usually light various firecrackers or fireworks.

On the Lebaran day, after performing Eid prayer in the morning, people dressed in their new or best clothes will gather to greet their family and neighbors. It is common to greet people with "*Selamat Idul Fitri*," which means "Happy Eid." Muslims also greet one another with "*mohon maaf lahir dan batin,*" which means "Forgive my physical and emotional wrongdoings," because Idul Fitri is not only for celebrations but also a time for atonement to ask for forgiveness for sins that may have been committed but were cleansed as a result of the fasting in the Muslim month of Ramadan. During this Eid morning to afternoon, the zakat alms for the poor are usually distributed in the mosques.

Families usually will have a special Lebaran meal; special dishes will be served, such as ketupat, opor ayam, rendang, sambal goreng ati, sayur lodeh, and lemang (a type of glutinous rice cake cooked in bamboo). Various types of kue, cookies, and dodol sweet delicacies are also served during this day. Younger families usually visit their older neighbors or relatives to greet them with a "Happy Eid" and also to ask for forgiveness. Idul Fitri is a very joyous day for children, as adults give them money in colorful envelopes.

Ketupat is a popular traditional celebrative dish for Eid al-Fitr meal in Brunei, Indonesia, Malaysia, Singapore, and Southern Thailand.

It is customary for Muslim Indonesians to wear traditional cultural clothing on Eid al-Fitr. The Indonesian male outfit is known as *baju koko:* a collarless, long- or short-sleeved shirt with traditional embroidered designs, with a "kilt" *sarung* of songket, ikat, or similar woven, plaid cloth, and a headwear known as *songkok*. Alternatively, men may wear either Western-style business suits or more traditional, loose-fitting trousers with color-matched shirts, and a peci hat. Traditional female dress is known as *kebaya kurung*. It consists of, normally, a loose-fitting kebaya blouse (which may be enhanced with brocade and embroidery) and a long skirt, both of which may be batik, or the *sarung* skirt made of batik, ikat, or songket and either the *jilbab* (hijab) or its variant, the stiffened *kerudung*.

Later, it is common for many Muslims in Indonesia to visit the graves of loved ones. During this visit, they will clean the grave, recite Ya-Seen, a chapter (*sura*) from the Quran, and also perform the *tahlil* ceremony. In Indonesia there is a special ritual called *halal bi-halal*. This could be done during or several days after Idul Fitri. Usually core family and neighbors first during the first day of Idul Fitri, further relatives in the next day, and work colleagues in the days to weeks later after they get back to work. They will also seek reconciliation (if needed), and preserve or restore harmonious relations. The rest of the day is spent visiting relatives or serving visitors.

Hajj

The Hajj is the largest gathering of people in the world every year, and one of the five pillars of Islam, a religious duty that must be carried out by every able-bodied Muslim who can afford to do so at least once in his or her lifetime. The state of being physically and financially capable of performing the Hajj is called *istita'ah*, and a Muslim who fulfills this condition is called a *mustati*. The Hajj is a demonstration of the solidarity of the Muslim people, and their submission to God.

The pilgrimage occurs from the eighth to twelfth of Dhu al-Hijjah, the twelfth and last month of the Islamic calendar. Because the Islamic calendar is a lunar calendar, eleven days shorter than the Gregorian calendar used in the Western world, the Gregorian date of the Hajj changes from year to year. Ihram is the name given to the special spiritual state in which Muslims live while on the pilgrimage.

The Hajj is associated with the life of the Islamic Prophet Muhammad from the seventh century, but the ritual of pilgrimage to Mecca is considered by Muslims to stretch back thousands of years to the time of Abraham (Ibrahim). Pilgrims join processions of hundreds of thousands of people, who simultaneously converge on Mecca for the week of the Hajj, and perform a series of rituals: each person walks counter-clockwise seven times around the Ka'aba, the cube-shaped building, which acts as the Muslim direction of prayer; runs back and forth between the hills of Al-Safa and Al-Marwah; drinks from the Zamzam Well; goes to the plains of Mount Arafat to stand in vigil; and throws stones in a ritual Stoning of the Devil. The pilgrims then shave their heads, perform a ritual of animal sacrifice, and celebrate the three-day global festival of Eid al-Adha.

History

The Hajj is based on a pilgrimage that was ancient even in the time of Muhammad in the seventh century. According to tradition, elements of the Hajj trace back to the time of Abraham (Ibrahim), around 2000 BC. Abraham's wife, Sarah, was unable to conceive, and upon her request, Abraham had taken their female servant, Hagar, as a second wife. Hagar bore Abraham a son, Ishmael. It is believed that Abraham was ordered by God to leave Hagar (Hājar) and Ishmael ('Ismā'īl) alone in the desert. Looking for shelter, food, and water, Hagar ran back and forth between the hills of Safa and Marwa seven times with her son. In desperation, she laid the baby on the sand and begged for God›s assistance. The baby cried and hit the ground with his heel (some versions of the story say that the angel Gabriel [Jibrail] scraped his foot or the tip of his wing along the ground), and the Zamzam Well miraculously sprang forth.

Preparations

During the Hajj, male pilgrims are required to dress only in the *ihram*, a garment consisting of two sheets of white, unhemmed cloth, with the top draped over the torso and the bottom secured by a white sash, plus a pair of sandals. Women are simply required to maintain their hijab—normal, modest dress, which does not cover the hands or face.

Hazza Abu Rabia / Adapted from "Hajj" at en.wikipedia.org / CC BY-SA 3.0

The Ihram is meant to show equality of all pilgrims, in front of God: there is no difference between a prince and a pauper. Ihram is also symbolic for holy virtue and pardon from all past sins. A place designated for changing into Ihram is called a *Miqat*.

While wearing the Ihram, a pilgrim may not shave, clip his or her nails, wear perfume, swear or quarrel, have sexual relations, uproot or damage plants, kill or harm wild animals, cover the head (for men) or the face and hands (for women), marry, wear shoes over the ankles, or carry weapons.

Rites

Upon arrival in Mecca, the pilgrim, now known as a *Hajji*, performs a series of ritual acts symbolic of the lives of Ibrahim (or Abraham in English) and his wife Hajar (or Hagar in English). The acts also symbolize the solidarity of Muslims worldwide.

The greater Hajj (*al-hajj al-akbar*) begins on the eighth day of the twelfth lunar month of Dhu al-Hijjah. On the first day of the Hajj (the eighth day of the month), if pilgrims are not already wearing ihram clothing upon their arrival, they put on this clothing and then leave Mecca for the nearby town of Mina, where they spend the rest of the day. The Saudi government has put up thousands of large, white tents at Mina to provide accommodations for all the pilgrims.

Tawaf

The pilgrims perform their first *Tawaf*, which involves all of the pilgrims visiting the Kaaba and walking seven times counterclockwise around the Kaaba. They may also kiss the Black Stone (Al Hajar Al Aswad) on each circuit. If kissing the stone is not possible because of the crowds, they may simply point toward the stone on each circuit with their right hand. In each complete circuit a pilgrim says, "Here I am at Thy service, O Lord, here I am. Here I am at Thy service, and Thou hast no partners. Thine alone is All Praise and All Bounty, and Thine alone is The Sovereignty. Thou hast no partners ("Labbaik Allahumma Labbaik. Labbaik, La Shareek Laka, Labbaik. Innal Hamdah, Wan Nematah, Laka wal Mulk, La Shareek Laka")", with seven circuits constituting a complete Tawaf. The place where pilgrims walk is known as Mutaaf. Only the first three shouts are compulsory, but almost all perform them seven times.

The Tawaf is normally performed all at once. Eating is not permitted, but the drinking of water is allowed because of the risk of dehydration. Men are encouraged to perform the first three circuits at a hurried pace, followed by four times, more closely, at a leisurely pace.

After the completion of Tawaf, all the pilgrims have to offer two Rakaat prayers at the Place of Abraham (Muqaam Ibrahim), a site inside the mosque that is near the Kaaba. However, again because of large crowds during the days of Hajj, they may instead pray anywhere in the mosque.

Although the circuits around the Kaaba are traditionally done on the ground level, Tawaf is now also performed on the first floor and roof of the mosque because of the large crowd.

After Tawaf on the same day, the pilgrims perform sa`i, running or walking seven times between the hills of Safa and Marwah. This is a reenactment of the frantic search for water for her son Ishmael by Abraham's wife and Ishmael's mother, Hajar. As she searched, the Zamzam Well was revealed to her by an angel, who hit the ground with his heel (or brushed the ground with the tip of his wing), upon which the water of the Zamzam started gushing from the ground. The back-and-forth circuit of the pilgrims used to be in the open air, but is now entirely enclosed by the Masjid al-Haram mosque, and can be accessed via air-conditioned tunnels. Pilgrims are advised to walk the circuit, though two green pillars mark a short section of the path where they are allowed to run. There is also an internal "express lane" for the disabled. As part of this ritual the pilgrims also drink water from the Zamzam Well, which is made available in coolers throughout the mosque. After the visit to the mosque on this day of the Hajj, the pilgrims then return to their tents.

Arafat

The next morning, on the eighth of Dhu al-Hijjah, the pilgrims proceed to Mina, where they spend the night in prayer.

On the ninth day, they leave Mina for Mt. Arafat, where they stand in contemplative vigil and pray and recite the Quran, near a hill from which Muhammad gave his last sermon; this mountain is called Jabal Al Rahmah (The Hill of Forgiveness, Mount Arafat). This is known as Wuquf, considered the highlight of the Hajjah. Pilgrims must spend the afternoon within a defined area on the plain of Arafat until after sunset. No specific rituals or prayers are required during the stay at Arafat, although many pilgrims spend time praying, and thinking about the course of their lives. A pilgrim's Hajj is considered invalid if he or she does not spend the afternoon on Arafat.

Muzdalifah

As soon as the sun sets, the pilgrims leave Arafat for Muzdalifah, an area between Arafat and Mina. Pilgrims spend the night sleeping on the ground with open sky, and in the morning they gather pebbles for the next day's ritual of the Stoning of the Devil (Shaitan) after returning to Mina.

Ramy Al-Jamarat

At Mina the pilgrims perform *Ramy al-Jamarat*, throwing stones to signify their defiance of the Devil. This symbolizes the trials experienced by Abraham while he was going to sacrifice his son as demanded by God. The Devil challenged him three times, and three times Abraham refused. Each pillar marks the location of one of these refusals. On the first occasion when Ramy al-Jamarat is performed, pilgrims stone the largest pillar, known as Jamrat'al'Aqabah. Pilgrims climb ramps to the multilevel Jamaraat Bridge, from which they can throw their pebbles at the jamarat. On the second occasion, the other pillars are stoned. The stoning consists of throwing seven pebbles. Because of the crowds, in 2004 the pillars were replaced by long walls, with catch basins below to collect the pebbles.

Eid Al-Adha

After the casting of stones, animals are slaughtered to commemorate the story of Abraham and Ishmael. Traditionally the pilgrims slaughtered the animal themselves, or oversaw the slaughtering. Today many pilgrims buy a sacrifice voucher in Mecca before the greater Hajj begins, which allows an animal to be slaughtered in their name on the tenth, without the pilgrim being physically present. Centralized butchers

Hazza Abu Rabia / Adapted from "Eid al-Adha" at en.wikipedia.org / CC BY-SA 3.0

sacrifice a single sheep for each pilgrim, or a camel can represent the sacrifice of seven people. The meat is then packaged and given to charity and shipped to poor people around the world. At the same time that the sacrifices occur at Mecca, Muslims worldwide perform similar sacrifices, in a four day global festival called *Eid al-Adha.*

Tawaf Al-Ifaadah

On this or the following day, the pilgrims revisit the Masjid al-Haram mosque in Mecca for another tawaf, to walk around the Kaaba. This is called Tawaf al-Ifadah, which symbolizes being in a hurry to respond to God and show love for Him, an obligatory part of the Hajj. The night of the tenth is spent back at Mina.

On the afternoon of the eleventh and again the following day, the pilgrims must again throw seven pebbles at each of the three jamarat in Mina.

Pilgrims must leave Mina for Mecca before sunset on the twelfth. If they are unable to leave Mina before sunset, they must perform the stoning ritual again on the thirteenth before returning to Mecca.

Tawaf Al-Wida

Finally, before leaving Mecca, pilgrims perform a farewell tawaf called the Tawaf al-Wida. Wida means "to bid farewell."

Journey to Medina

Some pilgrims choose to travel to the city of Medina and the Al-Masjid al-Nabawi (Mosque of the Prophet), which contains Muhammad's tomb and Riad ul Jannah, and also pay visit to the graves of Muhammad's companions, *Ummahāt ul-Muʾminīn* and *Ahl al-Bayt* in Al-Baqiʾ. The Quba Mosque and Masjid al-Qiblatain are also usually visited.

Umrah

Umrah can be performed any time of year, and unlike Hajj, it is optional. Umrah does not contain as many steps as Hajj does. For Umrah preparation, Ihram is to be done. Tawaaf and Sai are to be completed as described above. Hair cutting as per the norm is the last step to symbolize that pilgrims are making a fresh start.

Eid Al-Adha

Eid al-Adha, "the festival of sacrifice," also called the Feast of the Sacrifice, the Major Festival, and the Greater Eid, is an important religious holiday celebrated by Muslims worldwide to honor the willingness of the prophet ʾIbrāhīm (Abraham) to sacrifice his young firstborn son Ismāʿīl (Ishmael) as an act of submission to God's command and his son's acceptance to being sacrificed, before God intervened to provide Abraham with a lamb to sacrifice instead. In the lunar Islamic calendar, Eid al-Adha falls on the tenth day of Dhu al-Hijjah and lasts for four days. In the international Gregorian calendar, the dates vary from year to year, drifting approximately eleven days earlier each year.

Eid al-Adha is the latter of the two Eid holidays, the former being Eid al-Fitr. The basis for the Eid al-Adha comes from the 196th verse of the second sura of the Quran. The word Eid appears once in the fifth sura of the Quran, with the meaning "solemn festival."

Like Eid al-Fitr, Eid al-Adha begins with a Sunnah prayer of two rakats followed by a sermon (*khutbah*). Eid al-Adha celebrations start after the descent of the Hajj from Mount Arafat, a hill east of Mecca. Ritual observance of the holiday lasts until sunset of the twelfth day of Dhu al-Hijjah. Eid sacrifice may take place until sunset on the thirteenth day of Dhu al-Hijjah. The days of Eid have been singled out in the Hadith as "days of remembrance." The days of Tashriq are from the Fajr prayer of the ninth of Dhul Hijjah up to the Asr prayer of the thirteenth of Dhul Hijjah (five days and four nights). This equals twenty-three prayers: five on the ninth through twelfth, which equal twenty, and three on the thirteenth.

Origin

According to Islamic tradition, approximately four thousand years ago, the valley of Mecca (in what is now Saudi Arabia) was a dry, rocky, and uninhabited place. Abraham ('Ibraheem in Arabic) was instructed to bring his Egyptian wife Hājar (Hāgar) and Ismā'īl (Ishmael), his only child at the time, to Arabia from the land of Canaan by God's command.

As Abraham was preparing for his return journey back to Canaan, Hajar asked him, "Did God order you to leave us here? Or are you leaving us here to die?" Abraham turned around to face his wife. He was so sad that he could not say anything. He pointed to the sky, showing that God commanded him to do so. Hajar said, "Then God will not waste us; you can go." Though Abraham had left a large quantity of food and water with Hajar and Ishmael, the supplies quickly ran out, and within a few days the two began to feel the pangs of hunger and dehydration.

Hajar ran up and down between two hills called Al-Safa and Al-Marwah seven times, in her desperate quest for water. Exhausted, she finally collapsed beside her baby Ishmael and prayed to God for deliverance. Miraculously, a spring of water gushed forth from the earth at the feet of baby Ishmael. Other accounts have the angel Gabriel (Jibrail) striking the earth and causing the spring to flow in abundance. With this secure water supply, known as the Zamzam Well, they not only were able to provide for their own needs, but were also able to trade water with passing nomads for food and supplies.

Years later, Abraham was instructed by God to return from Canaan to build a place of worship adjacent to Hagar's well (the Zamzam Well). Abraham and Ishmael constructed a stone and mortar structure—known as the Kaaba—which was to be the gathering place for all who wished to strengthen their faith in God. As the years passed, Ishmael was blessed with Prophethood (*Nubuwwah*) and gave the nomads of the desert his message of submission to God. After many centuries, Mecca became a thriving desert city and a major center for trade, thanks to its reliable water source, the well of Zamzam.

One of the main trials of Abraham's life was to face the command of God to devote his dearest possession, his only son. Upon hearing this command, he prepared to submit to God's will. During this preparation, Satan (Shaitan) tempted Abraham and his family by trying to dissuade them from carrying out God's commandment, and Ibrahim drove Satan away by throwing pebbles at him. In commemoration of their rejection of Satan, stones are thrown at symbolic pillars signifying Satan during the Hajj rites.

When Ismā'īl was about thirteen years old (Abraham being ninety-nine years old), God decided to test their faith in public. Abraham had a recurring dream, in which God was commanding him to offer his son as a sacrifice—an unimaginable act—which God had granted him after many years of deep prayer.

Abraham knew that the dreams of the prophets were divinely inspired, and one of the ways in which God communicated with his prophets. When the intent of the dreams became clear to him, Abraham decided to fulfill God's command and offer Ishmael for sacrifice.

Although Abraham was ready to sacrifice his dearest for God's sake, he could not just go and drag his son to the place of sacrifice without his consent. Ishmael had to be consulted as to whether he was willing to give up his life as fulfillment to God's command. This consultation would be a major test of Ishmael's maturity in faith, love for and commitment to God, and willingness to obey his father and sacrifice his own life for the sake of God.

Abraham presented the matter to his son and asked for his opinion about the dreams of slaughtering him. Ishmael did not show any hesitation or reservation, even for a moment. He said, "Father, do what you have been commanded. You will find me, Insha'Allah [God willing], to be very patient." His mature response, his deep insight into the nature of his father's dreams, his commitment to God, and ultimately his willingness to sacrifice his own life for the sake of God were all unprecedented.

When Abraham attempted to cut Ishmael's throat, he was astonished to see that Ishmael was unharmed, and, instead, he found a dead ram that was slaughtered. Abraham had passed the test by his willingness to carry out God's command.

This is mentioned in the Quran as follows:

> "O my Lord! Grant me a righteous (son)!" So We gave him the good news of a boy, possessing forbearance. And when (his son) was old enough to walk and work with him, (Abraham) said: "O my dear son, I see in vision that I offer you in sacrifice: Now see what is your view!" (The son) said: "O my father! Do what you are commanded; if Allah wills, you will find me one practising patience and steadfastness!" So when they both submitted and he threw him down upon his forehead, We called out to him saying: O Ibraheem! You have indeed fulfilled the vision; surely thus do We reward those who do good. Most surely this was a manifest trial. And We ransomed him with a momentous sacrifice. And We perpetuated (praise) to him among the later generations. "Peace and salutation to Abraham!" Thus indeed do We reward those who do right. Surely he was one of Our believing servants.

As a reward for this sacrifice, God then granted Abraham the good news of the birth of his second son, Is-haaq (Isaac):

> And We gave him the good news of Is-haaq, a prophet from among the righteous.

Abraham had shown that his love for God superseded all others: that he would lay down his own life or the lives of those dearest to him in submission to God's command. Muslims commemorate this ultimate act of sacrifice every year during Eid al-Adha.

Eid Prayers

Muslims go to the Masjid to pray the prayer of the Eid.

Who Must Attend?

According to some fiqh (traditional Islamic law), although there is some disagreement, the following should attend:

1. Men, who should go to mosque—more precisely, eidgah (a field where Eid prayer is held)—to perform Eid prayer; it is sunnat e muakkadah (a confirmed sunnat). Menstruating women have to stay away from the prayer, but should witness goodness and the gathering of the Muslims.
2. Residents, which excludes travelers.
3. Those in good health.

When Is It Performed?

The Eid al-Adha prayer is performed any time after the sun completely rises up to just before the entering of Zuhr time, on the tenth of Dhul Hijjah. In the event of a natural disaster, the prayer may be delayed to the eleventh of Dhul Hijjah and then to the twelfth of Dhul Hijjah.

The Sunnah of Preparation

In keeping with the tradition of the Prophet Muhammad, Muslims are encouraged to prepare themselves for the occasion of Eid. Below is a list of things Muslims are recommended to do in preparation for the Eid al-Adha festival:

1. Make wudu (ablution) and offer Salat al-Fajr (the pre-sunrise prayer).
2. Prepare for personal cleanliness—take care of details of clothing, etc.
3. Dress up, putting on new clothes or the best ones available.

Rituals of the Eid Prayers

Scholars differ concerning the ruling on Eid prayers. There are three scholarly points of view:

1. That Eid prayer is Sunnah mu'akkadah (recommended). This is the view of Imam Maalik and Imam al-Shaafa'i.
2. That it is a Fard Kifaya (communal obligation). This is the view of Imam Ahmad.
3. That it is Wajib on all Muslim men (a duty for each Muslim and obligatory for men); those who do not do it with no excuse are sinning thereby. This is the view of Imam Abu Haneefah, and was also narrated from Imam Ahmad.

Eid prayers must be offered in congregation. It consists of two rakats (units) with seven Takbirs in the first Raka'ah and five Takbirs in the second Raka'ah. For Sunni Muslims, Salat al-Eid differs from the five daily canonical prayers in that no adhan (call to prayer) or iqama (call) is pronounced for the two Eid prayers. The Salaat (prayer) is then followed by the Khutbah, or sermon, by the Imam.

At the conclusion of the prayers and sermon, Muslims embrace and exchange greetings with one other (Eid Mubarak), give gifts (Eidi) to children, and visit one another. Many Muslims also take this opportunity to invite their non-Muslims friends, neighbors, coworkers, and classmates to their Eid festivities to better acquaint them with Islam and Muslim culture.

Salāt al-Jumuʿah, Friday Prayer

Jumuʾah (also rendered *jumʾah*; *ṣalāt al-jumuʿah*, "Friday prayer") is a congregational prayer (*salah*) that Muslims hold every Friday, just after noon in the place of *dhuhr*. Muslims pray ordinarily five times each day according to the sun's sky path, regardless of clock time. It is mentioned in the Quran as follows:

> O ye who believe! When the call is proclaimed to prayer on Friday (the Day of Assembly, *yawma 'l-jumuʿati*), hasten earnestly to the Remembrance of Allah, and leave off business (and traffic): That is best for you if ye but knew! And when the Prayer is finished, then may ye disperse through the land, and seek of the Bounty of Allah: and celebrate the Praises of Allah often (and without stint): that ye may prosper.
>
> —Quran, sura 62 (Al-Jumua), ayat 9–10

The *jumuʿah* prayer is half the *ẓuhr* (dhuhr) prayer, for convenience, preceded by a khuṭbah (a sermon as a technical replacement of the two reduced *rakaʿāt* of the ordinary *ẓuhr* (dhuhr) prayer), and followed by a congregational prayer, led by the imam. In most cases the khaṭīb also serves as the imam. Attendance is strictly incumbent upon all adult males who are legal residents of the locality.

The muezzin (*muʾadhdhin*) makes the call to prayer, called the adhan, usually fifteen to twenty minutes prior to the start of Jumʾah. When the khaṭīb takes his place on the minbar, a second adhan is made. The khaṭīb is supposed to deliver two sermons, stopping and sitting briefly between them. In practice, the first sermon is longer and contains most of the content. The second sermon is very brief and concludes with a dua, after which the muezzin calls the iqama. This signals the start of the main two rak'at prayer of Jumʾah.

The communal prayers have higher compliance of worshippers, as compared to the noncommunal ritual prayers. In Turkey, for example, the ritual prayers are performed regularly by 44 percent, whereas Friday prayers are regularly attended by 56 percent (25 percent responded that they sometimes attended, and 19 percent responded that they never did).

From hadith:

> Narrated Abu Huraira: The Prophet said, "On every Friday the angels take their stand at every gate of the mosques to write the names of the people chronologically (i.e., according to the time of their arrival for the Friday prayer) and when the Imam sits (on the pulpit), they fold up their scrolls and get ready to listen to the sermon."
> —Collected by Muhammad al-Bukhari, *Sahih al-Bukhari*[5]

Muslim ibn al-Hajjaj an-Naysaburi relates that the Islamic prophet Muhammad used to read Surah 87 (Al-Ala) and Surah 88, (Al-Ghashiya), in Eid prayers and also in Friday prayers. If one of the festivals fell on a Friday, the Prophet would have made sure to read these two Surahs in the prayers.

Hazza Abu Rabia / Adapted from "Jumu'ah" at en.wikipedia.org / CC BY-SA 3.0

6

Marriage in Islam

Laws and Customs

by Hazza Abu Rabia

T he role of women in Islam is an extremely debated and discussed topic in Western society today. An area of Islam that clearly demonstrates the rights of women is in marriage. Islamic marriage laws are clear in their intention to give women rights, monetary gains, and freedom in case of divorce. In the West, however, these benefits are not understood and are oftentimes ignored by the media and by critics of Islam. The reasoning behind this is the extreme difference between Western culture and the culture of Islam. While many in the West claim that Islam discriminates against women or that women do not have rights under Islam and under Islamically ruled governments, study of the religion and customs proves otherwise. Contrary to popular Western beliefs, Islam maintains a great love and respect for women that is absent from Judaism and Christianity's histories. To back up their claims, critics of the religion will often claim that the Prophet mistreated women and will use the stories of his wives Safiyya and Aisha. However, these stories are often misinterpreted and when told in the west often ignore the rights enjoyed by the wives of the Prophet and further ignore the traditions that are used in modern times in Islamic marriage. Islamic marriage laws were based on the ideas of reformation within the flawed societies of the past and the development of a partnership between men and women in the family unit.

The Quran and its teachings significantly changed the pattern of history with regards to the roles of men and women in the family unit. With the development of Islamic law and the teachings of the Prophet

Muhammad, new roles were developed for men and women and a new understanding of how they should relate to one another developed, especially in the sense of legal rights for women.

"In pre-Islamic Arabian society, the basic family unit was the patriarchal agnatic clan, a group of people descended directly in the male line from a common ancestor and under the authority of the eldest male or chief member of the family. This was an extended family of several generations, and several groups of married couples and their offspring, with collaterals and clients, were all considered part of one household. Status, duties, and rights stemmed entirely from the clan. Property was regulated by the customs of the group. Marriages were arranged by the heads of the families with a view to the interests of the families rather than the wishes of the couple to be married. Women were of inferior status and were not full members of the group. A good marriage brought honor to the clan; if its female members were violated, the clan was dishonored. The group was responsible for defending the other members and making restitution in case of any crime committed by a member. However, alongside the agnatic clan, various forms of polyandrous marriage of one woman to several men with varying degrees of permanence and responsibility for paternity, including temporary 'marriages,' were also known in Arabia. Polygamous arrangements varied from multiple wives in one residence to arrangements in which a man had several wives living with their own tribes whom he would visit on a rotating basis. No single norm was universally accepted. It was increasingly difficult to hold people to the ideal obligations regarding the distribution of property, the protection of women, or the guardianship of children. In these confused conditions, Qura'nic teachings attempted to strengthen the patriarchal agnatic clan. The Qura'nic rules against incest were crucial for the viability of group life, for biological heredity, and for the creation of marriage bonds between families. Divorce, though still relatively easy, was discouraged. Polyandrous marriages were condemned because they undermined patriarchal family stability. Since the family descended through its male heirs, the Quran provided rules to assure knowledge of paternity. For example, in the event of divorce, a woman could remarry after having three menstrual periods" (Lapidus, pp. 24–25).

The roots of Islamic marriage laws prior to the development of Islam based themselves in the idea of a strong, family unit. However, while Islam encourages strong familial bonds through prayer and through respect, the bonds of the past were based in the idea of ownership of women and children like property, blood relations and feuds, and in the use of marriage as a social contract to ensure good relations between tribes. Men did not have to maintain their responsibilities towards their wives and children as they do under Islamic law. They could marry several women and leave them alone to raise the children among their own tribe while going off to visit other wives. The responsibility for women and children fell upon the shoulders of the tribe they belonged to, not to the husband they married or the father of the children. The loyalty and responsibility of a male in pre-Islamic times was to his tribe, not to his wife and children. The Quran outlines rules and expectations for marriage, children, property, and personal rights. By doing this, the Quran did more than just list the rights that are inherent to all who follow Islam but also created a sense of unity among the Arab people. Rather than individual laws and customs per tribe, the Quran gives all people who follow Islam guidelines that demand personal responsibility in exchange for unity and equality. While some actions of the past still remain to this day, such as polygamous marriage, there are laws that dictate when this is necessary and how to live in such a situation. There are also laws outlined by the Quran that clearly outline the roles of the husband and wife or wives within the marriage and give them personal freedoms that were not allowed in the pre-Islamic eras, especially under Christianity and Judaism.

To begin to understand Islamic marriage laws one must first understand the importance of a woman or wife in Islam in comparison to the importance of a wife in Christianity or Judaism. Muhammad was quoted as saying, "The world and all things in it are valuable; but the most valuable thing in the world is a virtuous woman" (thinkexist.com) and "Women are the twin halves of men" (thinkexist.com). The Quran and the teachings of Muhammad all declare women as valuable and as important figures with rights equitable to those of men. In contrast, Christianity and Judaism claim that women are lesser than men and are gateways to evil. They also state that women were created from men, making them inherently subordinate to males. However, the Quran disputes this. The Quran describes how love and peace are to come from there being both males and females. It also describes women as partners with men, not as servants or lesser than human beings. However, there is often a misunderstanding of the Quran by those who do not study its teachings carefully. If one carefully examines the words of the Quran, what is described is not the same inequality that is described in the Bible but rather a partnership.

> "Men have been given the duty to protect and support women. God has given preference to one gender over another in certain duties. Men have been given preference in being providers of women and women are given preference in caring for a child. Even if divorce separates a man from his wife, he has to seek her help in caring for the child or if another female agrees (Koran 2:233). Men are told to spend of their property on women and not to ask the woman for anything, even if she happens to be rich" (Asadi, p. 71).

This outlined partnership protects the interests of the female when other religions do not acknowledge her as having importance except in passing. It also gives women the rights to their children which until recently was not always a given. In Western cultures, a man could exercise an iron fist over his family and force his wife to do his bidding over the children rather than actually taking part in raising them. The relationships of Christianity and of Judaism were about power and control of a man over a woman and used God as an excuse for these injustices. The West often portrays Muslims as following the marriage laws of someone that they misunderstand and believe was wrong to his wives and took advantage of them. Often, opponents to Islam will cite the stories of Aisha or Safiyya. However, these stories are complex and often misunderstood. Often, Aisha is portrayed as a victim, as a child who was forced into a marriage with an older man. But several parts of the story are left out. While Aisha was indeed young when the Prophet and her were wed, there is little evidence that tells of her actual age. What is known is that she was the Prophet's only virgin wife and was quite possibly his most loyal follower after the death of his first wife. There is absolutely no evidence that suggests that Aisha was a victim or captive of the Prophet but a massive amount of evidence shows her great love, respect, and admiration for him. Indeed, up until her death Aisha taught about his teachings and about the greatness of what God had shared with the Prophet (muslim.org). Others claim that the Prophet used the Quran to gain wives in an unsavory manner. They often will cite how the Prophet killed the father and husband of his wife Safiyyah prior to his marriage to her. What is left out is that her anger subsided when the Prophet apologized to her to such an extent that she forgave him and soon loved him (answering-christianity.com). Soon the two developed a partnership and Safiyyah is even quoted as saying that she wished she could take the place of the Prophet on his deathbed (answering-christianity. com). Opponents to Islam misrepresent the stories of these two wives of the Prophet and claim that he used his wives as objects or trophies and did not respect them and that therefore that must mean that the

Quran encourages this as well. However, the Quran offers an entirely new perspective on relationships and marriage by giving guidelines on how to build a relationship that is fair, for God, and out of love and respect. The Prophet and his wives taught this lesson throughout their lives and it lives on in the Quran. Islamic laws from the Quran regarding marriage cover the bases of children, divorce, infidelity, and personal responsibility, all ideas that are often ignored by the cultures of those who purposefully misrepresent Islam.

The laws of marriage in Islam not only created a partnership between men and women and established women's rights but also developed the society and economy in a way that was significantly more modern than the rest of the world. While the pre-Islamic times had not developed laws that protected and benefitted all involved, the laws outlined in the Quran offered the chance at redemption and at a new beginning for the societies living in the Middle East. The new ideas of self-identity and personal responsibility had a profound effect on the lives of those who embraced Islam. Also, now that women were allowed more rights and were able to have monetary gains the economic strength of a family unit was also beginning to develop.

> "Furthermore, in the context of the patriarchal family the Quran provided for moral and spiritual reform and introduced a new freedom and dignity to individual family members. In particular, it enhanced the status of women and children, who were no longer to be considered merely chattels of potential warriors but individuals with rights and needs of their own. For the benefit of women, marriage was recognized as having important spiritual and religious values. It was a relationship sanctioned by the will of Allah. The Quran urged respect for their modesty and privacy, that they be treated as feeling persons. The Quran also granted women certain specific rights that they did not enjoy in pre-Islamic Arabia. A woman was now able to hold property in her own name, and was not expected to contribute to the support of the household from her own property. She was given the right to inherit up to a quarter of her husband's estate, and, in case of divorce, retained the agreed-upon bridal gift" (Lapidus, pp. 25–26).

The new rights gained by women and children under Islam allowed for the expansion of the idea of a community united through the common beliefs of Islam. The differing customs, laws and beliefs of varying tribes throughout the past were now greatly changed by the new ideas of unity, partnership, and mutual respect. Laws that did not specifically pertain to marriage in the past now took on a new meaning under the laws of Islam.

Property laws in Islam affect the marriage as well. In Christian, Western cultures and in pre-Islamic times women and children were considered the property of a man or of a tribe. They did not maintain personal freedoms nor did they maintain rights within their own marriages. In Christian, Western cultures, a woman would begin her life living under the law of her father, then under the law of her husband, and if her husband died before her, a woman would then live under the law of her son. If no man in her family would support her then she was forced to live on the street as a beggar or find a way to support herself. Any woman that managed to become successful on her own with a business or other legitimate prospect was ostracized from the community. However, after the introduction of the Quran to history significant developments were made in women's rights in the Middle East. These developments were a part of the marriage laws that are still in use today.

> "When a man marries a woman, he has to give a substantial part of his property (according to his means) to the woman as a 'marriage gift (Mahar),' stated as a man's duty unto God (Koran 4:24). A woman doesn't have to give anything to a man even if she is rich. It is for this reason primarily

that the Koran asks that out of a parent's property the son gets twice that of the daughter (Koran 4:11). It is expected that the daughter would marry and get a man's property as marriage gift and not have to worry about providing for herself, as it's the man's duty to provide for her. The son on the other hand would Islamically be expected not only to provide for his potential wife but also give a major part of his property to her as marriage gift" (Asadi, p. 75).

These laws and customs have given Muslim women rights in their marriages for centuries while Western women have still not entirely maintained rights within their own marriages to this day. It would be untrue to say that all Islamic marriages follow the law of the Quran, as some tribes and men will attempt to "modify" the truth to suit their personal means but these instances are examples of men purposefully misusing the Quran, not following God's Word and the word of the Prophet. If followed correctly, the Quran's laws enable men and women to have fair rights and opportunities to become partners in a marriage that they both freely choose to be in and feel comfortable and happy in.

Polygamous marriage is also a subject that the Quran gives specific guidelines for. While Polygamous marriage is often the subject of much scrutiny, history shows it as being not for power or status, as is commonly believed of Islam, but for situations in which the quality of life for a large number of women is deteriorating as there are not enough men to become husbands and fathers and the groups as a whole suffers as a result. In order to expand the group and give unmarried women a family of their own, Islam allows polygamous marriages. However, the stipulations for this are that all the wives involved must be treated equally by their husband, no favoritism is allowed. Also, a man cannot have more than four wives at one time. These rules help to prevent the polygamous marriages from becoming competitions and women being prizes or trophies to obtain, rather than women to love and live with. However, Christianity and Judaism have a love/hate relationship with the concept of polygamy. The concept of polygamy is attempted by some Christian groups, such as the Mormons, but these individuals are arrested and their families are taken apart if they attempt such a thing in the Western world.

"There is nothing in Christianity or Judaism against polygamy. Indeed the Old Testament assumes that marriages will be polygamous and laws are constructed based on that assumption. For example, Exodus 21:10 in the Bible states: 'If he take to him another wife, her food, her raiment, and her duty of marriage shall he not diminish' (The Bible, Exodus 21:10). There is not a word attributed to Jesus in the New Testament which disallows polygamy. Paul forbade bishops and deacons from marrying more than one wife (1 Timothy 3:2), this implicitly suggests that others were allowed polygamy …The Koran severely restricted the open practice of polygamy. There is just one statement in the Koran that deals with polygamy, yet it is misused and inflated by both Muslims and non-Muslims. It states: 'And if you fear that you will not be able to deal justly with the oppressed women (Yatama-literally, the orphans among women), then marry from among them two or three or four, but if you fear you won't be just (even then), then marry only one (Koran 4:3).' The Koran states explicitly above that polygamy is allowed only if the women you marry: 1. Belong among oppressed (orphan) women. Men cannot pick and choose from 'any' women who they want as a second wife. 2. Polygamy is to be practiced only if marriage would be social justice to such women ('if you fear that you will not be able to deal justly,' says the Koran), justice that they are otherwise denied. 3. If marrying more than one cannot bring such justice than polygamy is not allowed. Thus the Koran severely restricts and restricted in Arabia, the open practice of polygamy in society" (Asadi, pp. 77–78).

While polygamy is practiced openly in the Arab world, it is not always common. Many men choose to remain with their one wife, and this choice is not considered weak by the Quran but it is a personal choice allowed by the Quran. Exactly how common Islamic polygamous marriages are depends on the location of the couple (i.e. Saudi Arabia would have significantly more polygamous marriages than the U.S. as polygamy is legal there and illegal here).

There are significant differences between modern Islamic marriages depending on location. Marriages between Muslims in the West will hold true to the law of Islam and to most traditions but will occasionally stray into more Western styles and traditions. There are also differences in marriage customs depending on location in the East as well. The customs of Indonesian Muslims are different than those of the Palestinians and the Palestinian customs differ from those of the Indians and so on. Commonly in the Muslim world, there would be few meetings between a man and woman before marriage. Any meetings that would occur would be chaperoned to protect the purity of the couple. Often the chaperone is a male relative of the bride. However, while these customs vary very little between countries, there are other customs that are unique to the area the marriage is taking place. For example, while weddings in Egypt are more familial affairs, weddings in Iran are very public. Occasionally in Iran, a wedding may consist of two, three, or even more couples so that they may all share the cost of this very expensive event. Fertility symbols are also used in Iranian weddings. Items such as eggs and shelled nuts are often at Iranian weddings in order to encourage fertility among the couple(s). Another cultural difference in Islamic weddings is in Indonesia. While in other Islamic areas anyone can preside over a wedding, in Indonesia a government official and a religious official must be present and conduct the ceremony. A tradition in Morocco that is very similar to the traditions of the West is the "furnishing party." In the United States a bridal shower is an all-female event in which friends and relatives give the bride gifts for her new home so that after the wedding she can be ready for her wifely duties. In Morocco, a "furnishing party" takes place five days before the wedding and is an event dedicated to the decorating and setting up of the new couple's soon to be home (hilalplaza.com). The varying and rich traditions of Muslim weddings represent the varying cultures that have embraced Islam around the world.

If one was to plan an Islamic wedding in the West, it would be even more important to carefully plan and follow the laws of Islam as it is not only more difficult due to the location but due to the overwhelming influences of Western culture and their marriage customs. There are many marriage websites to assist with the planning for those who are unfamiliar with the Islamic law and customs just as there are mosques and imams who are able to assist in understanding the law (although it is rare for an Islamic marriage to take place in a mosque). Popular wedding websites, such as theknot.com, offer tips, instructions, and advice to Western, Muslim couples looking to have a traditional Islamic wedding. According to theknot.com, a couple must follow these directions in order to have a proper Islamic wedding in the West.

"The only requirement for Muslim weddings is the signing of a marriage contract. Marriage traditions differ depending on culture, Islamic sect, and observance of gender separation rules. Most marriages are not held in mosques, and men and women remain separate during the ceremony and reception. Since Islam sanctions no official clergy, any Muslim who understands Islamic tradition can officiate a wedding. If you are having your wedding in mosque, many have marriage officers, called *qazi* or *madhun*, who can oversee the marriage. The marriage contract includes a meher-a formal statement specifying the monetary amount the groom will give the bride. There are two parts to the meher: a prompt due before the marriage is consummated and a deferred amount given to the bride throughout her life. Today, many couples use the ring as the prompt because the groom presents it during the ceremony. The deferred amount can be a small sum—a formality—or an actual gift of money, land, jewelry, or even an education. The gift belongs to the bride to use as the pleases, unless the marriage breaks up before consummation. The meher is considered the bride's security and guarantee of freedom within the marriage. The marriage contract is signed in a nikah ceremony, in which the groom or his representative proposes to the bride in front of at least two witnesses, stating the details of the meher. The bride and groom demonstrate their free will by repeating the word qabul ('I accept,' in Arabic) three times. Then the couple and two male witnesses sign the contract, making the marriage legal according to civil and religious law. Following traditional Islamic customs, the bride and groom may share a piece of sweet fruit, such as a date. If men and women are separated for the ceremony, a male representative called a wali acts in the bride's behalf during the nikah. The officiant may add an additional religious ceremony following the nikah, which usually includes the recitation of the *Fatihah—the first chapter of the Quran—and* durud (blessings). Most Muslim couples do not recite vows; rather, they listen as their officiant speaks about the meaning of marriage and their responsibilities to each other and to Allah ..." (www.theknot.com).

Other online resources, such as ehow.com, give similar information to those looking to celebrate a traditional Islamic wedding. Other wedding traditions include: inviting the poor, keeping men and women separate if there is to be social interaction, and serving traditional chicken, fish, rice, and candied almonds (www.eHow.com). The importance of maintaining the traditions of an Islamic wedding while in the West is so that the wedding reflects on the Qura'nic teachings that are not as commonly associated with everyday life in Western cultures. Keeping many of, if not all, the traditions even while away from an area where they are common, maintains the religious aspects of the wedding itself and the religious lives that will be led by the bride and groom.

Unfortunately, no matter what the culture or religion is, there are some marriages that do not achieve success as others do. The Quran is very clear in its description of divorce as well as marriage. While Christianity, especially Roman Catholicism, ostracizes the divorced, the Quran offers an alternative. "The Koran by giving women a right to initiate divorce is truly revolutionary. The New Testament, in the supposed words of Jesus, makes divorce an offense similar to adultery, permissible only when the woman has cheated on the husband (Matthew 5:32). The Old Testament states that only a man can initiate divorce (Deuteronomy 24:11). The Koran, contrary to that states: '... If you both fear that you won't be able to keep within the boundaries of God in marriage, there is no harm is she ransom herself ...' (Koran 2:229). The ransom of course be the return of the initial property that the man gave her when she got married to him (the mahar)" (Asadi, p. 80). The Quranic laws that make women equal partners in the marriage also make them equal partners in divorce. While Christian beliefs often blame or ostracize the woman for "failing," the male is quickly forgiven. The Quran gives women more freedom in their relationship and gives them an opportunity to leave if they feel the marriage is not working. This prevents women from being treated as property within the marriage as they have an equal opportunity to end it as well as the man. Also, in contrast with Western society is the acknowledgement that divorce is the end to something that should have been done in God's name and for the right reasons. In the West, divorce is done quickly and often severely damages the family unit as there are few preordained laws that explain the steps that should be taken to initiate a divorce.

"The Koran's method of divorce is simple yet very functional. If mind is set on divorce, a divorce statement is written and pronounced in the presence of witnesses (Koran 65:2). Then there is a three month break in which both parties stay together as husband and wife, so that time be given to reconsider (Koran 2:228). After the three month period, if the man initiated the divorce, he can either take the wife back, if she wants to remain in the marriage, or part. If he takes her back he can initiate divorce only once more in his life with the same woman. If he takes her back the second time, then he has lost his rights to initiate divorce in the same relationship ever again (Koran 2:229). A woman can buyout her divorce by surrendering the property that was given her by the husband whenever she thinks the marriage won't work out. All through this process, the Koran suggests that help be sought by arbitration (Koran 4:35), one person from the man's side and one from the woman's" (Asadi, pp. 80–81).

These laws and guidelines regarding divorce are remarkably similar to what is considered new and modern regarding divorce in Western culture. However, the Quran has given women rights in divorce and has encouraged positive reconciliation. The Quran does not demand that those who are divorced be ostracized by the community but be helped in an attempt to reconcile and accepted even if a divorce does occur. The divorces cannot be quick and not thought out, as is commonly misperceived. A divorce in Islam is a serious matter that represents the end to something that was a partnership and development of a family, it is not a crime like it is in other cultures or religious groups.

The importance of marriage is indisputable in any culture, religion, or country. However, it is how each religion and country deals marriage that can create misunderstandings between cultures and countries. While the West chooses to interpret Islamic weddings as polygamous unions where the women are prizes rather than partners, in reality a marriage in Islam is based on family, unity, and God. While the United States faces a 50 percent divorce rate and hundreds of thousands of unwed mothers and "missing" fathers, the laws set forth by the Quran protect and help to prevent some of these unfortunate circumstances. The Quran was centuries ahead of the rest of the world in its views on the equality of women and on the importance of marriage for spiritual gains rather than just for money or property reasons. Women married in Islam are given greater rights in their lives and in their own marriages. They can divorce, maintain property and money without their husband's input or control over it, they have an important role in raising the children and teaching them, and are allowed educations and even jobs. It was only within the past hundred years or so that women in the United States, the supposed "land of the free," were even given the most basic of rights in their marriages. In order for Western women to have even obtained those rights they had to fight, protest, and many even had to die for the cause before women's rights were taken seriously in the United States. However, the Quran acknowledges that women's rights are inherent with their humanity. The Quran gives women the control in their lives that women in the West had to work to earn, they were not considered inherent rights. While the West is busy condemning Islam, it forgets to look into one of its most basic of traditions, marriage, to see just how the Quran has expanded the rights of over a billion people in the world and how marriage laws in particular, are an example of a beautiful tradition that maintains its beauty not through the amount of money spent on it or the number of television shows dramatizing it but through the ideas of partnership and love.

Works Cited

"Age of Aisha (ra) at Time of Marriage." *The Lahore Ahmadiyya Movement in Islam*. Web. 8 May 2011. http://www.muslim.org/islam/aisha-age.htm.

Asadi, Muhammed A. *Islam & Christianity: Conflict or Conciliation? a Comparative and Textual Analysis of the Koran & the Bible*. San Jose Calif.: Writers Club, 2001. Print.

Contributor, An EHow. "How to Honor Islamic Wedding Traditions | EHow.com." *EHow | How to Videos, Articles & More —Trusted Advice for the Curious Life | EHow.com*. Web. 8 May 2011. http://www.ehow.com/how_2228308_honor-islamic-wedding-traditions.html.

Lapidus, Ira Marvin. *A History of Islamic Societies*. Cambridge: Cambridge University Press, 2010. Print.

"Morocco Moroccan Wedding Customs." *Hilal Plaza*. Web. 8 May 2011. http://www.hilalplaza.com/morocco-wedding-customs.html.

"Muhammad Quotes." *Find the Famous Quotes You Need, ThinkExist.com Quotations*. Web. 8 May 2011. http://thinkexist.com/quotes/muhammad/.

Schaer, Robin B. "Ceremony: Muslim Wedding Rituals—TheKnot.com." *Wedding Dresses—Wedding Engagement—Wedding Ideas—Wedding Planning—TheKnot.com*. Web. 8 May 2011. <http://wedding.theknot.com/wedding-planning/wedding-ceremony/articles/muslim-wedding-ceremony-rituals.aspx?MsdVisit=1>.

Zawadi, Bassam. "Safiyyah, the Wife of Muhammad." Web. 8 May 2011. http://www.answering-christianity.com/bassam_zawadi/safiyyah_the_wife_of_the_prophet.htm.

7

The Muslim Life-Cycle

by Reuven Firestone

Muslims throughout the world practice a number of rites and ceremonies that recognize the stages of life. These rituals developed from the native cultures upon which Islam took root as well as formal religious requirements of Islam, so they differ quite markedly from one area to the next. In fact, many life-cycle rituals that are recognized popularly as Islamic are actually cultural rather than religious. The three common life-stages that are shared throughout the Muslim world are circumcision, marriage, and death, but we shall examine some other practices that have absorbed religious overtones despite their being cultural in origin.

Birth, Naming, and Circumcision

The Qur'an does not require any particular ritual associated with birth or the first period of life, but there are some prophetic traditions and customs that suggest certain activities. Muhammad is purported to have articulated the call to prayer in the right ear of his newborn grandson, Hasan, and the similar call that is made in the mosque just before the prayer service in his left. It became customary, therefore, for a male

Reuven Firestone, "The Muslim Life-Cycle," *An Introduction to Islam for Jews*, pp. 210–224. Copyright © 2010 by The Jewish Publication Society. Reprinted with permission by University of Nebraska Press.

relative or pious individual to do the same for a newborn after it has been washed and swaddled. The opening chapter of the Qur'an is then recited for the protection and health of the baby, and people often bring gifts.

A special ceremony and sacrifice called `aqīqa` occurs on the 7th day after birth (or later for some). The purpose is to give thanks to God, to express joy at the birth of a child, and to announce the birth publicly. The word is associated with the sacrifice or with the child's hair that is often shaved off on this occasion. The root meaning in Arabic comes from the verb "to split" or "to rip" and means roughly, "being irreverent or disobedient" (`uqūq` means "disobedience" or "recalcitrance"). It is possible that the custom emerged from a cultural wish to demonstrate the religious obedience of the parents or to forestall lack of obedience of the child. In any case, the ritual sacrifice is the responsibility of the parents or grandparents and is considered "recommended" by most jurists but not mandatory. In most places, two sheep are sacrificed for a boy and one for a girl, but an egalitarian trend recommends only one for a girl or a boy, based on a tradition that Muhammad sacrificed one lamb for each of his grandsons, Hasan and Husayn. The meat of the animal is divided like the sacrifice at the end of the *Hajj* period, one third for the poor, one third for friends, and one third for the family. But one may also give all the meat to the needy. For those who shave the infant's hair

---

MUSLIM NAMES

According to both the Bible and the Qur'an, one of the first human acts was that of naming (Gen. 2:18–20, Q.2:30–33). While the actual story is told somewhat differently in each scripture, they agree on the significance of names—knowing names and giving names. Naming is important in most cultures—perhaps in every culture—because the giving of a name provides grounding for a newborn child in family, history, culture, values, and religion. Just as Jewish names have special meaning in relation to Jewish tradition, family tradition, and ritual practice, so do Muslim names provide a special grounding for belonging and for meaning within the religious context of Islam.

Most Muslim names are Arabic in origin because of the Arabic linguistic environment out of which Islam and the Qur'an first emerged. Persian became another medium for naming because of the influence of its culture on developing Islam, and Turkish became a third medium for Muslim names. Jews and Christians who lived in Arabic-speaking lands often took on Arabic names too, though they rarely took on religious names known from Islamic religious history. The exception to that is the vernacular use among Jews and Christians of biblical names that occur in the Qur'an in Arabic. Perhaps the most common are Mūsā for Moshe, Yūsuf for Yosef, and Ya`qūb for Yakov.

---

there is a custom to give charity of equal value to the weight in silver of their baby's hair. Another custom is to circumcise the baby boy at seven days, although this specific timing for the circumcision is only a custom.

It is common to name the baby on the occasion of the `aqīqa`, though it is not required, and some name the baby at birth or shortly thereafter. There are some common customs regarding names. It is conventional and fully accepted to name children after living or deceased relatives or after famous or pious individuals. Muhammad is said to have recommended for boys the name Abdallah (servant of God) or Abd al-Raḥmān (servant of the Merciful), and perhaps the most common name for boys is Muhammad,

Ahmad, or Mahmūd (all from the same root as the name Muhammad). Girls may be named after wives of the Prophet or other saintly persons in Muslim history.

As in Judaism and in the Hindu traditions, the birth mother is rendered ritually impure as a result of childbirth. According to Islamic custom, she is excused from ritual duties for 40 days. In the Bible (Lev. 12:1–8), the birth mother remains in a state of ritual impurity of 33 days for a male and 66 days for a female, after which she must bring a lamb as a sacrifice. In some Muslim circles, the 40th day after birth, which marks the end of the period of ritual impurity, is an occasion for celebration.

As the child gets older and begins to speak, it is taught religious formulas and phrases like the *basmalah* and other phrases and devotional statements. The Qur'an is the basis around which most religious learning revolves, so children are encouraged to learn and memorize sections of the Qur'an. If the child has a gifted memory it will be taught to know the entire Qur'an by heart. If the child attends a religious day school it will learn the Islamic religious sciences, and if the child attends a nonreligious school, it will usually learn Islam in afternoon programs and Friday schools. In the United States, a growing network of Islamic day schools is growing, and there are also afternoon Islamic schools and "Sunday schools" for children attending public school.

As mentioned above ("Law versus Custom"), male circumcision is a universal expectation of Islam even though it is not mentioned in the Qur'an. The circumcision is often performed by a person whose job is to conduct such procedures, though today it is often performed in a hospital or clinic. The Arabic name for circumcisor is *khātin* or *muṭahhir*, who functions as a barber-surgeon, somewhat parallel to the Jewish *mohel*, though in the Jewish profession the person must also be learned in the intricacies of Jewish law and ritual associated with the procedure, whereas there is less need to know legal religious technicalities in the Islamic equivalent.

Marriage and Sexuality

Asceticism is frowned upon in Islam, and that includes celibacy. In the first *hadith* of the section on marriage in the most authoritative *Hadith* collection of Al-Bukhari, Muhammad is confronted by three men who ask how the Prophet worshiped. When they heard Muhammad's message they felt that they had to change their ways in order for their sins to be forgiven, so after leaving his presense, each one undertook to engage in some ascetic act that they hoped would merit forgiveness. One said, "I will forever pray through the night." Another said, "I will fast forever and never break it." The last one said, "I will refrain from women and never marry." When Muhammad heard what they had said, he sought them out and said to them, "Are you the ones who said that? By God, I have more fear and consciousness of God than you, yet I fast and break my fast, I pray and then go to sleep, and I marry. Whoever disapproves of my practice is not a follower." Another authoritative *hadith* from the same collection is often cited in relation to marriage. One day a group of young men with few resources available to them that would enable marriage were sitting with the Prophet. "The Messenger of God said to us, 'O young people! Whoever has the means to marry should do so for it will lower one's gaze and strengthen his control, and whoever is unable to marry should fast, for it is exhausting.'"

Sexual pleasure, per se, is neither prohibited nor frowned upon in Islam. Sheikh Yusuf al-Qaradawi, whom I have cited previously and takes a moderately traditional position, writes the following.

Sex is a strong driving force in the human being which demands satisfaction and fulfillment. Human beings have responded to the demands of the sexual appetite in three different ways: (1) One way is to satisfy one's sexual need freely with whomever is available and whenever one pleases … (2) The second approach is to suppress, and try to annihilate, the sexual drive … (3) The third approach is to regulate the satisfaction of this urge, allowing it to operate within certain limits, neither suppressing nor giving it free rein. This is the stand of the revealed religions, which have instituted marriage and have prohibited fornication and adultery. In particular, Islam duly recognizes the role of the sexual drive, facilitates its satisfaction through lawful marriage, and just as it strictly prohibits sex outside of marriage … , it also prohibits celibacy and the shunning of women. This is the just and intermediate position. If marriage were not permitted, the sexual instinct would not play its role in the continuation of the human species; while if fornication and adultery were not prohibited, the foundation of the family would be eroded. Unquestionably, it is only in the shade of a stable family that mercy, love, affection, and the capacity to sacrifice for others develop in a human being, emotions without which a cohesive society cannot come into being. Thus, if there had been no family system, there would have been no society through which mankind would be able to progress toward perfection.

Some Muslim modernists would note that Qaradawi is writing more about men than about women, and would bemoan the tendency of Muslim religious scholars to express more concern about the sexual rights of the male gender than the female. Nevertheless, both the Qur'an and the tradition make clear that the purpose of sexual relations is not restricted to procreation but includes the right to satisfy one's sexual desire and to channel it in a positive direction.

It should be noted here that Islam forbids homosexual relations, though this is challenged currently by some gay and lesbian Muslim activists who are calling for a review of the issues. The Qur'an refers to male homosexuality five times in references to the behavior of Lot's people (Q.7:80–84, 11:78–81, 26:162–168, 27:55–57, and 29:28–30), and perhaps another time in Qur'an 4:15–16. The term in 4:15 is abomination (*fāhisha*), which most interpreters understand as heterosexual adultery or fornication (*zinā*). A minority opinion understands the references to indicate female and male homosexual relations. All these references are negative.

In the qur'anic descriptions of paradise there is reference to "immortal boys" in Qur'an 56:17 and 76:19, or perhaps "immortal children," and "young men" as cupbearers to those who merit entrance. The exegetical tradition does not suggest that these have a homosexual function, but some literary works do, sometimes with humor. In later legal discussions, an analogy is sometimes made with the use of wine in paradise that is permitted while forbidden in the life of this world.

Marriage

Islam directs all physical sexual engagement to the institution of marriage. The Qur'an is often cited in support of this. "Wed those among you who are unmarried, and the righteous among your male and female slaves. If they are poor, God will provide for them from His bounty. God is infinite, all knowing. Those who cannot find [the means for] marriage should be chaste until God provides for them from His bounty" (Q.24:32–33).

The Qur'an has much to say about marriage and gender relations, and these have been interpreted to convey a range of meaning. On the one hand, a famous verse seems to require only the satisfaction of the male: "Your wives are a cultivable field for you, so enter your field as you wish … " (Q.2:223). Other verses such as Qur'an 2:187 are cited to support sexual mutuality: "It is permitted to you to have sex with your wives on the night of a fast. They are a garment for you and you are a garment for them … so lie with them and seek out what God has decreed for you" (Q.2:187). In one Qur'an verse that seems to be rarely cited (possibly because it seems to critique Muhammad who was later assumed to be immune from error), God actually appears to condemn the Prophet for failing to satisfy the sexual desires of his wives: "O Prophet! Why do you prohibit what God has permitted for you, striving for the satisfaction of your wives? God is forgiving, merciful!" (Q.66:1).

These and many other verses have been interpreted in a variety of ways by traditional and modern Qur'an scholars and jurists to support diverse views. Cultural sensibilities and traditions are often deeply interwoven with religious values, and it is often impossible to separate the two. Moreover, the various schools of law differ over many of the details associated with the institution of marriage. For the purposes of this introduction to Islam, I can only treat the most basic consensus positions, though I hope to make it clear that as with so many other subjects, Islam is not monolithic on matters of marriage, sexuality, and women's issues.

Most marriages in the Muslim world, including in the West, are arranged by the parents of the bride, and often the groom as well. The male, however, tends to be much more active than the female in seeking a mate. Unlike the woman, he may engage in the process on his own. A woman who has not been married previously is usually represented by a guardian who may be her father or other close male relative. If none are available, a male adult may be appointed for the purpose. It is the male guardian who will sign the wedding contract for the wife, who essentially assigns him power of attorney. Potential marriage partners may visit with each other before the wedding, but never without chaperons. Islam prohibits a man and woman who are not related in such a way that they may not marry to be alone together. It is becoming increasingly common to see young couples sitting together and talking in very public, sometimes crowded places in the Muslim world in order to meet and get to know each other. Dating and courtship as known in the West is not generally acceptable.

Arranged marriages are expected in Islam, but no marriage is possible without the consent of both partners. An authoritative *hadith* states, "The Prophet said, 'A widow may not be given away in marriage unless she consent and a virgin may not be given away in marriage unless she agrees.' They asked, 'O messenger of God! How can we know her permission?' He answered, 'Her silence [indicates her permission].'" That is followed by another *hadith*: "Khansā' bint Khidām al-Anṣāriyya said that her father gave her in marriage when she was a widow, but she did not like that, so she went to the Messenger of God and he declared the father's arrangement invalid." Despite such protection, the fact is that traditional Islamic marriages are family affairs that carry the stresses and influences of more individuals than only the two parties who will become husband and wife. Sometimes this works out for the best, as the high divorce rate in the West might attest. But sometimes the pressures can force people to marry against their will, or at least against the will of the woman.

The Marriage Contract

Marriage is not a sacrament in the Christian sense, but carries more the sense of a revocable legal agreement as in the Jewish sense of marriage. As in Judaism, it is a relationship based on a formal contract. The term referenced in passing in the Qur'an is *"mithāq ghalīz,"* which should be translated as "a powerful contract" (Q.4:21). The contract in essence legalizes sexual relations between the partners and includes a number of stipulations for each. The most basic is mutual good treatment, which is not legally defined. Each partner has rights and duties, which are differentiated by gender but are interrelated. If one partner fails his or her responsibility, that partner may jeopardize his or her claim to a particular right.

The husband's first duty is to pay a sum of wealth, often in gold jewelry, to his wife. This is called the *mahr* and has a parallel in the Bible (*mohar:* Gen. 34:12, Exod. 22:16). There is no set amount, but whatever is pledged becomes legally hers and she may save, spend, or invest it however she chooses. In exchange for the *mahr*, the husband receives power or authority over the marriage or over the contract. This is often understood as control over the relationship, including the sexual rights of the relationship, which therefore grants the husband the right to end the marriage by pronouncing repudiation of the contract. If the wife wishes to end the marriage, she must essentially buy out the contract by paying legal compensation. There are also grounds for divorce that vary between the schools of law, through which the wife may seek a judicial decision.

The wife also has the right to lodging, clothing, and support (compare Exod. 21:10). If her husband has other wives, she also has the right to an equal share of her husband's time. In exchange for the husband's support of his wife, jurists hold that a husband has the right to restrict her movements and to expect that she be available for sexual intimacy. A wife who does not comply may legally loose her right to support as well as any claim to a portion of her husband's time.

Some jurists accept added stipulations in the contract designed to secure more rights and privileges for the wife. The most common are that the husband will not take any additional wives or relocate from the wife's home town. The Hanbali school holds that if the husband violates such added stipulations, the wife has the right to dissolve her marriage, but the other schools do not accept the validity of these two clauses. They may be included in the marriage contract but are not enforceable unless the husband had delegated to her a right to divorce on grounds that one of the stipulations was breached. Another way to validate them is for the husband to pronounce a suspended divorce, which would take effect automatically if he violated one of them. The effect of this is to protect the binding power of the husband while providing more protection for the personal needs of the wife.

The complex issues associated with the rights and duties of husband andwife through a legal contract find a close parallel in the traditional Jewish system. For many Jews as well as Muslims, the traditional system is an acceptable way of establishing and guaranteeing rights and responsibilities for both partners. For those who would work toward equalizing the rights and independence of the wife, some wish to work within the parameters established by the legal basis of the traditional marriage contract. Others object to the overall framework of differentiated rights and duties or to unequal male prerogatives, and for these, modifications to the traditional marriage contract cannot resolve the problems. They call for a fundamental rethinking of the legal presumptions in the marriage contract and the particular style of relationship that such a contract tends to promote.

Wedding ceremonies vary significantly throughout the Muslim world. Even between upper and lower Egypt or between the Atlas Mountains and the coastal cities of Morocco, regional customs make the actual wedding ceremonies quite diverse. They vary even more between the many different regions and ethnic groups among Muslims living in Arab lands, Indonesia and Malaysia, India and Pakistan, Central Asia, Sub-Saharan Africa, and China. Public celebrations with bright and colorful decorations, contracts, henna ceremonies, deal-making, and other preparations join families as well as individuals; and the music, wedding banquets, and parties may easily last for more than a week after the official wedding contract is signed.

I have witnessed many kinds of wedding bands, dancing horses, huge fireworks displays, celebratory gunfire of automatic weapons, and even modest parades of the groom or the groom and his bride to their new home together.

Polygamy

Unlike the Bible, which has no limit to the number of wives a man may take, the Qur'an limits the number to four at the same time. In reference to the treatment of orphans the Qur'an says, "If you fear that you will not deal fairly with orphans, then marry those women who seem good to you—two, three or four. But if you fear that you will not be just, then one, or [a woman] whom your right hands possess. That is the best to avoid being unjust" (Q.4:3). Later in the same chapter and using the same language, the Qur'an conveys the message, "You will never be able to be just with wives even if you try" (Q.4:129).

Muhammad had special dispensation to take more than four wives (Q.33:50–51). The tradition literature mentions that he took wives to save them from destitution and that women came to him with the hopes that he would take them into his entourage. The Qur'an, however, eventually forbade him in Q.33:52 from taking additional wives: "No more wives are permitted to you. … "

The traditional commentaries claim that polygamy was a common practice in the pre-Islamic period and that the Qur'an provided limits and special protection for multiple wives that were not available prior to this revelation, but some modern scholars believe that polygamy was actually a qur'anic innovation that was responding to the unfair treatment of female dependents who were neglected by their guardians in Medina. In any case, Qur'an 4:129 would seem to suggest a preference for monogamy in the Qur'an.

Contraception

Because Islam forbids sexual relations outside of marriage, the classic discussions about birth control focus on contraception between husband and wife. The Qur'an does not treat contraception directly, but Muslims who oppose contraception often cite the following verses treating infanticide for support: "Do not kill your children out of fear of poverty. We will provide for them and for you" (Q.6:151, 17:31). Others cite Qur'an 42:49–50: "To God belongs the dominion of the heavens and the earth. He creates whatever He wills, giving to whomever He wills a female [child] and giving to whomever He wills a male [child]; or He combines them male and female, and He makes barren whomever he wills, for He is omniscient, powerful."

Most of the law schools allow contraception under certain conditions. Coitus interruptus (`azl) was practiced by pre-Islamic Arabs and continued to be used during time of the Prophet with his knowledge. In one authoritative *hadith*, Muhammad is asked whether in the case of legally acquired female captives the contraceptive technique of `azl is permitted. He responded, "You are not required to refrain from it. There is no soul that God determines should be born that will not be born." The practice of withdrawal may diminish the sexual gratification of the female partner, and it is also entirely the prerogative of the male partner who must be sensitive to his impending ejaculation. Some authorities, therefore, such as Ahmad ibn Hanbal (d.855, the originator of the Hanbali legal school) required the consent of the wife for contraception because she has the right of sexual enjoyment and to be a part of the decision of having a child. The form of contraception mentioned in the *Hadith* is `*azl*, but some modern jurists accept other forms as well.

Abortion

Abortion is *ijhāḍ* in Arabic, but as in other systems, it is related to miscarriage, which in Arabic means "losing [lit. "the falling of"] the fetus or "having been slipped out". The Qur'an does not include these terms, so the jurists extrapolated from the two central verses forbidding infanticide mentioned above (Q.6:151, 17:31). The *Hadith* rarely mentions *ijhāḍ*, but occasionally references miscarriage caused by violence to a woman rather than intentional abortion. In the *Hadith* references, the question is what damages must be paid to the woman, and the answer is the payment of a male or female slave.

From this the jurists derived the general consensus that the killing of a fetus is not permissible as soon as one can speak of it as a formed person. The payment of blood money is required if the baby is aborted alive and then dies, while a fine of lesser amount is to be paid if it is aborted dead. There is no agreement among legal scholars as to when the fetus would be considered a fully formed person. In fact, there are substantial differences between the four legal schools, not only over at what point in the pregnancy abortion would be forbidden, but also over the conditions that would allow interfering with the natural processes of pregnancy and birth. All agree that abortion is permissible up to 40 days, while the Hanafi and Shafi`i schools allow up to 120 days. The schools apply certain conditions in some cases, such as that both parents agree to the procedure or that the mother fears she may run out of milk under the physical stress of a new pregnancy.

Exceptions to these limits are made by some authorities if the life of the mother is endangered, based on Qur'an 2:233: "No mother should be harmed on account of a child of hers." According to Qaradawi's reading of the jurists, "If ... after the baby is completely formed, it is reliably established that the continuation of the pregnancy would necessarily result in the death of the mother, then, in accordance with the general principle of the Shari`ah, that of choosing the lesser of two evils, abortion must be performed."

Divorce

Divorce (*ṭalāq*) is of course not a necessary part of the Islamic life cycle. In fact, although fully legal, it is not common. This is due partly to the fact that marriage ties families as well as individuals together, and family pressures tend to foil the possible desire of the partners themselves to divorce. Nevertheless, sometimes the relationship between husband and wife becomes extremely strained, as is recognized in the Qur'an. In a discussion about difficulties in relationship between a married couple, the Qur'an teaches the following: "And if you fear dissention between them, then send an arbitrator from his family and from hers. If they wish to reconcile, then God will bring agreement between them, for God is knowing, aware" (Q.4:35). Arbitration is not always successful in bringing understanding to a marriage relationship. The Qur'an has a lot to say about divorce, and it reflects the patriarchal society out of which Islam emerged in 7th century Arabia. Divorce is accepted, but it is the prerogative of the husband; he initiates the proceedings. A divorced woman must wait for three menstrual cycles before remarrying (Q.2:228) in order to maintain that she is not pregnant, because the father of the child is entitled to paternity and to raise the child. The Qur'an is explicit that the husband is a rank above the wife in this regard (Q.2:227–232), but it also provides certain protections for the woman. At issue here is the difficult problem of paternal responsibility and privilege over the children as well as the same over the wife.

After the husband declares a divorce, there is a required waiting period called `*idda* (from the root meaning "to count") of four months (Q.2:226) during which the wife may not remarry and actually must remain in the home of the husband. They are nevertheless officially divorced by the husband's declaration. During the `*idda* period they may be reconciled without the requirement of remarriage, but after the period has passed they are officially divorced. Based on Qur'an 2:229, the husband may reconcile with his wife twice, but if he declares the woman divorced a third time it is a permanent enactment that cannot be undone without the writing up of a new marriage contract. The wife's expenses during the waiting period are the responsibility of the husband. She cannot be expelled from her place of residence and any harassment on the part of the husband may constitute a criminal as well as amoral offense. In case of divorce, the young children remain in the custody of their divorced mother but the father is responsible for their maintenance.

The wife can also divorce her husband if that is stipulated in the marriage contract, say, for taking another wife. This type of divorce is called "delegated divorce." Marriage can also be dissolved through mutual consent, though it is actually the husband's prerogative to make it official. The problem for women is that it is almost impossible by traditional procedures for a woman to initiate a successful divorce. This, by the way, is a problem that is found also in the traditional Jewish community, and various attempts by secular courts to enable the rights of women in this regard have not been satisfactory. There is also a form of divorce mentioned above among the protections of the wife called *khul`* ("removal" or "repudiation"), through which the wife essentially buys out her wedding contract, but this is usually accepted only with the husband's permission and can elicit the husband making extortionate demands. There are other forms of divorce as well, such as *li`ān* (mutual cursing) or a kind of annulment called *faskh* or *tafrīq*. All tend to favor the husband over the wife.

A recent Egyptian law, approved by the chief jurist of the most respected institution of Islamic jurisprudence in Egypt and perhaps the entire Sunni Muslim world, Al-Azhar, provides an alternate approach. Beginning in March 2000, Egypt has granted the wife the right to obtain a *khul`* divorce without the husband's consent if she returns the full dowry that she received at marriage. By the middle of the first year after the law was passed, some 3,000 petitions seeking divorce under these provisions had been filed in Cairo, a city of some 18 million residents.

Inheritance

The Muslim law of inheritance is quite complex and cannot be explored here in any detail. It is based on Qur'an 4:11–12: "God directs you concerning your children: the male gets the equivalent of the portion of two females, but if they are more than two daughters, they get two thirds of what one leaves. If there is only one, she gets half. … " The verses continue to outline a complex set of relations and percentages of inheritance, which is made much more complicated in the juridical literature. A person may make a will, but that can affect only up to one third of the estate, the remainder regulated by the legal formulas. The net result, if one compares the system with that of the Hebrew Bible, is significantly better for women because they are fully entitled to inherit, though at a reduced rate of men (cf. Num. 27:8–11). The system seems to have been developed in an environment that was not agrarian because it is impossible for any single inheritor to retain an unequally large portion of land. Land becomes divided equally along with other forms of wealth.

The result has often been to divide viable land-holdings into increasingly smaller shares among survivors in each generation until it becomes difficult or even impossible for sustainable farming through inheritance. Lands must then be purchased outside of the family plot, which then makes the farming all that much more difficult. The same problem applies to businesses that often become unviable after one or two generations.

One way to get around the problem is through the institution of the charitable trust or foundation (*waqf*). This avoids some of the problems of inheritance division, but it also dissolves the business that generated the income in the first place. The *waqf* was designed to fund public institutions such as mosques, schools, hospitals, market buildings, and libraries. The advantage for the family is that relatives may be employed to administer the institution that is funded, thereby creating and maintaining jobs for generations of family members. *Waqfs* remain private and not open to government interference. This very independence sometimes causes difficulties, because if the funds dry up, the property may end up abandoned and taken out of circulation without the ability of government to possess it for refurbishing.

Death, Burial, and Mourning

As with many other Islamic rituals, death practices tend to vary from place to place and reflect the cultures over which Islam became dominant. It is customary to turn the dying person's face in the direction of the *qibla* (toward Mecca) if possible, and to recite the *shahāda*. This is equivalent to the Jewish custom of reciting *Shema* at the moment before death.

It is also customary to recite chapter 36 of the Qur'an, called *yā sīn*, which treats resurrection of the dead and final judgment in comforting terms. "It is We who will revive the dead and record what they have sent before and what they have left. We have made an accounting for everything in a clear book" (Q.36:12). Of particular consolation are verses 51–58: "The trumpet will sound and they will rush out of their graves to their Lord, crying out, 'woe is us! Who roused us from our bed? This is what the Merciful One promised. The messengers spoke the truth!' In only one shout they are present before Us. So on that day no soul will be wronged in the least, nor shall you be rewarded except for what you have done. Those destined for the Garden are joyful today for their activity, they and their spouses reclining on couches, joyful there, having all they desire. 'Peace,' spoken from a merciful Lord."

As soon as possible after death, the body is washed and prepared for burial. As in Judaism, embalming is not permitted. The washing is the final ablution for the deceased. It is particularly meritorious to be engaged in this act, men performing it for men and women for women except for children or spouses, who may be washed by their mates or parents regardless of gender. Usually, the body is washed three times, the hair combed and, if long, braided. The body is then dried and perfumed, and then wrapped in a simple white cotton shroud. A coffin is not necessary but is permitted. The point is that it be simple and no costly materials be used. If the deceased is a martyr, the body is not washed. It is assumed that the martyr's death purifies, and the martyr is immediately entered into heaven.

The body may be carried to the mosque, taken to any clean place, or remain at the home for the funeral service (*janāza*). The body in a coffin or on a bier is placed in front of the worshipers, and the service is led by a close male relative or a professional or appointed imam. The funeral service is performed standing and there are no prostrations. It includes four *takbīrs*, the opening chapter of the Qur'an, and any number of variants of supplications for Muhammad, on behalf of the deceased, and for all Muslims. An example might be something like "O God! Grant forgiveness to our living and to our dead, and to those who are present and to those who are absent, and to our young and our old folk, and to our males and females. O God! Whomever you grant to live from among us, help him to live in God; and whom of us you cause to die, help him to die in faith. O God! Do not deprive us of the reward for patience on his loss, and do not make us subject to travail after him." Prayers are recited for the forgiveness of the deceased's sins (unless it is a child who is assumed to be pure of sin). The prayer service ends with the normal conclusion of *taslīm* facing right and then left.

The body should be buried on the day of death, if at all possible. If the death occurs in the afternoon or evening, it may be buried the following day, if necessary. After completing the *jināza* prayers, the body is taken to the cemetery. Mourners walk in front or beside the bier; those who are riding or driving follow it. The funeral procession proceeds in silence, if possible.

The grave should be deep and the body should face Mecca. When lowering the body, a prayer-statement may be recited: "In the name of God and with God, and according to the *sunna* of the messenger of God upon whom be the blessings and peace of God." Other prayers may be offered as well, and it is common to recite Qur'an 20:55 which follows a reference to God having created the earth as a bed or couch to lie on: "We created you from it and We shall return you to it, and We shall bring you forth from it another time." A stone, brick, or amount of soil is placed under the head of the deceased to raise it up. After placing the body in the grave, the attendees fill the pit with soil and raise the level to about a foot above the level of the surrounding earth. This may be followed by another recitation of the *Fātiḥa*. There are, of course, any number of variations in the ritual, depending on custom, denomination, and location.

The official period of intense mourning is three days, during which loved ones and close relatives receive visitors and condolences and avoid decorative clothing and jewelry. A lesser level of mourning continues until the end of 40 days after burial. During this period, there may be special meals, prayers, and Qur'an recitations to honor and remember the dead. Widows observe an extended mourning period, four months and 10 days long, based on Qur'an 2:234. During this time, a widow is not to remarry, move from her home, or wear decorative clothing, jewelry, or perfume.

The grave itself may or may not be marked or decorated. As noted above in the discussion of "Wahhabi" and similar expressions of Islam, any embellishment of graves is highly disapproved of by some groups. Nevertheless, it is common to have grave markers, and anyone who has visited Cairo and seen the City of the Dead must be impressed by the many necropolises and mausoleums that are customary in Egypt. It is considered meritorious to visit cemeteries and meditate on the meaning of life and death.

Before ending this section on the life-cycle, it is fitting to revisit the Islamic notion of final judgment. We have observed how resurrection of the dead is a basic creed of Islam. That resurrection will occur at the end of days, when all souls will be subject to a final divine judgment and then eternity in heaven or hell. The period between death and resurrection is called *barzakh*, which means "interval" or "gap" and derives from Qur'an 23:99–100: "Until death comes to one of them, he will say, 'My Lord, send me back that I may do right by what I have neglected.' No way! That is only talk. Before them is a gap until the day they will be resurrected." In the tradition and folk literatures, this is a period during which the angel of death or his assistants will separate the soul from the body, either painlessly or harshly depending on how righteous the person was while living. Three events are said to make up this period: the separation of the soul from the body, an interrogation of faith for the soul by the angels Nakīr and Munkar, and then possible torment or horror of the grave. As strange as these events may seem to Jews unfamiliar with Islamic eschatology, an interesting *hadith* appears in a number of authoritative sources that suggests that the Jews of Medina had a very similar notion.

Muhammad's youngest wife `Ā'isha said: The Messenger of God came to me [once] when a Jewish woman was with me, and she said: 'Did you know that you will be tested in the grave?' `Ā'isha continued: The Messenger of God was frightened [in response] and said: 'It is the Jews who will be tested!' `Ā'isha said: We stayed together some nights, and then the Messenger of God said: Did you know that I was given a revelation that you will be tested in the grave? `Ā'isha said: Thereafter I heard the Apostle of God seeking refuge from the torment of the grave.

8

Ṣūfī Devotion

by Andrew Rippin

T he question of the origins of Sufism (*taṣawwuf*), the mystical aspect within Islam, and its devotees, the Ṣūfīs, seems to have attracted its own particular type of dispute within the academic study of Islam. The reason for this dispute would appear to go back once again to a memory of medieval (and later) polemic between Christians and Muslims. Christians have often pictured Islam as a very sensually based religion: Muḥammad's multiple marriages, the Qurʾān's very physical and sensual portrayal of heaven and its rewards, and Islam's permitting of polygamy and enjoining holy war (*jihād*) have all been featured in these kinds of characterizations. At the same time, however, Christians have been very well aware of a profound ascetic-mystical trend in Islam. Abū Ḥamīd al-Ghazālī (d. 1111), for example, one of the most famous of all Ṣūfīs, became well known in the medieval west especially in his philosophic guise; this was true of a variety of other mystically inspired writers also. In trying to reconcile the two natures perceived within Islam, the implicit suggestion given by some early writers on the subject was that the mystical trend could not be inherent in Islam but must have come from Christianity, a far more elevated religion in their view.

It is the case, then, that raising the question of the origins of Sufism today is no less controversial than the question of the origins of the entire religion of Islam, because behind the questions lies the aura, if not the attitude, of medieval polemic. To suggest that Islamic mysticism is, in fact, a borrowing from outside

Andrew Rippin, "Sufi Devotion," *Muslims*, pp. 136–148. Copyright © 2005 by Taylor & Francis Group LLC. Reprinted with permission.

raises the spectre of the denial of the intrinsically spiritual nature of Islam and thence of the spiritual nature of Muslims themselves.

The question of origins here is twofold. The basic point, much argued by Ṣūfīs themselves in their search for the legitimization of their spiritual quest, is whether Islam as a religion contained within itself a spiritual-ascetic tendency from the very beginning; that is, does Islam inherently see that the mystical way (defined, for the time being, as the quest for some intimacy with God as induced through certain practices of a meditative, repetitive or self-denying nature) is the ideal life that should be aimed for? From the Islamic perspective, is that lifestyle inherently pleasing to God?

The second issue is one concerning the origins of Sufism itself. Regardless of where the original spiritual-ascetic impulse came from, were the practices, aspirations and the mode of expression used by the Ṣūfīs elements developed within Islam or were they the result of influences from another source (be that Christian, Indian, Iranian or whatever) and adapted to an Islamic style?

The Source of Sufism in Islam

The problem with answering the first question is, of course, one of interpretation. How do we judge an issue such as "inherent asceticism"? Some would say that a basic world-denying attitude is a part of Judaism, Christianity and Islam, especially because the overall tradition has been influenced by the radical dualism of Manichaeism with its distrust of the material world. This attitude is difficult to reconcile, however, with the picture of Islam and Judaism especially as "nomocratic," where a very practical attitude towards life in the here and now, as manifested in the law, is a prime characteristic of the religion. The other aspect of the problem is the common one found in all elements of the origins of Islam and that is the lack of contemporary sources. There simply are no ascertainably early sources which give us a glimpse of a spiritual-ascetic lifestyle from before the ninth century, in common with the lack of documentary evidence for the beginnings of Islam in general.

Muslim arguments on the subject revolve around the citation of the Qurʾān and elements of the *ḥadīth* and the *Sīra*, the life story of Muḥammad, which indicate the possibility of, if not the positive encouragement and enactment of, the ascetic ideal. This approach fully answers the question from the internal Muslim perspective. The Qurʾān and Muḥammad, as Ṣūfīs have always said, support the mystical quest. Statements concerning God are popularly cited, for example, Qurʾān 2/186, "Whenever My servants ask you about Me, I am near to answer the call of the caller," and Qurʾān 50/16, "We [God] are closer to him [humanity] than his jugular vein!" Looking inward, therefore, becomes the goal and the quest, although Qurʾān 2/115, "wherever you may turn, there is the face of God," adds another dimension to the quest. The wandering way of life of the early ascetic is supported in Qurʾān 29/20, "Travel in the land and see how He began creation." Qurʾān 9/123 asserts, "God is with the godfearing" whose way of life is echoed in the Quranic refrain to remember God always (for example, Qurʾān 33/41, "You who believe, remember God often"). The "light verse," Qurʾān 24/35, is the most famous of all verses for Ṣūfī speculation and its very presence in the Qurʾān is often claimed to be proof of the need for the mystic way:

> God is the light of the heavens and the earth. The likeness of His light is as a niche in which there
> is a lamp; the lamp is in a glass; the glass is just as if it were a glittering star kindled from a blessed

tree, an olive neither Eastern nor Western, whose oil will almost glow though the fire has never touched it. Light upon light, God guides His light to anyone He wishes.

As for Muḥammad, his whole experience of revelation and his preparation towards receiving it are seen as models for the ascetic life and its product. This is also true of other Quranic figures, especially Moses and al-Khiḍr whose stories, as told in *sūra* 18, have been elaborated into accounts of the mystic quest. Many of the traditions about Muḥammad most favoured by the Ṣūfīs are not to be found in the major *ḥadīth* collections, generally having been rejected by the collectors as unsound, but the Ṣūfīs kept their traditions going among their own circles. Many aphorisms are found on Muḥammad's lips which are applicable to the Ṣūfī quest, and Muḥammad is also portrayed as following an ascetic way of life. The latter traditions found their way into works such as the *Kitāb al-Zuhd* ("The Book of Ascetic Practices") of Ibn Ḥanbal (d. 855), the eponym of the legal school, who is often seen as a supporter of the early ascetic movement. Poverty especially became an ideal espoused by Muḥammad. For example, Ibn Ḥanbal cites the tradition from ʿĀʾisha who "was asked what the Messenger of God did in his house. She replied, 'He patched clothes, fixed sandals, and did similar things'." ʿĀʾisha also reported that when Muḥammad died, "he did not leave a dinar or a dirham, nor any sheep or cattle, nor did he bequeath anything."

Even more productive for the Ṣūfīs has been the story of the *miʿrāj*, Muḥammad's night journey (based around Qurʾān 17/1), which is seen as a tale of the supreme mystical experience to which every mystic aspires. While the basic account is found in all orthodox sources about Muḥammad, starting in germ form in Muḥammad's early biographer Ibn Isḥāq, the Ṣūfī understanding and interpretation of the account are, of course, unique. The emphasis frequently falls on the role of the journey as a prophetic initiation, leading the way for all mystics after Muḥammad to journey to their own union with the divine presence, not as prophets but as saints or "friends of God."

Interestingly, there is a marked anti-ascetic tendency within the Sunnī books of *ḥadīth*, especially focusing on the rejection of Christian monasticism. For example, these reports are often used in Islam to support the notion that even Ṣūfīs should marry. Other such elements include a rejection of forty-day food restrictions and pleas against poverty (even to the point of denying excessive charity). Most of this material can be seen as anti-Christian in tendency and as reflecting the tension that Muslims felt over the status of ascetic tendencies in early Islam.

However, all of this attention to the Qurʾān, *Sīra* and *ḥadīth* on the part of the Ṣūfīs simply indicates that they have, like all other Muslims, always gone back to the prime sources of Islam for inspiration as well as justification of their position; in that way they are no different from the jurists in the quest to define the law as closely as possible, for example. For modern historians to take "objective" facts from this type of material and attempt to reconstruct a picture of mystical trends in early Islam is to commit the error of anachronistic reading of the texts; one is clearly looking at the texts through the eyes of later people and we learn nothing from them of the earliest meaning given to these sources. The most that may be concluded from this part of the discussion, therefore, is simply to say that Muslims have found the life story of Muḥammad and the Qurʾān itself to be vital sources in their mystical quest. One would not want to discount the possibility that even the early versions of the biography (*Sīra*) of Muḥammad have been affected by early mystics and thus reflect some of their concerns and desires, as is reflected also in the *ḥadīth* literature with its books devoted to *zuhd*, asceticism, as practised by Muḥammad. That the Qurʾān might, in fact, contain such ascetic elements is a possibility that needs to be entertained; however, whether the pieces of the Qurʾān which suggest this background was always understood that way by Muslims, and where those pieces of the Qurʾān actually originated, are vexing questions which still must be faced by scholarship.

Sources of Ṣūfī Practice

The solution to this first aspect of the problem of the origins of Sufism, then, would seem to be to put aside the questions about the inherent spiritual asceticism of Islam and perhaps simply admit that the understanding of the nature of God as contained within the Judaeo-Christian-Muslim tradition is one which is potentially amenable to the mystical way of life. There only remains, then, the second question of the development of what we may truly call Sufism in Islam, the influences upon it and its role in the emergence of Islam. For the early period there is the major problem of definition, of how to determine for example, whether Ibn Ḥanbal should be considered a Ṣūfī or simply an ascetic Muslim, given his encouragement of that way of life. That he should have combined this role with one of the upholding of traditionalism is significant, of course; one of his works which displays ascetic tendencies is the above-mentioned *Kitāb al-Zuhd*, a collection of traditions about the life of Muḥammad. Indeed, for the earliest period, this emphasis on asceticism is the primary element that one can isolate with certainty as the forerunner of the later mystical way. The evidence suggests that it was in the early to mid-ninth century that these sorts of tendencies found their expression in written form; it was only later in that century that this became combined with speculative thought, producing as a result a true system of mysticism, which may accurately and meaningfully be called Sufism. The dating of this era for the emergence of Sufism is confirmed within juridical works, where the disdain for the ascetic way of life is displayed and a resultant attempt on the part of the jurists to restrict its scope can clearly be seen; the end of the eighth century and early in the ninth century appears to be the era for the greatest disputes on this matter.

Certainly, the influence of Christianity on the foundation of asceticism in Islam is clear in some of the earliest writings. Al-Muḥāsibī (d. 857), for example, has been shown to have borrowed heavily from the New Testament for various sayings and commendations of the Ṣūfī way of life. As well, the practice of wearing woollen garments called *ṣūf*, by means of which it is popularly believed that the term "Ṣūfī" (meaning "those who wear rough woollen garments") was coined, is said to have been done in imitation of Christian hermits; this was carried out in order to serve as an indication of poverty as well as being an ascetic practice in and by itself.

The development of a mystical litany was also a part of the early enunciation of the movement. Termed *dhikr*, the practice was connected by the Ṣūfīs to the Quranic injunction to "mention God often," as in Qurʾān 33/21. The developed form of this litany consists of the constant repetition of various phrases, often *lā ilāhᵃ illā ʾllāh*, "There is no god but God." This practice serves as the focal point of devotions for virtually every Ṣūfī group. Christian modes of worship once again may have provided some of the impetus for this particular element.

Doctrinally, the early mystics are held to have been devoted to the notion of *tawakkul*, "total trust" in God. The characteristics are complete indifference to the world and its affairs and a full dependence upon God supplying the needs of the individual; this attitude was said to demonstrate one's total trust in the power and mercy of God who will supply those needs. A total lack of possessions and deprivation of any bodily comforts were the marks of such a person. This trend is often seen to have been influenced by Christianity also, that being a tendency of monasticism in the church.

Given the geographical contexts in which Islamic asceticism is generally seen to have emerged—Baghdad, in the environment of the Christian heritage, and Khurasan, a former Buddhist centre—it is not surprising that elements of various religions, especially Christianity as the above examples show, should be present; little would seem to be gained by denying it. However, it has frequently been pointed out that the ascetic lifestyle in Islam developed with a certain overt political motivation. Once again in Islam, a religious position appears to have been used as a rallying point for rebellion against the ruling powers. The whole early ascetic inclination is frequently pictured as a renunciation and rejection of the political strife in the formative Islamic period. The early mystics were the true Muslims who held onto the Islamic spirit in the face of the manipulation of the religion by the ruling powers for their own purposes. The emphasis on *tawakkul* would be pictured in marked contrast to the efforts of all other Muslims to secure their places on earth rather than in heaven, at least from the perspective of the mystics. Al-Ḥasan al-Baṣrī (d. 728), famous for his role in the theological debates discussed in Chapter 5, emerges in the literature as one of the central figures of this type of spirituality, going to the extent of denying the value of existence in this world and speaking of the hereafter as the realm free of the contamination of political self-interest. Revolutionary involvement in the political arena was not sanctioned by al-Ḥasan al-Baṣrī, even if that could have meant replacing an unjust ruler with a pious one; the slow persuasion of rulers was about the best that could be hoped for in the effort to improve the lot of all Muslims in the community.

Overall, then, the argument certainly can be made for "foreign influences" on the development of Sufism but, without a doubt, modern scholarship sees the internal tensions of the Muslim community as crucial in the emergence of early ascetic tendencies.

Development of Sufism

The ninth century was marked by a rapid progression of mystics, each famous for adding a certain element to the emergent mystical viewpoint and creating the central tenets of Sufism. Under the influence of neo-Platonism, at least according to some writers, mystical doctrines of the love of God, the beatific vision of the mystical experience, gnosis as the goal of the experience, the image of the mystical ascension, the absorption into God and the theory of the mystical states are all seen to emerge.

Al-Junayd (d. 910), a pupil of al-Muḥāsibī, is often given the credit for establishing a true system of mystical speculation, bringing together the insights of his predecessors and creating a lasting system for all subsequent generations. He is credited with the elaboration of the doctrine of *fanāʾ*, the goal of the mystic in "dying in one's self," "passing away" or "absorption" into God, supported by the Quranic, "All that is on the earth will disappear while your Lord's face abides, majestic, splendid" (Qurʾān 55/26–7). The mystic quest is based on the need to return to God, the state in which humanity was before creation. *Baqāʾ*, the "continuance," is the existence of the mystic after *fanāʾ*, when he or she lives in God. Al-Junayd combined this goal with an ethical theory which demanded of the mystic who has reached the state of "absorption" a return to society; this was so that the individual would make clear "the evidence of [God's] grace to him, so that the lights of His gifts in the return of his individual characteristics scintillate and attract the community to him who appreciate him." This meant, for al-Junayd, that the Ṣūfī had the responsibility to return to his community life and fulfil all the obligations of Muslim existence; the knowledge of the individual's absorption into the divine remains a "secret treasure" which shines through the person in everything done in the world.

Al-Ḥallāj

Contemporary with al-Junayd was al-Ḥallāj (d. 922) who, likewise, was convinced of the necessity of the mystic quest, but who was condemned to death for the blasphemy of considering that individuals could recognize their God-nature through mystical experience. Stories relate that al-Ḥallāj proclaimed, "I am the Truth," which was taken to mean that he felt himself actually to be God incarnate in the world. Such Ṣūfis (another early example is al-Basṭāmī, d. 875) have come to be termed "intoxicated" as compared to the "sober" mysticism of al-Junayd, for they had become so overcome by the mystical experience that existence, as such, had no meaning to them; their utterances became the focal point of their understanding of their experiences and vice versa. The ethical aspect of al-Junayd's doctrine became submerged within their experiences.

Later Developments

These authors were only starting to develop a truly systematic picture of Sufism; it fell to authors such as Abū Naṣr al-Sarrāj (d. 988) in the following century to construct general accounts of Sufism, its history and its meaning in the Islamic context. Al-Sarrāj wrote in his *Kitāb al-Lumaʿ* of the legitimacy of Ṣūfi practice, based upon the precedent of Muḥammad and his companions. With this, he combined a great deal of definitional material in an attempt to distil the essence of the mystical path as it existed in his time. He states, for example:

> The meaning of "passing away" and "continuance" … is the passing away of ignorance into the abiding condition of knowledge and the passing away of disobedience into the abiding state of obedience, and the passing away of indifference into the state of continual worship, and the passing away of the consideration of the actions of the servant, which are temporary, into the vision of the Divine Grace, which is the eternal.

The eleventh century brought greater systematization to the theoretical basis of Sufism in the writings of al-Qushayrī (d. 1072). Writing in 1046, al-Qushayrī was concerned with demonstrating that Sufism was not in conflict with Sunnī Islam. Part of this proof was provided by the biography of many prominent Ṣūfis. He also presented a picture of the theory of the stations through which a Ṣūfi passes on his or her mystic quest and the states which God may grace the mystic with during that quest. Such had already been detailed by al-Sarrāj before him, but al-Qushayrī added further detail to the schema. Forty-five terms are used to describe the quest, starting with *tawba*, "repentance," which is seen as the manifestation of the conscious desire to follow the mystic way, through "patience," "constant awareness of God" and "satisfaction with God," culminating in "gnosis," "love" and "yearning to be with God."

Abu Ḥamīd al-Ghazālī used the basis established by earlier Ṣūfi theorists for promoting the assimilation of Sufism into orthodoxy in developing his own arguments; his magnum opus, *Iḥyāʾ ʿUlūm al-Dīn*, the "Revivification of the Religious Sciences," written between 1099 and 1102, tried to accomplish just what its title suggests: bring life back into the orthodox "religious sciences" through the inspiration of Sufism. In the process, Sufism itself would be seen to gain total legitimacy as being an essential part of the Islamic way of life. His work is divided into four sections. The first, "worship," concentrates on the "inner meaning" of the rituals of Islam. The second, "personal behaviour," sees the progression from religious law to mystical training as intimately linked. The third, "deadly sins," details the discipline needed for the mystic quest. Finally, the fourth, "the way to salvation," concentrates on the interpretation of spiritual experience. This progress in the life of the individual reflects al-Ghazālī's overall view of life and the mystic quest:

> If, then, you ask, What is the Beginning of Guidance in order that I may test my soul thereby? know that the beginning of guidance is outward piety and the end of guidance is inward piety. Only through piety is anything really achieved; only the pious are guided. Piety designates carrying out the commands of God most high and turning aside from what He prohibits. …

The Ṣūfī orders

The tendency towards increased intellectual support and the systematization of Sufism was developed even further in the Ṣūfī orders, which are based on the principle of the relationship between the master and the pupil. The authority of the master who has ascended through the stages of the mystic must be accepted wholly by the pupil, for only with guidance will the union with God be possible. The foundation of the *ṭarīqa*, the "way" or "path," and later coming to mean the "order" or "brotherhood," emerged as a way of providing a practical and structured way for the initiate to be guided through the stages of mystical experience. Beginning as an informal group, companionship with an acknowledged master was the focal point of the *ṭarīqa*. Groups emerged early on, centred in dwellings known as *ribāṭs*, *khānqāh*s, *khalwa*s or *zāwiya*s, all meaning "Ṣūfī retreats," in one part or another of the Muslim world. Such retreats were not organized in any particular way, however; the participants simply wandered from one such place to another. In the eleventh century the institutionalized *ṭarīqa* movement received a boost with the Seljuq reorganization of the *madrasa*, the Islamic school, and the provision of support and supervision of Ṣūfī dwellings at the same time. This trend was encouraged even further by the success of al-Ghazālī's work in bringing Sufism into the fold of orthodoxy. The process culminated in the thirteenth century with the emergence of special centres of Ṣūfī training; focused on the activities and way of a single man, a centre would perpetuate the name, teaching, exercises and rule of life of that person. The *ṭarīqa* was handed down through the *isnād* or *silsila* of the *shaykh*, the leader of the order, passing on to the spiritual heirs of that person. The initiate swore allegiance to the *shaykh*, and thereby became linked to the spiritual chain. Often incorporated into these *silsila*s were famous Ṣūfīs of the past, such as al-Junayd and al-Bastāmī; the initial stage of the chain is frequently Muḥammad and from him ʿAlī, although this does not necessarily indicate any Shīʿī leanings on the part of the groups.

All such *ṭarīqa*s, formally at the very least, accept the law and ritual of orthodox Islam as binding. In this way, they provide a supplement to the Islamic way of life, rather than a true "alternative vision," although, obviously, their view of the true nature of Islam and its purpose is different from those who remain outside the *ṭarīqa*. The point remained, however, that in order for the *ṭarīqa*s to ensure their acceptance by orthodoxy (i.e. the jurists), the attention to the externals of Islamic life continued to be necessary.

The major *ṭarīqa*s in classical Islam were the Suhrawardiyya, the Qādiriyya, the Rifāʿiyya, the Yasawiyya, the Kubrāwiyya, the Čishtiyya, the Shādhiliyya, the Badawiyya, the Mawlawiyya (Mevlevi) and the

Naqshbandiyya. These groups trace their foundations to various persons who lived in the twelfth and thirteenth centuries.

The Practices of the Ṣūfī Orders

Taking the Qādiriyya as an example of the *ṭarīqa* phenomenon, one may see the role these institutions played in the fostering of the Ṣūfī attitude. ʿAbd al-Qādir al-Jīlānī, the *shaykh* of the movement, was born in Jilan in Persia in 1077 and went to Baghdad at the age of eighteen; there he became a popular preacher within the Ḥanbalī tradition at the age of about fifty, and he died in 1166. There is no evidence that he ever consciously set out to form a Ṣūfī school, although the legends told in great profusion about his life certainly want to picture him as a Ṣūfī miracle worker. The following story is reported by a disciple of al-Jīlānī:

> Once, while I was still a young man, I entered the presence of Shaykh ʿAbd al-Qādir (may Allah be well pleased with him), together with a large group. I had with me a book that dealt with questions of abstract philosophy and the speculative sciences of spirituality. As soon as we entered his presence, the Shaykh spoke to me—to me personally, not to the group as a whole—and before he had examined the book, or asked me about its contents, he said, "That book of yours is a bad companion. You had better go and give it a thorough wash!" I reacted to this by deciding to leave his presence, drop the book into some receptacle or other, and then refrain from carrying it with me after that, for fear of offending the Shaykh. My lower self could not accept the idea of giving it a wash, because I had developed quite a fondness for it, and some of its theories and principles had stimulated my intellectual curiosity. I was about to get up and leave, intending to carry out this plan of action, but the Shaykh gave me such a stare, like someone regarding me with incredulous amazement, that I simply could not get up. I felt trapped in a state of paralysis, but then he said to me, "Hand me that book of yours!" So I opened it, and lo and behold, there was nothing inside it but blank paper, with not a single letter written on it! I gave it to the Shaykh, and he thumbed through its pages, then he said, "This is 'The Book of the Excellent Merits of the Qurʾān' by Muḥamad Ibn al-Durays." When he handed it back to me, I saw that it was indeed that book, written in a most handsome calligraphic script! The Shaykh then said to me, "Are you ready to turn in repentance from saying with your tongue what is not in your heart?" I said, "Yes, O my master." So he told me to stand up. I obediently rose to my feet, and I had forgotten all about philosophy and the principles of spirituality! They had been totally erased from my inner being, as if they had never captured my interest."

It was to the two sons of ʿAbd al-Qādir that the formation of the school actually fell and, by the year 1300, centres existed in Iraq and Syria, with the major expansion coming in the fifteenth century. ʿAbd al-Qādir himself is famed as a saint and the belief in his power of intercession is what has made the *ṭarīqa* a significant presence throughout the Islamic world.

The Qādiriyya's practices reflect the beliefs of the group itself but also the general Ṣūfī stance on the role of the master and the efficacy of various mystical practices. The initiation procedure contains the promise to "recite the *dhikr* in obedience to the dictates of the *shaykh*" and the *shaykh* accepts the initiate "as a son." The *dhikr* itself is recited by the group seated in front of the *shaykh* and repeated hundreds of times. The novice members repeat *lā ilāhᵃ illā ʾllāh*, "There is no god but God," 165 times, while the more advanced members repeat a series of statements praising God and ʿAbd al-Qādir 121 times, followed by 100 repetitions of *sūra* 36, 41 repetitions of *sūra* 72, 121 repetitions of *sūra* 110, 8 repetitions of *sūra* 1 and topped off by 1 recitation of *sūra* 112. All this is done under the control of the *shaykh* at a pace which increases as it goes on, until individual members, potentially, have a mystic experience appropriate to the level of their spiritual advancement.

Ibn ʿArabī

Muḥyīʾl-Dīn ibn ʿArabī represents the culmination of another strand within Islamic Sufism. Born in Spain in 1165, he travelled throughout North Africa and the Middle East, becoming initiated into Sufism in 1194, and eventually dying in Damascus in 1240. He was a prolific author and wrote *al-Futuḥāt al-Makkiyya*, "The Meccan Revelations," a Ṣūfī encyclopaedia, and *Fuṣūṣ al-Ḥikam*, "The Bezels of Wisdom," his most famous work which summarizes his vision. A difficult writer to comprehend, without a doubt, he was fully educated in the Islamic sciences and brought to his work a vast quantity of learning.

His thought represents a true theosophy, believing in the essential unity between humanity and God. Having brought speculative Sufism to its apogee through his emphasis on gnosis (*maʿrifa*) as the way to the experience of truth, Ibn ʿArabī has been accused of monism, of denying the reality of the separation between God and His creation. The doctrine of God's transcendence is often held to be essential to Muslim orthodox theology, denying as it does any possibility of the incarnation of God in the world, a consequence of its ancient polemic with Christianity. In theory, the theosophical Ṣūfīs got around the problem with the notion of "the reality of Muḥammad" in control of the universe, that being the power to which the Ṣūfīs could aspire in their mystical quest. Ibn ʿArabī argued for the doctrine of *waḥdat al-wujūd*, the "unity of being," where certain implications seem hard to avoid: being and existence are all one and are combined in God; being which is apart from God exists only by virtue of His will, but was, prior to its being made separate, one with God; the "perfect human" (*al-insān al-kāmil*) is the one who knows of oneness with God, who loves God, and who is loved by God. For Ibn al-ʿArabī, the concept of the *barzakh*, the barrier and bridge between material existence and the divine world referred to in Qurʾān 25/53 and 55/20 in a metaphor of "the place where the two seas join," is of central importance because that is the realm of existence in which humans play a critical role. The ability, or even the necessity, for humans to bridge that gap both in life and in death provides the unity of being but preserves the conceptual tension between the immanence and transcendence of God.

The Role of Sufism

The influence of Ibn ʿArabī, despite the complexity of his thought, has been enormous, not only on all Sufism from that point on, but also in the modern scholarly world, which is still trying to get to grips with his ideas. But Sufism was not only of this elevated intellectual type, for the role of the brotherhoods in bringing Sufism closer to the popular level cannot be underestimated. It was the efforts of the brotherhoods which spread Islam into many far-flung corners of the contemporary Muslim world, often facilitated by means of mystical poetry and aided by a tolerant attitude towards local religious practices as long as they were accompanied by the basic spiritual impulse of Islam in its Ṣūfī guise. Such attitudes within Sufism are often seen as key to empowering local culture through its association with the worldly powerful religion of Islam; furthermore, the empowerment of social groups, notably women, has often been facilitated by Sufism especially given the exclusion of females from many aspects of normative, formal Islam. As well, Sufism has served throughout its history as a source of general religious revival for Muslims, breathing life into institutions when they tended to reach the point of self-suffocation. While many of the orthodox have remained deeply suspicious of many Ṣūfī practices and, at certain points in history (most notably with Ibn Taymiyya, d. 1328), renewal of Islam has been sought by means of a purge of non-mainstream Ṣūfī influences, Sufism has remained alive and well, catering to those who picture life in terms of the "mystic quest."

9

The Shīʿa

by Andrew Rippin

Islam remained, for the most part, remarkably unified in its religious manifestations during the classical period. It is only the split between the legal and theological schools already discussed and what is known as the Shīʿa of ʿAlī that has produced any degree of cleavage and only the latter which has produced a true sense of an "alternative vision" of Islam. Of course, such nomenclature reflects only the statistical reality that there are (and have always been) more Muslims who, by virtue of their legal and theological school practices, would be defined as members of the *ahl al-sunna* than there are and have been Shīʿite Muslims. Few Muslims would approach these differences as a "choice" to be made on the individual level; rather, in the existence of the Shīʿa and the Sunnīs, we are confronted with the outcome of inner Muslim debates which resulted in different enunciations of Islam and in variant claims over the legitimate (and thus from each group's perspective, normative) nature of Islam in the world. It may be asserted, thus, that the Shīʿa represent an alternative vision of Islam in the sense that they do indeed hold to different tenets on some very significant points within Muslim theory, dogma and practice.

A number of treatises were written by various Muslim authors which detailed a tendency toward sectarianism within the faith, which would seem to contradict the preceding statement. Famous works by

Andrew Rippin, "The Shia," *Muslims*, pp. 121-135. Copyright © 2005 by Taylor & Francis Group LLC. Reprinted with permission.

al-Baghdādī (d. 1037) and al-Shahrastānī (d. 1153) provide lists of the seventy-three "groups" into which the Islamic community fractured. Shīʿī writers such al-Nawbakhtī (d. between 912 and 922) did similarly. These works, however, reflect less what would normally be considered true variation in expression of Islamic identity, and more a documentation of variations on specific points of Muslim theology. The books are a part of a tendency towards classification of all sorts of sundry matters, which was common in classical Islamic times. They also reflect an interpretation and justification of a tradition ascribed to Muḥammad which speaks of his community dividing into seventy-three (or seventy-one or seventy-two) parts. The important concluding statement of this tradition provides its significance: only one of these groups will actually be saved in the hereafter. It was the job of the authors of these texts, then, to enumerate the multiplicity of groups, while, at the same time, providing a clear definition of the group which would be saved: that group, of course, being identical with the author's own allegiances. In some instances, one suspects that, in these books, political rebels have been made into theologically based heretics, thus once again reinforcing the traditional picture of a well-defined "Islam" as existing from the very earliest times.

One of the groups detailed by these "heresiographers," a group divided into numerous sub-divisions according to their classificatory schemes, was the Shīʿa of ʿAlī. Once again, how many of these groups really existed as clearly identified units is questionable and certainly few of them actually survived for any substantial period of time. Several main groupings did become prominent, however.

The Shīʿī Understanding of its Origins

As was mentioned in the discussion of the rise of theology, the Shīʿa pictures its roots back in the days of ʿAlī ibn Abī Ṭālib and the early caliphs. The Shīʿa, or "party," of ʿAlī consisted of those who defended his right to rule the early community in the civil war with Muʿāwiya. They claimed, on the basis of statements of Muḥammad and by virtue of ʿAlī's relationship to Muḥammad (being his cousin and son-in-law), that he had a legitimate claim to rule. Much is made of traditions from Muḥammad, accepted by both the Sunnīs and the Shīʿa, in which ʿAlī is designated as having a special relationship to Muḥammad. Al-Tirmidhī (author of one of the canonical Sunnī books of *ḥadīth)* reports: "The prophet said in reply to someone who had complained about ʿAlī: 'What do you think of one who loves God and his prophet and who in turn is loved by God and his prophet?'" Also transmitted is: "The most loved of women to the prophet of God is Fāṭima [ʿAlī's wife, Muḥammad's daughter] and the most loved of men is ʿAlī." Such traditions, however, tend to fall into a general category of discussion of the "merits of the companions" found in all *ḥadīth* literature, in which each of the early followers of Islam is honoured. In this way, their authority as "founding fathers," and subsequently as transmitters of *ḥadīth*, was enhanced, and it seems likely that this was the function of such reports in the beginning. It was only when ʿAlī as an individual had his persona enhanced by the Shīʿa that such reports acquired a greater significance. It would appear, however, that this must have taken place to a great extent after traditions enhancing ʿAlī's position were already in circulation in the early community; ʿAlī's position within the family of Muḥammad is probably sufficient to explain why early sources would consider him an especially prominent person.

From the Shīʿī perspective, there was more at stake in the whole debate, however, for example concerning the nature of the rule of the early community. Was the leader to be one who combined religious with political authority? Or, with the death of Muḥammad, had religious authority passed to each individual believing Muslim? It remains a matter of debate among scholars as to whether ʿAlī received his earliest support because of a nascent belief in his religious significance (which thus suggested that he had authority in religious matters, an element which becomes fully developed among the later Shī'a as we shall see), or whether this was a purely political manoeuvre which later became coloured with religious significance.

However, as was the case for theology, these debates among scholars essentially accept the Muslim accounts at their face value and argue over the various aspects of them, rather than appreciating the ideological viewpoint from which such material was compiled. These debates still work from the standpoint of acceptance of the data provided about the early period and that data's impulse to demonstrate a legitimating and detailed view of Islamic origins.

The Shī'a and the Qur'ān

Most significant in the stance of the Shī'a, vis-à-vis their origins, is their general acceptance of the text of the Qur'ān virtually intact, in line with the Sunnīs. While there certainly have been tendencies within the Shī'ī community to debate the accuracy of the text as they have it and even a tendency to suggest modifications to the text—citing additions, omissions, changes and alterations to the version promulgated by 'Uthmān—this sort of activity has been relatively restrained. Much of the contemplated modification to the Quranic text is of such a nature as to take place within the legitimated (from the Sunnī perspective) range of "variant readings." An example of this is found in Qur'ān 3/110, "You are the best community which has been produced for humanity," such that rather than being read *umma*, "community," the Shī'a have read the word as *a'imma* and taken it as referring to the leaders of the Shī'ī community, the Imāms. What this may be taken to suggest is that the differentiation between the Sunnīs and the Shī'a arose only after the promulgation of an established text of the Qur'ān for all such arguments depend upon a text of the Qur'ān which is fixed and well known.

This view of the historical development of the Sunnīs and the Shī'a fits in with the account of the rise of Islam and the caliph's authority given earlier in this book. A fully variant text of the Qur'ān in the hands of the Shī'a would have indicated an earlier establishment of the Shī'a than the evidence concerning the rise of Islam as a whole might otherwise suggest. It might also have suggested a "fixed" text of the Qur'ān being established early on, to which the Shī'a responded with their own version. However, since the Shī'a do *not* have their own Qur'ān, both the late establishment of the Shī'a and the Sunnī community as two interpretations of Islam, and the establishment of a fully fixed text of the Qur'ān prior to that division, are historically possible.

The Shī'a and *Hadīth*

The other significant element in understanding the rise of the Shī'a is the observation that the Shī'a have a distinct body of *hadīth* material, much of it traced back to or through the early leaders of the Shī'ī community or, at the very least, containing variants compared to the Sunnī community's versions. In its written form, this material started to emerge during the ninth century. Given the function of the *hadīth* in Islam in general, the existence of a separate body of material indicates that the central matter of dispute causing the separation of the Sunnī community and the Shī'a was one of ultimate authority in the community as a whole and within each group separately. In the early unified community, the caliph appears to have had complete authority, as was discussed earlier in Chapter 4. With the rise of the learned classes in the eighth century, the disputes over authority became more pronounced. The Sunnī community emerged with its trust placed in fixed written sources of authority, leaving what became the Shīʿī group continuing to hold to authority vested in an individual.

The Authority of the Shīʿī Imām

This understanding of the development of authority makes sense of what is the most prominent and distinct element in the Shīʿa, and that is the person of the Imām. Designated by Muḥammad, ʿAlī was the first Imām for the Shīʿa; this was seen as the designation of a spiritual position, not one of temporal power, and thus the inability of the Imāms in later times to seize power within the community was of no particular concern to their followers. The function of the Imām was to guide his followers by explaining and clarifying the divine law, as well as to direct those believers in the inner spiritual path of Islam. This he was able to do because of his close connection to God, facilitated by *ilhām,* "inspiration" (as distinct from *waḥy,* "revelation," which is the mode through which scripture is produced), and the knowledge passed on to him by the one who designated him. God's mercy and justice indicate that there can never be a time when the world is without an Imām, for, if that were so, people would have no guidance and there would be no proof available of God's beneficence towards His creation. The Imām is thus termed the *ḥujja,* "proof," and *hādī,* "guide." The people who were to be Imāms were designated by God from the beginning of creation, and were even viewed as pre-existent in the form of primordial light according to some mystically flavoured interpretations. They are, as a consequence of these ideas, seen as sinless and the best of all creation. The actual existence of an Imām is to be taken as part of God's beneficence towards humanity, for he facilitates the salvation of God's creation by providing a sure guide in the world and a certain answer to issues of dispute.

The most prominent branch of the Shīʿa, known as the "Twelvers" (in Arabic *Ithnā ʿashariyya*) or more generically as the Imāmīs, identifies a chain of twelve men through whom the line of authority passed in the formative centuries of Islam. These people were designated by their predecessors and their birth was generally pictured as accompanied by various miraculous signs, confirming this designation. That the clear delineation of this line was, up to a certain point, *ex post facto* would appear likely and is even evidenced by mid-tenth century Shīʿī sources who speak of people in their community being unsure of the identity of the Imām. It will only have been when the need for authority emerged within the community that the tracing back of a chain of authority (as in the *isnād* of a *ḥadīth*) would have actually been necessary. The established line of the twelve Imāms is as follows:

ʿAlī ibn abī Ṭālib, d. 661

Ḥasan, his son, d. 669

Ḥusayn, ʿAlī's second son, d. 680

Zayn al-ʿĀbidīn, his son, d. 712 or 713

Muḥammad al-Bāqir, his son, d. 735

Jaʿfar al-Ṣādiq, his son, d. 765

Mūsā al-Kāẓim, his son, d. 799

ʿAlī al-Riḍā, his son, d. 818

Muḥammad al-Taqī al-Jawād, his son, d. 835

ʿAlī al-Hādī, his son, d. 868

Ḥasan al-ʿAskarī, his son, d. 873 or 874

Muḥammad al-Mahdī, his son, born 868

The Formation of the Shīʿa

Jaʿfar al-Ṣādiq appears to have been the pivotal figure through whom the Shīʿa actually came into existence as a religious movement. Up to that point, the best that one may suppose is that rival groups, whose primary focus was in the political arena, existed in the community; some of these groups saw their right to rule traced back to ʿAlī. As with the emergence of the whole system of Islam itself, the particular elements manifested in the Shīʿa took time to evolve, even though the sources themselves wish to project the origins back to the earliest period. The rise of the ʿAbbāsid caliphate, making its appeal to persons in sympathy with the rights of ʿAlī, would coincide with the dates of Jaʿfar al-Ṣādiq. It is with the sixth Imām and his designated successor, Mūsā al-Kāẓim, that the incipient notions of the Imamate would appear to have originated, based on the information provided by various heresiographical works and Shīʿī tradition itself, which sees Jaʿfar as the formative spokesman. One crucial element here is the establishment of a procedure for the designation of the Imām, rather than that person being determined by a process of battle; the Shīʿī platform can then defend a quietist attitude despite a lineage which would suggest a need to usurp rule in the world; this also had the effect of cutting off a tendency towards the proliferation of rival claimants to the position of Imām. Another crucial element was the Imām's receipt of esoteric knowledge passed on from the previous Imām. Regardless of these early elements, it is only in the time of the twelfth Imām that we actually have any Shīʿī sources which provide us with detailed information on the Shīʿa and their beliefs, and it is clear that it is in the post-twelfth Imām period that the Shīʿa as we know it today actually came into being.

The Occultation of the Last Imām

The twelfth Imām is said to have disappeared and to have entered into his "lesser occultation," being hidden from the view of the world. He designated a series of four persons (in parallel to the first four caliphs perhaps) to whom he communicated his commands; this situation lasted from 874 until 941. He then entered into his "greater occultation" in which condition he no longer communicates with the world. This notion of occultation is a necessary consequence of the line of Imāms ending at a particular point in history. If humanity cannot be without an Imām and the line of Imāms has ended, then the last Imām cannot be dead but must be alive; otherwise, a substitute for him must exist. Known as the *ghayba*, the occultation will last until God determines its end. The return of the twelfth Imām in the role of the messianic Mahdī is awaited; this will occur shortly before the day of judgement. At that time, he will be manifested on earth and will lead the righteous into battle against the forces of evil. Finally, good will triumph over evil, and the Imām will subsequently rule over the world in a period of peace.

The notion that there should be twelve Imāms and that the twelfth should permanently "disappear" took some time to solidify within the Shīʿa. Certainly, authors writing at the time of the twelfth Imām appear to have expected the line to continue beyond him. Although they admitted that at the time he was "hiding," he was clearly expected to show himself once again. Indeed, the presence of the Imām as a "proof" and a "guidance" was deemed essential and was the major element in polemic against the Sunnī schools which the Shīʿa felt were adrift with no guidance. It would appear to be the case, however, that other Shīʿī groups had already developed the notions of a limited chain of Imāms and of the last one "disappearing." All that was really happening, then, was that the Imāmī group was employing already circulating ideas as an explanation of events taking place in their "twelver-Shīʿī" line. By the time of the Shīʿī writer al-Kulaynī (d. *c*.941), the idea of there being a line of twelve Imāms was established, although, for the rest of the century, authors still found it necessary to compose works which would explain and defend this notion of an occulted Imām. Arguments in favour of there being a line of only twelve Imāms were found in Quranic references to the number twelve (e.g. twelve months in the year, Qurʾān 9/36) and in Shīʿī and Sunnī traditions which talk of Muḥammad naming twelve successors, which in Sunnī sources are found in texts written in a period before the occultation of the twelfth Imām and perhaps reflect notions regarding "twelve" as a number symbolic of restoration, fulfilment and authority, as in the twelve tribes of Israel and the twelve disciples of Jesus.

There seem to be political reasons lying behind the idea of the "disappearance" of the twelfth Imām which account for it becoming a successful doctrine in Shīʿī circles. As long as the Imām was physically present in the world, he represented a threat, albeit ineffectual, to the ruling powers. The Shīʿa found themselves virtually always persecuted under the rule of the ʿAbbāsids. Removing the worldly reality of the Imām, after enduring some one hundred years of ʿAbbāsid rule, was a way of securing a continued existence for the group, but also may be linked to a growing sense of material prosperity among certain groups of Shīʿīs which they were unwilling to forego. Cooperation with the ruling powers was far easier without the Imām present, but believing in his "occultation" meant that one's loyalty to him did not have to diminish; cooperation with the rulers brought power as well as a more comfortable existence, something which took place under the pro-Shīʿī Buwayhids and clearly separated political and religious dimensions of existence. The Shīʿī doctrine of *taqiyya* ("religious dissimulation"), by which it was considered acceptable to conceal one's true allegiance in the face of adversity, fitted in with this situation and attitude. It is likely also that, as with Sunnī Islam, a rise in the status and power of the ʿulamāʾ, "the learned or scholarly classes," put pressure on the Imām whose actual presence proved inconvenient for the learned classes and their expectations and aspirations. As well, for all practical purposes, by the time of the twelfth Imām, the ʿulamāʾ had taken over positions of effective authority anyway, the Imām himself generally being kept out of contact with the vast majority of his followers; it was dangerous for the Imām to be in public view, due to his political pretensions. The authority of the learned classes after the *ghayba* resided in the basis of their knowledge of the traditions transmitted by the Imāms. Thus the emergence of the books of *ḥadīth* at approximately the time of the lesser occultation is to be expected.

Shīʿī Theology

Much of developed Shīʿī theology follows that of the Muʿtazila, discussed earlier in Chapter 5, with a few crucial differences. It is significant to note that, in a sense, the Shīʿa represents a re-emergence of Muʿtazilī thought which appears to have lost much of its popular appeal in the Sunnī world in the preceding century or so. The significance and meaning of the Imamate were the major factors which separated the Muʿtazila and the Shīʿa. Further significant differences are really a consequence of this stance. One of the Imām's functions is to intercede on behalf of his followers in the hereafter; this function runs counter to the Muʿtazilī insistence on "the punishment and the threat" as applying to all persons, consistent with their perception of the justice of God. Likewise, for the Shīʿa, there can be no "intermediate position," that of the hypocrite, applicable to those who appear to sin in their actions but declare their belief; those who declare their allegiance to the Imām are quite clearly members of the community and must be accepted as such. Other than these elements, the theological doctrines are familiar: belief in divine unity and justice, in the role of prophethood and the bringing of the law by sinless prophets, and in the resurrection at the end of time.

The Shīʿa did not always hold this theological position, however; the debates in the post-*ghayba* period clearly show an evolution from a tradition-based system to a more fully rationalistic one. Prior to that, however, in the very early period, the information regarding the situation is even less clear and provides at least some evidence of an even greater measure of shift in theological doctrine. However, the fact of the matter remains that there are no sources which can be trusted to be fully reliable, to give us information on the doctrinal stance of the Shīʿa prior to the tenth century. Some scholars have made the suggestion that any sources internal to the group itself suffered destruction at the hands of the later Shīʿa who found the early doctrines unacceptable. The degree to which these early doctrines were contrary to later ones is suggested, perhaps, by Sunnī sources, specifically al-Khayyāṭ (writing around 882) and al-Ashʿarī (writing around 912). The doctrines of these early groups, dubbed the *ghulāt*, "the exaggerators," included notions of the transmigration of souls, an anthropomorphic conception of God, God's willing of the evil deeds of humanity, and the possibility of alteration in God's will. At one point, it is also held that some believed in the absolute divine nature of the Imām, although the later Sunnī sources perhaps reflect the lessening of this doctrine for they no longer make that accusation. The trouble here is that the Sunnī sources are clearly polemical in tone and approach, and the items of doctrine with which the *ghulāt* are associated are precisely those items which bring about the greatest reprobation from the Sunnī schools; to represent these doctrines as being held by the largest Shīʿī school at the time may well be a case of attempting to mislead deliberately.

Ibn Babawayh

By the tenth century, when the Buwayhid dynasty took over in Baghdad and made the ʿAbbāsid caliph simply a tributary to the ruler, the Shīʿa had become a political force and a clearer picture of its theological stance starts to emerge. Ibn Babawayh (d. 991) appears to have been one of the leading figures in this movement. He wrote against the notion of anthropomorphism—which certainly suggests that some Shīʿīs still held to such doctrines—and, by the end of his life, also seemed convinced that humanity has a degree of free will under God's law:

> Our belief concerning human actions is that they are created … , in the sense that Allah possesses foreknowledge … , and not in the sense that Allah compels mankind to act in a particular manner by creating a certain disposition. … And the meaning of this is that Allah has never ceased to be aware of the potentialities … of human beings.

At an earlier stage of his life, however, Ibn Babawayh held to a firmer predestinarian position. What marks all of his works is a reliance on tradition rather than reason and a total rejection of the stance of *kalām* ("The partisans of the *kalām* will perish and the Muslims will be saved"); this is similar to the stance of al-Ashʿarī in the Sunnī world who was reacting to the full force of Muʿtazilī doctrine. Ibn Babawayh, on the other hand, came before the major impact of Muʿtazilī thought among the Shīʿa, although some tendency in the direction of rationalism is to be noted in writers from earlier in the tenth century.

Later Theologians

Muʿtazilī theology proper came into the Shīʿa through the work of al-Shaykh al-Mufīd (d. 1022), al-Sharīf al-Murtaḍā (d. 1044) and al-Ṭūsī (d. 1067). While the basis for the particulars of the Muʿtazilī position was already firmly established in the Shīʿa (and, some would say, was there since the time of Jaʿfar al-Ṣādiq), it is these authors who emphasized the use of reason in support of the doctrine, seeing the need to defend the religion on that basis. Al-Shaykh al-Mufīd argues for a less radical type of Muʿtazilī stance than some of the later authors; he avoids saying that people are the actual "creators" of their own acts and that the Qurʾān is created. Rather, he says that the Qurʾān "originated in time" and acts are "produced" or "made." God's actions in the world are always in the best interests of humanity (this being provided as an explanation of evil in the world). Overall, al-Shaykh al-Mufīd attempted to avoid going beyond what he sees as the limits of Quranic phraseology in enunciating his theology.

With the later authors, the position became more radical, with reason becoming the basis of all doctrine rather than being the tool by which authoritative doctrine could be defended and enhanced, as it was for al-Shaykh al-Mufīd. Al-Murtaḍā may best be thought of as the Shīʿī al-Ashʿarī in the sense that his writings became the basis for all later Shīʿī exposition of theology, being the virtually unquestioned source.

Why the Shīʿa adopted this rationalist position in theology would appear to be connected to the need for authority. While the Imām was in the world, the source of authority for the Shīʿī community was clear: it was the Imām; being an authoritative source was the very purpose of his presence in the world. The Sunnīs were, in the Shīʿī view, reduced to mere conjecture on all elements of their religion. With the *ghayba* of the twelfth Imām, authority first came through the series of four representatives who were able to put questions to the Imām and bring back answers. With the greater occultation, however, this could no longer happen, although the appearance of the Imām to a worthy individual, either in reality or in a dream, was at least held to be possible. In the absence of the Imām, then, authority was in the hands of the learned classes. But this was no better than the Sunnī position, which the Shīʿa had criticized for having no sound basis. Muʿtazilī theology provided a way around this problem, by suggesting that reason alone could provide the certitude which is required. Deduction based on reason, therefore, rather than tradition as used by the Sunnīs, was the ideal replacement for the Imām, whose rulings would only conform to the laws of reason anyway. As the line of Shīʿī thought developed, al-Murtaḍā argued that reason could prove the necessity of the existence of the Imām in the first place, providing the proof for the key element of Shīʿī thought that the Muʿtazila lacked. He argued that the office of the Imām was necessary and that

> [t]he way to prove its necessity is reason, contrary to the doctrine of the Muʿtazilites and their like. It is necessary only for bringing those who are under moral obligation close to what is for their interests and for keeping them far from what is harmful.

Shīʿī Legal Thought and Practice

In the legal field, a late development is quite clear also, as in theology. The tenth-century work by al-Kulaynī, *al-Kāfī fī ʿIlm al-Dīn* ("The Sufficient in the Knowledge of Religion"), marks a pivotal point in the emergence of defined Shīʿī law. This work gathers together traditions, either from the Imāms or from Muḥammad and transmitted through the Imāms, which serve as the basis for all discussions (both legal and theological) in this period. The writing of the book is significant and contains, by its very composition, a polemical element. The book clearly wants to argue that the Imām in the world is no more. No longer can that source of authority be utilized, and the Shīʿa, like the Sunnīs, must turn to written sources to substantiate their position. The writing of a work such as al-Kulaynī's marks a stage in the emergence of the Shīʿa in which the learned classes, who had control of the sources, were starting to assert their authority; in such a way, it was ensured that any potential claimants to the position of the Imām were effectively silenced. Al-Kulaynī's book is one of four, the others written by Ibn Babawayh and al-Ṭūsī (the latter having two to his credit), which are considered the counterparts to the six authoritative collections of *ḥadīth* in the Sunnī world.

Without the Imām, or his representatives, in the world, the specific duties assigned to him were said to be lapsed. These included leading the holy war (*jihād*), division of the booty of war, leading the Friday prayer, putting juridical decisions into effect, imposing legal penalties, and receiving the religious taxes. The absence of the Imām left the community leaderless, and it fell to al-Ṭūsī in the eleventh century to enunciate a theory of juridical authority being in the hands of those knowledgeable in jurisprudence, the *fuqahāʾ*. Even then, the role of the jurists was limited and it took several centuries and a number of other theorists to develop a more encompassing theory; it was only in the sixteenth century that the *fuqahāʾ* took over all the duties of the occulted Imām, with the exception of offensive *jihād* which, it was determined, could only be undertaken by the Imām himself.

The absoluteness of this delegation of the authority of the Imām was tempered by the theological speculation over the return of the twelfth Imām. This expected return, though, was of little practical concern to the jurists whose role was to create a legal system with no reference to a living Imām, only to one who existed theologically.

The actual theoretical development of the principles of Shīʿī jurisprudence was, for the most part, late in being written (fourteenth to sixteenth centuries), at least in comparison with the much earlier Sunnī development. To some extent, therefore, the Shīʿa depended upon the principles already enunciated within Sunnī thought in order to develop the legal basis of their society; the differences between the two are, as a result, quite slight. The Shīʿa, in this view, are little more than another legal school, parallel to the four major Sunnī schools. Minor differences occur in the prayer ritual and the fast of Ramaḍān, but these are precisely of a nature which would be seen as a variation between schools of law. Friday noon prayer is not as important to the Shīʿa because of the absence of the Imām who is supposed to lead that prayer, although this became a problem of some seriousness in juridical discussions. Various practices are enjoined, such as visiting the tombs of the Imāms, and these visits are conducted with extensive rituals on a par with those of the *ḥajj*.

There are, of course, some significant differences between Sunnī and Shīʿī practices. The phenomenon of "temporary marriage," *mutʿa*, considered to be referred to in Qurʾān 4/24, is specifically forbidden in the Sunnī world, where any limit put on the length of a marriage makes a marriage contract null and void. Divorce and inheritance laws also vary. Most striking is a different form of the *shahāda* employed at some points in Shīʿī history. The phrase, "I testify that ʿAlī is the *walī* ['friend'] of God" is added to the two-part Sunnī witness to faith; this is, however, a fairly late addition, mention of it not being made in the earliest texts of Shīʿī law other than that of Ibn Babawayh, who condemns its usage. The sixteenth century saw arguments in favour of its employment, urged probably by the political aims of the rulers at that time, the Safavids, who instituted the Shīʿī position as the state religion of Iran in 1501. The argument for the basis of the statement as opposed to its ritual employment, however, is to be found quite early in Shīʿī thought, for example in al-Kulaynī who argues that the belief in the *wilāya* of ʿAlī is a fundamental tenet of the Shīʿa, and that the belief simply in "There is no god but God and Muḥammad is the messenger of God" is not sufficient to ensure salvation; clearly, the third element of the testimony is needed in the belief of the individual, even if in this early period it was not actually part of the ritual repetition of the *shahāda*.

Additionally, Ibn Babawayh reports the following tradition about Fāṭima bint Asad, the mother of ʿAlī. Muḥammad is quoted as saying that immediately after her death:

> She was asked about her Lord, and she said, "My Lord is Allāh". And she was asked about her Prophet and she replied, "Muḥammad". And she was asked about her Imām and *walī* and she faltered and paused. And I said to her, "Thy son, thy son". So she said, "My Imām is my son". Thereupon they [the two questioning angels who appear to everyone after death] departed from her and said, "We have no power over you … ".

Undoubtedly, it was the pressure of Sunnī condemnation which did not allow this statement to enter the Shīʿī *shahāda* from the very beginning and it was only after many centuries that it was actually approved under more propitious political circumstances.

A prominent celebration which is not found in the Sunnī world revolves around the commemoration of the death of Ḥusayn, the son of ʿAlī. Culminating on the tenth day of the first month of the year, Muḥarram, the day of ʿAshurāʾ, it observes the day of the death of Ḥusayn and his followers which took place at the hands of the forces of the Umayyad ruler Yazīd. This occurred in the year 680. Martyrdom to the cause of the party of ʿAlī became the operative motif in understanding Ḥusayn's death and the celebration of this became the central event of the Shīʿī religious calendar. Visitation of sacred places, especially the tomb of Ḥusayn in Karbala, play an important role in the celebrations on this day. Generally, these ritual differences between the Shīʿa and the Sunnīs have gained symbolic value for the Shīʿa in terms of providing a distinct (and, implicitly, correct) religious identity, especially in times of political antagonism with the Sunnī world.

Variants of the Shīʿa

Given that a fundamental notion among the Shīʿa was the necessity of the identification of an Imām in each generation, it is hardly surprising that rival claimants appeared at various points in history. We thus see the emergence of several branches within the Shīʿa, each of which differed over the line of descent of authority at a certain historical moment. The Ismāʿīlīs, Zaydīs and Druze (Durūz in Arabic) are three such prominent groups. Some of these splits account for their origins in terms of differences over political strategy. The Zaydīs, for example, picture their origins in armed revolt against the Umayyad rulers. They were formed as a group in support of Zayd ibn ʿAlī, a grandson of Ḥusayn ibn ʿAlī, who was defeated and killed in 740. While in certain situations these small offshoots of the Shīʿa have proven politically volatile, throughout a good portion of history they have been politically quiescent, looking forward to the end of time and the return of the Mahdī. This simply goes along with the doctrine of the occultation of the Imām when faced with the political realities of the historical situation. The Ismāʿīlīs are particularly noted for their "inner" interpretations of much of Muslim practice, looking to make the point that the law was to benefit the soul as well as the body. For them, the person of the Imām is a key link to God who provides the authoritative interpretation of all Islamic matters.

The central issue which separates all of the Shīʿa of the Sunnīs, then, is this issue of the Imām and his role. The answer to this was not, for the Shīʿa, straightforward because of issues related to identifying the person of the Imām and dealing with his absence (in those branches of the Shīʿa which held to that idea). As is always the case, historical contexts affected the way in which this doctrine evolved but it is clear that the fundamental disagreement between Muslims over the nature of community leadership had a long-lasting and profound effect upon the unity of the *umma*.

Part II

Islam in the Contemporary Arab World

10

The Making of the Modern Middle East

by Dona Stewart

T he origins of the modern Middle East lay not only in the aftermath of the Ottoman Empire, whose territories were carved up and placed under European control, but in the growth of new ideas that emerged prior to World War I. Particularly important was the idea of nationalism and a desire for independence among local inhabitants in the region. At the same time European interests in the Middle East, economic and political, deepened. Indeed, though the Ottoman Empire spanned over 500 years, by the seventeenth century it was a decidedly different empire, in its form and function, from the one led by Suleyman that had challenged European control of Vienna.

The Transformation of the Ottoman Empire

The 'decline' of the Ottoman Empire, once an accepted premise by scholars, is now a disputed issue. Instead, the reasons for Ottoman loss of dominance vis-à-vis Europe, and the internal challenges this created, must be understood. In the seventeenth century, the Ottoman Empire's territorial expansion was halted by growing European military strength. The Ottomans lost control of Hungary through conflict with the Hapsburgs and lost Black Sea territories to the Russians. At the same time, they had to guard their eastern flank against Safavid expansion.

Dona Stewart, "The Making of the Modern Middle East," *The Middle East Today*, pp. 86–101. Copyright © 2009 by Taylor & Francis Group LLC. Reprinted with permission.

The discovery of the New World profoundly changed the global economy and system of trade, to the detriment of the Ottomans. New sea-based trade routes lessened the significance of the overland routes under Ottoman control. The discovery of vast amounts of silver in the New World also created inflationary pressures, reducing the value of the imperial treasury. Moreover, an industrializing and expansionist Europe established colonies overseas to secure sources of raw materials and markets for their finished products. In this way Europe accumulated vast amounts of capital. Meanwhile, demand for goods manufactured by the Ottomans declined, and revenues shrank. The Ottoman Empire also became a supplier of raw materials to Europe, and a market for its products. The empire took numerous loans from European institutions and became deeply indebted, rendering it unable to support key institutions, including the military.

To counter its loss of competitiveness, the empire entered into a series of reforms and modernization policies beginning in the mid-nineteenth century. The reforms, known as the *Tanzimat* ('reorganization'), were intended both to modernize and to Westernize the empire. The establishment of Ottoman embassies in London, Paris, Berlin and Vienna under Sultan Selim III (1789–1806), though short-lived, enabled the transmission of European ideas to the Ottoman elite that would shape the country's future. Reforms included modernization of the military, overhaul of the banking system, the creation of universities, and the incorporation of French law into the empire's legal code. In addition, factories were built to replace production by craftsmen. The result of these reforms was to create 'institutional dualism', in which traditional institutions continued to exist alongside new, modern ones (Cleveland 2004). For example, Islamic schools co-existed alongside those with 'modern', Western-based curricula. This dualism broadened an already existing divide between the poor, who had little access to any institutions, and elite populations. The dualism also reinforced clashes within the upper class over the desired shape and form of Ottoman society, either as one influenced heavily by institutions and practices based heavily on religion and tradition, or as one based on modernization heavily influenced by emulation of Western practices.

Perhaps the most significant outcome of the reforms was the introduction of a constitution in 1876, under Sultan Abdul Hamid II, which introduced an elected chamber of deputies and a senate, appointed by the sultan. Despite creating institutions to expand participation in governance, the constitution did little to limit the powers of the sultan. By 1878, Abdul Hamid II had disbanded the chamber of deputies and ruled without limit.

During his harsh reign, the empire brutally attacked Armenian Christians seeking an independent state within Ottoman territory and crushed an uprising against the Ottomans on the island of Crete, prompting Greece to declare war. With Western intervention, Crete gained its autonomy. The empire also lost control of the Balkans. By the end of Abdul Hamid II's thirty-year reign, the Ottoman territories were much less diverse. The concept of 'Ottomanism', and the embrace of all religions within the empire, was replaced with pan-Islam, and the idea of the empire as guardian of Islam.

However, the European-inspired idea of parliamentary limits on the monarchy was not forgotten, and Abdul Hamid II's actions helped fuel a growing dissident movement among the new middle-class elite. These dissenters, known collectively as the Young Turks, promoted the principles of secular society and constitutionalism. Often, they themselves held government positions, from which they challenged traditional Ottoman rule. They were active in a secret political movement, led by students in the military, called the Committee of Union and Progress that succeeded in restoring the constitution in 1908 and would be pivotal in the creation of modern Turkey after World War I.

This period also witnessed an overall decentralization of power within the empire as power was ceded to local authorities. Under Muhammad Ali (1769–1849), then governor of the Ottoman province, Egypt launched an extensive modernization program. Ali's ultimate goal was to achieve independence from the Ottomans and establish his own dynasty. Extensive military and commercial reforms were designed to modernize Egypt's economic, military, educational and administrative systems. Higher education was modeled after European standards; new institutions were created for the study of medicine, engineering and the sciences. From the graduates of these institutions a cadre of civil servants took over administration of the state, using Arabic rather than Ottoman Turkish. Close commercial and trade ties were formed with European states, while European military technology, training methods and practices were adopted. Egypt developed an industrial sector, producing items ranging from guns to textiles while developing commercial agriculture based on cotton cultivation. Muhammad Ali also removed his greatest rival for power, the Mamluks, massacring them after a banquet at his citadel. Muhammad Ali revolted against the Ottomans, and after armed conflict gained recognition as the hereditary ruler of Egypt—another territorial loss for the empire.

His successor, Ismail Pasha (1863–9), continued Egypt's modernization program, though many of his schemes sank the country deep into debt. Ismail Pasha was deeply enamored of Western culture and institutions. He remade Cairo, draining marshland near the Nile to create new districts laid out in European form. A grand boulevard was cut from the historic Islamic city to connect this new district. Here, European-style villas were created, along with parks lit by 500 gas lights. Streets were laid out in a radial pattern, mimicking Hausmann's plans for Paris, and an opera house built. Ismail Pasha is famously quoted as saying 'My country is no longer in Africa … it is now in Europe!' (Vatikiotis 1991: 73).

European Penetration of the Middle East

By the seventeenth century, the European commercial and political presence had increased significantly in the Middle East. They had forced the Ottomans to sign a series of agreements, known as the Capitulations, exempting Europeans from Ottoman taxes and granting them preferential tariff rates. To fund their modernization plans, the Ottomans borrowed extensively from Europe. Over a twenty-year period beginning in 1854, they borrowed approximately 180 million English pounds (Owen and Pamuk 1999). By 1876 the empire was failing to make payments, and lost its financial independence when an external board of creditors was created to assure repayment of European debt.

Though brief, France's occupation of Egypt (1798–1801), touched off by the Napoleonic expedition to Egypt, heralded a new era of European political and military control. Few parts of the Middle East were unaffected by European political rivalry. Having already established control over much of India by the 1860s, Britain sought to secure the routes to this jewel of their empire. With Aden (1839) under its control, Britain sought alliances along the Persian Gulf, signing treaties with Bahrain (1880), Muscat (1891), the Trucial Coast (1892) and Kuwait (1899). In 1882, Britain occupied Egypt, in an effort to safeguard the Suez Canal and thwart French ambitions to reclaim control of the country.

France established an empire in North Africa, establishing control first over Algiers (1830), Tunisia (1881) and Morocco (1912). Italy belatedly entered the colonial fray, acquiring the Ottoman province of Tripoli in 1911. Though the end of World War I marks the imposition of a formal system of European control, under the League of Nations mandate system, European control was already well established in the region. Indeed, the Ottoman Empire was itself deeply embroiled in a growing European rivalry which pitted Britain and France against Germany. Ottoman involvement in this rivalry ultimately brought about its downfall.

World War I and the End of the Ottoman Empire

World War I erupted in Europe in June 1914 following the Austrian invasion of Serbia in response to the assassination of Archduke Ferdinand in Sarajevo. This invasion activated a system of military alliances between the European countries, so that by August most of Europe had entered the war.

The Ottomans had a secret alliance with the Germans, as a means to counter Russian interests in Ottoman territories, and entered the war on the side of the Central Powers, composed of Austria-Hungary, Germany and Italy. They fought against the Alliance of the Triple Entente composed of Britain, France and Russia and referred to as the Allies.

Box 10.1
T. E. Lawrence and the Arab Revolt

Perhaps no figure in modern Middle Eastern history is more legendary than Thomas Edward Lawrence (1888–1935), known as 'Lawrence of Arabia'. An Arabic-speaker who often dressed in robes, Lawrence was a passionate advocate for Arab independence.

As a university student, Lawrence spent much time in the Middle East and worked on numerous archaeological sites after graduation. With the outbreak of World War I, Lawrence enlisted and was posted to British Military Intelligence in Cairo, Egypt.

With his linguistic skills, and his experience in the region, Lawrence was assigned to make contact with Arab nationalists and gain their assistance in fighting the Ottoman Turks. Lawrence worked closely with Emir Feisal (later king of Iraq), the son of Sharif Hussein of Mecca to coordinate Arab military attacks. These attacks, known as the Arab Revolt, significantly undermined the Ottoman ability to advance on British forces and hold territory.

The Arab forces kept a large number of Ottoman troops tied down in Medina, to keep them from fighting the British in Palestine. They also seized the strategic port of Aqaba, opening a supply line for deeper British advanced into Syria. Finally, Arab forces repeatedly attacked the Hejaz railway, a key communications and supply channel for Ottoman forces.

Following the war, Lawrence became a strong advocate for Arab self-determination and for fulfillment of the promises made to them during wartime. With Feisal, he appeared at the Paris Peace Conference in 1919 to promote this cause. He was frustrated and bitterly disappointed with the conference's outcome, which established the League of Nations mandates.

Lawrence continued his military career in the Royal Air Force, but used a new name as a highly popular documentary about his role in the Arab Revolt raised his public profile. He also devoted himself to writing. His book *The Seven Pillars of Wisdom* is a rich and detailed account of the Arab Revolt and his role in it.

Lawrence's tragic death, at the age of 46, contributed to the legend surrounding him. His death occurred as he swerved his motorcycle to avoid hitting two young cyclists.

The Middle East was an epicenter of military activity during World War I. The Ottomans fought the Russians on their eastern flank. Meanwhile, the Allies attempted to seize Istanbul. The ensuing battle at Gallipoli exacted heavy casualties among the Allies, who were eventually forced to withdraw. At Gallipoli a young Ottoman colonel, Mustafa Kemal, displayed strong military leadership; later his leadership would define modern Turkey. The Allies were more successful in Mesopotamia, conquering Baghdad and seizing southern Iraq in order to defend Iranian oil fields and protect the passages to India.

On their western flank, Ottoman forces attacked the British based in Egypt and Palestine, and attempted to seize the strategically important Suez Canal. The British war effort was aided by local Arab guerrilla forces who sought the opportunity to throw off Turkish rule. Led by the legendary T. E. Lawrence and Feisal, the son of Sharif Hussein of Mecca, the informal forces of the Arab Revolt proved effective against the sultan's armies. The Arab irregular forces disrupted the Ottoman supply lines, rendering the railroad unusable and seizing the key port of Aqaba. In October 1918, they captured Damascus.

The involvement of Arab forces was the result of an alliance between the British and Sharif Hussein bin Ali, the emir of Mecca and guardian of the holy cities of Mecca and Medina. This position was a key post within the Ottoman Empire; from it Hussein, a direct descendant of the Prophet Muhammad, was able to build a large network of tribal alliances. In exchange for his support against the Ottomans, Hussein sought the creation of an independent Arab state composed of the Arabian peninsula, Greater Syria (Lebanon and Palestine) and the provinces of Iraq. In a series of ten letters the British High Commissioner in Egypt, Sir Henry McMahon, while excluding the territories of Syria and Iraq, agreed that 'Great Britain is prepared to recognize and uphold the independence of the Arabs in all the regions lying within the frontiers proposed by the Sharif of Mecca' (Cleveland 2004: 160).

Though the Arabs anticipated the creation of an independent Arab state following Ottoman defeat, this goal was in direct conflict with a secret agreement between the British and the French, signed in 1916, to divide Ottoman territories between them. Under the Sykes-Picot Agreement, Britain would control a zone in the southern portion of Mesopotamia (Iraq) and an area stretching from Gaza to Kirkuk. The French area of control included the Syrian coast and interior, and portions of southeastern Turkey and northern Iraq. Palestine was to be under international administration (Map 10.1). The document became public in 1917, following the Bolshevik revolution in Russia, to the embarrassment of the British and the French.

The defeat of the Central Powers resulted in the Ottoman Empire's unconditional surrender, on October 31, 1918, ending over 400 years of continuous rule by the sultanate.

Drawing the New Map of the Middle East

The new borders of the Middle East were drawn largely in Paris, where world leaders, including US president Woodrow Wilson, British prime minister David Lloyd George and French foreign minister Georges Clemenceau, met to divide the territories of the defeated German, Austria-Hungarian and Ottoman empires. The Paris Peace Conference of 1919, held at Versailles, was a massive undertaking meant to resolve competing claims on the territories that belonged to the defeated. Deliberations lasted six months; and, though World War II would cause further border modifications, the postwar settlement left a lasting imprint. This is particularly true in the Middle East, where vast Ottoman territories were divided, laying the foundation for the modern state system.

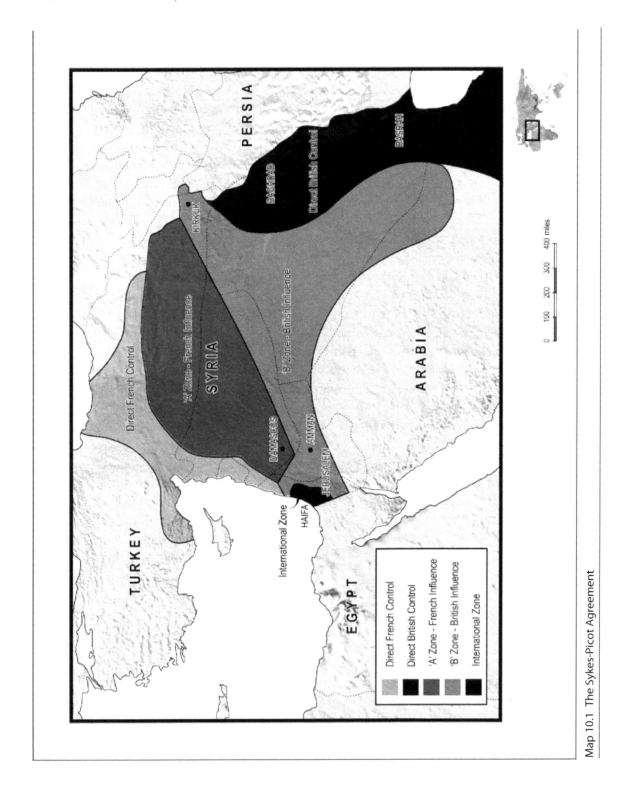

Map 10.1 The Sykes-Picot Agreement

Emerging Nationalism

Both Britain and France held pre-existing interests in the former Ottoman territories, as indicated in the Sykes-Picot Agreement. The French had longstanding connections to Syria and the Levantine coast, with its Maronite population. Britain sought to turn oil-rich Mesopotamia into a single state, including the key cities of Baghdad, Basra and Mosul. Britain also sought Palestine, which was to be a homeland for the Jewish people. In 1917, British foreign secretary Arthur Balfour had written to Lord Walter Rothschild, a leader of Britain's Jewish community, informing him of Britain's support for a Jewish 'national home' in Palestine. The Balfour Declaration further stipulated that it be 'clearly understood that nothing shall be done which may prejudice the civil and religious rights of existing non-Jewish communities in Palestine'. This position was, of course, in direct conflict with the promises made to Sharif Hussein.

Box 10.2

The League of Nations Mandate System

The League of Nations was established in the aftermath of World War I, in part to set up a framework through which conflicts could be resolved through a system of collective security and negotiation rather than by warfare.

The mandates system was designed for the administration of the territories held by the Ottoman Empire and Imperial Germany prior to their defeat in the war. The mandates were administered by some of the Great Powers, namely Britain and France, involved in the war. As the mandatory power was required to answer to the League of Nations, and submit reports on the mandate territory's progress, the mandates were not officially colonies, though in many ways they functioned as such.

All of the mandates in the Middle East were Class A Mandates. These territories were 'provisionally recognized as independent nations' and were expected to reach independence with the advice and assistance of the mandatory power. The United Kingdom was given the mandates for Iraq, Palestine and Transjordan; France had control over Lebanon and Syria. In truth the preparations made for independence, both political and economic, often tended to favor the mandatory power rather than lay the framework for true self-sufficiency at independence.

Class B Mandates were concerned with former German territories in sub-Saharan Africa, such as Tanganyika and Kamerun. These territories were considered much less ready for independence and needed substantial development and control. For the Class C Mandates, which included Southwest Africa and islands in the South Pacific, there was no real prospect of independence.

In 1945 the League of Nations, which had failed to prevent another world war, was supplanted by the newly formed United Nations. The remaining mandates became UN Trust Territories. In the Middle East only the British Palestine mandate remained; UN attempts to find a solution based on separate Jewish and Arab states failed. In 1948 the British pulled out, and Jews in Palestine declared the creation of Israel. This led to the first war between Israel and the Arabs.

Box 10.3

Isaiah Bowman: American Geographers at Versailles

The American entry into World War I, which tipped the balance in the conflict, leading to the Allied victory, assured the US a place in the postwar settlement process. Even before the end of the war, Woodrow Wilson led the negotiations with Germany. But it was the ideas in Wilson's Fourteen Points that came to influence the work of the peace-makers, trying to create a permanent and lasting peace. Included in Wilson's Fourteen Points were the idea of territorial nationalism and the readjustment of the boundaries of European states and protection of various nationalities in the former Ottoman Turkey. In essence, Wilson's plan sought to eliminate future conflict by resolving competing ethnic-based territorial claims.

Determining these claims, and accurately locating them on the ground, was a monumental task. To begin, Wilson assembled a team of America's top geographers. The group was known first as 'The Inquiry' and later, at the Paris Peace Conference, as the 'American Committee to Negotiate Peace'. The group collected extensive amounts of geographical data, attempting to create political units based on scientific principles rather than on warfare. The American Geographical Society archive holds over 530 maps related to the Paris Peace Conference, many of which were produced by the Inquiry.

Difference, particularly between ethnic groups, was thought to be at the root of political instability. Cartographic techniques such as thematic mapping were used to map differences in language, religion and ethnic affiliation. A major question was to which political unit did each group of people belong. In doing so, the work of the Inquiry divided populations into categories based on the concept of 'race'. Race, however, was perceived as a socio-cultural concept, and the Inquiry sought to make a racial map of Europe and Turkey, showing national boundaries as well as 'mixed' and 'doubtful' zones. In this manner the peace-makers made adjustments to Europe's territory.

This level of scientific inquiry only applied to the territories of Europe and parts of Turkey, where the characteristics and desires of the population were given great consideration. In the former Ottoman territories of the Middle East, whose fate was determined largely at the San Remo Conference in 1920, the ethnic composition of the inhabitants and their history were not taken into consideration in creating the League of Nations mandates.

Wilson's team was headed by geographer Isaiah Bowman, who held the title of chief territorial advisor to the president. Bowman (1878–1950) was director of the American Geographical Society for twenty years and served as editor of the *Journal of Geography* and associate editor of the *Geographical Review*. The author of over sixteen books, largely on issues in political geography, he served as the president of Johns Hopkins University for thirteen years.

Crampton, J. (2006) 'The cartographic calculation of space: race mapping and the Balkans at the Paris Peace Conference of 1919'. *Social and Cultural Geography*, 7: 731–52.

In determining the post-Ottoman borders and installing a system of external control by European governments, the peace-makers at Versailles often failed to acknowledge the wishes and desires of the local population (MacMillan 2001). This position was contrary to that established in President Wilson's famous 'Fourteen Points' speech of 1918 that laid out the principles for creating lasting peace in Europe. In this speech he called for an independent and sovereign state to exist in the Turkish part of the former Ottoman empire, and 'the other nationalities which are now under Turkish rule should be assured an undoubted security of life and an absolutely unmolested opportunity of autonomous development'. Many in the Middle East, including Arabs, Kurds and Armenians, interpreted Wilson's words as a guarantee of their right to self-determination. However, their nationalist aspirations remained largely unfulfilled. The disposition of Ottoman territory, though discussed in Paris, was not completed until 1920 at the Conference of San Remo and embodied in the Treaty of Sèvres (Map 10.2).

The Armenians were Christians who had lived under the rule of various empires, including the Byzantines, Persians and Ottomans, following the demise of an independent Armenian state in 1375. A large Armenian population existed inside the Ottoman Empire; they had previously been subject to attacks by both the sultanate, who saw Armenian nationalism as a threat to the empire, and Kurds, who viewed Armenian nationalism as a threat to their own nationalist aspirations. The Western world reacted in horror and sympathy to the massacre of Armenians carried out in 1915–16. Despite rhetorical support for the plight of the Armenians, and vast campaigns in Europe and the US to collect funds for Armenian refugees, the peace-makers at Versailles did not back the idea of an independent Armenia to be created from the ashes of the Ottoman Empire. Following Ottoman defeat, Armenia declared independence in 1918; and, though the Treaty of Sèvres, which ultimately disposed of Ottoman territory, provided for an independent Armenia, no steps were taken to ensure its survival. Without a protector to save it from reoccupation by the newly independent Turkey, Armenia was absorbed by the Soviet Union in 1922.

The nationalist aspirations of the Kurds, who sought an independent Kurdistan, were similarly dashed. It is clear that the peace-makers knew little about the Kurds, whose identity is based largely on a shared ethnic identification and Kurdish linguistic bond. Kurds are predominantly Sunni Muslim, but can also be Shia or Christian. Though Britain initially supported the idea of Kurdistan, as a means to provide a buffer state to protect Mesopotamia and its oil, the Kurds rebelled against the idea of a Kurdistan under British protection. In the end, though an autonomous Kurdistan did appear on the maps of the Treaty of Sèvres, the rise of a strong republic of Turkey, under the leadership of Kemal Ataturk (Mustafa Kemal), meant the end to Kurdish nationalist dreams.

Despite Wilson's lofty language in the Fourteen Points speech, Arabs were little represented at the postwar settlement talks. By all accounts, Feisal's reception in Paris was chilly, with Balfour stating (MacMillan 2001: 380): 'I am quite unable to see why Heaven or any other Power should object to our telling the Moslem what he ought to think.' No Arabs, including Palestinian Arabs, were present at San Remo. In essence, the Arabs were expected to do as they were told.

Though Sharif Hussein's son, Feisal, accompanied by T. E. Lawrence, journeyed to the Paris conference to speak for Arab independence and for fulfillment of the promises the Arabs felt were made by McMahon, it did little to ensure Arab self-determination. In Paris, they found little support from the British and great resistance by the French. By 1918, Feisal, in anticipation of the peace settlement, had already begun to establish an independent state in Syria, a great threat to French interests. With Palestine held by the British, and Syria by the French, Hussein's wartime support was rewarded by the creation of Transjordan, an autonomous area inside the British Palestine mandate. His eldest son, Abdullah, was placed on the throne. The British did not abandon Feisal; in 1921 they made him king of the newly created Iraq.

A new entity, Transjordan, was created under British rule, included within the British mandate of Palestine. The British mandate included the area of historic Palestine, including Jerusalem, though its boundaries had never been precisely determined, and areas previously belonging to the Ottoman province

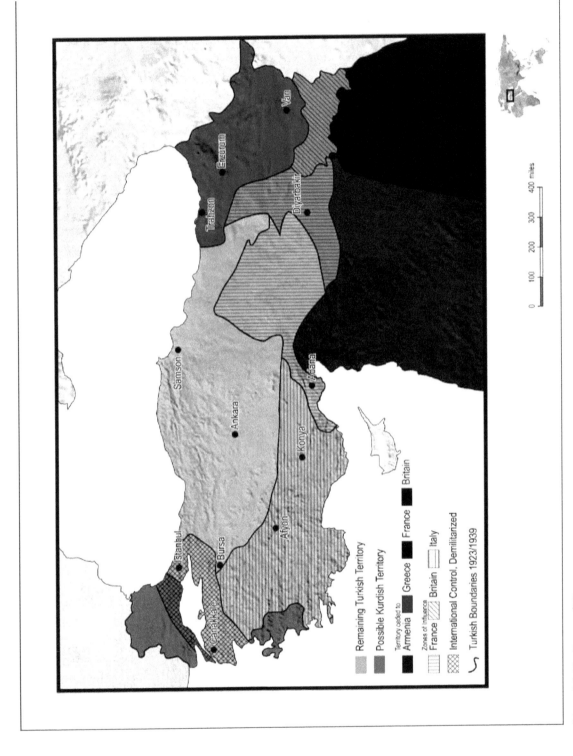

Map 10.2 The Treaty of Sèvres

of Syria. The Transjordan, the precursor to modern Jordan, was also included in this mandate. The British placed Sharif Hussein of Mecca, their ally during World War I, on Transjordan's throne.

The vast Ottoman territories were reduced to a small portion of the Anatolian peninsula around the city of Ankara. Italy and Greece controlled the southern and southeastern portion of the peninsula, including the coasts. Constantinople (now Istanbul), an international zone, was occupied by Allied troops. The settlement was designed to ensure that the Ottoman Empire never again rose to rival Europe, or threatened

---

Box 10.4
The Armenian Genocide

Between 1915 and 1917 approximately 1 million of Turkey's Christian Armenians were killed or deported. They died from starvation, exhaustion on forced marches, bludgeoning and rape. At the time, no word existed in the English language to describe killings on such a scale, and the apparent attempt to eliminate an entire people.

Ottoman Turkey entered World War I on the side of Germany, fighting against Russia, Britain and France. The 'Young Turk' government of the Ottoman Empire feared its Armenian population, numbering approximately 2 million, would betray Turkey. The Armenian Christian population had existed in the area for 3000 years, and under the Ottoman *millet* system was a protected minority (*dhimmis*). Though Russia encouraged the Armenians to revolt, and a few did, the vast majority remained loyal.

The genocide of the Armenians was led by the government, and was an intentional act to rid Turkey of its 'Armenian problem' and not an unexpected outcome of fighting associated with the war. The government ordered the deportation of Armenians, closed their schools and desecrated its churches. In Constantinople, and in cities throughout Turkey, leading Armenian citizens and intellectuals were executed.

The events were covered up, and denied by Turkey and her ally Germany. However, as word leaked out, the international community did nothing to stop the killing. The US ambassador in Turkey, State Department officials, returning missionaries and even former president Theodore Roosevelt urged President Woodrow Wilson to take action. Wilson failed to denounce the 'race murder' as the US had not yet entered the war and he sought to preserve American neutrality. Through the American Near East Relief Committee, the US did provide $110 million in humanitarian aid to the survivors.

Though Britain, France and Russia (though not the United States) wanted to see the perpetrators of the genocide tried by an international tribunal, this tribunal never took place. Military tribunals in Turkey convicted two senior Ottoman officials for their involvement in the killings; they were sentenced to hard labor and death by hanging. Others, who had escaped from Turkey, were sentenced *in absentia*.

Over two decades later, the crime of systematic elimination of a people was given a name: genocide. It is derived from the Greek *geno*, meaning race or tribe, and the Latin *cide*, meaning killing. It was coined by Raphael Lemkin, who survived the Holocaust and sought to find a name that could capture the scale of these crimes. The Armenian genocide is often recognized as the first true genocide, though the Turkish government does not describe the events as genocide. The subject of the Armenian genocide remains contested in Turkey.

Power, S. (2002) *A Problem from Hell: America and the Age of Genocide*. New York: Basic Books.

European interests in the Middle East. The Ottoman parliament was disbanded, the CUP of Young Turks fled, and the Allies took control of Ottoman finances. Though the sultan continued to rule officially, all decisions were made in cooperation with the Allies.

The Creation of Modern Turkey

The settlement imposed by the Treaty of Sèvres fed a Turkish nationalist movement that had its roots in the reform period. The occupation of the Ottoman heartland, and of Istanbul in particular, by foreign troops inspired a strong reaction from the local Turkish population. Even before the treaty was concluded, resistance movements formed that would challenge the implementation of the Treaty of Sèvres. Under the leadership of Mustafa Kemal, a fledgling national resistance was formed whose main goal was to achieve Turkish sovereignty over areas with a Turkish majority. By 1920, they had formed a government in Ankara, with Mustafa Kemal as president, to represent the Turkish people. A national assembly, composed of local representatives and members of the parliament previously disbanded, was formed and quickly adopted a constitution.

Under the leadership of Mustafa Kemal, Turkish military strength grew, and easily dislodged Greek forces in southern Turkey in 1922. With Kemal's troops threatening to engage the British in Istanbul, the two parties agreed to renegotiate the terms of the Treaty of Sèvres. In the renegotiations, Turkish representatives pushed for adoption of the principles in the National Pact, which stated the right of full Turkish sovereignty over the remaining portions of the empire with a Turkish majority. The final treaty, the Treaty of Lausanne, largely adhered to this principle and restored Turkish control over the entire Anatolian peninsula, including Istanbul. On November 1, 1922 the sultanate was abolished, and the Republic of Turkey was created the following year. Mustafa Kemal (Ataturk) was its first president.

Egyptian Nationalism

The British occupied Egypt in 1882 in order to protect the Suez Canal, prevent French involvement in the region, and rein in an economic crisis that had forced foreign monitoring of Egypt's economy. The arrival of British troops also quelled a nationalist revolt, led by an Army colonel, Ahmed Urabi, and other officers. Urabi sought to establish a popularly elected legislature that would control Egypt's budget and the heavy taxation on the poor needed to maintain the khedive's high spending levels and debt payments. British troops, after defeating the nationalist troops, restored the khedive to power.

Britain's subsequent occupation had a profound effect on the Egyptian economy and political system, increasing its dependence on Britain and thereby spurring the growth of Egyptian nationalism. Though Egypt technically remained an Ottoman province, and was not formally a British protectorate, Britain assumed control of its internal and external affairs. The power of the khedive paled in comparison with that of the British consul general, Lord Cromer, who oversaw a vast network of British civil servants and administrators who served as—highly paid—advisors in Egyptian government ministries. Britain controlled the budget and the decision-making.

This fueled tension with the well-educated Egyptian elites, who had benefited from the educational reforms during previous modernization and wished to administer their own country. Britain's involvement in the Sudan further enraged nationalists.

An economic crisis, as a result of a global recession, badly hurt exports of cotton, which had become Egypt's dominant crop under British policy. Farm incomes plummeted, creating unrest in the countryside. At the same time, nationalists voiced their opposition in the press. The wounding of the wife of a village prayer leader in the rural area of Dinshaway in June 1906 by five British officers on a pigeon-shooting outing touched off local protests. In the ensuing trial by British authorities, meant to dissuade others from protesting, thirty-two peasants were convicted of premeditated murder (and four executed). The Dinshaway incident further inflamed nationalists, of both Islamic and secular ideologies.

The hardships borne by the Egyptian population during World War I, when 100,000 British troops were stationed in Egypt, further stirred nationalist sentiments. Following the war, Egypt officially became a British protectorate, increasing British control. In 1919 riots erupted throughout the country following the British expulsion of popular nationalist leader Saad Zaghlul. In 1922, Britain, unable to reestablish control over Egypt, unilaterally granted it independence. Though Egypt then established a parliament and elected Saad Zaghlul as its first prime minister, the monarchy continued to exert ultimate authority and maintained a close relationship with the British. Full realization of nationalist goals would not happen until 1952 when a revolution led by military officers overthrew the monarchy.

Box 10.5
Ataturk: The Father of Modern Turkey

The characteristics and structure of modern Turkey were profoundly influenced by Mustafa Kemal (1881–1938), also known as Ataturk.

A successful military officer, Kemal served Ottoman Turkey in the battle of Gallipoli in 1915. Though the Allies eventually prevailed, the battle was a formative event in the development of modern Turkish nationalism. After the war, Kemal led the nationalist movement and the series of military conflicts against Greece, the United States and the French, who sought to implement the provisions of the Treaty of Sèvres. Kemal ignored the treaty, whose provisions included an autonomous state for the Armenians, and led the creation of a new, modern Turkey.

As Turkey's first president, Kemal sought to break ties with the Ottoman past. He moved the capital from Istanbul (Constantinople) to Ankara. Turkey became a republic, ending over 500 years of hereditary rule by sultans. A National Assembly was elected by all males aged 18 or older. Women received full political rights, including the right to vote and to serve in parliament, in 1934—well before women in many European countries. The president was elected by the national assembly from amongst their membership.

Secularism was chief among the principles of the new state. Ataturk closed the religious schools, eliminated the Ministry of Religious Endowments, and instituted a legal code based on Swiss and other European law, rather than on *sharia*. Islam, followed by the vast majority of Turks, was seen as a personal belief system, separate from the state. To this end, he abolished the caliphate, by which the Ottomans had claimed leadership of the Muslim world. Polygamy, acceptable under Islam, was outlawed, and the Sufi religious orders were driven out. Sunday replaced Friday as the day of rest. Kemal also took steps to reduce the power of the religious leadership.

Box 10.5 (Continued)

His efforts to modernize Turkey's economy were only partially successful. He attempted industrialization through state-led capitalism, targeting specifically the textile and steel industries. The decision, in 1928, to replace the Arabic alphabet with the Latin to write Turkish is credited with raising national literacy levels to over 90 percent, one of the highest in the region. Today, this combination of secularism, high educational attainment and an open economy has made Turkey an economic leader in the region.

Kemal was criticized for the rapid pace of his reforms and the loss of traditional Turkish culture to one based on modernity and European influences. The reforms were also seen as bringing greater benefit to urban elites than to the peasantry. Moreover, there was little tolerance for opposition to his plan.

In 1935, Turkey's National Assembly bestowed upon him the title 'Father of the Turks', or Ataturk. He died in November 1938 at the age of 57. The true test of the system he put in place was the smooth transition to his successor, a strong supporter of Kemalist ideology, Ismet Inonu. Kemal remains a major symbol of Turkish nationalism; his portrait can be found in government offices and private businesses throughout Turkey.

The Iranian Constitutional Revolution

The constitutional revolution in Iran marks both the first of the constitutional and parliamentary revolutions that swept through the Middle East in the pre-World War I era and the end of the Qajar hereditary dynasty that had succeeded the Safavids and ruled Persia since 1781.

From the late nineteenth century, Russian expansion in central Asia and British hegemony over India had pressed Iran on both sides. By 1907 the British and the Russians had signed an agreement dividing the country into spheres of influence between them. Both Russia and the British sought to control the country's oil resources and strategic ports. Lavish spending by the monarch, Shah Muzzafir al-Din (1898–1906), had led to Iran's economic dependence on both Britain and Russia; the central government could function only with the aid of foreign loans. To repay these loans Britain had forced a series of highly unpopular concessions on the monarchy. One of the earliest gave the British a monopoly on the production, domestic sale and export of tobacco in 1891. Highly unpopular, the concessions heightened nationalist sentiments, which were led by the religious leaders (*ulama*). Widespread protests forced the shah to repeal the concessions the following year. The repeal of the concessions illustrates a common tendency in Iranian politics: that of the religious leaders to enforce the populist will.

By the turn of the century a diverse group of merchants, religious leaders and intellectuals constituted a growing nationalist movement. The granting of an oil concession to the British, known as the D'Arcy concession, further angered the nationalists. The terms of the concession gave the British control of Iranian oil reserves for sixty years, with Iran receiving only 16 percent of the net profits. Widespread protests erupted in 1905, focused on limiting the powers of a highly unpopular monarch. Protests ended in 1906, following the shah's agreement to convene a constitutional assembly (*Majlis*).

The *Majlis* created an elected legislature and reduced the power of the shah, especially over financial issues. The status of Islam was secured by the *Majlis*, which reaffirmed Twelver Shiism as the official state religion and the *sharia* as the basis for law. By 1908 the country was caught up in a civil war between those who backed the monarchy, and sought to restore its power, and the constitutionalists. Britain and Russia both entered Iran to protect their economic interests. Though the parliament continued to function, it did so under the watchful eye of foreign powers.

The interwar period saw a short-lived return of the monarchy, when Reza Pahlavi, the minister of war, led troops into Tehran in 1921, forcing the government to resign. The Qajar shah named him prime minister and sought exile in Europe. In 1926 a puppet *Majlis* crowned Reza Pahlavi the new Shah of Persia. With this, the Qajar dynasty ended, and the Pahlavi dynasty was established.

Reza Shah embarked on an extensive modernization and Westernization program. The country's name was changed from Persia to Iran, to evoke images of the nation's past. Nearly all institutions, including the military and educational systems, were modernized in European tradition. The shah sought to emulate the secularization of European society, banning Iranian dress, the all-concealing *chador* worn by women, and the veil. The wearing of hats and European dress became compulsory.

Reza Shah also reduced the power of the religious leaders, in part by creating a new legal system based on French law, which required judges to hold degrees from European-style institutions rather than from Islamic schools. He also seized much land belonging to the religious endowment system.

Reza Shah's rule was highly authoritarian; criticism was suppressed through the use of harsh punishments and the secret police. The press was controlled, and Reza Shah accumulated vast wealth and greatly expanded his land holdings.

World War II saw another round of European intervention in Iran. Despite Reza Shah's attempts to keep it neutral, both Britain and the Soviet Union feared he would support the Germans. Both Britain and the USSR invaded in 1941, forcing Reza Shah to abdicate his throne. His son, Mohammad Reza Pahlavi, took the throne.

Moving Toward Independence

The dawn of the twentieth century brought great change to the Middle East. By mid-century the old empires were gone and new borders drawn. European control was formalized through League of Nations (subsequently United Nations) mandates. The countries of the region were increasingly characterized by 'institutional dualism', by which European institutions were created alongside traditional, such as European courts alongside Islamic ones.

The penetration of European institutions into society at the hands of rulers who sought to emulate Europe, or who had become deeply indebted to the European powers, helped foster a growing sense of nationalism. By the end of World War II, it was becoming more difficult for Europe to exert control over their colonies. In a few short years most of the countries in the region would reach independence within a new world order defined by the rising strength of the United States and the Soviet Union.

Box 10.6
The Rise (and Fall) of Arab Nationalism

While nationalist movements developed in the individual countries of the region, such as Egypt and Syria, a form of nationalism with a broader mandate, to unite all Arabs, also grew. The Arab nationalists sought to increase the strength of the Arab countries through uniting them in solidarity against their major foe, the imperialist powers and Israel. They argued that imperialism had artificially divided the Arabs, a single people, into many states. Through political unity, and the creation of a single Arab state, he Arab world would be reinvigorated and recharged. The loss of the 1948 war with Israel could be attributed to the division of the Arabs into many states.

Box 10.6 (*Continued*)

Many of the intellectual ideas behind Arab nationalism can be traced to the writings of Michel Aflaq, a Syrian and co-founder of the Ba'ath party. The Ba'ath party is a secular nationalist organization, founded in Syria in 1947. It had branches in many countries, including Iraq; however, after an internal disagreement, the Iraqi Ba'ath party split from the Syrian in 1963. According to Aflaq, the Arab fatherland was an indivisible economic and political unit.

But no one did more to advance the cause of Arab nationalism than Egyptian president Gamal Abdel Nasser, who served as the self-proclaimed leader of the Arab world in the 1950s and 1960s. A charismatic leader, Nasser's anti-imperialist rhetoric against both the US and the USSR, and his anti-Israel statements, made him enormously popular in Egypt and throughout the Arab world. On the international stage he was active in the Non-aligned Movement, along with Nehru of India and Tito of Yugoslavia. The NAM is an anti-imperialist, anti-colonialist and anti-Zionist organization of states. In 1956 he nationalized the Suez Canal, further bolstering his anti-imperialist credentials. He was strongly committed to the idea of a single Arab state (led by Egypt, of course); and, in 1958, Egypt and Syria joined to form the United Arab Republic. The union was short-lived, lasting for only three years.

In 1967, Nasser led the Arab states in an war against Israel (see Chapter 6). The war, which caused further territorial losses to Israel, was a disastrous defeat for the Arabs. In its aftermath, Nasser attempted to resign. Millions of Egyptians poured into the streets to demand his return to office.

Though Nasser remained in office, Arab nationalism, which peaked in the 1950s, began to wane. A number of factors contributed to its decline. The Arab defeat in 1967, which underscored the permanence of a strong Israel in the region, and demonstrated the weakness of the Arab militaries, dealt a huge psychological blow.

A further reason was the dismantling of European control over the region, removing imperialism as Arab nationalism's major rallying cry. By the 1960s, much of the Arab world was independent; even Algeria had managed to shake off French control, though at a great price.

Without imperialism to provide a common enemy, internal cohesion among the Arab states, which had always been problematic, worsened. Nasser, reeling from his defeat, began verbally to attack other Arab governments, reducing his stature as leader of the Arab world Increasingly the Arab states began to focus on their own internal needs, such as rapid population growth and economic stagnation, rather than on the unrealized dream of Arab nationalism.

As Arab nationalism, grounded in secular thought, had been unable to deliver on its promises, new ideologies gained ground. Islamist thought began to grow in popularity as it offered a different, religion-based, path for raising the conditions faced by the population in these newly independent countries. Islamists lashed out at the explicitly secular nationalist governments. Saddam Hussein in Iraq carried the mantle of Arab nationalism in the latter part of the twentieth century. His execution can perhaps been seen as the 'last gasp' of Arab nationalism.

Dawisha, A. (2003) *Arab Nationalism in the Twentieth Century: From Triumph to Despair.* Princeton, NJ: Princeton University Press.

Kaplan, R. (2007) 'Arab nationalism's last gasp', *The Los Angeles Times* (Opinion), January 7.

Summary of Main Points

- By the sixteenth century the Ottoman Empire was losing its global position to new competition from Europe and the New World.
- To combat this loss of competitiveness, the Ottoman Empire instituted a series of modernizing reforms.
- These reforms increased European control over the MENA in the eighteenth and nineteenth centuries which grew as European countries competed with each other to control the region.
- The post-World War II settlement created the modern system of states in the MENA and placed most of them under direct European control.
- During this time, nationalist ideas emerged and grew, laying the foundation for independence movements.
- Modern Turkey was created out of the remains of the Ottoman Empire and under the leadership of Ataturk established a strong secular republic.
- In Iran, the Pahlavi dynasty was established, while Russia and Britain each sought to control the country.

Suggestions for Further Reading

Cleveland, W. (2004) *A History of the Modern Middle East*, 3rd edn. Boulder, Colo.: Westview Press. A comprehensive and authoritative history of the Middle East since the rise of Islam.

Fisk, R. (2005) *The Great War for Civilisation: The Conquest of the Middle East*. New York: Vintage Books. This sweeping account of the region's modern history, augmented by the author's personal accounts, adds a much-needed dimension beyond what history books can provide. The author is an award-winning journalist with thirty years' experience in the region.

Fromkin, D. (1989) *A Peace to End All Peace: Creating the Modern Middle East, 1914–1922*. New York: Holt. The classic and highly detailed account of the demise of the Ottoman Empire. Fromkin does an excellent job of demonstrating how the postwar settlements contributed to instability in the region.

Hodgson, M. (1974) *The Venture of Islam*. Vol. 3, *The Gunpowder Empires and Modern Times*. Chicago, Ill.: University of Chicago Press. Historian Hodgson coined the term 'gunpowder empires' to explain the rise of empires, beginning with China, based on advances in weaponry. In this book he explores the links between state formation and gunpowder in the Middle East.

Keddi, N. (2006) *Modern Iran: Roots and Results of a Revolution*. New Haven, Conn.: Yale University Press. Traces the roots of the Iranian revolution and its ideology through to the present. Essential reading for understanding modern Iran.

MacMillan, M. (2001) *Paris 1919: Six Months That Changed the World*. New York: Random House. A highly detailed account of the peace conference at Versailles following the end of World War I. See especially chapters 26–9 that cover the end of the Ottoman Empire, the creation of new Arab states and the roots of modern Turkey.

Myntti, C. (2003) *Paris along the Nile: Architecture from the Belle Epoque*. New York: American University in Cairo Press. Packed with photographs, this volume documents the historic, and threatened, architecture of 'European' Cairo.

Owen, R. and Pamuk, S. (1999) *A History of Middle East Economies in the Twentieth Century.* Cambridge, Mass.: Harvard University Press. See especially Chapter 2 for a discussion of Egypt's economic dependency.

Palmer, A. (1993) *The Decline and Fall of the Ottoman Empire.* London: John Murray. Extensive examination of the decline of the empire and possible explanations.

Tyldesley, J. (2005) *Egypt: How a Lost Civilization Was Rediscovered.* Berkeley, Calif.: University of California Press. A light-hearted look at the archaeological frenzy touched off by the Napoleonic expedition to Egypt.

Vatikiotis, P. J. (1991) *The History of Modern Egypt: From Muhammad Ali to Mubarak*, 4th edn. Baltimore, Md: Johns Hopkins University Press. Set against the backdrop of growing nationalism and European penetration, this volume provides insight into the critical decades before Egyptian independence.

Zurcher, E. (2004) *Turkey: A Modern History.* London: I.B. Tauris. Traces the development of the Republic of Turkey, the implementation of Ataturk's reforms and current challenges.

11

Religion in the Middle East

by David S. Sorenson

It is called the Dome of the Rock in reference to where it stands: the shimmering dome rises above an octagonal building sheathed in decorative tiles, built on a rocky outcrop where Jews and Christians believe Abraham offered Isaac for sacrifice, and Muslims believe the Prophet Muhammad ascended to heaven to receive the last of God's messages to his Muslim community. The Dome towers over the Western Wall, the remnant of what Jews believe was the Second Temple, and is but a short distance from the Church of the Holy Sepulcher, the believed site of the death and resurrection of Jesus Christ. To visit these sites is to step from one set of religious beliefs to another to another, culling the remarkable similarities of belief that the embrace of politics has obscured if not obliterated.

Religion is a key to understanding politics in the Middle East, as it is elsewhere in the world. No one can truly understand European politics, for example, without understanding the history and role of Catholic and Protestant faith in Europe, or understand Indian politics without understanding Hinduism. In the Middle East, religion has a pronounced impact on society and politics. As George Sfeir describes it, "In Arab Muslim societies, where tradition is closely identified with religion, the constitutional declarations of basic freedoms, themselves a product of the modern liberal state, are more often than not

David S. Sorenson, "Religion in the Middle East," *Introduction to the Modern Middle East*, pp. 42–72. Copyright © 2007 by *Perseus Books Group*. Reprinted with permission.

frustrated, not so much by the actions of oppressive governments (although that cannot be completely dismissed), as by the contradictions in the legal culture between traditional religious values and the newly adopted attributes of the modern state." Barakat notes that "rulers throughout Arab history have used religion to discourage rebellion (*fitna*) on behalf of unity of the community, or *umma*, and the need to safeguard it against internal and external threats. Political actors use religion to undermine liberal and radical opposition and to justify repressive policies. Traditional governments and authoritarian rulers have attempted to establish their legitimacy and authority by the strict application of the Sharia in alliance with religious movements." Religion shapes not only Muslim Middle Eastern countries but also predominately Jewish Israel. As Ira Sharkansky observes, "Perhaps the most fundamental reason for there being a thick mixture of politics and religion in Israel is that there is a great similarity in the underlying characteristics of religion and politics."

The vast majority of the people who live in the Middle East belong to one of the three monotheistic religions: Islam, Judaism, or Christianity. Islam has by far the largest number of adherents, with all countries in the Middle East except Israel having Muslim majorities. Lebanon is the only other Middle Eastern country with a significant non-Muslim population; around 30 percent of Lebanese are Christians. In the rest of the Middle East, Christians are a small minority. In Israel, where Christianity originated, only 3 percent of the present population is Christian; in Egypt, Christians probably constitute around 5–9 percent of the population.

Religion as a Source of Political Belief

Religious beliefs and practices have a profound impact on both political philosophy and the formation of political institutions. Practically every national government in the world borrows from religious teachings. Some regimes link politics and religion because of a conviction that religion demands such ties. Other regimes use religion to bolster claims of political legitimacy. Religion provides powerful symbols ("In God We Trust," or "There is no God but God, and Muhammad is his Messenger") to support the image that divinity supports and protects the political system and its rulers. Some symbols support democracy—Vox populi, vox dei ("The voice of the people is the voice of God")—while others support dictatorship and repression (Spanish dictator Francisco Franco pointed to Pope Pius XI's positive comparison between Spanish Nationalists and the Crusaders).

In many societies, political beliefs become the source of law. Almost all law existing in Middle Eastern countries stems at least partially from religious belief. In some countries religious law is the law, as in Saudi Arabia, where the Sharia informs jurisprudence. In other Middle Eastern countries, religious groups pressure their governments to adopt religious law, leading to compromises where at least some of the legal code derives from religious belief. Thus in many Arab countries and in Israel, religious codes form the basis of family law.

Religion as a Source of Conflict

Some portray religion as a source of war and internal conflict in the Middle East. Religion may contribute to the passions that ignite war, and it may inspire warriors to fight. Egyptian soldiers shouted "God is great" as they crossed the Suez Canal to fight the Israelis on the other side in 1973. However, wars are mostly fought for power, in response to fear, or for wealth or the glory that victory can bring. These factors have all contributed to war in the Middle East. That the participants belong to different religions may give the appearance that they are fighting over those beliefs. But that is no more the case than the US-Japanese war between 1941 and 1945 was a struggle between Christianity and Shinto.

All three monotheistic religions exist in the Middle East, although Islam is by far the majority religion. However, it is much less well understood in the West than are the other two faiths.

Islam

Islam is the recognized title of the religion whose adherents believe that God revealed testimony to the Prophet Muhammad during his lifetime. Those messages, recorded as the Holy Quran, along with lessons from the life of the Prophet, make up the core beliefs of Islam. The term Islam in Arabic translates as "to submit," meaning that devotees of Islam submit to the will of God, in Arabic, Allah. A Muslim is one who believes in and adheres to the basic tenants of Islam. A majority of the world's Muslims are not Arabs (Arabs constitute around 20 percent of the total Muslim population); considerable numbers of Muslims live in Pakistan, Southeast Asia (Indonesia is the world's largest Muslim country), Turkey, China, and the former republics of the Soviet Union. Altogether, there are around 1 billion Muslims in the world. However, no matter where they are, they acknowledge the importance of the Arab roots of the religion by facing Mecca when they pray, and almost all of them will travel to that city sometime in their lifetime.

Large majorities of the world's Muslims follow five fundamental practices:

- The *shahadah*, or testament of faith (literally, "there is no God but God, and Muhammad is his Messenger.")
- Prayer, or *salat*, five times a day at prescribed times
- Observance, or *siyam*, of the holy month of Ramadan, during which time Muslims must not eat, drink, smoke, or engage in sex during daylight hours
- Performance of the *hajj*, the religious journey to the city of Mecca at least once during one's lifetime
- *Zakat*, or alms giving, sharing personal wealth with those less fortunate

There are other beliefs and practices in Islam, though not all Muslims universally accept them. They include:

- A taboo against eating pork, which is widely followed by Muslims (and Jews as well).
- A taboo against the consumption of alcohol, followed selectively in the Muslim world. In some Muslim countries, laws prohibit the production, sale, or consumption of alcohol. This is the case in some Gulf countries like Saudi Arabia and Kuwait, although neighboring Bahrain and the United Arab Emirates allow alcohol. Most Islamic countries allow for the production and sale of wine, beer, and in the eastern Mediterranean, a distilled beverage called *arak* (or *raki* in Turkish), though in many of those countries, there is Islamist pressure to curtail alcohol consumption.
- Sabbath observed on Friday.
- Abandoning Islam once one is a Muslim—apostasy—is equivalent to treason.

- A prohibition on charging interest on money loaned, which some Muslims consider as exploitative and unfair risk sharing. In some Islamic countries, banks must find other ways to be profitable, including imposing service charges or to pay returns from profit/loss returns. Other Islamic countries allow the charging of interest on loans (see Chapter 3 for more on Islamic banking).
- A prohibition on portraying Allah or the Prophet, often taken from the Quran Suras 41 to 52. The angry reaction in many Muslim countries to cartoons in a Danish newspaper in 2006 unfavorably depicting Muhammad was an expression of this belief.
- A belief that Muhammad was the final messenger from God.
- A belief that the Quran is the last word from Allah revealed to Muhammad in Arabia because the community of Arabs there had become ignorant of God's earlier messages to Adam, Abraham, Moses, and Jesus. They view these earlier figures as messengers. Jesus is controversial. Muslims hold that if one accepts the phrase "there is no God but God," then by definition God cannot have progeny. They hold that Jesus was human and was chosen by God to reveal earlier messages to humankind. They also believe that God would not let a messenger die by crucifixion.

Sources of Islamic Faith

There are two prime sources of Islamic belief—the Quran and the Hadith, or sayings of the Prophet.

The Quran

The holy book for Muslims is the Quran, the written collection of the revelations given by Allah to Muhammad. The Quran has never been revised, for to do so would be to alter the unalterable word of Allah. It contains 114 chapters, or suras, arranged in order of the length of each sura, with the longer chapters coming first. Muslims believe that the true Quran exists only in the Arabic language. They claim that God sought an Arabic speaker to reveal messages that Arabs later wrote in Arabic script. Thus many non-Arabs learn written Arabic so that they can read the Quran in its purest language. Some Muslims regard Arabic itself as sacred script, and to ensure that human feet cannot trample a piece of Arab writing, carefully discard old Arabic newspapers so that they do not wind up on the street.

There is discussion about the authority of the Quran, as there is about other holy texts. Some argue that its interpretation should be literary rather than literal. The Quranic texts contain contradictions, as for example between the earlier and later revelations. Thus the Quran may be understood to have different meanings, as opposed to absolute law, a single meaning in its suras. Such a view, known as *Mutazilism*, argues that while God created the universe, that act did not predispose human actions, and thus Mutazilism accepts human determination of self-conduct. The opposing view, known as Asharism, argues that people acquire actions from God, though God is not responsible for the outcome of evil actions, which are the responsibility of humans alone, thus negating self-will. Asharism as a doctrine prevailed in discussions on Islamic theology after the twelfth century, though its rationalist views became more prevalent in the Shiite community.

The Hadith

The other sources of Islamic belief are the Hadith, or traditions from the life of the Prophet. Muslims emulate such traditions where they can, believing that Muhammad was "the perfect man" since Allah chose him to receive the Quran; thus early followers collected these sayings and actions. Muslims believe that the life of the Prophet holds lessons for them, since it was Muhammad whom Allah chose to receive the messages recorded in the Quran. The lessons extracted from that life became the Sunna, or "way" of the Prophet.

As in all recorded oral tradition, disputes arise among Muslim scholars about the meaning of particular hadith, particularly where they appear to contradict the Quran. Since others recorded the hadiths, their veracity depends on the interpreter, and the degree that a particular hadith may be traced directly to the Prophet. In cases where a hadith does contradict the Quran, the Quran takes precedence, as it is believed to be the direct word of God.

Muhammad was born in the trading city of Mecca in 570 CE. A merchant uncle adopted him after Muhammad's parents died at an early age. When he reached adulthood, he became a merchant and a notable citizen in Mecca. He married a widow, Khadija, and had two daughters, one of whom, Fatima, would marry his cousin Ali. After Khadija's death, Muhammad married again, and at one time had eleven wives, partly to cement ties to local tribes.

Muhammad was a contemplative man who sometimes left the bustle of the city to meditate in a cave south of Mecca. There, according to tradition, around 610 CE, the Angel Gabriel visited him and told that he had been chosen to receive God's word. For the next twenty years, he continued to receive messages that he initially revealed only to a small group of followers. Those followers of Muhammad would later record these messages as the Quran in the time of Caliph Umar. Part of the message was to disseminate the messages to community members and bring them into the flock. However, many citizens in Mecca resisted Muhammad's teaching, and he had to fight to preserve his small flock.

Islamic tradition holds that in his later years, Muhammad journeyed by night on a mythical animal to Jerusalem, where he ascended to heaven to receive the final revelations. The Dome of the Rock now marks the site where Muslims believe he started his ascension, known as the *miraj*. They consider it the third holiest place in Islam, after the mosques in Mecca and Medina. Control over this place, which now contains both the Dome of the Rock and Al-Aqsa Mosque, is a bitter issue between Israel and the Palestinians. The Palestinians, who are predominately Muslim, argue that as Muslims they should have sovereign control over the mosques and the land on which they stand (see Chapters 11 and 14 for more on this issue).

Sunni and Shiite: Branches of Islam

Like Christianity and Judaism, Islam's followers are divided into sects, the most important of which are Sunni and Shiite. A majority of Muslims are Sunni, but around 10 to 15 percent of the world's Muslims are Shiite. They constitute a large majority of Muslims in Iran, and are in the majority in Bahrain and Iraq.

The Origins of Sunni-Shiite Differences

At the time of the Prophet's death in 632 CE, there was no human successor to lead the small band of Muslim followers. The Muslim community (or *umma*) thus selected the Prophet's closest companion and father-in-law Abu Bakr (the father of Aisha, Muhammad's last wife) as his successor, or caliph. While some cite evidence that the Prophet expected Ali to succeed him, factors like clan rivalry led to the choice of Abu

Bakr. But he died after only two years, when the *umma* chose the second caliph, Umar ibn al-Khattab. He ruled for ten years and led the conquest of Jerusalem. When Umar died in 644 CE (killed by a Persian prisoner of war), the third caliph, Uthman ibn Affan, a member of the Umayya clan, served until 656, when he was murdered by an Egyptian soldier who may have been the son of Abu Bakr.

Finally a relative of the Prophet, Ali ibn abi Talib, the husband of Muhammad's daughter Fatima by Khadija and Muhammad's cousin, was chosen as the successor. A rival from the Umayyad clan, Muawiya, a cousin of Caliph Uthman, challenged the selection. Muawiya had moved to Damascus with another group of Muslims, including Aisha, who had a dispute with Ali. Mu'awiya believed that those who murdered Uthman supported the succession of Ali. After initially defeating the rebels at the battle of the Camel at Basra in 656, Ali agreed to discuss the succession decision after his forces and those of Muawiya met at the battle of Siffin in 657. Ali's soldiers showed little will to fight after Muawiya's troops posted Qurans on their spears, and thus negotiations began between the parties that would last a year. This enraged one of Ali's followers, who murdered him in 661 CE. The succession first passed to Ali's eldest son, Hasan, but he declined the title and moved to Mecca. Ali's second son, Hussein ibn Ali, then took up his father's cause and moved to the city of Karbala (or Kerbala), now in southern Iraq. Muawiya died in 680 and his son Yazid succeeded him. Hussein ibn Ali refused to recognize Yazid as caliph and decided to eliminate him as a rival. He sent an army to Karbala, and in 680 CE Yazid's forces defeated the small group under Hussein ibn Ali and beheaded its leader. The survivors, now calling themselves the Partisans of Ali, or Shia Ali (later shortened to Shia), never again challenged the dominant role of the Sunni until the modern era, thus indicating the significance of the 2005 elections in Iraq.

This may seem like a small incident in the scope of human history. However, as Ajami notes, "Kerbala cast a long shadow; for the faithful it annulled time and distance. Succeeding generations had told and embellished the tale, giving it their sense of separateness and political dispossession." It also contributes to a sense among the Shiites that their role is to continue the tradition of suffering and martyrdom epitomized by Ali and his son.

The Shiites

Both Sunnis and Shiites practice the fundamentals of Islam, though they may differ in details. For both, the Quran is their holy book, and the hadiths guide them. Yet there are differences that date back to the question of succession after the death of the Prophet in 632 CE. They remain divided on the selection of the early caliphs, even though the caliphate disappeared, either in 1517 with the Mamluk defeat by the Ottomans, or in 1924 when Turkey's new leader Mustafa Kemal formally abolished the post. The Sunni followed the first three caliphs and ultimately rejected the selection of Ali as the fourth "rightly guided caliph." They take their name from the phrase *ahl al–Sunna wa-l-jammaah,* which in Arabic means "peoples of custom and community." They believe in the election of the caliph by members of that community, while the Shiites believe that the caliph, whom they refer to as the "imamship" is nonelective and should remain within the family of the Prophet. That distinction has blurred over the centuries, but it has also led to another distinction between Sunnis and Shiites. The Shiites have a formal leadership structure while the Sunnis do not. In Sunni practice, an *imam* or prayer leader leads the prayers in the mosque, but that person can be chosen from among the community. In Shiite tradition the imam (coming from the term "righteous individual," or *al-imama*) is more than a prayer leader. He (only males can become imams) is also considered a jurist, particularly for members of the Twelver Shiite community (see below). However, all Shiites hold that the role of Imam as a jurist (*qadi*), and thus a political leader, is important. The jurist must understand the Quran in all its manifestations (including the "five pairings" of verses), and the various forms of hadith.

The formal clerical structure normally found in Shiite Islam is:

- Grand Ayatollah (Ayatollah uzma) or "Great Sign of God"
- Ayatollah (Sign of God)
- Hojat al-Islam (Authority on Islam)
- Mubellegh a-Risala (Carrier of the Message)
- Mujtahid (a graduate of a religious seminary)
- Talib ilm (a religious student)

The Shiites are further divided into subsects, usually based on which imam they follow:

- The Zaydi, found largely in Yemen, believe that the true line of succession ended with Zayd ibn Ali, the fifth imam and grandson of al-Hussein. The Zaydi have no tradition of a hidden imam and instead hold that the imamate can continue, even though the Zaydis in Yemen (the majority there) are currently without a religious leader.

  A majority of Shiites disagree, believing instead that succession passed to the sixth imam, Jafar al-Sadiq, the son of the fifth imam Muhammad al-Baqir, who had a pronounced influence on the development of Shiite law. The Shiites disagree, though, on the next path to succession, with one group holding that Jafar's son Ismail is the rightful successor, while the larger majority believe that the true successor is the twelfth imam. Consequently there are two other Shiite groups.

- The Ismaili, or "Seveners," who believe that the seventh Imam, Ismail, was the last true Shiite descendant of the Prophet. Their early leader Ubayd Allah attempted unsuccessfully to conquer Syria and then fled to Tunisia, which he did conquer in 909, declaring himself the Mahdi. He named his dynasty the Fatimid (after the Prophet's daughter Fatima, to whom he claimed kinship). The Fatimids conquered Egypt in 969 and ruled there until Salah al-Din defeated them in 1171. Most Ismaili now live in India, with few left in the Middle East.

- The Imamiyya, or "Twelvers," believe that the correct line of succession runs through the ninth, tenth, and eleventh imams (Muhammad al-Jawad, who died in 818, Ali al-Hadi, who died in 868, and Hassan al-Askari, who died in 874), to al-Askari's son, the twelfth imam, Muhammad al-Mahdi (born Abu-Qasim Muhammad ibn Hasan), who "disappeared" or "was hidden" (or went into "occultation") in 874, at around age eight, near Samarra in modern Iraq, but will someday return to establish a perfect Islamic society on earth. The reason for occultation involves the danger to imams and occultation continues because of the threat. Occultation became a tradition largely in the tenth century when the reality of a living imam would have attracted messianic attention away from the Twelver leaders, who thus claimed that their imam was alive but "hidden." They are the largest Shiite group. They include in their traditions the practice of *kalam*, or free will developed by Muhammad ibn Muhammad al-Harithi which carries forward to this day. According to Heinz Halm, "The success of the Iranian Shi'a today cannot be understood without taking this into account."

The Sunni

The Sunni branch of Islam is the largest Muslim group, constituting around 85 percent of the world's total Islamic population. Common to the Sunnis is a belief that the "rightly guided" caliphs were successors but not spiritual leaders. Thus the Sunnis expected their leaders to be responsive to the guidance of those schooled in Islam but not to be clerics. Like the Shiites, Sunnis differ among themselves. One distinction lies in the different schools of Sunni Islamic law, or jurisprudence. The distinction helps explain certain regional differences in Sunni behavior, for example, the more conservative attitude in Saudi Arabia versus the more liberal mores in Morocco.

Schools of Sunni Jurisprudence

Islamic law, designed to regulate the behavior of both individual Muslims and the Muslim community, has many sources. The most basic is the Quran itself, and the hadith and the sunna. Juridical renderings also come from religious scholars (*ijamaa*) through analogy (*qeyas*) and reasoning (*ijtihad*). However, confusion arose in the Umayyad period when *qadis,* or religious judges, had considerable leeway to interpret the law. By the eighth century, legal scholars attempted to provide legal guidance, and those efforts resulted in four Sunni schools of law.

The *Hanafi* school, named after its founder, Abu Hanifa (d. 767 CE), has spread throughout the Middle East, except the Arabian Peninsula and Iran, and is the most liberal of the schools, except in areas regarding women and personal status. It emphasizes the role of reason and independent judgment, or *ijtihad*. Abu Hanifa was once a student of Jafar al-Sadiq, the Sixth Imam in the Shiite imamate line, suggesting possible Shiite influence in the Hanafi school.

The *Maliki* school came from the teachings of Malik ibn Abnas (d. 796 CE), who emphasized the importance of public welfare and the public interest. The Maliki school is most commonly found in the Maghreb and sub-Saharan Africa.

The *Shafi* school follows Muhammad al-Shafi (d. 819 CE) and his emphasis on the importance of legal doctrine, and upon methodology for determining the authenticity of the Prophet's reports (sayings and practices). Shafi adherents also hold that it is important to avoid deviation through reason from those sayings and practices deemed authentic. Adherents of the Shafi school are found in Egypt, Yemen, East Africa, and Southeast Asia, and a majority of Kurds (a linguistic group discussed later in this chapter) are followers of the Shafi school.

The *Hanbali* school is the most conservative of the four, originating in the teachings of Ahmad ibn Hanbal (d. 855 CE). It is most influential in Saudi Arabia and Qatar. The teachings of ibn Hanbal emphasize the oneness of God (*tawhid*) and particularly the banning of unacceptable innovations (*bida*). The Hanbali school, like the Hanafi, does allow for *ijtihad* in matters not covered by religious text. It also emphasized the body of a woman as "sexually provocative and private," thus leading to the requirement for full body and face covering for women in conservative Hanbali-influenced countries like Saudi Arabia.

The Schism Between Sunni and Shiite

Despite such theological and differences of praxis, Keddie notes that before the Persian Safavid dynasty (1501–1722 CE), the Shiite and Sunni communities coexisted in relative harmony. But after forcible Shiite conversions of Persian Sunnis and persecution of the Shiites by the Ottomans, the fissures between the two communities widened greatly. The Sunni realm gained power over the Shiite dynasties by the middle of the eleventh century, particularly after the Seljuq Turks occupied Baghdad around 1055, replacing the Twelver Shiite leaders who considered Baghdad their intellectual center.

Is there still a schism between the followers of Shiite and Sunni Islam? Despite efforts to cement ties between the two interpretations (like the 1959 *fatwa,* or religious instruction, by the Sunni Al-Azhar University in Cairo declaring Shia the fifth school of Sunni Islamic jurisprudence), problems continue. They occur mostly in Islamic countries where Shiites are a significant minority or majority of the population. They remain targets of oppression and discrimination in some majority Sunni Middle Eastern countries, forcing some to engage in the practice of *taqiyya,* or hiding one's true beliefs. In Saudi Arabia, for example, where Shiites may be 8 percent of the total population, intolerance from the majority al-Muwahiddun (Wahhabi in the West) regime remains a problem. The problem is more serious in Iraq, where the minority Sunni regime of Saddam Hussein waged open warfare on the Shiites in the south until its elimination in 2003. The long-standing resentment by Iraqi Shi-ites against the Sunnis remains. After the 2003 ouster of Saddam Hussein and American-led efforts to install a majoritarian government, Shiite and Sunni militias formed and attacked each other's populations, with Sunnis fearing a loss of traditional dominance and Shiites trying to gain and hold what they believed was their rightful place in Iraq after centuries of Sunni domination. In some Sunni neighborhoods, citizens adapted the Shiite practice of *taqiyya,* dressing like Shiites and putting pictures of Hussein and Ali in their houses in an effort to escape the Shiite militias.

Other Islamic Sects

Not all sects claiming Muslim identity abide by the practices noted above; the Sufi, Druze, and Alawi are exceptions.

The Sufi

Most religions have elements of mysticism within their corpus, and Islam is no exception. The most notable mystics in Islam are the Sufi, who date back to the teachings of Hasan al-Basri (643–728) and Rabia al-Adawiyya (d. 801), the latter attracting a circle of followers because of her asceticism. Sometimes described as an esoteric version of Shia, the Sufi work to achieve a spiritual sense of the meaning of God, often resorting to repeated prayer, music, dance (including the dance of the so-called whirling dervishes symbolizing the order of the universe), and the teachings of Sufi masters. Such masters reflect a Sufi belief in the requirement for the "perfect man" (or *qutb*) to serve as an intermediary between God and humans, reflecting a similarity to the concept of the Shi'a imams. These masters often head Sufi orders, where disciples learn Sufi practices of religious self-discovery, including how to sweep aside worldly concerns and practices to truly know the meaning of God's will. Some masters (or *pir*) became missionaries and were responsible for the spread of Islam into Africa and Southeast Asia, far more so than the Arab merchants who traded there. In modern times, some Sufi have risen to political prominence—Recep Tayyip Erdodan, the prime minister of Turkey, is Sufi.

The Sufi may be either Sunni or Shiite, but most Sufi live in Sunni areas. However, whatever the preference, some Sufi practices go beyond the normal practice of both streams of Islam. A common Sufi practice involves the construction of shrines at the tombs of saints, a custom heterodox Muslims eschew. Some Sufi believe that a pilgrimage to such a shrine can substitute for the *hajj,* a view also at odds with traditional Muslim practice. The Sufi have no formal structure and rarely have structured ties to regimes. Consequently the Sufi may benefit when regimes relax or cut ties to religious leaders, as happened in Turkey under and after Kemal Ataturk, whose secularation of Turkish social and political space allowed certain Sufi groups to develop strong networks in business, politics, the media, and welfare services.

The Druze

The Druze live mostly in Lebanon and Syria, with a smaller number in Israel. They do not perform the *hajj* or observe Ramadan, and thus many Muslims do not regard them as true Muslims. They refer to themselves as al-Mowahideen (roughly "monotheist"). The name "Druze" came from the westernized name of a Druze preacher named Nashtakin al-Darzis, though contemporary Druze consider his teachings blasphemous.

The Druze date back to the ninth century CE, when Darzis and Hamza ibn Ali ibn Ahmad proclaimed that God had become human and taken the form of man, al-Hakim bi-amr Allah, between 996 and 1021 CE in Fatimid Cairo. They further believe that Hamza ibn Ali was a reincarnation of many prophets, including Christ, Plato, Aristotle, and Adam, and revealed the truth to all Mowahideen who took an oath to accept and advance those truths. After the death of Druze leader Baha al-Din in 1031, the Druze decided not to accept converts, and thus Druze may marry only other Druze. Their beliefs include a single god (thus no Holy Trinity), the truth in a book known as Kitab al-Hikma, which contains not only Quranic verses but other beliefs as well, including reincarnation (the concept of heaven and hell are believed to be spiritual and not virtual).

Israeli policy treats the Israeli Druze differently from Israeli Muslims in that the Druze are eligible for military service while Muslims are not. Some argue that because the Druze keep their religious practices secret, they are not real Muslims but are practicing *taqiyya*. This interpretation, as Parsons notes, means that while the Druze "may seem to be participating in Muslim Arab culture, they are in fact just pretending. They are practicing taqiyya."

> Fog and sleet fill the valley, making the platforms on each side difficult to see. The dim figures of several people appear on the Syrian side of the valley, while off in the distance a wagon draws slowly down the narrow road from the Golani Druze village on the occupied Israeli side. Figures emerge from the wagon and shouting begins from one of the platforms. One figure calls out the attributes of his son or daughter (it is too misty to tell) over the fierce wind to the other side, from which someone in turn shouts the qualities of his offspring. This is the only place where Druze families in Golan can arrange a marriage between their progeny and the offspring of Druze parents in Syria. It is called the "shouting place," and it represents the only avenue out of occupied Golan for the 18,000 or so Druze who still live there, for only marriage to a Syrian Druze allows one to leave. The outcome of this particular shout was uncertain, but it was clear from the effort on that bone-chilling day that the stakes for both families were very high.

The Alawi

The Alawi (Alawiyun, anglicized to Alawi Nusayriyah, or Alawi, or Alawite; Alevi in Turkish) date to at least the teachings of Hussein ibn Hamadan al-Khasibi, a Twelver Shiite who died around 957. The Alawi are found mostly in Syria and Turkey, and hold secret religious observances that cause other Muslims to regard them largely as pagan. The problem was especially keen for Syrian President Hafiz al-Asad, and later his son Bashar, who came from the Syrian Alawi community. Hafiz al-Asad asked a Shiite cleric in Lebanon, Musa al-Sadr, for a religious ruling (*fatwa*) declaring that the Alawi were actually Shiite Muslims. The term

"Alawi" roughly means a follower of Ali ibn Abi Talib, the son-in-law of the Prophet, so the Shiite tie is clearly implied, if not evident to other Shiites. The Alawi belong to a Shiite group known as the Ghulat, or exaggerators, who consider Ali beyond veneration as the son-in-law of the Prophet, a manifestation of the deity. They did not consider themselves descendants of the family of Ali, but rather gatekeepers. The office of *bab*, or "gate," is still significant in the Alawi faith. After the arrival of the Crusaders in the eleventh century, certain Christian ideas seem to have permeated the Alawi. They adopted the concept of a Trinity (not a part of Islam), with Ali as the meaning and essence (*mana*), Muhammad as the outward exoteric name (*ism*), and Salman al-Farsi as the gate to Ali's esoteric essence (*bab*). They also celebrate Christian feast days such as Christmas, Epiphany, and Pentecost. The Alawi hold mass-type ceremonies during which the congregation chants hymns, also not an Islamic practice. Finally, most Alawi believe in reincarnation, although it is more restricted than in Hindu belief.

The attacks on the Alawi began with Ahmad ibn Taymiyya (d. 1328), an early critic of Islamist laxity, who claimed that the Alawi drank wine, believed in reincarnation, and considered Ali ibn Abi Talib as a god. The Hanbali school banned Sunni marriage with the Alawi. However the Alawi benefited when the Ottoman governor of Syria created a separate administration for them in the nineteenth century, and the French built a unique armed force from Alawi soldiers in former Ottoman territories, giving them the special military status that carried over into modern Syria. Today an Alawi elite rules Syria, though this elite also includes members of other branches of Islam as well as some Christians (see Chapter 12).

The Bahai

The Bahai sect is more recent, dating to the 1860s in Persia. The Bahai are inspired by the teachings of Mirza Hussein Ali, who took the name Bahaullah, and taught that God has manifested himself in the forms of Abraham, Moses, Jesus Christ, Buddha, Muhammad, and in Bahaullah himself. These teachings include the unity of God across all religions, equality of the world's people (including the equality of men and women), eradication of poverty, avoidance of politics, and abstinence from drugs and alcohol. The Bahai claim to be Muslim because they recognize the Quran as the word of God revealed to Muhammad. However, they recognize other messengers, and they do not perform the Five Pillars of Islam. The faith attracted Iranian Jews, Zoroastrians, and Shiites seeking a more modern faith. However, Bahai beliefs and practices came under attack in Iran after the 1979 revolution (and before that in other countries like Egypt and Morocco), and followers there faced widespread persecution. According to Bahai officials, the Iranian government has killed over 200 of their faithful. Many have fled Iran, and now their main temple is in Haifa, Israel.

Islam and Politics

Early Muslim thinking on politics consisted largely of a code of good conduct for rulers based on norms developed from the early ideas on Islamic communities. Emphasis was on obedience to authority, and, as Brown notes, "the weight of Muslim tradition was on the side of political submission." During the caliphate periods, Islamic political theory concentrated largely on the leadership qualifications for rulers, and contained little guidance on such matters as state administration, and almost no mention of individual rights. Islamic politics evolved through the caliphate periods into modernity and confrontation with European colonialism. What Tibbi calls Islamic modernism began in the nineteenth century, seeking fusion with Western ideas to resist colonialism, and developed in parallel with other movements, like the Wahhabist elements from Muhammad al-Wahab seeking to purify Islam, the idea of a relatively secular Muslim state. All these movements ultimately affected political Islam.

During the times of Caliphs Uthman and Ali, a group calling itself the Kharijites or Khariji revolted against Ali when he agreed to mediate a challenge to the legitimacy of his succession, and they continued to revolt against the Umayyad and Ab-basid caliphates. They emphasized a strict literal interpretation of the Quran as well as an egalitarian society. Kharijite doctrine also emphasized jihad, or holy war, as the Sixth Pillar of Islam. The Khariji later split into factions (divided over, among other issues, the legitimacy of violence against sinners), and one faction under the guidance of Abd Allah ibn Ibad of Basra became the Ibadi around 680. These Ibadis (taking the name of ibn Ibad), eschewed violence, believed in redemption, and agreed to live with other Muslims who differed from their strict moral code. Some Ibadis left Iraq and settled in Oman, where they remain today as the majority religion (See Chapter 6). Others live in remote parts of Algeria, Libya, and Tunisia.

Contemporary Islamist Ideas

Islam as a political resistance movement dates to the early caliphs. It waned but later revived, largely in response to European incursions. Twentieth-century Islamist thinkers built on earlier traditions, with particularly important links to Taqi al-Din Ahmad ibn Taymiyya who wrote after the Mongols sacked Baghdad in 1258, calling for a return to the fundamentals of Islam in the face of outside threats and an emphasis on the importance of revelation over reason. Ibn Taymiyya also rejected the Shiite importance of imams, claiming they had no more authority than any other Muslim to interpret religious tradition. One prominent scholar who followed ibn Taymiyya in the twentieth century was Said Qutb, an important figure in the Egyptian Muslim Brotherhood. Qutb, writing in the early 1950s, argued that Muslims lived in a period of ignorance (*jahiliyya*) of Islam, similar to pre-Islamic times, and he called on a new "Quranic generation" to build a modern Islamic community on the remains of nationalism as the Prophet built his community on the remains of paganism. Noted Qutb, "The basis of our economic life is usury, our laws permit rather than punish oppression, the *zakat* is not obligatory, and is not spent in the requisite ways. We permit the extravagance and the luxury that Islam prohibits." For Qutb, *tawhid* should be the basis of Islamic society, to include its laws and a refusal to submit to un-Islamic authorities or nontextual laws, though Qutb accepts the possibility of contemporary understandings of religious text, which separates Qutb from some of the more fundamental Salafiyyists (see below). Hassan al-Banna, born in Egypt in the same year as Said Qutb, founded Egypt's Muslim Brothers in 1928 with a vision similar to that of Qutb. Al-Banna's anti-British sentiments pushed him to admire Hitler and Mussolini, but his primary message to Egypt's Muslims was not that they needed to resist alien domination, but that they needed to turn back from the brink of *jahiliyya*, the period of pre-Islamic existence or ignorance, that many Salifiyyists argued would return without a continual and emphatic Islamic purification by its adherents.

Ruhollah Khomeini, who became the supreme ruler of Iran in 1979, held similar views on secular government, writing scathing criticism of the ruling Pahlavi family's claim to nationalism based on the modernist nationalism views of Turkish Republic founder Kemal Ataturk. These and other Islamist theorists also rejected the quasi-Marxist politics embraced by many Arab nationalists. Khomeini called for rule by the experts in Islamic jurisprudence, *the vilayat-i faqih,* who can carry out the same functions as would the

Imam, even though the *vilayat-i faqih* would not have the Imam's status. As Nasr points out, Khomeini studied, among other texts, Plato's philosopher-king template of governance and applied it accordingly.

Political Islamists have varying objectives, depending partially on their orientation. As noted above, most Shiite Islamists believe that the supreme leader of a country should be an Islamic figure (an ayatollah, for example), that the Sharia, or religious law, be the law of the state, and that a literal interpretation of the Quran be followed by society. Sunni Islamists tend to enforce Sharia but rarely have religious heads of state. One Sunni sheik in Egypt, when asked if he sought the elimination of Egypt's secular state, responded, "No, Islam is not a style of ruling. We don't want the president of the republic to be a sheik, only to have the Sharia as the law of the land." Still, Sharia requires interpretation from doctrine to particular circumstances. Is it to be viewed as immutable and unchanging, a reflection of its origins, or can it accommodate change? The duty of interpretation of the Sharia itself through *usul al-fiqh* or "method of study" by scholars to link specific events and facts to the Sharia, and to determine if the outcome stems from the Sharia itself or through reason, or *ijtihad.* However, as Masmoudi comments, *ijtihad,* or reasoning between a strict inter-pretation of Sharia and other principles (like mercy or justice) was common in the fifth century, but recent attempts to revive it have been "modest and not very successful." Thus Sharia construal may reflect a literal view of Islamic law in many Middle Eastern societies since, as Tibi notes, "the Islamic cultural system does not admit a category of 'change.'" Consequently political Islamists demand that the secular state should abide by their traditionalist views of Islam: formulate and enforce state laws that forbid the consumption or possession of alcohol and require women to dress modestly (often with head covered and veiled), for example, to further their view of Islam as a purifying force to drive out corrupt ideas and practices.

In many ways, political Islam becomes a replacement or an adjunct to the state, where the state is either weak or narrowly focused. Islamist movements supply education, food, and public protection where the state cannot or will not provide such things in adequate quantity. In Cairo, people living in sections devasted by an earthquake in 1992 waited for over two weeks for the government to respond, but the mosques showed up immediately with food, shelter, and medical care. In Lebanon's Shiite areas, the Islamist group Hizbollah supplies much of the daily needs for the poor. In Turkey, the Islamist-oriented AKP Party supplements the state: "In practices that would be familiar to Shiite Muslims in Lebanon or Palestinians in Gaza, women's groups go door to door offering aid, community centers offer women's literacy classes, and sports centers give free physical therapy to handicapped children."

The Salafiyya

Some Islamist movements set as their vision the life and times of the Prophet and the first three generations of the Islamic community, which serves as a guide for proper Islamic society. Such movements are known as the Salafiyya, or "pious ancestors." The Salafiyya are commonly associated with a return to a puritanical and conservative vision of Islam, but because early Islamic times saw a ferment of ideas and theological interpretations, the Salafiyyist tradition also included discussions of modernity. Such Salafiyyists as Jamal al-Din al-Afghani, Muhammad Abduh, and Rashid Rida, writing mostly between 1880 and 1935, argued in favor of *ijtihad* and a limited dialog with the West, particularly in areas where Islam did not provide adequate guidance; some modernists find early Quranic justifications for parliaments and constitutions. Yet other Salafiyyists drew inspiration from Ahmad ibn Taymiyya, noted above. They emphasize the original purity of Islam by focusing on the impurity and temptation offered by the West (and the United States in particular), and by the Islamic regimes supported by the West that, in the Salafi view, only pretend to be

Islamic. There is a particular emphasis against *shirk*, or the attribution of powers reserved only for God. Thus Salafiyyists attacked shrines to saints and assaulted the mosque erected to commemorate Hussein Ali (see above) because they regard the Shiites as apostates. The Salafiyyi also reject *ijtihad* because the practice might refute the original sources of Islamic belief, the Quran and the life and sayings of Muhammad.

These are the Islamist roots of the Egyptian Islamic Jihad and Osama bin Laden's al-Qaeda. In his application of Salafi thinking to both the Egyptian Islamic Jihad and al-Qaeda, Doran states that "the magnitude of the attacks on New York and Washington indicates that al-Qaeda does indeed believe itself to be fighting a war to save the umma from Satan, represented by secular Western culture." However, the Salafi do not limit their quest to circumscribing the impact of Western culture on Muslims, but also campaign against "un-Islamic" practices in their own societies. Thus unveiled women or men who consume alcohol may become the victims of a Salafi attack, as happened in Morocco in 2003 when half a dozen people died at the hands of Salafiyya Jihadia, some with their throats slit.

Besides al-Qaeda, the best-known form of Salafiyya is the Wahhabi or, properly, the Muwahiddun or "Unitarian" interpretation of Sunni Islam, which differs from mainstream Salafiyyism in that it is far less tolerant of religious diversity. This stems from the influence of *tawhid* and its stress on the unity of God and the destruction of all that challenges that unity. The origins of this offshoot of Sunni Islam are in its name, from Muhammad ibn Abd al-Wahhab, a scholar whose puritanical teachings and interpretations of the Hanbali school influenced the al-Saud family of Saudi Arabia, and today form the basis of Saudi Arabian Islam (see Chapter 5). However, since many Muslims object to taking the name of a person for an Islamic sect, the formal name for its adherents is Muwahiddun. While Saudi Arabia is the most noteworthy example of Muwahiddun influence, it is also spreading into Central Asia and other parts of the Islamic world. It is the chosen Islamic interpretation of Osama bin Laden, the Saudi Arabian–born leader of al-Qaeda, who uses its strong opposition to *bida* (see above) to motive followers into extreme deeds. It would be mistaken, however, to regard the Muwahiddun, al-Qaeda, and other Salafiyya groups as in agreement on theology or politics. The Saudi Arabian regime is itself under attack by al-Qaeda and other Salafiyyist groups have tried to discredit beliefs and practices of the Muwahiddun. Others attack it because they believe that it rests on false premises. One Saudi Arabian theologian, whose views have drawn the ire of the Saudi government, argues that the authoritarian tradition in Saudi Arabia (and presumably other authoritarian countries) comes from the Umayyad rulers. Says Hassan al-Maleky, "The salafis blindly defend the Umayyads despite their many injustices." The Muwahiddun also believe that only the ruler may declare the permissibility of jihad whereas al-Qaeda argues that rulers may become apostate, and thus al-Qaeda members may declare jihad, even against rulers regarded as apostates.

While the roots of Muwahiddun belief lie in the Hanbali school, there are additional components to the sect. Its contempt for Shiites is greater than in other Salafiyyist groups. From its origins it attacked Shiite communities in eastern Arabia (in 1788–1792) and between 1801 and 1811 repeatedly attacked and destroyed Shiite shrines at Karbala and Najaf, as well as the Shiite communities in Bahrain, until Ottoman Governor Midhat Pasha annexed the island in 1871.

Hizb ut-Tahrir and the Caliphate Movement

Efforts to restore the Islamic caliphate date back to Arab efforts to restore the Mam-luk caliphate after its defeat in the early sixteenth century. In 1953 a Palestinian judge, Taqiuddin al-Nabhani, founded Hizb ut-Tahrir, or Party of Liberation, as he believed that the Muslim Brotherhood was not radical enough to cope with growing Western and Israeli power in the region. According to Palestinian intellectual Abdullah

Azzam, "If the enemy has entered Muslim lands, the jihad becomes an individual obligation," linking jihad (see below) as a means to restore lost Muslim lands.

Hizb ut-Tahrir beliefs emphasize that the problems of the Muslim *umma* date to the loss of both the Mamluk and Ottoman caliphate (the latter in 1924), and thus project a strategy to convert Muslims to the concept of a caliphate that would unite them in the face of threats from the world outside Islam. Hizb ut-Tahrir is more active in Central Asia than in the Middle East, and numerous Arab governments and Turkey have banned the movement. While its message has been used by others (including al-Qaeda), other Islamists widely reject it, preferring to focus attention on more modern problems.

Islam as a Reactive Force

The reaction to the Islamic revolution in Iran surprised observers in the West (and elsewhere), and particularly in the academic world. Academic models of revolution stressed leadership by the "modernizers" like Nasser or Kwame Nkrumah of Ghana, who offered their own vision of a postcolonial society. However, as Benard and Khalilzad note, such models were too simplistic, failing to understand the political attractiveness of a religion that emphasizes opposition to illegitimate authority. Islam emphasizes a purity of rule as well as spirit, and Islamic reformers find a powerful message in its humility and its calls to not only Islamic leaders but also the Islamic faithful in general to take responsibility for combating evil. The world outside the Islamic community became a world of temptation, filled with alcohol, sexuality, and an obsession with the material over the spiritual. For its protectors who see the world this way, the purpose of Islam is not to spread the faith to those who do not have it (because only God can determine who should be a Muslim), but rather to protect the Islamic community from inducements from outside the *umma*. For reactive Islam, though, members of the *umma* do have a responsibility for policing conformity with what they believe is proper Islamic conduct, thus they believe in the right of *takfir*, the obligation to excommunicate Muslims from the *umma* for behaviors and beliefs that counter what the reactivists hold proper.

The difficulty of any reactive movement is that it rarely has anything positive to offer in place of what it opposes. Islamists are able to organize opposition but few alternatives. Doran notes that "apart from insisting on the implementation of the Sharia, demanding social justice, and turning the umma into the only legitimate political community, radical Salafis have precious little to offer in response to the mundane problems that people and governments face in the modern world."

The Perception of External Threat

Islam is the newest of the three monotheistic religions (although it is over 1,400 years old), and Muslims feel a challenge from the other established religions, particularly Christianity and Judaism. Early Muslims believed that the established religions would not tolerate a competitor for the faithful. This was one reason why Muslim armies spread into areas where Christians, Jews, pagans, and Persian Sassanians held sway. That campaign began in 632 CE and lasted for a century, bringing much of the known world under Islamic control. That drive, and others that followed (the Ottoman campaigns into central Europe in the sixteenth and seventeen centuries, for example), raised the specter that the Islamic community was bent on spreading Islam by force into the non-Islamic world, a concern that remains today. Bernard Lewis, in commenting on the Ayatollah Khomeini's denunciation of the United States as the Great Satan, said, "America was by then perceived—rightly—as the leader of what we like to call 'the free world.' Then, as in the past, this world of unbelievers was seen as the only serious force rivaling and preventing the divinely ordained spread and triumph of Islam." In the modern era, many Muslims still express fear that the Islamic world remains under siege from the outside world, especially the so-called Christian world. That assault is not simply physical and political but also cultural. It is the things that corrupt a conservative belief system—alcohol, unveiled women, slot machines, and the emphasis of the material over the spiritual. Muslims view the West as the source of not only the temptations themselves, but also the political and economic power to spread them through the Muslim world.

The Nature of Jihad

The jihad aspect of Islam is one of its more controversial characteristics. The question is about the purpose and essence of jihad: is it to spread Islam to nonbelievers, eliminate all unbelievers, or defend Islam from its enemies? Is it against apostasy, or is it primarily concerned with the internal human struggle against evil? The answer is all of these, though scholars disagree about the validity of the latter goal. The Quran calls for a literal struggle by Muslims against nonbelievers, and certain hadiths call for the propagation of Islam through combat. It can also mean striving for excellence, and in one Arab-English dictionary, it translates to "fight, battle, holy war (against the infidels) as a religious duty." The earliest calls for jihad came after the death of the Prophet, when some Muslim converts left the faith to return to paganism, and the Muslim armies under Abu Bakr swept into these apostates' homelands. John Esposito casts the word contextually, "Muslims are enjoined to struggle (jihad) to implement their belief, to lead a good life, to defend religion, to contribute to the development of a just Islamic society throughout the world." "To lead the good life" is sometimes referred to as the "greater jihad" and means that the most important jihad for Muslims is the resistance of personal temptation. David Cook argues, though, that this definition is bereft of support in Islamic thought except in some Sufi traditions, and that jihad is warfare against the enemies of Islam, authorized by a Muslim who had the legitimate right to authorize jihad.

The defensive nature of jihad has its origins in the Quran, which states, "Fight in the cause of Allah those who fight you … and fight them on until there is no more tumult or oppression." However, does this passage (and others like it) call for a defensive struggle against the enemies of Islam? Are the enemies of Islam those who actually attack the Islamic community, or those who might attack it? Some suggest that it sanctifies an aggressive holy war to spread Islam, and that the Prophet and his followers started such wars to spread Islam across much of the known world by the early eighth century. The Quran provides a different context. In Sura 8:39 it calls for Muslims to "fight … till there is no fitna and the religion is God's entirely," where *fitna* describes either infidelity or polytheism but not other religions. However, the Arab Muslim militaries that swept into the Byzantine world in the seventh century did not force conversions of Christians and Jews once they came under Islamic rule. Both goals may lie at the root of early Islamic expansion. The conquest of Syria included the religious goal of conquering Jerusalem and Hebron, which is location of the tomb of Abraham (Ibrahim). However, early Muslim leaders also understood the commercial value of Syria with its trade routes. These leaders also wanted to convert the nomadic tribes in Syria to Islam before the Christian Byzantines could recruit them to build a coalition of tribes against the Muslims to the south. Later, when the Muslim armies swept across the Straits of Gibraltar into Spain and then across the Pyrenees into central France, the objective was again believed by Europeans of the time (and since) to have been an effort to spread Islam into Europe by force. However, as Cardini notes, "The Muslim commander Abd ar-Rahmen wanted … to plunder Saint-Martin, the national sanctuary of the Franks. It was probably never his intention to proceed any further, and he did not have the military might to do so." Should it be surprising that Muslims might have the same objective for conquest as any other conqueror: plunder? Plunder, after all, in the days before income taxes, was a major source of income to maintain the empire. Muslims could be as crassly materialistic as other leaders of the time, even as they might use religious passion as a cover.

The question also arises as to who may call for jihad. Was it legitimate for a respected Islamic jurist or warrior to call for jihad, for example? Could someone like Osama bin Laden demand jihad from all Muslims against Americans, as he did prior to the terrorist attack against the United States on September 11, 2001? Saudi Arabian scholar Muhammad al-Salem says not. "This is not about jihad," he states, referring to bin Laden's declaration. "Nobody has the right to declare war. It is done through the leadership." Hizbollah leader Sheik Muhammad Hussein Fadlallah echoes that sentiment, claiming that the September 11 attacks were against Sharia law, and that the attackers were not martyrs as bin Laden claimed, but "merely suicides" because they killed innocent civilians. He accused bin Laden of relying on "personal psychological needs" rather than on Quranic texts. Other Islamist critics of the global (or "far") jihad of bin Laden include ranking members of al-Jama al-Islamiyya, like Karam Zuhdi and Mohammed Essam Derbala, who criticize the September 11 attacks as violating Islamic prohibitions on killing civilians as well as strengthening the hand of the United States and other Western powers as they increased their presence in the Islamic world after the al-Qaeda attacks.

Martyrdom

Martyrdom (*shahid*) status in Islam is normally accorded to those who die in the defense of Islam, in battle, or through individual actions. Martyrdom brings the reward of an immediate journey to Paradise and, in some Islamic traditions, marriage to maidens, though, as Bonner notes, such a privilege is accorded to all righteous Muslims and not just those who die in battle or take their lives in defense of Islam. The martyrdom tradition is particularly significant for the Shiites, who venerate Ali and his son Hussein who died in defense of the Shiite claim to succeed the Prophet.

Some Islamists link Islam to the concept of martyrdom, or choosing actions likely to take the life of the martyr in the name of defending Islam from its enemies. Those who choose martyrdom through acts likely or certain to cause their death believe that Allah actually made the choice, and that the result of martyrdom is immediate passage to Paradise without judgment. Some Islamists argue that martyrdom is not suicide, since Islam prohibits the act, but rather consider it a weapon against a stronger opponent. Others argue that Muhammad used the term *shahid* in a way closer to the Christian concept of "confessor," and that it was later Islamic interpreters who provided the contextual identity of death by choice in battle. There are few Quranic references to martyrdom, but some that are used include, "And some people sell themselves for the sake of Allah's favor," or "Indeed you will find them (evil-doers) of all people the most attached to life," both from Sura 2 but nowhere in the Quran are Muslims directed to kill themselves to defend Islam.

Islamic Reformation

Islamic reformation emphasizes moderation, toleration, and adaptation to modernity. For example, Muhammad Shahrur argues that for too long conservative religious jurists have shackled the development of Islam, and that Islam must grow beyond adherence to the old ways and practices. Reform, or "liberal," Islam emphasizes limited government and individual rights, resembling in many ways classical European liberalism. Its roots took hold in Egypt, where scholars and writers like Muhammad al-Ghazzaly, Fahmy

Huwaidy, and Kamal Abul Madg critiqued the ideas of the militant Islamists. They noted that their embrace of hadiths was inconsistent with the more tolerant passages in the Quran, thus permitting wrongful interpretation by militant opportunists. Instead, the "new Islamists embrace the importance of *ijtihad* and the equality of peoples, criticizing the unequal treatment of women (and Shi'a by some radical Salafiyyists)."[103] Iranian thinker Abdol Karim Soroush criticizes the *ulama* for developing ideological positions outside of the Quran to justify their power. Tunisian leader Habib Bourguiba represented reformist Islam, and his emphasis on *ijtihad* allowed him to interpret Islam as favorable to Tunisian modernity. This "reformation" may grow as more Muslims move up the education ladder, and the ability of local Islamic leaders to control information wanes in the face of the information age. However, Muslims who discuss Islamic reformation run the risk of being labeled apostates for suggesting an alteration of standard interpretations of the Quran and the life of the Prophet by their more conservative peers.

For some scholars, democratization offers the prospect that open political systems will attempt to accommodate religious-based politics with secular movements, often as a part of common interest coalition building. The expectation is that religious movements will moderate their positions when sharing political space with actors whose agendas differ from their own. The calculus is that leaders and followers of religious movements would rather be in the political tent, even if the payments for such inclusion are smaller because of compromise and minority position, than to be outside and excluded altogether. The evidence does not entirely support inclusion expectations in the Middle East, however. Clark found that the Jordanian Islamist Action Front (IAF) refused to compromise in its coalition with the Higher Committee for the Coordination of National Opposition Parties on issues involving women that the IAF claimed were against religious rulings. Schwedler finds that the IAF did moderate on a broader set of issues, while the Yemeni Islamist Islah Party retained it positions without much moderation, though this may have reflected the personal position of its leaders as much as it did Islah followers. Given that Islah did poorly in the 2006 Yemeni elections when the ruling General People's Congress coopted some Islah issues, Islah's future may not include further participation in electoral politics. By contrast, the moderate Islamist Adalet ve Kalkynma Partisi (Justice and Development, or AKP) has moderated its stance as the dominant party in Turkish politics, following in part on the lessons of the Refah Partisi (Welfare Party), which the military outlawed in 1998 because it did not moderate enough for its political tastes. Turkey also has a tradition of political compromise, which several military coups have enhanced.

Islam And Democracy

Islam, as the major religion in the Middle East, clearly affects political practice there. Some argue that Islamic practices and beliefs sanction democracy, while others claim that Islam is fundamentally antidemocratic.

Democracy emphasizes collective decision making, the rule of law, and the accountability of leaders to the polity. The earliest versions of Islamic practice emphasized consultation (*shura*) within the *umma* for significant decisions like choice of leadership. The Quran contains numerous references to the desirability of democracy and participation by the *umma*.

There is evidence of early democratic practices within Islam. Within the centralized rule of the tribe, consultation with elders was a part of tribal routine. The elders would meet and discuss a variety of issues in an effort to reach consensus over how to address them. As urbanization grew in the Arab world, the practice, known as the *majlis* or *shura* tradition, continued. Today the *majlis* continues, particularly in the Persian Gulf, as a way to connect ruler and ruled. Provincial governors in Saudi Arabia, city mayors, and national government ministers all hold *majlis* on a regular basis, and citizens come to petition them for favors or redress of a grievance. In some Arab countries, the *majlis* tradition forms a kind of democracy that connects citizens to their rulers more directly than might be the case in a parliamentary democracy. However, not all agree that the *majlis* or *shura* tradition means that Islam is inherently democratic. The Islamic modernist scholar Mohamed Talbi claims that the *shura* tradition is pre-Islamic, and that certain ethical principles that are both Islamic and universal are what actually connect Islam to democracy.

Tunisian Islamist thinker Rachid Ghannouchi argues that the roots of democracy lie in medieval Europe, which in turn got its influence from earlier Islamic civilizations. Ghannouchi also argues that suspending democracy in Islamic societies would only give rise to radical and ultimately unstable politics. Turkish Islamist leader Recep Erdoğan, who became Turkey's prime minister in 2002, stated that Islam is not an obstacle for democracy. Democracy includes Turks who are devout and those who are not. Finally, a comparison of Christian and Muslim populations on the World Values survey suggested that both Christians and Muslims hold democracy to be highly desirable as a political system, though they differ on social values such as abortion, gender equality, and gay rights.

One interpretation of Islam is that it is inherently undemocratic because the source of laws is the Quran, and the duty of good Muslims is to obey them rather than to debate them. The ruler in a classic Islamic polity is obligated to demonstrate fidelity to God's wishes as revealed in the Quran and to uphold the Sharia, or religious law. Such commitments constitute authority to rule rather than popular sovereignty. As a liberal member of the Kuwaiti parliament asked as his legislature debated a motion to adopt the Sharia as Kuwait's legal code, "How can you be a democrat and follow a fatwa?" Algerian Islamist Ali Belhaj views democracy as a contrived instrument placing popular will above the cohesion of the *ulama*. There is also the weight of tradition in many Muslim countries, where during the Islamic empires the *ulama* generally supported authoritarian rule, thus placing the religious establishment in the position of defenders of authoritarian rule. Islam does not recognize the principle of separation of church and state, which some argue is almost mandatory to prevent the hijacking of democratic processes by religious leaders who argue that the ultimate source of political authority is God, not the people.

However, as Stepan observes, half of the world's Muslims live in partial or complete democracies, in such places as Pakistan, Turkey, and Indonesia, but "there are no democracies in the Islamic countries of the Arab world." Thus the real barrier to democracy may be Arab culture rather than Islam. In the Arab world, tribal traditions emphasize the role of chiefs and other elders as leaders who rule through experience and wisdom, rather than being elected by the tribe. Such roles in some cases remain necessary because of the harsh challenges of the desert environment and the need to draw on the wisdom of elders without question.

The *majlis* heritage may explain the limits to democracy in the Gulf states, but it does not necessarily extend to the rest of the Arab world. Here traditional thinking about Islam and leadership may also play a role in reinforcing current beliefs in the value of authoritarian rule. As Charles Butterworth notes, most students in Arab countries from elementary schools to universities study formal principles of the state that take their meaning from the Quran. Students of politics read the works of Alfarabi or Averroes (ibn Rushd), or Nizam al-Mulk, who, in contrast to some Western thinkers like Rousseau or Locke, espouse a belief that few citizens are capable of good governance, and that the universe of God must be understood and not simply overcome. Bernard Lewis reinforces the "reluctance to democratize" argument by noting that the few Islamic rulers to attempt some type of constitutional government did so in "not so much imitation as propitiation, not of their own subjects but of the European powers whose political pressure they feared and whose fi-nancial support they wanted." However, to suggest that this adoption of democratic standards was blind imitation imposed by fear is to downplay the reality that some of these same European powers failed to create the prerequisites for democracy in the Middle East in the first place.

Islam and Pluralism

Islamic tradition often limits political participation in predominately Islamic countries to Muslims. That tradition places great importance on the notion of the umma as a distinct and special entity. The *umma* received preferential treatment by Islamic leaders, usually at the expense of other religious communities. Yet there is evidence of tolerance and even a desire for the well-being of other religious groups by Muslims. Abdulaziz Sachedina argues that the Quran refers to the need for a pluralist society, to include believers and nonbelievers alike. The problem, he argues, is that Muslim jurists regarded pluralism as a source of instability to the Islamic order, despite the teachings of the Quran. The Fatimid Caliph al-Hafiz wrote in 1136, "We believe that we should spread wide the mantle of justice and benevolence and embrace the different religious communities with mercy and compassion. Measure to improve conditions should include Muslims and non-Muslims alike, who should be provided everything they might hope for in the way of peace and security." Centuries later, Abdou Filali-Ansary argued for a liberal pluralist vision of Islam, stating, "Islam, properly understood, is not a system of social and political regulation [that] frees up space for cultures and nations in the modern sense of these words to lay the foundations of collective identity … and opens the way to a full respect for civic spheres in which Muslims can coexist as equal citizens with non-Muslims." Mahdi, interpreting the work of Islamic philosopher al-Farabi, claims that "democracy is a composite regime: various groups, aiming at the ends characterizing the other regimes, exist side by side and pursue different ways of life … and they are free to fulfill their distinct aims independently or in cooperation with others." Not all Muslim scholars hold such views. Ibn Hazm has a much more restricted position that non-Muslim *dhimmi* (meaning roughly "protected status") could have such status only if they recognized the status of the Prophet for the Arabs and honored him, while other writers emphasize the secondary status of the *dhimmi* and, for example, prohibit Muslims from consuming meat slaughtered by *dhimmi*.

Jews living in predominately Islamic areas were traditionally subject to certain restrictions, such as paying a tax (or *jizya*) to the Muslim community, or in their dress or in the buildings they constructed. Some Islamic dynasties, such as the Al-mohads in Morocco or the Safavids in Persia, were particularly harsh in their treatment of Jews. However, it is also true that Jews were often integrated into Islamic communities, even serving as court physicians and advisers to Islamic courts.

Islam is the majority religion in the Middle East, but it is not the only one. Israel is around 80 percent Jewish, and Lebanon has a large number of Christians. Around 12 percent of Syria's population is Christian. Iran has a small population of Zoroastrianians, whose beliefs predate Islam.

Judaism in the Middle East

Of the world's three monotheistic religions, Judaism is the oldest. It dates to the time when tradition holds that Abraham left the city of Ur in modern Iraq at God's command for the Promised Land, which was to be the home of the Jewish people. However, famine drove them to Egypt, where they multiplied until driven out. That same tradition holds that the Jews, led by Moses, received the Ten Commandments on their journey of return to the Promised Land, and entered it after the death of Moses. Under Joshua, they drove out the Canaanites in retaliation for Canaanite attacks against the Jews as they tried earlier to enter Israel. Israel thus became a theocracy as well as a home for the Jews, and the tradition of political Judaism grew from that time.

As in Islam, the Jewish religion has a few core beliefs, and numerous differing interpretations of faith. The Thirteen Articles of Faith capture the essence of Jewish belief, which include the following beliefs: there is only one God; God has no physical shape or form; there have been no other gods before God; humankind must worship God directly; the prophets were sent by God; God gave the Law of Moses to the Jewish people; good is rewarded and evil is punished; God is supreme ruler of the world; there will be a Messiah and one must never cease to believe in his eventual coming; the coming of the Messiah will bring about a resurrection of the dead.

Jewish Law

Jewish law, or Halacha, stems from the five books of Moses, which became the Torah, and the Talmud, which is an interpretation of Jewish history by early rabbis (collected around 200 CE). The nature of the Torah in particular divides Orthodox from Reform Judaism, as noted below.

As in Islam, a large majority of Jews follow ritualistic practices, including observation of the Sabbath (which starts on Friday at sundown and continues to sundown on Saturday), and other religious holy days (including Passover and Rosh Hashanah, the most important). Other practices include male circumcision, a prohibition against eating certain foods (pork, for one, as in Islam), and taboos regarding such things as death, menstruation, sex, and childbirth. In modern times, Jews differ considerably on actual practice, which are more common among Conservative Jews than Reform (see below).

Jewish Sects

Before around 1700 CE, there were few differences in the beliefs and practices of Judaism, and local customs and cultures often shaped such practices. However, when exposed to the currents of change in eighteenth-century Europe, Jews there began to separate into divisions. There are three such divisions common to Judaism: Orthodox, Conservative, and Reform.

Orthodoxy is distinguished by its emphasis on orthopraxy, or faithful adherence to the belief that both the Torah and the oral law (or Mishnah) are divinely inspired and fully authoritative. Orthodoxy also requires adherence to the code of Shulhan Arukh, demanding daily religious observance. Those who hold Orthodox views see themselves as the only true followers of the Jewish faith and traditions. They believe that God issued the Torah, and that it must thus be accepted literally.

Within the Orthodox tradition, there are several subdivisions. The Modern Orthodox largely adopt the position that they can coexist with others who are not like-minded while at the same time maintaining observance of Jewish law in their daily lives. In Israel, they are often referred to as observant Jews, to distinguish them from the ultra-Orthodox, who believe that the Orthodox community must live separately from those not of their faith. They have built settlements in the Occupied Territories, or live in separate neighborhoods in Israel proper, such as Mea Shearim in Jerusalem. The ultra-Orthodox themselves are subdivided into several groups, with most identifying with the Hasidism.

The Hasidim draw from the teachings of the Ukrainian folk preacher Israel ben-Eliezer Baal Shem Tov, known often by his acronym Besht, who gathered a flock of followers around 1735 CE. The Hasidic ideal, for who follow it, was panentheism: God is the ultimate and only reality; the world is illusory. Fundamental to Hasidic practice is the doctrine of the *tsaddik*, a channel through which all godly grace flows, leading to a permanent and uninterrupted thought of God in all that one does. Such an accomplishment is approachable by the close study of a rebbe, or communal leader. Some of these leaders came close to associating Hasidism with mysticism and miracles, though other Hasidic leaders and non-Hasidic Jews denounced such teachings. Hasidic Jews set aside much time for religious study, and consequently the Hasidim have gained an exemption from working and from the military draft. For some Hasidic interpreters, religious study is an essential ingredient for political leadership. As Rabbi Yehoshua Shapira put it in a speech denouncing Ariel Sharon's planned Gaza disengagement (see Chapter 14), "I do not believe in a leader who does not come from the *beit midrash* (religious study house). The spirit can come only from the beit midrash."

In Hasidic practice, the Yiddish language is widely spoken, and even the dress is distinctive. Hasidic men wear the wide-brimmed fur hat (with 13 sable tails representing the 13 qualities of Divine Mercy), while letting their hair drop into side locks in the old Polish style. Hasidic women dress in traditional modest clothing. The Hasidim believe in the importance of living in one's own community, and thus reserve neighborhoods in towns and cities that are exclusive to them. Signs posted at the entrance to such neighborhoods warn immodestly dressed visitors not to enter, and caution against driving vehicles there on the Sabbath.

Jewish Mysticism

As in Islam, there is a Jewish mystical tradition, often epitomized by the Kabbalah school, which Rabbi Yitzhak Kadouri led until his death in January 2006. His visions reportedly paved the way for the choice of Moshe Katsav as Israeli president in 2000 as well as Israeli rejection of a deal with Syria to return the Golan (see Chapter 14). Kabbalah emphasizes the importance of revelation to particular individuals of the specific meanings of ancient Jewish texts, giving rise to the importance of such figures as Kadouri.

Judaism and Politics

Like all other religions, Judaism provides political lessons from its recorded writs. Judaism was the early basis for Israeli statehood, though the role of Judaism in modern Israel remains a subject of intense debate. Two Jewish religious traditions, liberty and equality, have roots in the Torah and in prophets such as Amos, Micah, and Isaiah. Other lessons flow from the history of Judaism and particularly from its early history.

Sicherman argues that Judaism is the covenant between God and the people of Israel, where the Israelis are promised security and prosperity in exchange for fidelity to the commandments of God. This belief is the major tenet behind the Zionist commitment to the Promised Land (see Chapter 14) and to Jerusalem in particular, which still inspires arguments about its place in the founding of Judaism. However, God not only bestows title to land but can also take it away for immoral behavior, as in the case of the Canaanites, who lost title to the land that became Israel, according to Jewish interpretation, when they polluted it with idolatry. Moreover, the Torah eschews pacifism and instead commands preemptive action against and death for those who kill a member of the Jewish faith. For Jews who believe in a literal interpretation of the Torah, compromise with anyone outside the community of the Chosen People is difficult to accept. Some conservative strains, particularly those influenced by the ideas of Rabbi Avraham Yitzhak Kook and his son Zvi Yehuda Kook, claim that any compromise over land occupied by Jews is violation of Jewish sacred writ. Followers of the Kook interpretations were in the vanguard of protests against the evacuation of Gaza in 2005. For others, though, relations with neighbors are to be respectful, and violating a treaty is tantamount to profaning God's name.

Prime Minister David Ben Gurion understood that interreligious strife could weaken Israel, and thus in June 1947 he wrote a letter outlining the policy that Israel follows today with respect to Jewish religious observance. It includes the following provisions: The Jewish Sabbath, Saturday, is the official day of rest. No national public transportation is run on the Sabbath. The religious school system is funded by the state. Rabbinical courts apply the Halacha (religious law) to personal matters, such as marriage and divorce.

The Law of Return, passed by the Knesset in 1950, was supplanted by a new law allowing any person claiming to be a Jew to immigrate to Israel and become a citizen on the basis or his or her Jewishness. So while Israeli nationality could be granted to non-Jews (as a result of the Nationality Law of 1952 which granted Israeli citizenship to those living in Israel in 1948, including Muslims and Christians), only Jews could become new citizens of Israel. However, a sharp debate developed inside Israel over Jewish identity, particularly over sects that do not accept rabbinical law, or groups like the Ethiopian and Somalian Falasha Jews, whose practice of Judaism differs from mainstream customs. It continues to be an issue for the Orthodox in particular, who invalidate any conversion to Judaism by Reform or Conservative congregations because they do not use Jewish law as the sole means of conversion.

Christianity in the Middle East

The events in the life of Christ took place by tradition in the Middle East, but Christian thinkers and leaders shaped Christian thought, practice, and authority largely in Europe, with the exception of the Orthodox Church in Asia Minor. This is one of the reasons why Christians who live in the present Middle East remain largely outside of mainstream Christianity. The three main branches of Christianity worldwide—Catholic, Eastern Orthodox, and Protestant—have relatively few adherents in the Middle East, and Christianity itself is a minority religion there. The largest Christian sects in the Middle East include the Copts of Egypt, the Maronites, the Nestorians, and the Chaldeans.

The Coptic Faith

The Coptic Church dates back to the teachings of St. Mark in the first century CE. St. Mark arrived in Alexandria, Egypt, where he preached and wrote until 68 CE, when the Romans crucified him for his beliefs. The Copts have contributed much to Christianity, including the Nicene Creed (authored by Coptic Pope Athanasius), the oldest catechetical school in the world (in Alexandria), and monasticism (first practiced by Copts). However, other Christian sects accused the Copts (wrongfully, it turned out) of believing in monophysitism. This view, in contrast to the belief in the dual nature of Christ (equally human and equally divine) was the focus of discussion at the Council of Chalcedon, held in 451 near Constantinople. At Chalcedon, the accusations of monophysitic belief against the Copts engendered a break from both the Catholic and Orthodox Churches that exists to this day. The Copts disdain the charge of monophysitism, claiming that either their Pope Dioscurus failed to convince the Council, or that the Council wanted to punish the Copts for believing in the separation of church and state. Perhaps confusion arose from their claim that while the perfection of Christ's humanity and the perfection of his divinity were separate, both are united in what Copts refer to as "the nature of the incarnate word," as preached by St. Cyril of Alexandria.

The Copts suffered persecution in Egypt after Chalcedon by Christians until Islamic conquerors arrived in 641 CE. After that, they found themselves coexisting with their Islamic rulers, sometimes under an uneasy but peaceful truce, and sometimes under attack. Chapter 10 covers their history in Egypt.

The Maronite Faith

Around 410 CE a group in Syria formed a Christian religious order consecrating the memory of St. Maron (or Maro), a hermit monk known for his life of prayer. Forced to accept monophysitism under Byzantine Emperor Heraclius in an effort to unite all Middle Eastern Christians against the Islamic invaders, the Maronite leaders claimed at the Council of Chalcedon that their doctrine actually rejected monophysitism.

After Islam came to the eastern Mediterranean in 636, the Maronites began to leave Syria for the mountainous area of Lebanon, and the first Maronite church began there in 749. The mountains of Lebanon provided sanctuary for the Maronites until the coming of the Crusaders, whom the Maronites eagerly welcomed. That contact with the Catholic Crusaders began to link the Maronites to the Church, and in 1215, the Maronite patriarch visited Rome and participated in an Ecumenical Council. In 1584 Pope Gregory XIII founded the Maronite College in Rome, further strengthening ties to Catholicism. While the Ottomans restricted contact between the Maronites in Lebanon and Catholic Rome, France made Lebanon a protectorate under the guise of assisting fellow Catholics. Despite such ties, Maronites do have some independent traditions, such as selecting their own patriarch, allowing some clergy to marry, and conducting the liturgy in the Syriac language.

Other Christian Denominations in the Middle East

There are small groups of Nestorian Christians in the Arab world and in Iran. They were inspired by Nestorius, once the patriarch of Constantinople, then banished to the Libyan desert after the Council of Ephesus in 431. Iraq has a small population of Chaldeans (a group once affiliated with the Nestorians but separated in the sixteenth century, when Catholic Pope Eugene II declared their affiliation with Catholicism).

Christianity and Politics in the Middle East

Some charismatic Christians have attempted to gain converts from Israel's Jewish population, and the Israeli government has deported several Christian ministers found to be engaged in active conversions. However, other evangelical Christians outside of Israel have become strong supporters of Israel, particularly since the 1967 conquest of the holy sites in Jerusalem. Some believe that the temple must be rebuilt on its purported original site on the Temple Mount (Haram al-Sharif) in order to initiate the final battle of Armageddon and the thousand-year reign of Christ on earth. If such beliefs inspire an effort to rebuild the ancient Jewish temple, the reaction in the Islamic world will be fierce, since the old Temple stood on ground now occupied by the Dome of the Rock and Al-Aqsa Mosque.

Zoroastrianism

This is an ancient religion whose origins are uncertain. The name comes from its founder, Zarathushtra, or Zoroaster, who lived sometime between 1000 and 600 BCE, possibly in India. The sacred text of Zoroastrianism, the Avesta, refers to one god and a concept of dualism that describes two universes, one good and one evil. The religion took root in Persia, and its followers managed to coexist with the Muslims when they arrived, since Muslims first considered Zoroastrianism a monotheistic religion. Later Zoroastrian practices, however, shifted to polytheistic traditions. Its followers remain in Iran, but they have faced persecution for centuries, and now make up less than 1 percent of the Iranian population.

Yazidism

This is a small religion with perhaps not more than 100,000 followers scattered in rural parts of Iraq (where the majority live), Syria, and Iran. Most Yazidi are ethnic Kurds. The Yazidi faith appears to draw from Islam, Judaism, Nestorian Christianity, and Zoroastrianism for its doctrine, though the Yazidi understanding of God is considerably different from those religions. The Yazidi worship Malak Taus, who is believed to rule the universe in the form of a peacock angel, and pay homage to Sheikh Adi, a twelfth-century mystic. Because the Yazidi do not believe in sin and argue that the devil was forgiven and has repented, they are sometimes accused erroneously of devil worship. Followers of the 4,000-year-old religion tend to live in isolated villages, partly to avoid clashes with Muslims who regard them as infidels. In August 2007, over 250 Yazidis died in the Iraqi town of Qahataniya at the hands of suspected al-Qaeda suicide bombers.

Religion plays a significant role in Middle Eastern and North African politics, but its impact must be understood in conjunction with other sources of influence. Along with the legacy of history, religion combines with economic factors to shape political beliefs, practices, and preferences. The next chapter covers the connection between Middle Eastern politics and the economics of the region.

Suggested Readings

Ajami, Fouad. *The Vanished Imam: Musa Sadr and the Shiia of Lebanon.* Ithaca, NY: Cornell University Press, 1986.

Appleby, R. Scott, ed. *Spokesman for the Despised: Fundamentalist Leaders of the Middle East.* Chicago: University of Chicago Press, 1997.

Baker, Raymond William. *Sadat and After: Struggles for Egypt's Political Soul.* Cambridge, MA: Harvard University Press, 1990.

_____. *Islam Without Fear.* Cambridge, MA: Harvard University Press, 2003.

Betts, Robert Brenton. *The Druze.* New Haven, CT: Yale University Press, 1988.

Binder, Leonard. *Islamic Liberalism: A Critique of Development Ideas.* Chicago: University of Chicago Press, 1988.

Black, Antony. *The History of Islamic Political Thought.* New York: Routledge, 2001.

Bonner, Michael. *Jihad in Islamic History: Doctrines and Practice.* Princeton, NJ: Princeton University Press, 2006.

Brown, L. Carl. *Religion and the State: The Muslim Approach to Politics.* New York: Columbia University Press, 2000.

Bulliet, Richard W. *Islam: The View from the Edge.* New York: Columbia University Press, 1994.

Cook, David. *Understanding Jihad.* Berkeley: University of California Press, 2005.

Crone, Patricia. *God's Rule: Government and Islam*. New York: Columbia University Press, 2004.

Esposito, John L. *Islam: The Straight Path*. 3rd ed. New York: Oxford University Press, 2005.

_____. *The Islamic Threat: Myth or Reality?* New York: Oxford University Press, 1995.

Esposito, John L., and John O. Voll. *Makers of Contemporary Islam*. New York: Oxford University Press, 2001.

Gerges, Fawaz A. *The Far Enemy: Why Jihad Went Global*. Cambridge: Cambridge University Press, 2005.

Halm, Heinz. *Shi'ism*. 2nd ed. New York: Columbia University Press, 2004.

Hefner, Robert W., ed. *Remaking Muslim Politics: Pluralism, Constestation, Democratization*. Princeton, NJ: Princeton University Press, 2005.

Karsh, Efraim. *Islamic Imperialism: A History*. New Haven, CT: Yale University Press, 2006.

Kepel, Gilles. *Muslim Extremism in Egypt: The Prophet and the Pharaoh*. Berkeley: University of California Press, 1986.

_____. *Jihad: The Trail of Political Islam*. Cambridge, MA: Belknap, 2002.

_____. *The War for Muslim Minds*. Cambridge, MA: Belknap, 2004.

Lapidus, Ira M. *A History of Islamic Societies*. Cambridge: Cambridge University Press, 1988.

Lewis, Bernard. *The Jews of Islam*. Princeton, NJ: Princeton University Press, 1984.

_____. *What Went Wrong? Western Impact and Middle Eastern Response*. New York: Oxford University Press, 2003.

_____. *The Crisis of Islam: Holy War and Unholy Terror*. New York: Modern Library, 2003.

Majid, Anouar. *Freedom and Orthodoxy: Islam and Difference in the Post-Andalusian Age*. Stanford, CA: Stanford University Press, 2004.

Mayer, Ann Elizabeth. *Islam and Human Rights: Tradition and Politics*. Boulder, CO: West-view, 1991.

Momen, Moojan. *An Introduction to Shi'a Islam*. New Haven, CT: Yale University Press, 1985.

Munson, Henry. *Islam and Revolution in the Middle East*. New Haven, CT: Yale University Press, 1988.

Nasr, Vali. *The Shia Revival: How Conflicts Within Islam Will Shape the Future*. New York: Norton, 2006.

Norton, Augustus Richard. *Hezbollah: A Short History*. Princeton, NJ: Princeton University Press, 2007.

Piscatori, James P., ed. *Islamic Fundamentalism and the Gulf Crisis*. Chicago: University of Chicago Press, 1991.

Reuter, Christopher. *My Life as a Weapon: A Modern History of Suicide Bombing*. Princeton, NJ: Princeton University Press, 2004.

Roy, Olivier. *The Failure of Political Islam*. Cambridge, MA: Harvard University Press, 1994.

_____. *Globalized Islam: The Search for a New Ummah*. New York: Columbia University Press, 2004.

Schwedler, Jillian. *Faith in Moderation: Islamist Parties in Jordan and Yemen*. Cambridge: Cambridge University Press, 2006.

Tibi, Bassam. *Islam Between Culture and Politics*. New York: Palgrave, 2001.

Tsafrir, Nurit. *The History of an Islamic School of Law: The Early Spread of Hanafism*. Cambridge, MA: Harvard University Press, 2004.

Voll, John O. *Islam: Continuity and Change in the Modern World*. 2nd ed. Syracuse, NY: Syra-cuse University Press, 1994.

Watt, William Montgomery. *Islamic Political Thought*. New York: Columbia University Press, 1998.

12

Political Culture and the Crisis of Democracy in the Arab World

By Abdelwahab El-Affendi

When the scandal over the abuse of Iraqi prisoners in the Abu Ghraib prison broke out in early 2004, Seymour Hersh, one of the key figures behind the revelations, pointed to the irony that Abu Ghraib had been a notorious torture centre under the Saddam Hussein regime that was thoroughly looted and stripped even of windows and doors after the fall of the regime. The United States military took over the deserted building, gave it a thorough face lift, with 'the floors tiled, cells cleaned and repaired, and toilets, showers, and a new medical center added' (Hersh, 2004a). Then they proceeded to do exactly what the Saddam regime had done there before, only this time they took pictures to amuse themselves.

In the heated controversy that followed, the US authorities and mainstream media argued that the torture at Abu Ghraib was an aberration, the responsibility of only a 'handful of rogue elements' in the US military. However, many analysts argued that the abuses reflected the erosion of democratic and human rights standards in the post-9/11 era, and were linked to the overall US policies in Iraq, Afghanistan and Guantanamo, involving the widespread use of torture on terror suspects (Hersh, 2004b). Some even compared the process to the creeping Nazification of Germany in the 1930s (Rajiva, 2005).

Other observers compared this latest Western incursion into the Arab world to the first: that of Napoleon Bonaparte in 1898. That one also used the pretext of bringing 'liberty' to the Arabs, and ended equally

Abdelwahab El-Affendi, "Political Culture and the Crisis of Democracy in the Arab World," *Democracy in the Arab World*, pp. 11–40. Copyright © 2011 by Taylor & Francis Group LLC. Reprinted with permission.

disastrously. Two prominent US historians (Richard Bulliet of Columbia University and Juan Cole of the Global Americana Institute) made the comparison almost simultaneously in August 2007. Napoleon had 'proclaimed his intention of liberating the Egyptians from their Mamluk oppressors. And he brought an army of scholars and advisers with him to make the occupation of Egypt a model of European benevolence' (Bulliet, 2007). Both leaders displayed a 'tendency to believe their own propaganda' (or at least to keep repeating it long after it became completely implausible).

> Both leaders invaded and occupied a major Arabic-speaking Muslim country; both harbored dreams of a 'Greater Middle East'; both were surprised to find themselves enmeshed in long, bitter, debilitating guerrilla wars. Neither genuinely cared about grassroots democracy, but both found its symbols easy to invoke for gullible domestic publics. Substantial numbers of their new subjects quickly saw, however, that they faced occupations, not liberations.
>
> (Cole, 2007)

Napoleon's promise of liberation soon confronted the locals as 'an avalanche of bothersome regulations' and predatory practices aimed at raising revenue for the invaders (Flower, 1972: 48). When the people could take it no more and revolted, the advocates of liberty used the most brutal of tactics, including resorting to indiscriminate shelling of Cairo and even the mosque. Every rule in the book was broken, and all pretence of promoting liberty or respecting Islam was dropped. Al-Azhar was occupied and desecrated.

> Horses were tethered to the Kiblah, furniture was hurled around and the Koran kicked about the floor. El Djabarty, aghast, saw soldiers spit on the carpets, urinate on the walls, and litter the mosque with broken wine bottles … Heavy fines were imposed all round, and ten Sheikhs believed to have been implicated were stripped naked and shot in the Citadel.
>
> (Flower, 1972: 50)

Sound familiar? It could be Fallujah 2004, Hebron 1986, Hama 1982, or Halabja 1987.

1. Democracy, Liberalism, Occupation

This convergence of regime conduct across times and cultures should cast a sharp light on some of the unspoken assumptions that underpin much of the current discussions on democracy and democratization. One could cite numerous other examples, from the way the British conducted themselves in the face of the 1857 rebellion in India, through the French atrocities in Algeria, to Israel's behaviour today, to highlight aspects of this phenomenon, which I would like to call the 'Napoleon-Saddam Syndrome'. It is a condition that seems to infect rulers and other political actors in the region, regardless of their cultural background or origin, and suck them into a spiral of abuses, oppression, mounting resistance and more repression, leading to eventual collapse.

An inkling of the nature of this pathology can be found in remarks made by Israeli leaders who, in their attempt to defend Israeli's aggressive and often brutal behaviour towards the Palestinians by claiming that the Middle East is a brutal area where only the language of violence is understood, betray a sense of siege and isolation (Barak, 1999). The resulting paranoia is self-reinforcing; the actor who feels threatened by everyone around him acts in a manner that further alienates people and confirms his fears. Ironically, this paranoia is also shared by entrenched and increasingly beleaguered Arab regimes, and the excuses are comparable. When challenged about the horrendous abuses they engage in, Israeli officials often use the refrain: 'This is not Switzerland, you know.' Arab despots respond to mild suggestions that they moderate their abuses of human rights by quipping: 'If I were to do what you ask, the fundamentalists would take over ... Is that what you want?' This invariably silences the interlocutor, who quickly changes the subject (Zakaria, 2001).

Many theoreticians tend to follow the autocrats in emphasizing the role of the 'environment,' usually delineated in cultural terms. For example, Flower argues that Napoleon's problem was that his slogans about the 'rights of man' had little resonance with 'the inward-looking Egyptians' (Flower, 1972: 47), before giving a catalogue of the endless oppressive measures introduced by Napoleon under these slogans. This blaming of the victims suggests that it is not just Napoleon and Bush who tend to believe their own propaganda, but that many analysts do so as well. For the Egyptians did not rebel against the 'rights of man', but against unbearable oppression by an alien and insensitive power which ruled by force of arms.

To start, we can draw one logical conclusion from the encounters just mentioned: that the amount of repression needed to sustain a regime is proportional to the depth and breadth of rejection it faces from the people. That the US occupation forces in Iraq are having to use similar techniques of repression to the Ba'athist regime they displaced is a sign that they are facing comparable resistance from Iraqis. By definition, democracy should not face popular resistance, since democracy is rule by the people, which cannot be in revolt against itself. So if a certain order provokes a fierce resistance, that order is, by definition, not a democracy.

While there are many disagreements about defining democracy, David Beetham is right to argue that:

> Disputes about the meaning of democracy which purport to be conceptual disagreements are really disputes about how much democracy is either desirable or practicable; that is, about where the trade-off should come between democratic and other values.
>
> (Beetham, 1993: 55)

For Beetham, democracy can be defined as:

> A mode of decision-making about collectively binding rules and policies over which the people exercise control, and the most democratic arrangement to be where all members of the collectivity enjoy effective equal rights to take part in such decision-making directly—one, that is to say, which realizes to the greatest conceivable degree the principle of popular control and equality in its exercise. Democracy should properly be conceptualized as lying at one end of a spectrum, the other end of which is a system of rule where the people are totally excluded from the decision-making process and any control over it.
>
> (Beetham, 1993: 55)

There is a broad agreement on this conception of democracy as a political system 'in which the members regard themselves as political equals, as collectively sovereign, and possess all capacities, resources and institutions they need in order to govern themselves' (Dahl, 1989: 1). The theoretical disputes, as Beetham points out, revolve around rival and contestable claims as to how much democracy can be realized in a sustainable form. This is an important consideration since democracy has been 'a remarkably difficult form of government to create and sustain' (Held, 1993: 13).

Sustainability, or 'consolidation', is a key concern for theoreticians of democratic transitions, and is said to occur when democracy becomes 'the only game in town', i.e. 'when no significant political group seriously attempts to overthrow the democratic regime or to promote domestic or international violence in order to secede from the state' (Linz and Stepan, 1998: 49). One could argue that this requirement is too stringent, since it could imply that today's Spain or Britain during the IRA insurgency are not consolidated democracies. However, the general idea is that a democracy can be considered consolidated when such activities do not pose a serious threat to its stability. Linz and Stepan stipulate six conditions needed for a democracy to be consolidated: an authoritative state, a lively civil society, an autonomous political society, the prevalence of the rule of law, an effective state bureaucracy and an institutionalized economic society (Linz and Stepan, 1998: 51–8).

However, modern democracy has another dimension to it. As Bernard Crick puts it, what is usually meant by democracy today is 'a fusion (but quite often a confusion) of the idea of power of the people and the idea of legally guaranteed individual rights' (Crick, 1998: 257). More often described as 'liberal representative democracy' (Held, 1993: 18–20), to distinguish it from ancient direct democracies (like those of Athens) or from other forms that do not respect individual liberties, modern democracies are also referred to as 'constitutional democracies'. Liberal constitutionalism seeks to limit the powers of the state through guarantees of individual rights and private property. Liberalism ('a doctrine devoted to protecting the rights of the individual to life, liberty, property, and the pursuit of happiness': Plattner, 1999: 121) could and did exist without democracy, while constitutionalism could be, and has been, used to curb democracy. The designers of the American constitution in particular had used complex constitutional curbs on democratic rights (indirect elections of the president and senate, special role for the Supreme Court, etc.) in order to guard against the 'tyranny of the majority' as much as to guard against the tyranny of the few (Blondel, 1998: 74).

Given that liberalism contains principles that 'have been profoundly hostile to democracy', the evolution of modern democracy has been the 'history of successive struggles between liberals and various types of democrat over the extent and form of democratization' (Beetham, 1993: 58). In spite of this, the convergence was seen as inevitable, since liberalism's values of liberty and rights cannot long survive the denial of equal rights for all (Plattner, 1999: 122). In fact, attempts made to abolish some of the liberal features of modern democracies 'in the name of a more perfect democracy have only succeeded in undermining the democracy in whose name [these rights] were attacked' (Beetham, 1993: 57). To a large extent then, modern democracy can be seen as having been 'conceptualized and structured within the limits of liberalism' (Parekh, 1995: 165).

However, and of central relevance to our current investigation, the consciousness of the distinction and tension between liberalism and democracy has led to another startling conclusion. Taking as its premise the same point made above (that democracy and liberalism have become inseparable), some analysts have argued that in cases where democracy could lead to illiberal regimes (as was the case in the former Yugoslavia or some Arab and Muslim countries where Islamists could come to power), it might not be wise to promote democracy. Instead, some form of authoritarian liberalism should be championed (Miller, 1993; Zakaria, 1997; Plattner, 1999). From this perspective, it could be seen that what Napoleon and George W. Bush were trying to promote in the Arab world was not really democracy, but some form of authoritarian liberalism (cf. Cole, 2007). The claim that Arab culture is hostile to democracy has thus been reinterpreted to argue that Arabs are in fact hostile to liberalism.

2. The Basics of 'Culture Talk'

The appeal to culture as an explanatory variable determinant of social and political change, most recently publicized by Huntington's 'Clash of Civilizations' thesis, has a long pedigree, stretching back to Max Weber's famous citing of the 'Protestant Ethic' as the driving force behind modern capitalism (Wedeen, 2002: 713). Other theorists trace the genealogy back to de Tocqueville and even to Aristotle (Diamond, 1994: 10). The political culture approach has in recent years been eclipsed by rival approaches, after a brief ascendancy in the first half of the last century (Almond, 1994: pp. x–xi; Diamond, 1994: 1). Proponents of this approach stake the claim 'that we can identify distinctive and relatively stable distributions of political values, beliefs and understandings among populations' that can act as independent explanatory variables for political behaviour (Diamond, 1994: 1). In this regard, certain cultural attributes can cause democracy to flourish, including a level of individualism, moderation, pragmatism and mutual trust among the elite, coupled with an 'intelligent mistrust of leadership' (Diamond, 1994: 12). Central also is a solid commitment to the democratic process by all actors as stipulated above.

> This overriding commitment to democratic proceduralism is a critical political cultural condition for democracy. In combination with policy pragmatism and political tolerance, it promotes moderate partisanship, and these qualities together are most likely to limit the politicization of social life and the rancor of political intercourse.
>
> (Diamond, 1994: 11)

It is of course a truism to say that the culture of a society determines how individuals and groups conduct themselves publicly, especially if political culture is defined as 'a people's predominant beliefs, attitudes, values, ideals, sentiments, and evaluations about the political system of its country, and the role of the self in that system' (Diamond, 1994: 7). For if one includes evaluation of the political system in the definition of political culture, then the assertion about the influence of culture becomes a tautology. Nevertheless, attempts to identify causal links between political development and existing identifiable cultural traits in given societies face a number of problems. This is especially so when we add the assumptions that the components of this culture are widely shared, at least within the elite, and 'represent coherent patterns which fit together and are mutually reinforcing', and must also be constant over time and fairly resistant to change (Diamond, 1994: 8–9).

In view of numerous challenges to these assumptions, the recent revival of the political culture approach thus stakes only modest claims, rejecting outright the determinist version on theoretical and empirical grounds, since masses of evidence from field research and surveys continue to reveal that the causal relationship between culture and political behaviour is a two-way process, and political culture is seen as 'fairly plastic'. Determinism is rejected also on normative grounds, because belief in the rigidity of culture and a one-way causal relationship would condemn whole societies to perpetual lack of democracy (Diamond, 1994: 9–10). In addition, proponents of this modified political culture approach want to look at culture in terms of 'geological strata of history', where competing layers of cultural tradition coexist, and where the latest dominant traits have not completely eclipsed or supplanted earlier legacies (Diamond, 1994: 230–1). Put differently, this approach calls for a further dilution of the initial thesis by advising analysts to 'disaggregate political culture: look at subcultures (vertical and horizontal); look at elite cultures and mass culture' (Hudson, 1995: 73). Also, to understand political culture 'as a multi-layered phenomenon, amenable therefore to "geological" study: look at formal ideologies (on the "surface"), then at opinions (easily changeable), then at attitudes (less so), and finally try to plumb the deep structure of enduring collective values and orientations' (Hudson, 1995: 73).

These multiple qualifications look like the prudent preparation of multiple escape routes. But critics continue to reject these claims as 'either fundamentally tautological or empirically invalid' (Wedeen, 2002: 713). In any case, recent empirical studies on democratic transition 'explicitly dismiss the importance for transition of the prior consensus on democratic values', emphasizing instead splits within authoritarian regimes and the subsequent calculation by one faction 'that its interests are best served (or risks best minimized) by liberalization' (Diamond, 1994: 4–5). Acceptance of democratic norms evolves at a later stage, as a consequence of the compromises reached and the deals struck between former enemies. In a sense, it can be said that, apart from the elite commitment to democratic procedures (which may be initially instrumental and expedient) there may not be any specific preconditions for democracy. Moreover, many of the requirements postulated as preconditions for democracy may, in fact, be outcomes of democracy (Diamond, 1994: 15).

Any viable appeal to cultural explanations must take account of this interactive aspect of culture. While cultural norms and identities of necessity condition reactions to political challenges, political realities also condition culture. Culture as a process of meaning construction 'implies a social process through which people reproduce together the conditions of intelligibility that enable them to make sense of their worlds' (Wedeen, 2002: 717). The way, for example, ethnic identification evolves and shifts (even within similar groups) depends on many contextual factors as well as conscious choices (Wedeen, 2002: 724–5).

3. On Arab Political Culture and the 'Missing Bourgeoisie'

The political culture approach has been at its most problematic when applied in the Arab-Muslim context of 'Culture Talk', a discourse which 'assumes that every culture has a tangible essence that defines it, and … then explains politics as a consequence of that essence' (Mamdani, 2005). This discourse comes in two main versions.

> One thinks of premodern peoples as those who are not yet modern, who are either lagging behind or have yet to embark on the road to modernity. The other depicts the premodern as also the antimodern. Whereas the former conception encourages relations based on philanthropy, the latter notion is productive of fear and preemptive police or military action.
>
> (Mamdani, 2005: 18)

Both versions, however, look at culture, especially Muslim culture, as having 'no history, no politics, and no debates'. In both, 'history seems to have petrified into a lifeless custom of an antique people who inhabit antique lands' (Mamdani, 2005). This position has a political purpose. The message it seeks to send when it argues that the clash of Western powers with Arabs and Muslims is a clash of civilizations rather than a genuine political conflict (Lewis, 1990; Huntington, 1993), is that these people are not worthy of political engagement. Even if the alleged grievances are addressed (and here is a long list that starts with Palestine and does not end there) then these 'barbarians' would still remain hostile to the West. These arguments are additionally suspicious when they are promoted by experts known for their right-wing views and sympathies for Israel.

In some of its more recent recastings, the slightly more sophisticated thesis defines the problem in terms of a fundamental contrast between the world of jihad and the McWorld. The anti-modern world of 'jihad' ('the ancient forces of culture, geography, tradition, and community': Farazmand and Pinkowski, 2006: 70) and the commercialized 'McWorld' of high-tech consumerism and globalized pursuit of profit, may be antagonistic, but they are also interconnected. McWorld represents 'the natural culmination of a modernization process–some would call it Westernization—that has gone on since the Renaissance birth of modern science and its dominant paradigm of knowledge construed as power' (Barber, 2003: 156). It embodies the Enlightenment's 'trust in reason, its passion for liberty, and (not unrelated to that passion) its fascination with control' (Barber, 2003: 156). Jihad, by contrast, stands for forces of 'dogmatic and violent particularism' which seek to 'defend and deny, reject and repel modernity wherever they find it' (Barber, 2003: 7, 11). Needless to say, McWorld predominates in the modernized West, symbolized by America. 'Its template is American, its form style … It is about culture as a commodity, apparel as ideology' (Barber, 2003: 17). Jihad, by contrast, is found predominantly outside the West, or on its periphery and in small pockets within it.

Apart from the interesting (Freudian?) inversion which uses 'jihad' (a term that signifies the struggle in defense of universal truth) to symbolize parochialism, and a term derived from a Scottish clan name to symbolize universalism, this restatement of the old 'Orientalist' tautology (East is East and West is West) does not say very much. It does not explain why parochialism persists among some groups and not others. More important, it does not tell us why adopting certain lifestyles, such as eating certain types of food or wearing certain types of clothes, should have magical powers to transform people's perceptions and conduct in very radical ways.

In the end, we are finally referring to the Orientalist thesis proper, but in an even more simplistic form. In the Muslim world, where 'the struggle between Jihad and McWorld has been much more than a metaphor for tribalism or a worried antimodernism', empirical data appear to point to 'a certain lack of affinity between Islam and democracy' (Barber, 2003: 156). While fundamentalism is a phenomenon that has emerged in most religious traditions, 'only in Islam do fundamentalist tendencies appear to play a central role' (Barber, 2003: 206–7; cf. Manji, 2004).[1] In the end, it appears the long detour of jihad versus McWorld, to paraphrase Anderson (1995) on royal marriages and war in dynastic successions, leads back to the short route of Orientalist Culture Talk.

Hudson attempts to tackle the issue by dividing studies that apply the political culture approach to Arab politics into two categories: the reductionist (of which the Orientalists are the oldest and most influential) and the empiricist. The reductionists are given to 'grand generalizations' and plenty of stereotyping, tending to descend into absurd caricatures (Hudson, 1995: 65–7). While the empiricists have improved somewhat on the theses of '*ex cathedra* Orientalism and armchair psychology', they remain 'better at questions than answers' (Hudson, 1995: 70, 68). But in spite of all these misgivings, Hudson argues that to understand 'conditions such as legitimacy, liberalism or democracy it is hard to ignore culture … even if it is a residual variable after structural, economic and exogenous factors' (Hudson, 1995: 71–2). One has to tread carefully, however, observing the demands outlined earlier and avoiding reductionism and being 'methodologically multifaceted' (Hudson, 1995: 73).

Lisa Anderson is less charitable to the political culture crowd, accusing them of residual racism and extremely negative attitudes to their subject of study (Anderson, 1995: 79, 88–9). They either characterize Arabs as 'aliens' who are radically different from everyone else, blame Islam and the transcendental notions of divine sovereignty (and the failure to render unto Caesar what is rightly his), or dwell on tribal culture, patriarchy, patrimonialism, the informality of patterns of authority, etc. Their work is riddled with logical and epistemological flaws, reflecting 'an inability to think critically about change' (Anderson, 1995: 89).

Most of these writers fail to notice that the attitudes and behaviour patterns they refer to (when they are not mere projections or misreadings of the facts) are neither uncaused nor unchanging. To say with Hudson that 'it is infinitely difficult to govern in the face of a hostile, recalcitrant, skeptical populace' is to overlook the point that 'most of the people of the Arab world are quite right to be angry, reluctant and suspicious participants in politics' (Hudson, 1995: 86). As a consequence, to examine political change 'through the lens of political culture rather than structure may not be the most parsimonious vehicle' (Anderson, 1995: 86). In the end, 'the nature of political regimes in the Arab world, like those elsewhere in the world, can best be understood as reflections of the political economy of the countries in question, particularly the character of their integration into the world economy' (Anderson, 1995: 78).

A position which tries to link political economy and culture argues that the parochialism of the 'jihad world' and its resistance to democracy and modernization is a function of an underdeveloped bourgeoisie, or its lack of autonomy from state control (Waterbury, 1994; Salamé, 1994; Ayubi, 1995). This is also the reason why Arab and Muslim countries remain averse to liberalism, since liberalism has been historically associated with the rise of the bourgeoisie (Binder, 1988: 336–58). The rise of an indigenous bourgeoisie and a 'bourgeois revolution' is needed for liberalism and democracy to evolve in Muslim lands (Binder, 1988: 66–8). In the absence of such a revolution, democracy in the areas dominated by the parochial forces of 'jihad' tends to evolve into an 'illiberal democracy', making it perhaps imperative to experiment with spreading liberalism without democracy (Zakaria, 1997; Barber, 2003: 207–11).

To postpone democratization until liberalism evolves first, some form of 'guardianship' scheme (one could even call it *wilayat al-librali,* guardianship of the liberal, in contrast to *wilayat al-Faqih,* guardianship of the jurist) would be needed to guide the communities in question towards liberalism and democracy. A 'liberal autocracy', like the one the British ran in Hong Kong during most of the last century, could be the sort of guardianship scheme needed for this job (Zakaria, 1997). This also appears to be what the G8's 'Broader Middle East Initiative', launched in June 2004 to promote democracy in the Arab region, has boiled down to. The project envisages what amounts to a loose international guardianship which could help mould the region's despotic regimes into quasi-liberal autocracies (El-Affendi, 2005). After the debacles in Iraq and the success of Islamists in elections in Egypt and Palestine in late 2005 and early 2006, even this limited goal appears to have been abandoned.

However, like the argument about the rise of civil society as a precondition for democratization (Norton, 1995), this pinning of the hopes on an emerging bourgeoisie seems to beg the question where the 'Black Hole State' (AHDR, 2005) does not permit a space for civil society to function, and where 'the emerging private sectors in most Arab countries are still largely "clientalized" by the state, or else remain "informal" or underground' (Ayubi, 1995: 405).

4. The Perspectives of Arab Intellectuals

In spite of Said's demolition of Orientalism (and a plethora of other critiques[2]), a significant number of Arab intellectuals did not shy away from indulging in their own forms of 'Culture Talk'. This approach was given its most coherent (and, one could add, blatant) formulation in Hisham Sharabi's *Neopatriarchy* (1988), where he ascribed the longevity of Arab authoritarianism to the enduring patriarchical tendencies in Arab societies. According to Sharabi, patriarchy has been a feature of Arab culture since before Islam, which failed to modify it significantly. It has survived through the ages and managed to adapt itself to modernity, becoming 'neopatriarchy', combining both the enduring features of the old patriarchy with the relation of dependency vis-à-vis imperialist powers (Sharabi, 1992: 15–16, 45–66). Similar views are expressed by Khaldoun Al-Naqib, who uses the concept of tribalism to illustrate the same point. He defines tribalism as a hierarchical 'mode of organization' based on alliances as well as kin relationships, but also on an 'ethos', derived from 'primordial associations and loyalties existing deep within the consciousness of the group' (Al-Naqib, 1996: 9). However, Al-Naqib admits that 'tribalism', which he regards as the dominant organizing principle in many countries in the Arab East, is extremely adaptable to changing circumstances (Al-Naqib, 1996: 10–11, 20). This qualification squarely contradicts the central claim that Al-Naqib (following Sharabi) also makes about tribalism being so powerful that 'Islam has been unable to displace political tirbalism … to achieve the cohesion of the *umma* along moral principles' (Al-Naqib, 1996: 19).

Other writers such as Hasan Hanafi similarly argue that the problems we face in attempting to build free societies can be traced back to deep roots in our shared heritage, transmitted across generations through texts or direct oral inculcation (Hanafi, 1998: 176–9). These trends include literalism, authoritarianism (distilled through *Ash'arism*), rejection of the other, and the rejection of rationality (under the influence of thinkers such as Abu-Hamid al-Gazali, d. 1111) (Hanafi, 1998: 179–89).

This 'archaeological' digging in the past to explain the present makes too many assumptions about the universal acceptance, uniform exposure and internalization of particular views, which is not supported by historical evidence. The criticism of Sharabi's approach can also apply to Hanafi and similar schools. Like Hanafi, Sharabi, it has been correctly pointed out, indulges in sweeping generalizations for which he provides only sketchy and anecdotal evidence (Hamoudi, 2000: 18). He also neglects important facts regarding the role of mothers and the exposure of children to influences outside the home, such as schools or the media (Hamoudi, 2000: 18–21). Moreover, he fails to demonstrate any causal link or coherent interdependence between the traits he ascribes to neopatriarchy (for example, why should a society that embraces patriarchy—supposing that this was the case—tend to be irrational or lacking in initiative?).

Needless to say, this 'culturalist' conception does not induce its proponents to be enthusiastic supporters of democracy. For if the basic problem inheres in the culture, and therefore in the people, it would be useless to advocate democracy. The Orientalists are frank about this, as we see in Kedourie, who cites the fact that democracy has been tried and tested in the Arab world before and was a dismal failure, and who hence argues that the Arabs cannot understand, let alone embrace, democracy (Kedourie, 1994: 1–2).

The slightly more sophisticated stance expressed by Farid Zakaria (1997) and others entails demands for the setting up of a 'benevolent dictatorship' in each Arab country, to see it through to liberal maturity, a point made bluntly by an Arab intellectual (Elhadj, 2007).

Another Arab intellectual, speaking in 1979, reminded his audience that democracy had taken over 200 years to mature in the West, concluding that what is needed is not only to create the social and economic conditions for democracy first, but also to 'educate the people in a democratic way, and to train them to practice democracy until democracy becomes a value deeply ingrained in their souls' (Abdalla, 1998: 119). Another intellectual, El-Tahir Labib (in CAUS, 1998: 327) puts it thus: 'a backward society cannot but produce a backward socialism and cannot but produce a backward democracy'. Therefore, priority must be given to the revolutionary transformation of that society.

It has been noted that a significant section of Arab intellectuals made a (very reluctant) conversion to democratic ideals in the late 1970s and early 1980s (Ismael, 1995: 95). A deep sense of crisis that engulfed

Arab thought in the aftermath of the 1967 defeat by Israel was made more acute by the slide of most Arab regimes into an intolerably repressive mode. Cataclysmic events such as the Israeli invasion of Lebanon in 1982 and the Gulf War of 1990–1, which saw direct American hegemony imposed on the region, further enhanced this sense of crisis (Ismael, 1995: 93–6; Abu-Rabi, 2004: 50–2). An intellectual writing during that period (in 1983) tried to explain the sudden 'insistence on the issue of democracy in this period of our history by all political and intellectual trends in our homeland' by offering three reasons. First, the lesson of the previous decades was that the social and political gains sought by revolutionaries needed the masses to protect them; second, the regimes that promised economic development and Arab unity in exchange for suspension of human rights have achieved neither, and had become so gratuitously and brutally repressive that it had become impossible to tolerate the levels of violence they deploy against opponents; and, finally, the situation in the Arab world had deteriorated dramatically in the face of US-backed Israeli hegemony, leading to a marked increase in Arab dependency in all spheres (CAUS, 1998: 11–12).

How reluctant and incomplete this conversion to democracy was can be clearly seen from the very debates announcing it. In one such debate organized by the Centre for Arab Unity Studies in Beirut in 1979, one leading Algerian intellectual and diplomat (Lakhdar Ibrahimi) argued point blank that 'the democratic model operating in the West will not help us to achieve our goals in building a modern progressive society', mainly due to the general condition of dependency surrounding Arab societies (CAUS, 1998: 95–7). Also, the social conditions of Arab societies, plagued as they were by tribalism, sectarianism and ignorance, make it imperative to prioritize social transformation and social justice rather than formal democracy (CAUS, 1998: 81–3). Another intellectual speaking in the same debate (George Corm) argued that the admiration for democracy in Arab opinion clashes with the antipathy to all things Western and the attachment to values hostile to the individualism that is central to Western democratic norms (CAUS, 1998: 83). A number of intellectuals engaged in that debate accepted that the call for democracy has arisen in Arab thought and practice, not for its intrinsic qualities, but as a tool to achieve independence and development (CAUS, 1998: 97). Another added that the issue of democracy did not arise in the 1950s (during the Nasserist period in Egypt) due to the 'full confidence that power was in the hands of a resolute and able nationalist leadership' (Adil Hussein, in CAUS, 1998: 102). In answer to a point made earlier about managing the revolutionary transformation democratically, this same intellectual rejected the idea, arguing that revolutionary change is a protracted affair, occupying an extended period characterized by a fierce struggle, not only with the former ruling classes, but also 'against the consumerist norms among broad social groups, and against mentalities based traditionally on concepts that do not accord with the needs of development or independence, and so on' (CAUS, 1998: 102–3).

Similar ideas were repeated in other writings and debates during the years that followed. It is to be noted that discussions of democracy by Arab intellectuals, including that in the much celebrated *Arab Human Development Report*, rely heavily on Western concepts and sources in their definitions and explications (Al-Naqib, 1996; CAUS, 1998; Ayubi, 1995; Sadiki, 2004). Often there are differences between those who adopt radical leftist views and those who would like to follow the more traditional liberal line, even though the recent shift referred to above points to a convergence between the two positions. This has led to a criticism that this convergence is another problematic adoption of democracy as an ideology of salvation that is espoused equally irrationally (Tarabishi, 2006: 918). Like many other Arab intellectuals, Tarabishi adopts the Culture Talk stance, arguing that the problem is a social-intellectual, rather than a political, one. Giving freedom to the people could lead to the tyranny of the majority, given the multiple 'pathologies of Arab civil society' (Tarabishi, 2006: 16–18).

In a supreme irony, speakers in the above debates tended to heap tons of blame on the intellectuals who, it was alleged, 'failed dismally in performing any democratic role', or to maintain their independence vis-à-vis the ruling regimes (Corm, in CAUS, 1998: 84). Others were even more scathing, accusing intellectuals of becoming too pro-Western and alienated from the masses, or concerned merely with their individual interests. The intellectuals were generally socially and politically apathetic and/or (more seriously) preferred to act as agents of authoritarian regimes. Some intellectuals not only serve despotic regimes as propagandists and apologists, but even 'rationalize [repression] and push for it. [One has only to] survey the huge number of intellectuals dispersed throughout newspapers, magazines, media channels, publishing houses and research centers to become aware of this shameful reality' (Abdalla, 1998: 50–1).

These criticisms notwithstanding, a number of the intellectuals participating in those debates were already officials or sympathizers of regimes that were undemocratic. Many more went on to become ministers in cabinets that could not be described as democratic except by an extreme stretch of the imagination and terminology.

This probably provides the key understanding as to the nature of the democratic crisis in the Arab world. From the beginning, the concern in Arab and Muslim circles has not been with democracy as an intrinsic value, but as a means to something else. The fact that the early generation of Arab reformers like Rufa'a al-Tahtawi, Khayr al-Din al-Tunisi and Abd al-Rahman al-Kawakibi (and including Abduh) advocated *Islah* (reform) rather than democracy (Sadiki, 2004: 218–28) was due mainly to the sense of a need to give priority to communal survival over individual freedoms. It was the same with the revolutionaries of the post-war era. For that early generation and their latter day—more radical—successors, some key objectives were too important to be left at the mercy of democratic process. Both groups did not concentrate on empowering the people as an urgent necessity, for the priority was to empower communities or states.

The fact that the elite remained at best reluctant democrats is not a problem in itself, since studies of democratic transformation have consistently revealed that political actors more often than not opt for democracy as a last resort, or as the 'lesser evil' from their perspective. Only later does commitment to democracy evolve and solidify, receiving an unequivocal and enduring commitment from main actors. However, the problem in the Arab world is that rival political groups continue to entertain the view that many things are too important to entrust to the vagaries of a democratic process and the whims of the populace.

5. The Religious Dimension

The reluctant conversion to democracy among many former radicals coincided with the 'Islamic revival', which further complicated the renewed quest for democracy, and ensured that it would 'further divide rather than unite secular and religious visionaries and polarize their polities and societies' (Sadiki, 2004: 251). The debate on governance in the Arab world on the threshold of modernity became entangled from early on with the debate on what form of government is required by Islam. In its early form, the debate centred on the caliphate and whether it could be saved or restored (El-Affendi, 2008: 81–100). Additionally, this debate was also influenced by developments such as the Constitutional Revolution of 1905–6 in Iran, the first experiment of its kind in the Muslim world. Iran's brief success in establishing a constitutional monarchy modelled on the Belgian constitution, with an elected parliament incorporating a five-man council of *ulama* to vet all legislation for conformity with Shari'a, became an inspiration for modern Islamic thinkers since Rashid Rida (El-Affendi, 2004a: 172–94; El-Affendi, 2008: 83–96). The combination of a popular uprising demanding participation in decision-making, with a call for incorporation of Shari'a as a basis of legislation, was seen as proof that democracy and Islam are compatible (and it explains the phenomenon that baffled die-hard Culture Talk adepts such as Elie Kedourie, who argued that polls showing the majority of Egyptians demanding democracy and Shari'a are an indication that the Arabs do not understand what democracy is about: Kedourie, 1994: 1–2).

Out of that debate, a myriad of proposals emerged for forms of an 'Islamic' system of rule that usually combined an elected government with presumed safeguards to ensure that elected bodies would not transgress Shari'a. Many of the proponents of these models were reluctant to describe them as democratic. In fact, many were adamant that democracy and Islam were incompatible (El-Affendi, 2006). Maududi made the partial concession of calling his proposed system a 'theo-democracy', a partial democracy restricted by Islamic law (Adam, 1983: 117–26). This model was perfected in Khomeini's *wilayat al-faqih* (jurisdiction of the learned man) system currently being implemented in Iran. According to this formula, elected bodies should be constantly under the supervision of a *faqih*, a man of profound religious learning and integrity who has the power to overrule any decision deemed in contravention of Islamic law.

The emergence of Islamist visions of the state has become a hindrance to democratization on two counts. First, the Islamist–secularist divide has become the primary divide in Arab politics, hindering a democratic consensus and also giving autocratic regimes and their foreign backers excuses to avoid a commitment to democracy. The association of Islamism with violent resistance to Israel (Hamas, Hizbullah, etc.) and pro-Western regimes, not to mention terrorism, has been used as a pretext by Western powers not to support Arab democracy and, indeed, to endorse autocratic regimes.

Secondly, Islamist ideas and practices have themselves tended to be antidemocratic. Islamic rule in Iran and Sudan, and the anti-democratic models mentioned earlier, have tended both to build anti-democratic constituencies and to make democrats sceptical about the democratic commitments of Islamists, notwithstanding the fact that moderate Islamist groups have generally made these commitments.

As explained in some detail elsewhere,[3] the Islamist 'guardianship formulas' remain problematic because of a number of untenable assumptions underpinning them. For one thing, these formulas appear to assume that governance is essentially a judicial process, with the ruler assuming the role of a chief justice issuing rulings about conformity to law. That characterization of governance is too narrow. Governance is about much more than law enforcement, involving as it does the constant negotiation of rival demands, interests and perceptions. The skills required here are not merely those relevant to the task of determining conformity to law.

But even if we accept this characterization, it becomes difficult to reconcile the basic contradiction between two central presuppositions inherent in these models. At one level, treating the ruler as chief justice assumes that that Shari'a law has already been clarified and laid down sufficiently for a judge to implement. But in this case, the demand for a supremely pious and learned leader to help determine the law (and the wide area of discretion granted to him) becomes superfluous. That such an expert is called for seems to suggest that the law is not that clear, needing a special guide through its mazes. But if the law is not already laid down, a question arises as to whether one individual (or a small group of experts) is better placed to determine and expound on it than a larger pool of people, which is the essence of the anti-democratic prescriptions of the proponents of the model.

The anti-democratic ethos of these 'Islamic' models is underpinned by a further set of interconnected assumptions, starting with the common claim about Islamic teachings encompassing every facet of life, coupled with the claim that these teachings have already been clearly laid down in such a manner that the specific recommended 'Islamic' option in every case cannot be missed. In addition, it is assumed that all Islamic teachings could be subsumed under Shari'a, which must in turn be enforced by a public authority, or by the state. Finally, it is held that public opinion is not a reliable arbiter when seeking to determine what Islamic law dictates, and only specialized experts can tell us what the law is.

The problem with these assumptions is not only that Islamic teachings cannot be all subsumed under the law, but also that these teachings cannot be regarded as a long catalogue of 'off-the-shelf' rules that could be consulted on every occasion. In fact, Islamic teachings are not all legal injunctions, since the bulk are ethical norms requiring and offering a wide area of discretion and initiative. Also the myth that Islamic teachings cover every facet of life and offer ready guidance is contradicted by unequivocal Quranic verses demanding that believers should not ask too many questions of the Prophet (Quran 5: 101). This is, in turn, related to an incident when the Prophet became upset because one individual kept demanding unnecessary clarifications about a command he gave to perform a pilgrimage, prompting the Prophet to advise his audience not to risk burdening themselves with additional duties by asking for details.[4] This makes it clear that not only did Islam not have a rule for every conceivable situation, but that it is moreover a fundamental rule of Islam not to have such rules. This leaves the widest possible margin for initiative and fresh thinking on the most appropriate ethical conduct in all areas, including the area of governance, on which the texts say very little anyway.

The argument that an individual or a class of individuals is better placed to resolve matters of dispute than the community as a whole contradicts another fundamental Islamic tenet: that no priesthood is permitted or acceptable. The Quran condemns earlier religious communities for trusting too much in their 'priests and monks', to the extent that they have practically treated them as deities beside God (Quran 9: 31). It makes it clear time and time again that going astray by following the authority of 'our masters and nobles' is not an acceptable excuse in the eyes of God. Every individual is responsible for his/her own action, and only they are responsible (Quran 37: 28–35).

The Quranic injunctions against accepting authority (even presumed 'religious' authority) unquestioningly shift moral responsibility squarely onto the shoulders of the individual on the one hand, and the community as a whole on the other. This also rules out the prescription of the models generally offered as 'Islamic alternatives' to democracy. Ascribing 'religious authority' to an individual or a class contravenes the most fundamental Islamic tenet of all: the injunction against polytheism. A *khalifah* or a *faqih* who puts himself up as an absolute authority in fact claims divine powers for himself, an unacceptable situation that can only be negated if the individual in question becomes accountable to the community as a whole.

It would appear from the above that Islamic teachings are not only compatible with democracy, but demand it. For the assumption that the state, controlled by self-styled men of religion, is needed to guide the Muslim community to virtue, both robs the community of its autonomy without which it cannot perform its religious function and, more seriously, usurps God's own authority.

The challenge posed for Arab democracy by Islamist thought and practice is probably the most important one at the moment, and it needs to be tackled at several levels. The Islamists themselves need to revise their models in order to reflect Islam's true spirit, which is not only favourable to democracy, but is also, as we have shown above, one which finds democracy indispensable. Further, all political forces in the Arab world, including Islamists, need to build democratic coalitions constructed around mutual reassurances and understandings, with a commitment to peaceful coexistence and mutual recognition. This is necessary in order to deprive the despotic regimes of their divide-and-conquer advantage. Finally, a clear international stance in favour of democracy must be developed on the basis of the rejection of all excuses that maintain Arabs are not worthy of freedom for one reason or other. Nothing ever justifies the deprivation of whole peoples of their non-negotiable rights of self-determination and a life of freedom and security.

In particular, international support must be withdrawn from the militantly authoritarian 'secular fundamentalist' regimes which use opposition to Islamism as a pretext to deny fundamental rights. As Waines aptly put it,

> What is seldom acknowledged is that the strident authoritarian voices of contemporary religious fundamentalists have confronted for decades the powerful forces of secular fundamentalism, which have striven to eliminate them. One consequence of this has been the muting through co-optation by secular fundamentalists of the religiously authoritative voices of modernists.
>
> (Waines, 2003: 27)

While the Islamists certainly need to clean up their act in order to make a positive contribution to democratization, key obstacles to Arab democratization are the so-called 'eradicationists' (*Isti'saliyyin*), entrenched elites in countries like Algeria, Tunisia, Syria and Egypt who believe in the 'eradication' of Islamists by force, and in the process close all avenues of civil action in the name of combating fundamentalism.

6. The Search for Arab Democracy

The account above highlights some key issues impinging on the stubborn democracy deficit in the Arab world. The glaring absence of democracy in the Arab world is not in dispute. Between 1976 and 2006, not a single Arab country has been classified as free in the Freedom House annual survey. Polity IV scores tell a similar story. But it is not just the persistence of autocracy in the Arab world, but its depth. As Elbadawi and Makdisi (2007: 819) pointed out, 'even if we consider only authoritarian regimes, Arab dictatorships are the most oppressive, with a mean polity score of –7.8 compared to –5.2 for non-Arab regimes'.

> A similar story also emerges from comparing annual mean changes of Polity IV in and outside the Arab world … Out of 600 observations of change in the polity score for Arab states, only 31 of them are positive (i.e. associated with political liberalization or improved status of democracy).
>
> (Elbadawi and Makdisi, 2007: 819)

There are, of course, problems with both indexes, as they do not necessarily reflect accurately the existing conditions due to their reliance on subjective measures. Thus, unrealistically, the Polity IV index gives Libya a higher score than Qatar and UAE and equal to Bahrain, while Tunisia scores higher than Morocco.

More recently, Saliba Sarsar tried to develop a composite index that

> quantifies democratization through consideration of multiple variables: four variables address governance and representative government. These mark how heads of state and members of the legislature are selected, as well as political party development, suffrage, and the maturity of political rights and civil liberties. The annual Freedom House survey provides a fifth variable measuring media freedom. Measurements of religious liberty can be derived from US Department of State reports. A seventh addresses the observance of human rights with the information from Amnesty International, Human Rights Watch, and the US Department of State. The United Nations

Development Program's human development index provides a measurement of human development. The Heritage Foundation's index of economic freedom quantifies economic freedom. The status of democracy index assigns each of these nine variables 2 points for a total of 18 points. Each score ranges from 0 to 2, with 0 being nonexistent and 2 being the highest measurement.

(Sarsar, 2006)

On this basis, Arab states were ranked according to performance, with Morocco at the top, with 11 points, and Saudi Arabia at the bottom, with 2.5 in 1999. In the 2005 rankings, Saudi Arabia was given 4, but still remained at the bottom, while Morocco was downgraded to 8, leaving Jordan and Lebanon at the top spot with 10.5 each (the same ratings they had in 1999). Again, many of the rankings display anomalies, ranking Libya, Bahrain, Oman and Qatar on the same level (5 points; Qatar was raised to 6 in 2005), while Tunisia is given a score of 10 (9 in 2005), well above UAE (6) and one point above Kuwait (9, downgraded to 8.5 in 2005). At 8.5 points (downgraded to 7 in 2005), Syria also towers above most of these countries, and was level with Yemen (raised to 9 in 2005). Clearly, there is also something fundamentally wrong with this classification (Sarsar, 2006).[5]

However, the overall picture cannot be mistaken. The 2004 *Arab Human Development Report* (AHDR, 2005), confirms this reading, further noting the convergence of Arab regimes into an authoritarian model it dubs 'the Black Hole State', a polity that collapses on itself by concentrating power at the centre, normally in the hands of one person or a small clique, assisted by draconian measures and an overpowering repressive apparatus (AHDR, 2005: ch. 5).

In the 2003 report, the AHDR cited empirical evidence from the World Values Survey (WVS) that directly contradicts the Culture Talk explanation of the Arab situation. The survey has shown that the population of Arab countries values democracy as 'the best form of government', higher than any other region in the world. Its score in rejecting authoritarianism is also the highest, significantly higher, in fact, than the population of Western Europe in both scores (AHDR, 2003: 19). The 2004 report conducted surveys of its own that confirmed this inclination (AHDR, 2005: 89–98).

Other empirical analyses based on the WVS and other data further revealed that 'Islamic orientations and attachments have, at most, a very limited impact on views about democracy' (Tessler, 2002: 240). This was further confirmed by empirical research conducted specifically to test Francis Fukuyama's assertion that 'Islam has stood as a major barrier to democratization', using data from several Arab and Muslim countries (Al-Braizat, 2002). Again, the overwhelming evidence suggests that Arabs value democracy highly, and have no particular tolerance (as measured by attitude surveys) for authoritarianism, even among the religious, thus squarely disproving Fukuyama's claims (Al-Braizat, 2002: 280–6).

> The correlation between support for [democracy] as a very good way of governance and religiosity is insignificant although slightly positive. Predominantly Islamic societies show very high levels of support for [democracy] as a very good way of governing their countries, while simultaneously showing high levels of religiosity.
>
> (Al-Braizat, 2002: 281)

Al-Braizat goes further, finding a strong correlation between the Human Development Index (HDI) and the actual progress to democratization. While support for democracy in most Muslim countries remains high, actual democratization (as measured in years of uninterrupted democracy) correlates positively with HDI and negatively with religiosity (Al-Braizat, 2002: 288–90). Al-Braizat takes this to reflect a correlation between actual democratization and modern -ization, since he assumes a correlation between modernization and decline of religious observance, in line with classical modernization theory.

A similar stance in support of modernization theory is taken by Epstein *et al.* (2006), who take issue with the influential challenge by Przeworski *et al.* (2000) to the theory's central assumption regarding the correlation between modernization (as measured in terms of per capita GDP growth) and democratization. Przeworski and his associates tried to show that the positive association between high GDP and democracy only 'results from the reduced likelihood of modern countries sliding back, as it were, into undemocratic forms of government once having (randomly) become democratic' (Epstein *et al.*, 2006: 551).

Using polity scores, Epstein *et al.* (2006) try to disprove the Przeworski thesis by introducing a third category of partial democracies (Przeworski *et al.* use only two categories of democratic and authoritarian regimes). After correcting for some 'errors' in the Przeworski *et al.* models, they claim to have reestablished the finding that 'high incomes per capita significantly increased the likelihood of democratic regimes, both by enhancing the consolidation of existing democracies and by promoting transitions from authoritarian to democratic systems' (Epstein *et al.*, 2006: 566).

However, another study using the same polity scores has concluded that, regardless of its merits, the modernization hypothesis does not work in the Arab world (Elbadawi and Makdisi, 2007). In fact, the richer oil-producing Arab countries, whose per capita GDP is topped only by the OECD income levels, have consistently obtained the lowest polity scores, with some scoring −10 for prolonged periods. Ironically, while income levels in most Arab countries were higher than the median income in developing countries worldwide, Arab countries lagged behind developing countries in democracy as reflected in polity scores, while the sporadic spells of democratization occurred mainly in the poorer Arab countries (Elbadawi and Makdisi, 2007: 820–2).

The research by Elbadawi and Makdisi uncovers another interesting anomaly pertaining to the Arab world: that 'while regional military conflicts are positively associated with democracy … [with] conflicts usually lead[ing] to democratic transformation, the Arab region has been an exception' (Elbadawi and Makdisi, 2007: 828). The authors attribute this anomaly, represented by the tenacious hold on power by regimes after being defeated in war, to the fact that 'the highly polarized and emotional discourse created by the Arab–Israeli conflict and the perceived adversarial global power interventions in the region have provided potent arguments for authoritarian Arab regimes to escape accountability for disastrous failures, including major military defeats' (Elbadawi and Makdisi, 2007: 829).

7. Exceptionalism and the 'Missing Bourgeoisie'

This important insight takes us back to the Napoleon–Saddam Syndrome, the persistent pathology specific to the Arab region in particular and the Middle East in general. As noted, the remarks attributed to former Israeli Prime Minister Barak show that 'the highly polarized and emotional discourse' is not restricted to the Arab arena, while the sense of siege and isolation reflected in Barak's remarks also animates the discourse of entrenched and increasingly beleaguered Arab regimes to justify their brutality, by citing both foreign threats and the internal threat of chaos and mayhem. If we observe democratic norms and human rights, their argument goes, all will be lost. Enemies of the people (or civilization or religion or freedom) will take over (Zakaria, 2001).

The convergence in attitudes between the alien invaders and occupiers (Israelis, Americans in Iraq) and the local despots in advancing the claims that the Arab region is a brutal jungle where violence and repression are needed to keep order, betrays deeper structural similarities between the forces of alien occupation, and the indigenous post-colonial state which has inherited the colonial legacy and sought to perpetuate it. Rather than reflecting the cultural traits of the region, both structures betray their alien nature vis-à-vis the region and its peoples. As the Tunisian activist Moncef Marzouki (see below) and others argue, the current despotic Arab state has come to resemble an alien occupation.

While there is clearly a difference in the degree of alienation between foreign colonial forces (in particular, Israeli settler colonialism) and home-grown despotism, there are also some significant parallels. If Israel believes itself to be an alien entity facing rejection, the state in the Arab world is equally alien and at war with society (Ayubi, 1995: 442–4). The 'Black Hole State' is one that is engaged in trench warfare with the population under it, seeing in every move within civil society a threat, every independent economic development a mortal danger (AHDR, 2005).

Again, it is not the fact that the Arabs 'were rather slow in internalizing the concept of the state itself, or the "ethics" of public service and the attitudes of collective action' (Ayubi, 1995: 22). Rather, it is the fact that the state, 'an "imported commodity," partly under colonial pressure and partly under the influence of imitation and mimicry' (Ayubi, 1995: 21), continued to arrogate to itself the privileges and powers of the colonial state it had inherited. It jealously safeguarded its autonomy from society and has sought to rely more and more on foreign support.

This character of the state has made it precarious and vulnerable. In this regard, 'the violence of this state is in reality an indication of its weakness and fragility' rather than its strength (Ayubi, 1995: 23). In fact, violence and constant war against societies ensures that the result will be 'both a weak state and a weak society, with the forces of coercion and repression taking charge and acting largely on their own behalf' (Sluglett, 2007: 100).

The fact that a number of Arab states have come to resemble occupation powers is dialectically related to the tendency of some opposition groups to seek foreign support and even court foreign occupation (or presence) in their counties.[6] In Iraq, first the Kurds and later other Iraqis sought foreign protection against the brutalities of the former regime. In Libya and later in Sudan, the opposition sought foreign support to topple the regime and, in the case of Sudan, supported the presence of foreign troops to protect civilians. It thus appears that for at least certain opposition groups the regimes they oppose are seen as worse than foreign occupation.

The Arab situation is further complicated by a precarious and conflictual regional system, which had its local 'cold war' between radicals and conservatives between the 1950s and 1970s, and structural dependency on the outside world (Kerr, 1971; Al-Naqib, 1996: 45–56; Ayubi, 1995: 172). This combination of regional volatility and 'imperialist penetration' has coalesced to bring about the practical disintegration of the system following the Iraqi invasion of Kuwait in 1990, and the arrival of US-led foreign troops into the region. At the very moment when Soviet troops were leaving Eastern Europe to pave the way for independence and democratization, foreign troops were pouring into the region to back authoritarian regimes. More troops have since arrived and vast funds have also been deployed to support favoured regimes.

The aftermath of September 11 reinforced these trends. The USA and its allies became even more involved in the region's affairs; Israel under Sharon became even more repressive and nihilistic; regimes grew even more repressive, incompetent and devoid of legitimacy; and the region's people continued to feel even more resentment and frustration. The impression created by American leaders that the US intervention in the region would herald a new era of democratic reform, and their promises which inspired a few, including members of the 'liberal' opposition in Saudi Arabia, Kuwait and other Gulf states, and some opposition activists in Iraq, Syria, Egypt and elsewhere at the end of 1990,[7] lay in ruins, buried, together with many other hopes and promises, under the rubble of destroyed Palestinian homes and devastated Iraqi cities. Everything pointed to system meltdown.

In view of all this, it can be argued that the reason why the Middle East remains inhospitable to democracy is the same reason why it also remains inhospitable to the rise of an autonomous and influential bourgeoisie. The indigenous bourgeoisie bears the stamp of this war environment. Where the state acts as a 'protection racket', and manages the economy as if it was at war with important sections of society, the bourgeoisie will have to adapt and join the racketeers, despots or warlords. Otherwise, it stands no chance. In most Arab countries the state manipulates economic measures for political ends.

In any case, the region's ruling elite have sought to pre-empt the anticipated bourgeois revolution by engineering a 'bourgeois' revolution of their own. Emulating the model that evolved in the Gulf, the elites in other countries embarked on their own ingenious schemes of privatization: the state itself was now privatized, becoming the preserve of the ruling families and their allies in the ruling 'political parties', which are no more than coalitions of self-interest.

This trend has led to a convergence between monarchies and republics in the Arab Middle East, leading to the term *jumlukiyya* (coined by Saad Eddin Ibrahim), or monarchic-republic, to refer to the new privatized polity, where rule is 'all in the family', passing from father to son and shared within the family during the life of the founder of the ruling family. The old and new monarchies not only foster divisions by sect, class or ethnicity, but also work to create a new 'aristocracy', made up of a favoured class, segregated physically and emotionally from the masses of poor who are relegated to shanty towns, inner cities and rural areas. The phenomenon is akin to internal colonialism, with the privileged rich acting like a settler community. This has led one commentator to liken the new class to the Janissaries, or Memlukes, the professional 'mercenary' class of slave soldiers used by the ruling elites since the late Abbasid period as a tool of subjugating the populace (Umaymur, 2006). Another commentator who despaired of reform in his country was led to argue that this 'internal colonialism' made the function of political opposition redundant, calling instead for a culture and approach of (peaceful) resistance to this virtual colonialism (Marzouki, 2006).

More significantly, the new regimes appear to have in fact almost abolished the public-private distinction, leaving the state elite to treat both as a legitimate domain. In this regard, it is 'only the traditional artisan-commercial sector in some countries and the emerging so-called "Islamic business" sector in other countries that can claim a relative (but by no means absolute) degree of autonomy from the state' (Ayubi, 1995: 404). In any case, the rentier state has less need of the bourgeoisie than the latter has of the state.

Against this background, we need to be reminded that the appearance of an *independent* bourgeoisie signals the end result, and not the starting point, of the 'bourgeois revolution'. The bourgeoisie (and the mythical 'McWorld' of globalization) begin to have the magical powers ascribed to them only after many of the transformations ascribed to the bourgeoisie have already taken place. Political structures and cultural orientations which could oversee and underpin the atomization of society, the dissolution of feudal or traditional bonds, a massive urbanization, relative indifference to religious strictures, the pauperization and uprooting of farm labourers, etc., had to be already in place for capitalism to grow. In particular, a relatively impartial state which is not also a private business enterprise is absolutely essential.

This requires not only a 'disenchanted' world where 'rationality' rules, but also a trivialized world where actions and events are stripped of momentous significance. Secularization does not bring about indifference to religious issues; it is widespread indifference to religious issues that enables secularization. An 'enchanted' world is not only populated by spirits and spiritual individuals and communities, it is also haunted by taboos and horrors of 'unspeakable' acts: sacrilege, sexual deviance, threats to cultural identity and cohesion, etc. A disenchanted world, by contrast, is a bland universe of acts which are indifferently alike. The area of what is considered 'private', what is regarded by the state and society as a matter of indifference, expands to cover almost every aspect of personal and social conduct.

In the case of the Middle East, the trend has been moving in the other direction. It is true that in some countries economic liberalism has made some progress. In places like the United Arab Emirates, and in particular its thriving emirate of Dubai, the system has witnessed some reform and streamlining. While the 'family business' is still the largest one there is, the thriving economy is currently the most open in the Arab world. However, Dubai has been criticized for having achieved its success by becoming a site of runaway globalization where the creation of wealth is deliberately de-linked from citizenship rights (Devji, 2005). The nearby state of Qatar is also moving in the same direction of the liberalized bourgeois state, but has additionally institutionalized the distinction between the private wealth of the rulers and state revenues. It has also taken tentative steps towards institutionalizing democratic citizenship. However, in all these countries, some very important taboos remain, most significantly with regard to political action. Governments regard any unsanctioned attempts at political or civil society organization as a very serious matter.

In recent decades, the region has also witnessed twin processes of Islamization and traditionalization. The first phenomenon is now well known and has been extensively studied. It has been reflected both in increased personal religious observance and also in membership of Islamic activist groups. Such groups tend to endow more and more social activities with religious meaning, and either encourage or oppose them on this basis. Most of these activities relate to sexual mores and the public conduct of women (Islamic dress, mixed dancing, etc.). Simultaneously with this, and even prior to it, some governments adopted a reverse attitude of investing personal and social acts (such as the wearing of headscarves by women) with utmost political significance, and treating them as a most serious threat. This contagion has now moved to Europe and beyond with the headscarves and *niqab* controversies.

At the same time, regimes in the area began to deliberately revive and exploit traditionalist social structures, such as tribes, clans, sects and rural dignitaries and heads of families, in their bid to strengthen their hold on power and to further marginalize the rebellious intelligentsia from which came most of the opposition to their rule. Opposition groups also resorted to the mobilization of sectarian, ethnic and tribal identities in order to fight back, while ordinary citizens sought protection from the threat of the expanding authoritarian state in these traditional bonds, a process made more imperative by the deliberate weakening of any viable civil society mechanisms of defence or solidarity.

To top it off, the 'distorted' and 'dysfunctional' (from the perspective of free-market theorists) systems have been sustained and subsidized by a 'pyramid scheme' of complex local, regional and international alliances, which kept them going at an ever rising cost. We point here to the huge rents emanating from oil, aid, strategic assets, etc., as well as alliances with tribal or religious elites, the secular intelligentsia, sections of the military, Islamist groups, and sectarian or regional interests. The regimes that participated in the 1990–1 war on Iraq, for example, received massive foreign funding vital for their longevity at a time when dictatorships in Eastern Europe and elsewhere were unravelling.

The overall picture illustrates how the 'pyramid scheme' of distorting factors, which includes the input of major Western powers, operates to nullify any presumed impact of class polarization. While these factors apply mainly to the Arab political arena, they also apply to Israel, a heavily subsidized entity which is founded on very 'unbourgeois', if not anti-bourgeois, principles. The aspirations to build an exclusive religious-ethnic state in a hostile environment, and the paranoid sentiments inherited from memory of the Holocaust and the perceived threat of annihilation, cause Israel to embody the ethos of Barber's 'jihad'. Ironically, however, this 'jihad' is unsustainable without the heavy external subsidies and the complex networks of economic and political support which keep Israel plugged into McWorld. The resulting strong and modernized economy helps to subsidize a host of unproductive or counterproductive activities and make it financially attractive enough for bourgeois families to abandon the bastions of McWorld in Europe and the USA for a life on the frontline settlements on the hills of Judea. The generous flow of external resources has helped this extraordinary juxtaposition of jihad and McWorld. In the subsidized settlements, the profit motive and religious activism are satisfied in one move, and the salvation ideology meshes beautifully with the bourgeois economy.

The USA, which has had its own contingent of militias, Armageddonites and other jihadists since the 1970s (Barber, 2003; El-Affendi, 2004b), has been a long-term contributor to jihadism in the region. It funds and backs extremist settler groups in Israel as it had earlier backed jihadists in Afghanistan. Recently, Washington itself has begun to look and sound more like Jerusalem and Baghdad than Jefferson's capital. The Napoleon–Saddam Syndrome is catching up not only in Gaza, South Lebanon, Abu Ghraib and Baghdad's Green Zone, but also in Guantanamo and the Beltway. Dealing with the 'Middle Eastern Question' has thus become essential not only to bring peace and stability to the region, but also for the health of the world's major democracies.

As this author has explained in detail elsewhere, contrary to its declared announcements about promoting democracy in the Middle East, the real problem with US policy in the region has been its contravention of every democratic norm when dealing with the region's peoples (El-Affendi, 2005, 2004b). American jihadism in the region has triggered a powerful defensive reaction in the Muslim world, further undermining the prospects for democracy.

One can thus argue that the central issue relating to democratization in the Arab world pertains to the robustness of authoritarian regimes and their sources of power, given the nature of the alien state and the widespread opposition to despotism and alien control. As Eva Bellin perceptively put it:

> Thus, the solution to the puzzle of Middle Eastern and North African exceptionalism lies less in the absent prerequisites of democratization and more in present conditions that foster robust authoritarianism, specifically a robust coercive apparatus in these states. The will and capacity of the state's coercive apparatus to suppress democratic initiatives have extinguished the possibility of transition. Herein lies the region's true exceptionalism.
>
> (Bellin, 2004: 143)

The robustness of the coercive apparatus of the Arab state is derived from ample resources put at its disposal by the states (and their foreign backers); the reassurance and legitimacy provided by international networks of support; the patrimonial nature of the state; and its security apparatus, where private links of kin and patronage reinforce loyalty and demobilize the opposition. The beleaguered opposition is, in turn, weakened and discouraged from mounting campaigns due to the harsh measures deployed against it (Bellin, 2004: 144–7).

8. Conclusion

It can thus be concluded that neither a presumed cultural aversion to democracy nor an underdeveloped class structure can be said to be responsible for the turbulent politics of the Middle East. The structural causes of the region's dysfunctional politics stem from its 'haunted' (as opposed to 'disenchanted') character. Nothing here is permitted to be trivial or mundane. Every stone, every barren desert strip, is 'strategically important' or 'holy'. Every actor, including the USA and Israel, has a messianic project, a sacred cause, a vital interest. Nothing is treated as trivial or neutral. On the contrary, everything here, from food to dress, from language to cities, is invested with an irreplaceable value. As Reza Aslan points out, in this region, 'the personal is political, and religion is always both' (Aslan, 2005).

This has little to do with ingrained cultural traits and a lot to do with conscious political choices. The entrenched despotic regimes have deliberately (and sometimes inadvertently) engineered modes of polarization that would make their despotic ways look as if they are the last bulwark against the total disintegration of their countries. In their desperation to remain in power, even 'progressive' regimes (including the Ba'ath regimes in Iraq and Syria, and even the former Communist regime in Yemen) cultivated tribal or sectarian loyalties, and played group against group. By posing as arbiters between these polarized groups, they have engineered a latent civil war that continues by 'peaceful' means, refereed by a despot who continues to blackmail society with this threat. Like a terrorist with an explosive belt, the despot makes sure that, if he goes, the whole house will go up in flames.

The USA, Israel and other intruders have acted in the same way. These intruders brought over their own messianic projects to rival the region's resident messianism. A British minister recently argued that Afghanistan is now the 'new Cliffs of Dover', implying that ending the occupation there would be like abandoning Britain's southern coast! This echoes the rhetoric of Israeli officials about Jerusalem being the 'eternal and undivided capital of Israel', thus ruling out any compromise or negotiations. These foreign actors also emulate local despots in creating and fostering, in their desperation, polarized identities that end up holding them and everyone else hostage. This can be seen in the way sectarianism has been fostered in Iraq and encouraged in Lebanon.

This goes to support our point that the infectious 'Napoleon–Saddam Syndrome' is linked closely to the Machiavellian short-sightedness of political actors, including foreign actors. The frequent flare-ups that have raised the region's political temperatures to volcanic levels have a little to do with the region's history and a lot to do with its present. It is not only that we are faced here with a durable coalition of opportunist and messianic actors who believe that too much is at stake for one to bother about such mundane concerns as majority opinion, the rate of profit, budget deficit, bourgeois pleasures or even life itself. What is more alarming is that, in the shadow of these coalitions, extremely dangerous and disturbing structures of domination and disenfranchisement are becoming so entrenched and so alien that the amount of violence required to dislodge them will be phenomenal. Instead of progressing towards the open spaces of the bourgeois revolution, the systems here are recreating the Ancien Régime. The guillotine is sure to follow.

The despotic order in the Arab world is not a reflection of the region's cultural preferences. Had it been so, then there would have been no need for the extreme violence being deployed by regimes to maintain their grip on power. As Bellin rightly pointed out, the issue here is not the preferences of the locals, but the ability of the regimes to defy these preferences. This happens due to the patrimonial nature of the repressive apparatus, which combines sectarian and clannish links to isolate itself from the polarized society, and the ample resources and international support it enjoys. It is this extreme situation, and the mounting resistance to it, that fosters the polarization and extremism infecting the region.

From Napoleon to Bush, and the numerous local despots in between, the modern state in the Arab world (and its allies and adversaries, including Israel) is at war with the people. As the resistance to it mounted, it also worked to increase its repressive capacity, culminating in the 'Black Hole State' which tolerates no opposition and no independent civil society or economic sphere. As Ayubi and others rightly pointed out, this has also shaped opposition to these regimes. The Islamist or tribalist/ethnic character of the opposition reflects in part the nature of the enclaves the repressive state has failed to subjugate. The polarization and rising tension has become self-reinforcing. The regimes use the uncompromising stance of the radical opposition to convince the elite that it is the lesser of two evils, and to secure foreign support against the perceived threats of 'fundamentalism' and chaos.

There are nevertheless, positive signs. Arab intellectuals, politicians and civil society actors are realizing more and more that this situation is no longer tenable. Nascent coalitions of democrats, including moderate Islamists, are emerging to challenge authoritarian regimes. In spite of brutal crackdowns and deliberate attempts to sow divisions, the movements persist, and others are emulating their action. That is where the future of the Arab world lies.

Notes

1. For the record, we should note here that Barber tried to revise this thesis in a lecture delivered at the University of Westminster in May 2005 under the title: 'Islam and Democracy: Compatibility or Clash of Civilisations?'

2. See Said 1978, 1985, 2003.

3. See El-Affendi 2006.

4. According to a report in the authoritative compendiums of Bukhari and Muslim, 'the Prophet (peace be upon him) said in a sermon: "O people! Allah has prescribed Hajj for you, so you must perform it.' A man asked: 'Every year, O Prophet of Allah?" The Prophet (peace be upon him) remained silent. When the man repeated it thrice, the Prophet (peace be upon him) said: "Had I said 'yes', it would have become a yearly obligation, and this would have been beyond your power." Then he added: "Leave me alone so long as I leave you alone (i.e. do not pester me with questions about things which I omit and do not mention). Some people who lived before you were destroyed because they asked too many questions and disagreed with their Prophets. So when I command you to do something, do it to the best of your power, and if I forbid you from something, then just avoid it" (Bukhari and Muslim, quoted in Nasir al-Din al-Albani, 1995: 505).

5. The author does not indicate at what point a country would be considered democratic, but appears to suggest that no Arab country is fully democratic.

6. Related to this is the observation that, in some Arab countries, 'the rudimentary parliamentary regimes of the mandate period ... should continue to arouse a degree of nostalgia among those old enough to remember them' (Sluglett, 2007: 97).

7. Encouraged by promises given by US officials, a group of women demonstrated in Riyadh in late 1990 to demand the right to drive cars, while a group of forty 'liberal' personalities submitted a memorandum to the King in early 1991 asking for political reforms and more freedoms.

References

Abdalla, I. S. (1998) 'al-Muqawwimat al-Iqtisadiyya wa'l-Ijtima'iyya li'l-Dimuqratiyya fi'l-Watan al-'Arabi', in Hilal *et al.*, 1998: 105–21.

Abu-Rabi, I. M. (2004) *Contemporary Arab Thought: Studies in Post-1967 Arab Intellectual History*, London: Pluto Press.

Adam, C. J. (1983) 'Maududi and the Islamic State', in John Esposito (ed.), *Voices of Resurgent Islam*, Oxford: Oxford University Press: 99–123.

AHDR (Arab Human Development Report) (2002) *Arab Human Development Report 2002: Creating Opportunities for Future Generations*, New York: UNDP.

—— (2003) *Arab Human Development Report: Building a Knowledge Society*, New York: UNDP.

—— (2005) *Arab Human Development Report 2004: Towards Freedom in the Arab World*, New York: UNDP.

Al-Braizat, F. (2002) 'Muslims and Democracy, an Empirical Critique of Fukuyama's

Culturalist Approach', *International Journal of Comparative Sociology* 43/3–5: 269–99.

Al-Din al-Albani, N. (1995) *Silsilat al-Ahadith al-Sahiha*, vol. 2, Riyadh: Maktabat al-Ma'arif.

Almond, G. A. (1994) 'Foreword', in Diamond, 1994: pp. ix–xii.

Al-Naqib, K. (1996) *Sira' alqbilah wa'l-Dimuqratiyyah: Halat al-Kuwait*, London: Dar al-Saqi.

Anderson, L. (1995) 'Democracy in the Arab World: A Critique of the Arab Culture Approach', in Brynen *et al.*, 1995: 77–92.

Aslan, R. (2005) 'Aunt Kobra's Islamic Democracy', *The Boston Globe* (17 April). Online at: www.boston.com/news/globe/ideas/articles/2005/04/17/aunt_kobras_islamic_ democracy?pg=full

Ayubi, N. (1995) *Overstating the Arab State*, London: I. B. Tauris.

Barak, E. (1999) 'Speech to the National Defense College', 12 Aug. Online at: www. israel-mfa.gov.il/mfa/go.asp?MFAH0fh80 (Israel Foreign Ministry website).

Barber, B. R. (2003) *Jihad versus McWorld*, London: Corgi Books.

Beetham, D. (1993) 'Liberal Democracy and the Limits of Democratization', in Held, 1993: 55–73.

Bellin, E. (2004) 'The Robustness of Authoritarianism in the Middle East: Exceptionalism in Comparative Perspective', *Comparative Politics* 36/2 (Jan.):139–57.

Binder, L. (1988) *Islamic Liberalism: A Critique of Development Ideologies*, Chicago: University of Chicago Press.

Blondel, J. (1998) 'Democracy and Constitutionalism', in Inoguchi *et al.*, 1998: 71–86.

Brynen, R. *et al.*, eds (1995) *Political Liberalization and Democratization in the Arab World*, vol. 1, *Theoretical Perspectives*, Boulder, CO: Lynne Rienner.

Bulliet, R. (2007) 'Bush and Napoleon', *International Herald Tribune* (2 Aug.). Online at: www.nytimes.com/2007/08/02/opinion/02iht-edbulliet.1.6957129.html?r=1

CAUS (Centre for Arab Unity Studies) (1998) Centre for Arab Unity Studies 1998: *al. Dimugratiyya wa Huquq al.Insan fi%Watan a;'Arabi*, Beirut.

Cole, J. (2007) 'Bush's Napoleonic Folly', *The Nation* (24 Aug). Online at: www.global policy.org/component/content/article/168/36520.html

Crick, B. (1998) 'A Meditation on Democracy', in Inoguchi *et al.*, 1998: 255–65.

Dahl, R. (1989) *Democracy and its Critics*, New Haven, CT: Yale University Press.

Devji, F. (2005) *Landscapes of the Jihad: Militancy, Morality, Modernity*, Ithaca, NY: Cornell University Press.

Diamond, L., ed. (1994) *Political Culture and Democracy in Developing Countries*, Boulder, CO: Lynne Rienner.

El-Affendi, A. (2004a) 'On the State, Democracy and Pluralism', in Taji-Farouki and B. M. Nafi (eds), *Islamic Thought in the Twentieth Century*, London: I. B. Tauris: 172–94.

—— (2004b) 'Armageddon: The "Mother of All Empires" and its Middle Eastern Quagmire', in D. Held and M. Koenig-Archibugi (eds), *American Power in the 21st Century*, Queensland: Polity Press.

—— (2005) 'The Conquest of Muslim Hearts and Minds? Perspectives on U.S. Reform and Public Diplomacy Strategies', Brookings Project on US Policy towards the Islamic World, Working Paper, Sept.

—— (2006) 'Democracy and its (Muslim) Critics: An Islamic Alternative to Democracy?', in M. Khan (ed.), *Islamic Democratic Discourse*, Lanham, MD: Lexington Books: 227–56.

—— (2008) *Who Needs an Islamic State?* (2nd edn), London: Malaysian Think Tank London.

Elbadawi, I. and Makdisi, S. (2007) 'Explaining the Democracy Deficit in the Arab World', *Quarterly Review of Economics and Finance* 46/5 (Feb.).

Elhadj, E. (2007) *The Islamic Shield: Arab Resistance to Democratic and Religious Reforms*, Boca Raton, FL: Brown Walker Press.

Epstein, D. L., Bates, R., Goldstone, J., Kristensen, I., and O'Halloran, S. (2006) 'Democratic Transitions', *American Journal of Political Science* 50/3: 551–69.

Farazmand, A. and Pinkowski, J., eds (2006) *Handbook of Globalization, Governance, and Public Administration*, London: CRC Press.

Flower, R. (1972) *Napoleon to Nasser: The Story of Modern Egypt*, London: Tom Stacey.

Hamoudi, A. (2000) *al-Shaykh wa'l-murid: al-nasaq al-thaqafi li'l-sultah fi'l-mujtama at al-Arabiyah al-hadı̄thah,* tr. Abd al-Majı̄d Jahfah, Casablanca: Dar Tubqal.

Hanafi, H. 'Al-Judhur al-Tairikhiyya li-azmat al-Hurriyya wa'l-Dimuqratiyya fi Wujdanina al-Mu'asir', in Hilal *et al.*, 1998: 175–89.

Held, D. (ed.) (1993) *Prospects for Democracy*, Cambridge: Polity.

Hersh, S. (2004a) 'Annals of National Security: Torture at Abu Ghraib', *The New Yorker* (10 May). Online at: www.newyorker.com/archive/2004/05/10/040510fa_fact

—— (2004b) *Chain of Command: The Road from 9/11 to Abu Ghraib*, New York: Harper-Collins.

Hilal, A.(1998) 'Muqaddima: al-Dimuqratiyya wa Humum al-Insan al-'Arabi al-Mu'asir', in CAUS, 1998: 7–21.

Hudson, M. (1995) 'The Political Culture Approach to Arab Democratization: The Case for Bringing it Back in, Carefully', in Brynen *et al.*, 1995: 61–76.

Huntington, S. P. (1993) 'The Clash of Civilizations', *Foreign Affairs* (Summer): 22–49.

Inoguchi, T., Neman, E. and Keane, J., eds (1998) *The Changing Nature of Democracy*, Tokyo: United Nations University Press.

Ismael, S. (1995) 'Democracy in Contemporary Arab Intellectual Discourse', in Brynen *et al.*, 1995: 93–112.

Kedourie, E. (1994) *Democracy and Arab Political Culture*, Washington, DC: Washington Institute for Near East Policy.

Kerr, M. (1971) *The Arab Cold War: Gamal 'Abd Al-Nasir and his Rivals, 1958–1970*, London: Oxford University Press for the Royal Institute of International Affairs.

Lewis, B. (1990) 'The Roots of Muslim Rage', *Atlantic Monthly* (Sept.). Online at: www. theatlantic.com/doc/199009/muslim-rage

Linz, J. and Stepan, A. (1998) 'Towards Consolidated Democracy', in Inoguchi *et al.*, 1998: 48–67.

Mamdani, M. (2005) *Good Muslim, Bad Muslim: America, the Cold War, and the Roots of Terror*, New York: Three Leaves.

Manji, I. (2004) *The Trouble with Islam: A Muslim's Call for Reform in her Faith*, Edinburgh: Mainstream.

Marzouki, M. (2006) 'al-Muqawama: al-Hal wa'l-Wajib al-Akhir', *al-Ma'rifa* (10 Oct.). Online at: www.libya.alhora. com/forum/showthread.php?t=9218

Miller, J. (1993) 'The Challenge of Radical Islam', *Foreign Affairs* (Spring).

Norton, R. (1995) *Civil Society in the Middle East*, vols 1 and 2, Leiden: E. J. Brill.

Parekh, B. (1995) 'The Cultural Particularity of Liberal Democracy', in Held, 1993: 156–75.

Plattner, M. (1998) 'Liberalism and Democracy: Can't Have One without the Other', *Foreign Affairs* (March/April). Online at: www.foreignaffairs.org/19980301faresponse 1382/marc-f-plattner/liberalism-and-democracy-can-t-have-one-without-the-other. html

—— (1999) 'From Liberalism to Liberal Democracy', *Journal of Democracy*, 10/3 (July): 121–34.

Przeworski, A., Alvarez, M., Cheibub, J. and Limongi, F. (2000) *Democracy and Development*, New York: Cambridge University Press.

Rajiva, L. (2005) *The Language of Empire: Abu Ghraib and the American Media*, New York: Monthly Review Press.

Sadiki, L. (2004) *The Search for Arab Democracy: Discourses and Counter-Discourses*, London: C. Hurst.

Said, E. (1978) *Orientalism*, New York: Pantheon.

—— (1985) 'Orientalism Reconsidered', *Race Class* 27.

—— (2003) 'Orientalism 25 Years Later', *Counter Punch* (4 Aug.).

Salamé, G. (ed.) (1994) *Democracy without Democrats? The Renewal of Politics in the Muslim World*, London: I. B. Tauris.

Sarsar, S. (2006) 'Quantifying Arab Democracy: Democracy in the Middle East', *Middle East Quarterly* (Summer): 21–8. Online at: www.meforum.org/article/970

Sharabi, H. (1988) *Neopatriarchy: A Theory of Distorted Change in Arab Society*, New York: Oxford University Press.

—— (1992) *Al-Nizam al-Abawi,* Beirut: Centre for Arab Unity Studies.

Sluglett, P. (2007) 'The Ozymandias Syndrome: Questioning the Stability of Middle Eastern Regimes', in O. Schlumberger (ed.), *Debating Arab Authoritarianism: Dynamics and Durability in Nondemocratic Regimes*, Palo Alto, CA: Stanford University Press.

Tarabishi, G. (2006) *Hartaqat*, London: Dar al-Saqi.

Tessler, M. (2002) 'Do Islamic Orientations Influence Attitudes toward Democracy in the Arab World? Evidence from Egypt, Jordan Morocco, and Algeria', *International Journal of Comparative Sociology* 43/3–5: 229–49.

Umaymur, M. (2006) 'al-Inkishariyyun al-Judud wa Dhayl al-Asad', *Al-Quds al-Arabi* (20 Nov.): 18.

Waines, D. (2003) 'Religion and Modernity: Reflections on a Modern Debate', *ISIM Newsletter* (12 June): 27.

Waterbury, J. (1994) 'Democracy without Democrats? The Potential for Political Liberalization in the Middle East', in Salamé, 1994: 23–47.

Wedeen, L. (2002) 'Conceptualizing Culture: Possibilities for Political Science', *American Political Science Review* 96/4 (Dec.): 713–28.

Zakaria, F. (1997) 'The Rise of Illiberal Democracy', *Foreign Affairs* (Nov./Dec.).

—— (2001) 'How to Save the Arab World', *Newsweek* (24 Dec., US edn). Online at: www. fareedzakaria.com/articles/newsweek/122401_how.html

13

Al Jazeera

A Middle Eastern *Enfant Terrible* Goes Global

by Johanne Staugaard Johansen and Danielle Geara

"Al Jazeera is a fresh perspective—we tell it like it is," said the voice-over in Al Jazeera's promotional video. The media network's video also included clips from war zones, people in despair, and a well-groomed George Clooney endorsing Al Jazeera. The European broadcasting centre of Al Jazeera was based close to Hyde Park Corner in London, where red double-decker buses frequently passed by and some of London's most fashionable shopping areas could be found. From this centre daily meetings were held with the company's headquarters in Qatar to discuss which news to broadcast and which directions to take in terms of strategy and distribution.

Al Jazeera had attracted international attention for its frank style, its coverage of global issues with a focus on the people affected, and its attempt to become "the voice of the voiceless". Some praised Al Jazeera for adopting a different perspective and for its revolutionary achievement in becoming the first editorially independent news channel in the Middle East; others criticised it for being too controversial and sensational, and referred to it as "terrorist TV" because it had given air time to terrorist groups. (Exhibit F provides a selection of answers from a survey conducted in June 2009 regarding perceptions of Al Jazeera).

Johanne Staugaard Johansen and Danielle Geara, "Al Jazeera: A Middle Eastern Enfant Terrible Goes Global." Copyright © 2010 by INSEAD. Reprinted with permission.

Al Jazeera now faced the essential question: how sustainable was its success? In order to answer this question, Al Jazeera needed to address at least three key issues. Firstly, it had to determine how it could transform from a Pan-Arabic news channel into an international media network, and at the same time remain a strong player in an increasingly competitive media landscape in the Middle East. Secondly, it needed to identify how it could both leverage and demystify the original Al Jazeera brand when catering to global media consumers. And thirdly, Al Jazeera needed to establish how it would deal with its financial dependence on the Emir of Qatar going forward.

Al Jazeera's History

Establishing an Independent Pan-Arabic News Channel

The story of Al Jazeera began in Qatar in the mid 1990s. Thanks to Qatar's high-quality oil resources, prosperity and social progress had risen since the 1950s. In 1995, Sheikh Hamad bin Khalifa Al Thani had just come to power as the Emir and was eager to put Qatar on the map.

Parallel to the changing political climate in Qatar, the BBC had been working in Saudi Arabia to launch a Pan-Arabic news channel. However, when the Saudi government would not allow the BBC full editorial freedom, it made the decision to pull out. The BBC's failure to establish an independent news channel in Saudi Arabia prompted the Emir of Qatar to fill the gap in the market in a different way. It also meant that a number of journalists, producers and other people with experience in broadcasting were now available in the region.

The Emir of Qatar recognised the opportunity to create an independent and objective news channel that would stand in contrast to other channels in the region that were, at the time, influenced by government to varying extents. As a result, the satellite channel Al Jazeera ("The Island") was launched in Doha, Qatar in 1996. An initial US $150 million grant from the Emir of Qatar made the launch possible. Wadah Khanfar, Director General at Al Jazeera, pointed out:

> The vision mainly was to introduce to the Arab world free reporting that is distant from propaganda, and at the same time to give the Arab world the opportunity to express opinions. This is why our motive is to give all the opinions.

In 2006 Al Jazeera launched an English-language news channel. By 2009, Al Jazeera had established a global team of 3,000 employees in over 50 countries comprising 30 nationalities and 350 journalists, with headquarters based in Doha. The global team was connected via broadcasting centres based in London, Washington D.C. and Kuala Lumpur, in addition to approximately 70 bureaus located around the world. (Exhibit A provides an overview of Al Jazeera's worldwide locations).

Expansion of Product Offerings

From its launch in 1996 until early 2000s Al Jazeera essentially remained an Arabic news and current affairs satellite TV channel. Since then Al Jazeera expanded into a network with specialty TV channels in multiple languages and in several regions of the world. By 2009 its offering had become a mix of talk shows, news programming, news analysis and documentaries. In addition to the original flagship channel, Al Jazeera Arabic, the network comprised a range of speciality channels including:

- Al Jazeera Sports (2003)—Arabic-language sports channel,

- Al Jazeera Mobasher (2005)—live politics and public interest channel that broadcasts in real time without editing or commentary,
- Al Jazeera Children's Channel (2005)—children's channel for kids under 13,
- Al Jazeera English (2006)—24h English-language news channel,
- Al Jazeera Documentary Channel (2007)—Arabic-language documentary channel, and
- Baraem (2009)—most recently launched channel for pre-school kids (3-6 years old).

(Exhibit B provides an overview of the timeline of new channels launched by Al Jazeera).

The launch of Al Jazeera Sports had been particularly successful and the channel had quickly grown to become the most popular sports channel in the Middle East. It covered a wide range of major sporting events, such as the UEFA European Football Championship and the Olympics. Al Jazeera Sports also held exclusive broadcasting rights in the Middle East for major football leagues, including the Spanish La Liga and the Italian Serie A.

The most important new initiative following the launch of Al Jazeera had been the introduction of an English-language channel that targeted a global audience aimed at transforming Al Jazeera into an international media network. The idea was not to merely replicate the content in the original Arabic channel and broadcast it to an English-speaking audience, but to create a truly international channel, managed by a Western team and staffed with English speakers. "We do not aim for one demographic. We are aimed at anyone who wants a different take on world news and a questioning attitude to power," indicated Ben Rayner, executive producer at Al Jazeera English in London.

Al Jazeera English was launched in 2006. It was the first time an Arab media channel had broadcast news in English 24 hours a day. The initial plan was to provide an alternative to BBC and CNN, and to leverage on the increasingly powerful brand of Al Jazeera. Two and a half years after its launch, Al Jazeera English had grown to be much bigger than the Arab version and covered almost 140 million households compared to Al Jazeera Arabic's audience of 50 million households. Al Jazeera English was available worldwide in more than 100 countries. (Exhibit C provides list of editorial highlights of Al Jazeera English).

Market Developments

Although the Middle East was not homogenous, the countries of the region had some shared characteristics. The Middle East had a younger population on average than any other part of the world. Over 50% of the population in Yemen, Oman, Saudi Arabia, Jordan, Morocco and Egypt was estimated to be less than 25 years old, while in the remaining countries the under-25s made up 35% to 47% of the total population. Furthermore, in most countries the population was rapidly growing.[1] The Middle East was also experiencing growing GDPs across the region and economic growth had gradually created a larger middle class.

In terms of media, significant differences existed between Middle Eastern countries. Broadband penetration varied significantly across the region but was still very low in many countries (often less than 10%). In contrast, mobile technology and mobile phones were rapidly emerging as rival means of broadband access to internet content, and mobiles were also developing as an alternative way to watch television. However, generally TV was considered a very important source of information and news in the Middle East, reinforced by the fact that illiteracy was still widespread, rendering print media a less effective form of communication.

---

1 Arab Media Outlook, 2008–2012 (PricewaterhouseCoopers, 2009)

Although satellite television channels had originally been perceived as an entertainment alternative, they were increasingly seen as a more credible source of information than local media. According to Synovate's European Media and Marketing Study (EMS) in 2008 (June to September), the results of which were published on ArabianBusiness.com, top earning Arabs and regional decision makers preferred CNN for their English language news. Surveying the main income earners in the top 13% of Middle East households, CNN ranked number one in the Middle East for monthly reach, with 21% of the audience. BBC World News ranked second (15.6%), followed by Al Jazeera English (9%), CNBC (4.8%) and Euronews (3.6%)[2].

Legal restrictions on the press varied between countries, as did the level of state influence on the media. For example, Lebanon, Israel and Turkey afforded the press a relatively large degree of freedom and independence vis-à-vis most other countries in the region. The launch of Al Jazeera marked a breakthrough in Middle Eastern media environment because it was the first Middle Eastern news channel that was exempt from governmental control and was editorially independent. For example, it openly criticised monarchies in the region, and in this sense crossed many of the boundaries that had previously been commonly accepted. At various times in the past it had been banned from broadcasting in various countries including Iraq, Algeria, Morocco, Egypt and Saudi Arabia. At one time, Al Jazeera Arabic had been banned in every single country in the Middle East—except Israel.

Although periodically banned from broadcasting, it was popularly regarded as a reliable source of information. The Knowledge World Center for Polls reported that 96% of Arab academics found Al Jazeera to be a reliable source for news. (Exhibit D provides an overview of the viewer demographics of Al Jazeera Arabic. Exhibit E provides an estimate of the total potential audience of Al Jazeera in the Middle East).

Increased Competition

By 2009, Al Jazeera was no longer the only media network in the region that claimed to be independent and objective. Competitors were now both Arabic broadcasters such as Al Arabiya and Al Hurra, as well as the Arabic units of international broadcasters such as BBC Arabic, launched in 2008.

Al Arabiya, for instance, launched in 2003 and partly owned by the Saudi-owned and Dubai-based broadcaster Middle East Broadcasting Center (MBC), was perceived to be both credible and also more moderate than Al Jazeera, and had gained market share. The television network Al Hurra was created by the US government to compete directly with Al Jazeera Arabic. Launched by the Bush administration in an attempt to counter Al Jazeera's coverage of the invasion of Iraq, it had not yet succeeded in winning a big audience share.

For Al Jazeera English, in addition to BBC and CNN, competition now included CCTV-9, Channel News Asia, Deutsche Welle, EuroNews, France 24, Nile TV, Press TV and Russia Today. In a further sign of the increased level of competition in the Middle East, CNN was in the process of establishing a GCC hub (Gulf Cooperation Council[3]) with a base in Abu Dhabi, featuring daily live television broadcasts as well as handling regional advertising sales.

In addition to competition from rival television broadcasters, another important issue faced by Al Jazeera going forward was that its main competitors were no longer limited to television broadcasters but also included other media such as websites (e.g., CNN's website). Not only did Al Jazeera seem to be losing its first-mover advantage, in the future it needed to address competition from less traditional forms of media.

---

2 http://www.arabianbusiness.com/557309-top-earning-arabs-prefer-cnn-to-al-jazeera
3 Gulf Cooperation Council members: United Arab Emirates, Bahrain, Saudi Arabia, Oman, Qatar, Kuwait

Al Jazeera's Current Challenges

The Original Al Jazeera Brand: A beloved Enfant Terrible

Al Jazeera had succeeded in building a powerful brand. It was ranked among the five most powerful brands both globally and in Europe and Africa in 2004, according to Brandchannel, together with the prominent brands of Apple, Google, Ikea and Starbucks.[44] Forbes Arabia ranked Al Jazeera as the No. 1 Arab brand in a report on 'The Top 40 Arab Brands in 2006'.

Several factors had been essential in the development of the strong Al Jazeera brand:

The Voice of the Voiceless

Al Jazeera's presence in the neglected areas of the world and its use of local resources and local knowledge had contributed to the development of the company's brand. It attempted to be "the voice of the voiceless". Content was often exclusive and Al Jazeera sought to differentiate itself from other news channels by presenting evidence from "the ground" instead of reporting from a distance. Local correspondents reported news from all over the world, trying to give the impression of "native" coverage. "We want Africans to tell us about Africa and Asians to tell us about Asia," explained Nigel Parsons, former Managing Director of Al Jazeera English, in 2007.

Dealing with Taboos

An aura of truth had developed around Al Jazeera and it was seen as a channel that would "tell it like it is", due to the fact that it had been the first editorially independent channel in the region. Al Jazeera had confronted taboos such as homosexuality, women's issues and the wearing of the *hijab*. Moreover, Al Jazeera had invited Israeli officials to participate in talk shows, marking the first time Israeli politicians, intellectuals and journalists had appeared on an Arab news channel to speak about issues related to the Palestinian/Israeli conflict.

Covering the Wars in Iraq and Afghanistan

Some commentators claimed that Al Jazeera had established itself through reporting on the wars in Afghanistan and Iraq, and in this way had established a brand for itself. Al Jazeera's broadcast of the Osama bin Laden tapes following the events of September 11th 2001 had attracted significant international attention and had been an important part of the brand-building process. For example, the tapes had shown Osama bin Laden in an Afghan mountain hideout, and a bin Laden spokesman had delivered the message that, "The storm of airplanes will not be calmed." Moreover, bin Laden's messages had been transmitted without editing. Al Jazeera had also shown images of destruction and innocent victims as a result of US bombings.

In 2004, at the height of the Iraq war, then-Defense Secretary Donald Rumsfeld had accused Al-Jazeera (Arabic) of "vicious, inaccurate and inexcusable" reporting. Although some observers found its rhetoric anti-American, others applauded Al Jazeera for showing the conflict from another perspective. The question was whether Al Jazeera had gone too far and whether it had taken the right level of responsibility in broadcasting graphic war scenes.

---

4 www.brandchannel.com, http://www.brandchannel.com/features_effect.asp?pf_id=248

De-mystifying the Brand

Mark Jurkowitz, Associate Director of the Pew Research Center's Project for Excellence in Journalism, pointed out that when Al Jazeera English was launched in 2006, "There was a stigma attached to Al-Jazeera English, deserved or not, because of its relation to the Arabic version." So while the original Arabic brand remained essential for Al Jazeera's overall strength, Al Jazeera actively moved to de-mystify and soften its brand in order to become a global media player.

Al Jazeera English was different from the Arab version in several key ways. For example, the use of terminology varied between the two, with words such as "martyred" in the Arabic version replaced by "killed" in the English format. Al Jazeera English did not broadcast Islamic greetings or programmes, and showed fewer Arab faces on screen. Top talents from other networks were hired, including star journalists and reporters such as veteran BBC broadcaster David Frost, former BBC and CNN anchor Riz Khan, former CNN and BBC news anchorwoman and award-winning journalist Veronica Pedrosa. While the resulting rich palette of superstars from the news industry increased its credibility and popularity amongst viewers, there were concerns that this strategy could make it look like a collection of individuals and would fail to establish a distinct identity or a coherent discourse for the Al Jazeera brand.

Whilst some commentators had suggested standardising the two channels in order to strengthen Al Jazeera's competitive position, many felt this strategy was too risky. Al Jazeera therefore found itself needing to maintain a balance between being a revolutionary, controversial Arab brand on the one hand, and being an aspiring international player competing in the same league as CNN and BBC on the other.

Distribution Strategy

Al Jazeera could be accessed through satellite, cable, IP TV over ADSL, phone with Al Jazeera Mobile and the internet. It adopted an interactive approach towards consumers, inviting viewers to contribute on its website and TV talk-shows, as well as asking them to submit ideas for the company's logo through a logo design competition.

In one initiative aimed at extending its global reach, in January 2009, Al Jazeera released some of its broadcast quality footage from Gaza under a Creative Commons license. Contrary to the usual "All Rights Reserved" standard, the license invited third parties, including rival broadcasters, to reuse and remix the footage as long as Al Jazeera was credited.

Stepping into the US Market

Despite Al Jazeera's global successes, major cable providers in North America were reluctant to pick up Al Jazeera English. This was in part due to the reputation and controversy of its Arabic-language counterpart. Also, according to the Pew Research Center's Annual Report on News Media at the time, US cable networks spent only 8% of their time on foreign coverage in 2008.

Al Jazeera English multiplied its efforts among cable operators and consumers by launching a vast campaign through Facebook, blogs and dedicated websites such as http://iwantaljazeera.net. It understood that a possible first step into the attractive US market was to enter via the Canadian cable networks. Another possible route was via the internet. Al Jazeera English claimed that at least half of its web traffic, or 11 million visitors a month, came from North America-based IP addresses. Still, US television remained the primary source from which most Americans accessed their video news.

New Media

Al Jazeera actively pursued new media in its distribution strategy, not just in North America, but also in the Middle East and the emerging markets in general. For Al Jazeera, new media represented a bridge to both young people and to unreached geographies. Whilst internet penetration was low in the Middle East, Al Jazeera believed it represented a huge potential for the future, and its strategy of being innovative in terms of online presence and mobile applications was seen as a way to better target younger consumers who were generally considered more "new media friendly".

In addition to services like podcasts, a YouTube channel, a Facebook account, an iPhone application and multiple Twitter news feeds, Al Jazeera had launched a Twitter account and an interactive map of citizen-submitted reports to follow developments in Gaza. (Appendices G and H show Al Jazeera's distribution channels and new media initiatives).

Strategic Partnerships

Al Jazeera also pursued strategic partnerships to develop its reach. For example, in 2008 it announced a new deal with one of Asia's leading cable operators, Hong Kong Cable Limited, enabling it to broadcast in Hong Kong. In January 2009, Al Jazeera announced a partnership with Sony Ericsson, whereby RSS feeds of its news content would be pre-installed on four models of its mobile devices in both the Middle East and North Africa. Also in January 2009, Al Jazeera and *The Independent* announced a new partnership that brought Al Jazeera English video news bulletins to the web pages of the www.independent.co.uk, one of the leading British newspapers. Furthermore, in May 2009 Link TV—the largest independent television broadcaster in the US, devoted to providing diverse global perspectives on news and world culture not typically available on other US networks—announced that it would present a new global news hour including "World News" from Al Jazeera English.

These strategic alliances were consistent with Al Jazeera's objective of international expansion but they raised questions such as how these partnerships would affect the Al Jazeera brand and whether the partners were the right fit for Al Jazeera in terms of brand image and consumers.

Financial and Editorial Independence

Launched on the initiative of the Emir of Qatar, Al Jazeera continued to rely heavily on grants from the Emir as its main source of income, although it had originally aimed to become financially independent in 2001.

Advertising was limited on both its Arabic and English channels. Al Jazeera Arabic mainly attracted Qatari advertisers and had trouble attracting other advertisers. Al Jazeera English had chosen an approach of limited advertising and prided itself on favouring content over revenues. Whilst often cited as a weakness, the Emir's funding had clearly provided Al Jazeera with a large degree of independence from advertisers in terms of editorial content, as advertisers could potentially seek to influence the choice of programmes, content and style.

In addition to the grants and some limited advertising income, Al Jazeera also generated revenue through subscription-based sports channels, broadcasting deals with other companies and the sale of footage. Moreover, Al Jazeera had entered into a deal with Google to share advertising revenues from the Al Jazeera YouTube channel.

Nevertheless, financial support from the Emir remained the Achilles' heel of Al Jazeera, because it rendered it highly dependent on Qatar's financial health and political stability, as well as the goodwill of the Emir. Changes in the political or socio-economical situation in Qatar could oblige Al Jazeera to seek alternative sources of revenue to fund its operations.

Setting Strategies for the Future

Al Jazeera had, within only a few years, grown from a revolutionary Middle Eastern *enfant terrible* into an international media network. But the question now facing senior executives at Al Jazeera was: how sustainable was Al Jazeera's success?

Internationally, Al Jazeera's main differentiation strategy had been its reporting from neglected areas and being "the voice of the voiceless". However, if other big players in the news arena were to apply a similar focus, Al Jazeera might have difficulty keeping its competitive niche.

Another potential weakness stemmed from Al Jazeera's distinct style, considered by some to be wordy and depressing, and to focus too heavily on topics of death and destruction. This was linked to the fact that Al Jazeera insisted on showing "the ugly face of war" and avoided sanitizing the news. Al Jazeera was increasingly aware that viewers around the world wanted more positive stories, especially younger consumers.

A more general threat was seen to be the fact that some analysts questioned the future of the rolling news format of 24-hour TV satellite and cable channels, as many people were now turning to the internet for news. Whilst Al Jazeera had actively adopted new media initiatives, including making extensive use of the internet, questions remained as to how it could effectively monetize digital news broadcasts.

Going forward, Al Jazeera was also considering opportunities for new product development to gain a foothold in new markets. It had announced the planned launch of Al Jazeera in a number of other languages, including Al Jazeera Urdu, catering mainly to Pakistanis. It was felt that this would give Al Jazeera an opportunity to become "the CNN of the emergent markets".

Al Jazeera was also reported to have investigated the possibility of launching a newspaper and printing business. Whilst this move could be seen as surprising as the world witnessed the newspaper industry struggle, it seemed more relevant in the Middle East than elsewhere as printed news generally had more credibility than digitized news in the region.

Al Jazeera's senior executives needed to decide how to move forward and set strategies for the brand, the target markets and to address financial issues, including the heavy dependence on the Emir of Qatar. Firstly, they needed to decide whether they wanted to clearly separate the Arab and international Al Jazeera brands, or whether the original Arab link should be leveraged even more. Secondly, Al Jazeera needed to define a clear way ahead in terms of which markets and consumers to address and strategies to achieve this, especially with regard to the products it wanted to offer. Thirdly, it needed to deal with the question of vulnerability arising from its financial dependence on the Emir of Qatar.

How could the leadership within Al Jazeera ensure that going forward the controversial *enfant terrible* of the Arab world would become an internationally acclaimed and independent media network in the same league as giants such as CNN and the BBC?

Exhibit A
Al Jazeera Worldwide

Headquarters: Doha
Broadcast centres: Washington DC, London, Kuala Lumpur
Bureaus:

Abidjan	Delhi	Ndjamena
Almaty	Gaza	Nouakchott
Amman	Harare	Òslo
Ankara	Islamabad	Paris
Athens	Jakarta	Rabat
Baghdad	Jerusalem	Ramallah
Bahrain	Johannesburg	Sana'a
Beijing	Kabul	Sarajevo
Beirut	Khartoum	Sao Paolo
Berlin	Madrid	Sydney
Brussels	Manila	Tehran
Buenos Aires	Masqat	Tokyo
Cairo	Mogadishu	Tripoli
Caracas	Moscow	Tunis
Dakar	Nairobi	
Damascus	New York	
Dubai		

Source: "Al Jazeera—Setting the News Agenda", an Al Jazeera leaflet

Exhibit B

Al Jazeera Timeline

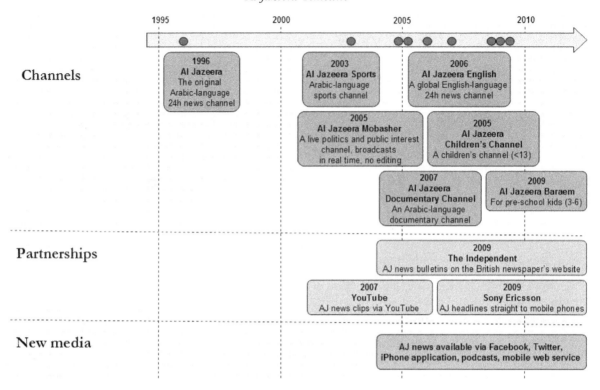

1996: Launch of **Al Jazeera**, the original Arabic-language 24h news channel.
Link: www.aljazeera.net/channel

2003: Launch of **Al Jazeera Sports**, an Arabic-language sports channel.
Link: www.aljazeerasport.net

2005: Launch of **Al Jazeera Mobasher**, a live politics and public interest channel, which broadcasts conferences in real time without editing or commentary.

2005: Launch of **Al Jazeera Children's Channel**, a children's interest channel (up to 13 years old).
Link: www.jcctv.net

2006: Launch of **Al Jazeera English**, a global English-language 24h news channel.

2007: Launch of **Al Jazeera Documentary Channel**, an Arabic-language documentary channel.
Link: www.doc.aljazeera.net

2009: Launch of **Baraem**, a channel for pre-school children (3–6 years old).
Link: www.baraem.tv

Exhibit C
Al Jazeera English Editorial Highlights

Below is a list of editorial highlights for Al Jazeera English compiled by Al Jazeera:

The War on Gaza

As the only international English language news network that broadcast from inside both Gaza and Israel, Al Jazeera provided live and comprehensive coverage of the war. With its unique access, Al Jazeera became the consistent and credible news source, both for viewers and other media. Al Jazeera had permanent bureaus in both Palestine and Israel.

Afghanistan

Al Jazeera had a fully staffed bureau in Afghanistan and provided comprehensive coverage from the start of the conflict and throughout the evolving situation. Al Jazeera teams covered the actions of both the NATO's International Security Assistance Force and the Taliban.

Russia/Georgia War

With journalists on the ground in Tbilisi, North and South Ossetia, and Moscow, Al Jazeera covered all sides of the complicated and fast-moving story of the Russia/Georgia war.

Myanmar Insurrection

Al Jazeera reported exclusively from inside Myanmar during the monks' uprising and the ensuing crackdown.

Myanmar Cyclone

Al Jazeera was one of the first networks on the ground inside Myanmar after the cyclone hit. Two Al Jazeera teams also reported from Bangkok as aid efforts built up.

The Assassination of Benazir Bhutto

Al Jazeera reported live within minutes of the assassination of Bhutto. Al Jazeera teams provided comprehensive coverage of the ensuing political dynamics after Bhutto's death as the country decided on a new leader.

Zimbabwe Elections

Al Jazeera reported from inside Zimbabwe as the people of the country voted for their president. The comprehensive reporting by Al Jazeera teams on the ground covered the political issues surrounding the election, including voter intimidation, the ensuing standoff and diplomatic attempts to resolve it.

Kenya Elections

Al Jazeera reporters covered the story of the elections live as the political deadlock began and the ensuing violence.

The US Presidential Elections

Al Jazeera offered comprehensive coverage of the US presidential candidates and the opinions of American voters. In addition to Stateside reporting, Al Jazeera explored in depth how the election would influence the rest of the world, and canvassed the opinions of people from around the globe.
Source: Al Jazeera Media Pack 2009, Al Jazeera English (Al Jazeera Network—Communications and Corporate Relations—2009

Exhibit D
Al Jazeera Arabic Viewer Demographic

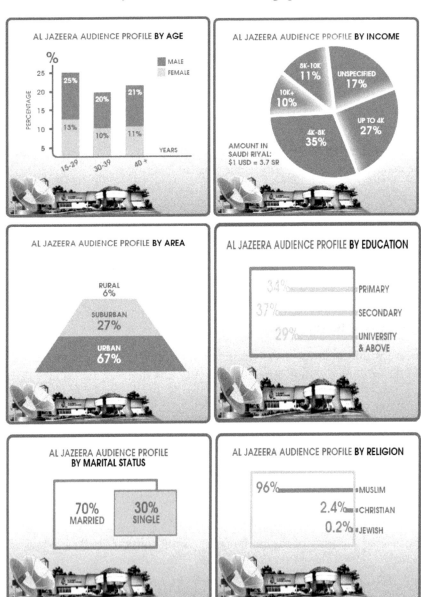

Source: http://www.allied-media.com/aljazeera/JAZdemog.html

Exhibit E

Al Jazeera Total Potential Audience

Country/ Region	Total Population	Arabs (%)	Total Adult Arabs (15y+)	Penetration (%)	Potential Audience
Algeria	32,818,500	99.0	21,833,492	24.0	5,240,038
Bahrain	667,238	73.0	346,804	43.7	151,553
Cyprus	771,657	3.2	19,285	25.0	4,821
Egypt	74,718,797	94.0	46,425,777	10.0	4,642,578
Europe	n/a	n/a	n/a	n/a	4,000,000
Iran	68,278,826	1.0	482,731	60.0	289,639
Iraq	24,683,313	75.0	10,977,903	47.0	5,159,615
Israel	6,116,533	19.9	889,766	47.0	418,190
Jordan	5,460,265	98.0	3,430,029	52.0	1,783,615
Kuwait	2,183,161	80.0	1,259,247	69.17	871,021
Lebanon	3,727,703	95.0	2,581,621	59.3	1,530,901
Libya	5,499,074	97.0	3,493,837	55.0	1,921,610
Morocco	31,689,265	99.1	20,977,913	39.2	8,223,342
Oman	2,807,125	75.0	1,216,889	59.0	717,964
Qatar	817,052	40.0	246,096	69.1	170,102
Saudi Arabia	24,293,844	90.0	12,615,793	51.2	6,463,071
Syria	17,585,540	90.3	9,750,162	38.0	3,705,062
Tunisia	9,924,742	98.0	7,100,160	23.0	1,633,037
Turkey	68,109,469	10.0	4,958,369	10.0	495,837
United Arab Emirates	2,484,818	40.0	728,549	52	378,845
United States	n/a	n/a	n/a	n/a	1,000,000
West Bank & Gaza Strip	3,512,062	88.6	1,680,311	99.0	1,663,508
Yemen	19,349,881	98.0	10,088,254	27.0	2,723,829
GRAND TOTAL	**405,498,865**		**161,102,989**		**53,208,177**

Source: http://www.allied-media.com/aljazeera/JAZdemog.html

Exhibit F

Survey, June 2009—Selection of Answers from 93 Respondents

What comes to mind when you think about Al Jazeera?

- "Arabic CNN"—*Canadian*
- "Best and most complete Arab news channel in the world. For any news about the Middle East, watch it for 15 minutes and you will know everything."—*Lebanese*
- "War reports. International recognition. Wide popularity"—*German*
- "Broadcasting images of Saddam Hussein with Western hostages during the first Gulf War."—*Brazilian*
- "Neutral, non-biased information"—*German*
- "The only times I hear about Al Jazeera is when a terrorist group uses it as a broadcast mechanism."—*American*
- "Governmental TV, biased, against the west, pro-Iranian, pro-Palestinian, good connection with terrorists and extreme Muslim."—*French*

What makes Al Jazeera different from other 24-hour news channels?

- "Arab perspective"—*Canadian*
- "Messages from Bin Laden are communicated through Al Jazeera."—*Dutch*
- "Independence from the Western view"—*South Korean*
- "Reality with no political distortion."—*NA*
- "Often controversial news coverage as the only ones that can access certain people and organisations."—*Colombian*
- "The counterpoint to the western television."—*Brazilian*
- "Access to zones where BBC/CNN don't go. Talks a lot about Africa (forgotten conflicts)."—*French*

What do you think are the weaknesses of Al Jazeera?

- "Public opinion outside sees it as biased towards the Arab world. Sadly, it is regarded by some North-Americans as tied to terrorism/ a voice for terrorists."—*Canadian*
- "Negative image due to heavy overload on war coverage."—*German*
- "Leaned towards *sensational* reporting in recent years due to the high competition with Al-Arabiya and other good quality media channels. "—*Moroccan*
- "One sided, partisan reporting."—*British*

Exhibit G

Al Jazeera's Distribution Channels

- Al Jazeera English is widely available on cable and satellite platforms throughout the world.
- Al Jazeera Arabic reaches approximately 50 million viewers.
- Al Jazeera English broadcasts to nearly 140 million households in more than 100 countries. A complete list of countries currently broadcasting AJE is available at: http://english.aljazeera.net/watchaje
- Al Jazeera English can be watched streaming live online at www.livestation.com/aje
- Al Jazeera is the most watched news channel on You Tube, receiving 2.5 million views per month.
- The Al Jazeera English website receives 22 million visits every month. Approximately half of the Al Jazeera English website traffic comes from the United States and Canada.
- A snapshot of Al Jazeera English's website, 21st June 2009:

UPDATED ON:
SUNDAY, JUNE 21, 2009
21:33 MECCA TIME, 18:33 GMT

FOOTBALL
Liga | SerieA | Qatari League

WATCH NOW
FRONT PAGE

AFRICA
AMERICAS
ASIA-PACIFIC
CENTRAL/S. ASIA
EUROPE
MIDDLE EAST

FOCUS
BUSINESS
SPORT
PROGRAMMES
WEATHER
YOUR VIEWS

SEARCH
ARABIC
ABOUT US

RSS

Tehran clashes 'left 13 dead'

State TV blames rioters and "terrorists" for deaths during crackdown on protests.

■ Video: Bloody scenes from Tehran
■ Video: Election divides clergy
■ Iran's disputed election
■ What next for Iran?
■ Your views: What now for Iran?
■ Q&A: Tweeting from Tehran

NEWS BULLETIN

IRAN IN CRISIS

Click on the video to see a larger version and more videos from Al Jazeera.

ALJAZEERA
TODAY'S SCHEDULE

WATCH AJE LIVE
Livestation

IN DEPTH

Iran condemns West's 'interference'
Ahmadinejad attacks the US and Britain for

'Jewish state' recognition urged
Israel's Barak says Arab acceptance a pre-

Sources: Al Jazeera Media Pack 2009, Al Jazeera English (Al Jazeera Network—Communications and Corporate Relations—2009) and Al Jazeera English's website http://english.aljazeera.net/

Exhibit H

Al Jazeera's New Media Initiatives

Facebook
The Al Jazeera Facebook Application allows you to keep up-to-date with all the news from Al Jazeera. You can also interact with programmes such as the Riz Khan show on Facebook

IM Bot
The Al Jazeera IM Bot allows you to receive breaking news directly to your email or Instant Messaging client. Just add aj.breaking@gmail.com to your IM Profile

Mobile Web Service
Get the latest News and Sport from Al Jazeera on your mobile. This service is now available in both Arabic and English. Simply go to http://m.aljazeera.net on your mobile.

iPhone Application
Read the latest news from Al Jazeera anytime, anywhere in an easy to read format for your iPhone or iPod Touch. Just tap in i.aljazeera.net into your browser and start reading.

Twitter
Let the news follow you wherever you are. Simply follow your desired news channel in order to receive the latest headlines via Twitter.

Sony Ericsson RSS
Al Jazeera and Sony Ericsson have partnered to bring the world's top stories straight to mobile phones through RSS feeds in both Arabic and English.

Podcasts
Subscribe to Al Jazeera podcasts to have your favourite Al Jazeera programmes delivered directly to you. Available through iTunes in Arabic and English.

YouTube
Al Jazeera on YouTube is the easiest way to watch Al Jazeera on the web. Go behind the glossy headlines with our diverse news reports and in-depth programming.

Special Projects
The team also produce special projects that use the latest technology. Previous projects include a Geo-Tracked journey through the Sahara using a GPS enabled mobile phone.

Sources: Al Jazeera Media Pack 2009, Al Jazeera English (Al Jazeera Network—Communications and Corporate Relations—2009) and Al Jazeera Labs (http://labs.aljazeera.net)

References

Links to articles about Al Jazeera:
- "Al Jazeera steps up global news offering", 13 May 2009, http://www.prweek.com/uk/News/MostRead/905594/Al-Jazeera-steps-global-news-offering/
- "Al-Jazeera, une chaîne pas comme les autres ! Une géopolitique de l'information au Moyen-Orient", July 2006, http://www.strategicsinternational.com/13_09.pdf
- "Behind the Scenes with Al-Jazeera, A Conversation with Mohammed el-Nawawy and Adel Iskander Farag", April 15, 2002, http://www.cceia.org/resources/transcripts/134.html

- Al Jazeera en Français—Jean-Marc Morandini http://www.universfreebox.com/article964.html
- "France 24 veut concurrencer Al Jazeera!" 28 Avril 2009, http://www.lexpressiondz.com/chron/2009-04-28/3/2410.html
- "Al-Jazeera: a top brand from Arabia?", http://www.360east.com/?p=113
- "Al Jazeera tough enough?" by Abram D. Sauer, April 28, 2003, http://www.brandchannel.com/features_profile.asp?pr_id=122
- Al Jazeera vs. Al Arabiya: are we getting sick of the former?, http://www.360east.com/?p=284
- "Inside Al Jazeera The World's Most Controversial TV Station", 3/4/02, http://media.www.harbus.org/media/storage/paper343/news/2002/03/04/WorldlyViews/In side.Al.Jazeera-196238.shtml
- "Al Jazeera: Turning up the heat", http://knowledge.insead.edu/aljazeera080105.cfm
- "Few in U.S. See Jazeera's Coverage of Gaza War", January 11, 2009, http://www.nytimes.com/2009/01/12/business/media/12jazeera.html?_r=1
- "The Internet and Middle East Studies, 1997", http://pws.prserv.net/hosaka/shuji/internet/The%20Internet%20and%20Middle%20East% 20Studies.htm
- "Al-Jazeera English to air in San Francisco", May 30, 2009, http://www.sfgate.com/cgi-bin/article.cgi?f=/c/a/2009/05/30/MNB617TH1T.DTL
- "Top earning Arabs prefer CNN to Al Jazeera, June 2009, http://www.arabianbusiness.com/557309-top-earning-arabs-prefer-cnn-to-al-jazeera
- "The international news will not be televised", June 2009, http://experts.foreignpolicy.com/posts/2009/06/04/the_international_news_will_not_be_televised

Information About Media in the Middle East

- Overview of newspapers in all countries: http://www.world-newspapers.com/
- Overview of online newspapers in all countries: http://www.onlinenewspapers.com/
- Middle East & North Africa Media Guide (MediaSource, 2009)
- BBC News' Country Profiles (including descriptions of media situations): http://news.bbc.co.uk/2/hi/country_profiles/default.stm
- "2009 Annual Arab Public Opinion Survey", Professor Shilbey Telhami, Anwar Sadat Chair for Peace and Development, University of Maryland and Zogby International: http://www.brookings.edu/~/media/Files/events/2009/0519_arab_opinion/2009_arab_publ ic_opinion_poll.pdf
- "Arab Media Outlook, 2008-2012", PricewaterhouseCoopers, 2009

14

Media Innovation in the Middle East

By Johanne Staugaard Johansen and Danielle Geara

In January 2010, the management team of MBC (Middle East Broadcasting Centre) assembled for a meeting about the Group's future strategy. They needed to decide how to take the company to the next level and into a new era.

So far, MBC had been an unbelievable success story. From its launch in 1991, it had developed under the leadership of the founder, Sheikh Waleed Al Ibrahim, from a single satellite channel into the leading media company in the Middle East. Over the years, MBC had launched eight popular TV channels, two radio stations, and several highly successful internet services (see Exhibit 1 for an overview of MBC's offerings). It had an audience of over 100 million regular viewers, and a 45% share of audience in Saudi Arabia, the key advertising market of the Middle East. Its flagship entertainment channel, MBC1, was the Arab World's number one family viewing channel. Furthermore, MBC was the only media group in the region that was both independent and commercially viable.

From the large windows of the meeting room, the 12 group directors had a view over Dubai's palm-fringed coastline, its cranes and tall buildings. Head of Strategy, Stephanie Holden, had just given a presentation on the newest developments in the media industry in the Middle East. Everybody in the room knew that things were going to change, both in the media industry in general and in the Middle East in particular. There was a variety of different opinions within the management group as people had widely differing

Johanne Staugaard Johansen and Danielle Geara, "Middle East Broadcasting Centre (MBC): Media Innovation in the Middle East." Copyright © 2010 by INSEAD. Reprinted with permission by The Case Centre and the authors.

backgrounds and histories with the company (See Exhibit 2). Some were strong creative and entrepreneurial forces, whereas others were more focused on strategy and business procedures. This diversity was seen as a main strength of the company but it guaranteed an intense discussion.

Despite their individual differences, it was clear to everybody in management that MBC faced several strategic challenges. How could the management team stimulate the continued growth of MBC, whilst avoiding the "incumbent trap?" How could they make sure that MBC stayed innovative with an entrepreneurial culture while remaining professional and coping with its increased size and complexity?

The Learning Years (1991–2002)

The Beginning

In 1991, Sheikh Waleed Al Ibrahim of Saudi Arabia established MBC in London as the first independent Pan-Arabic entertainment channel. The vacated Fulham offices of the UK satellite broadcaster BSB, which had merged with its competitor Sky, became MBC's first headquarters. In 1994, the company moved to a former warehouse of British Telecom in Battersea.

Although MBC's market was the Middle East, London was seen as a good starting point for MBC's activities because it had a booming TV industry and therefore a lot of media expertise and skilled people were available—resources that were scarce in the Middle East at that time. During the early years, MBC was mainly managed by western staff. Another reason for launching MBC out of London was the fact that it was seen as "neutral territory." By setting up the business in a non-Arab country, MBC was seen as being non partisan.

The Changing (Media) Landscape in the Middle East

From Scarcity to Multi-channel Platform

Only a decade earlier, the TV industry in the Middle East was almost non-existent, and what did exist was not very sophisticated. A turning point in the development of media in the region coincided with the dramatic growth of oil revenues from the 1970s, resulting in strong economic development. GDP soared from the 1990s, driven by high oil prices and economic diversification, which created higher levels of disposable income and fed both consumer media spending and advertising revenues.[1] For example from 2006 to 2007, nominal GDP grew 19.2% in Egypt and 16.2% in the UAE[2], gradually creating a larger middle class. Henceforth, the Gulf States could afford better education systems, broadcasting equipment, and the necessary electronic infrastructure.

Further transformation of the Middle East's media landscape took place during the 1990s with the start of satellite television. Initially, many governments tried to stall the roll-out of satellite TV, hoping to retain their control on what was broadcast. With the realisation that the development could not be stopped, they abandoned their attempts at resistance. By the mid 90s, half the population of Saudi Arabia were said to own satellite dishes; ten years later, in 2007, the figure had risen to 94%.

Most of the media companies in the Middle East were either family or government owned and financed. Levels of editorial independence varied across the region. For example, in Lebanon, and Turkey there was

---

1 Source: Arab Media Outlook, 2008-2012 (PricewaterhouseCoopers, 2009)

2 Source: Arab Media Outlook, 2008-2012 (PricewaterhouseCoopers, 2009) (International Monetary Fund, World Econommic Outlook Database, October 2008.

traditionally a larger degree of press freedom than elsewhere. Individual governments' influence was increasingly challenged by trans-national newspapers and the introduction of Pan-Arab satellite news channels, such as Al Jazeera, that was established in Qatar in 1996.

The new satellite stations—although linked to ruling families of the countries in which they were based—were more driven by commercial considerations[3] than the previous state-run media that remained the only option for TV viewers who had terrestrial antennas, and were often driven by a political agenda. The launch of satellite TV allowed consumers to choose between hundreds of channels, and although satellite television was primarily perceived as offering entertainment, it increasingly became a credible source of information.

Young and Growing Populations

The Middle East had a rapidly growing population.[4] Qatar and United Arab Emirates experienced high levels of immigration as expatriate workers were drawn in to work on major infrastructure projects. The region had a younger population on average than any other part of the world: over 50% of the population in Yemen, Oman, Saudi Arabia, Jordan, Morocco and Egypt were estimated to be under 25, while in the rest of the countries in the region the under-25s made up around 35–47% of the total population.[5] The youth segment was particularly receptive to new media. They adopted new technologies faster and experimented with new ways of accessing content. Moreover, they were likely to spend a higher proportion of their income on media consumption than older consumers. This unique demographic profile presented opportunities for online media owners, content developers, operators, and all parties along the media value chain.

Media Consumption

Media consumption in the Middle East was characterised by the fact that television was *the* most important source of entertainment. On average, people across the region watched 4.5 hours of television daily,[6] and this peaked during the month of Ramadan. Watching television was often a family activity, and formats that combined Western programming styles with local elements were very popular. One reason why television was an important source of information and entertainment in the region was the rate of literacy in some countries in the Middle East, ranging from 50% in Morocco to over 90% in Kuwait.[7] In markets where print media had a limited reach due to low literacy levels, television played a more important role.

Free-to-air (FTA) television had a dominant position in the Middle East, representing 82.5% of the total channels available.[8] The adoption of pay-TV in most of the Middle East was still weak, although in some of the wealthier countries, such the UAE, it had started to gain traction.[9] Consumers were generally satisfied with the content provided by FTA television, and the FTA media companies invested heavily in international formats and programming. Another major reason for FTA's dominance was the prevalence of piracy. Pirated DVDs made new movies via pay-TV less exclusive. Moreover, some decoders could gain free access to pay-TV via satellite.

---

3 Historicizing Arab blogs: Reflections on the transmission of ideas and information in Middle Eastern history. By Brian Ulrich, The Middle East Centre, University of Oxford
4 Source: Arab Media Outlook, 2008-2012 (PricewaterhouseCoopers, 2009)
5 Source: Arab Media Outlook, 2008-2012 (PricewaterhouseCoopers, 2009)
6 Source: Saudi Cum CTV 2008
7 Source: Arab Media Outlook, 2008-2012 (PricewaterhouseCoopers, 2009)
8 Source: Saudi Cum CTV 2008
9 Source: Arab Media Outlook, 2008-2012 (PricewaterhouseCoopers, 2009)

Competition

A host of new media companies, such as MBC, Rotana, the Abu Dhabi Media Company and LBC, were launched in the late 1980s and 1990s (see Exhibit 3). International content was brought to the region at the same time as several new channels with Arabic content started up. Many of these were targeted at specific consumer segments such as children, women and sports enthusiasts. During this period, the media in the Middle East became increasingly sophisticated.

Learning to Run a Media Company

While operating out of London, MBC was focused mainly on growing its flagship entertainment TV channel, MBC (later MBC 1). However, other innovations saw the light of day, including MBC's first radio channel, MBC FM, launched in 1994. In 1999, the acquisition of the rights to the TV show *Who wants to be a millionaire?"* proved to be a milestone for MBC. The show quickly gained a huge audience and put MBC on the map as a leading provider of family entertainment.

In 2000, MBC set up its first office in the Middle East, with the establishment of production facilities in Beirut. Production was more cost-effective in Lebanon than in London, and the pool of talent—both on-screen and off-screen—was at the time larger in Beirut than in the rest of the region.

During its London era, MBC was on a steep learning curve. It took some time to establish MBC as a professionally run media group, learning how to run a broadcasting channel, gaining experience, building a network within the media industry, and growing with the emerging satellite market as resistance to satellite gradually waned (see Exhibit 4). When the learning years came to an end, MBC had still only one analogue channel, one radio station, and a 19% share of the key advertising markets. Overall the company had yet to reach its commercial potential, although it seemed poised to expand at a rapid pace.

The Move to Dubai (2002)

On 7th March 2002, it was announced that MBC would move to Dubai. Sheikh Waleed Al Ibrahim decided that the company had learned the trade and was "ready to run." In Dubai, MBC would be closer to its audience and advertisers in the Middle East, in particular Saudi Arabia. The move would also lower costs as operating out of Dubai was significantly less costly than London. Furthermore, it meant that MBC would be able to hire more employees from the Middle Eastern region who had an intimate understanding of the market. The Middle East was defined as Egypt, Jordan, Lebanon, Syria, Iran, Iraq, and the countries of the Arabian Peninsula (Saudi Arabia, Bahrain, Kuwait, Oman, Qatar, United Arab Emirates[10] and Yemen).[11]

When the move became a reality, the majority of its employees in London decided to stay: 500 people left, 76 moved to Dubai, and 120 new people were hired. But MBC managed to keep the "DNA" of the company as it moved to the Arab world, both by retaining good practices that had been established in London—such as a systematic approach to HR management, including its non-discrimination policy—and keeping key people, including its main creative force. Key people who relocated to Dubai and became part of the management team included Najwa Safat (HR); Fadi Ismail (Production); Tim Riordan (TV); and Fadel Zahreddine

---

10 The seven emirates: Abu Dhabi, Ajman, Dubai, Fujairah, Ras al-Khaimah, Sharjah and Umm al-Quwain.
11 The Greater Middle East also included the North Africa countries (such as Algeria, Libya, Morocco, Sudan), and to the East included Afghanistan, Pakistan and Central Asian countries (such as Kazakhstan and Uzbekistan).

(Creative Services). They had been with MBC since the early days and had a thorough understanding of the company. All were present at the strategy meeting at Dubai headquarters in January 2010.

The move to Dubai marked the beginning of a new era. MBC moved from analogue to digital satellite distribution shortly afterwards, and began to break even financially. The company was ready to take more drastic steps and experiment with new ideas. MBC's culture was entrepreneurial and creative, although things could sometimes become chaotic as there were not too many established processes and no systematic information sharing.

The Expansion Years (2003-2007)

It seemed that almost from the minute MBC landed in Dubai, the company's "mad expansion" started. It profited from the fast growth of the (digital) satellite market in the Middle East, as well as from the growing advertising market. It also succeeded in securing rights for high-quality US content as it was the first broadcaster to spot that this content was available at a very low rate for the Arab market. At the end of this period of expansion, MBC had grown to eight TV channels, two radio stations, several internet activities, and 45% market share in Saudi Arabia.

From Standalone Channel to a Family of Digital Channels

MBC 2

A milestone in MBC's history was the launch of a second TV channel called "2" (later MBC2) in 2003. Until then, western movies had only been given a few slots per week on the main MBC channel. At a major TV content fair in April 2002, Tim Riordan, Head of TV, realised that there was more potential in broadcasting western movies, and that rights were available at very attractive rates. Riordan thought that a 24-hour free-to-air movie channel with western movies subtitled in Arabic could be a major opportunity for MBC. Although it was late at night, he immediately raised the idea with Sheikh Waleed, who indicated his support for opening a new channel if they could sign contracts with some of the major US studios. At the time, the Middle East was not an important market for Hollywood studios—simply a marginal market providing marginal profits. As a result, Riordan managed to negotiate some good long term deals and subtitled Hollywood movies turned out to be a huge success.

Al Arabiya

Not only did MBC launch the world's first 24-hour free-to-air movie channel 2 in 2003, it also supported the launch of the 24-hour news channel Al Arabiya. Al Arabiya was outside the MBC Group, but used the Group's assets and shared resources. Al Arabiya was a counterpoint to the Qatari news channel Al Jazeera (launched in 1996), which had a reputation for being controversial and independent, broadcasting "the ugly face of war", and being "the voice of the voiceless." MBC saw Al Arabiya as an alternative to Al Jazeera. It aimed to present a balanced picture and built a strong business section which brought in significant audiences, particularly during stock market booms. By 2010, Al Arabiya had a larger viewer audience in the Gulf than Al Jazeera, although the latter was perhaps better known globally due to its confrontational style and English version. The popularity of Al Arabiya in the region was one of the reasons why newly elected

US President Barack Obama chose to give his first ever television interview on becoming President to Al Arabiya in January 2009, giving a big boost to its credibility.

MBC 3, MBC 4, MBC Action, MBC Max, MBC Persia

In the years that followed, MBC rapidly expanded its products and services. When MBC purchased blockbusters from Hollywood studios, the movies came in so-called "output package" deals—it was standard industry practice to sell blockbusters only in a package with other movies and series that were less well known. MBC saw the opportunity to launch several new channels with this content, each with a specific brand identity and target audience. These channels included MBC 3 (2004) for children, and MBC 4 (2005), originally a non-movie fiction channel, but subsequently re-launched to target women more specifically with drama, comedy and entertainment shows. MBC added a second radio station to its portfolio in 2004. The company also launched MBC Action (2007), predominantly targeted at a young, male audience with high-octane action and reality shows, as well as MBC Persia (2008) and MBC Max (2008), which offered a wide range of movies with Farsi and Arabic subtitles respectively.

Shifting to a "Branded Approach"

In parallel to expanding its portfolio from a single channel to a family of digital channels, MBC also focused on developing its brand. MBC was now a group of channels with a strongly shared identity and shared group values, each with different characteristics. Each individual channel was clearly branded with its own logo, colour, look and feel that matched the content. For example, the yellow used for the MBC Action logo symbolised the yellow/black striped tape used to mark crime scenes in US action movies. In parallel with the individual brand identities, an overall MBC umbrella brand promise was introduced: "We see hope everywhere," which sent a positive message.

Outsourcing Advertising

In 2004, MBC took a bold decision with regards to advertising—and one which was unusual for a media company: it decided to outsource its advertising sales. The advertising market in the Middle East was very difficult and, despite recent growth, it was still small compared to the western world. Advertising expenditure per capita in the region was one of the lowest in the world: the Middle East represented approximately 4% of the world population but accounted for only 1% of global advertising expenditure. The most important market by far was the Kingdom of Saudi Arabia, hence MBC focused its advertising sales effort there.

One problem was the limited availability of consumer research and audience measurements, and that which was available was of poor quality. Consequently, it was unclear how many viewers a programme actually had. In the absence of a common and reliable rating methodology, advertisers lacked the critical tools to make efficient media buying decisions. The lack of transparency and consumer insights made it more difficult to develop campaigns and media strategies, and without accurate figures advertisers were reluctant to grow advertising budgets.

The major Pan-Arab advertisers were multinational companies in the fast-moving consumer goods market; food, beverages and telecommunications. Pan-regional advertising was predominantly spent on satellite TV. Only rarely did domestic brands use satellite TV as their advertising medium, as it was expensive and few local brands could justify the cost; they preferred to use the print medium.

MBC initially sold advertising itself, but found that growth was limited and operational complexity was high. Therefore, in 2004, MBC signed a 5-year deal with the Choueiri Group to handle advertising sales, This allowed MBC to concentrate on its core business—creating TV—and gave it income stability and predictability. The deal proved to be a major success. MBC gained a 45% viewer share in the Saudi market, whilst the "power ratio" (the share of the advertising market divided by the share of the viewer market) was consistently above 1.

Building up Own Content Capabilities

MBC built up its content capabilities significantly during the expansion years, via content acquisition, its own productions, and those of its subsidiary O3. It had huge success in acquiring Arabic content for MBC1, in particular drama and comedy programmes which boosted the ratings. MBC adapted western formats for its Arab audience, such as *Kalumna Nawaem*, which was inspired by various US talk shows, a concept whereby four women from different backgrounds in the Arab world discussed challenging topics. The talk show became one of the most popular programmes on MBC1. MBC also developed its own formats, using its production facilities in Beirut (bought in 2000), above all for entertainment shows and reality TV. Samar Akrouk, who had been with MBC since 1995, led the more than 70 production staff members in Beirut.

O3 Productions, a subsidiary of MBC from 2002, also came to play a major role in MBC's continued success during the expansion years. An independent production company but still part of the MBC Group, it was headed by Fadi Ismail, who had been with MBC since its beginnings in London. Although O3 Productions originally focused on producing documentaries, it rapidly expanded its activities to find and develop new genres. It handled the production, acquisition and dubbing of innovative fiction content. In this sense, O3 Productions had a very entrepreneurial feel to it, as Ismail noted: "We are the adventurous part of the group." O3 Productions mostly targeted its products at non-MBC1 channels. MBC1 remained a more conservative, Saudi, family-oriented channel, where it was important that content was appropriate for families to watch together without embarrassment. Other channels offered more room for experimentation.

New Media

MBC set up its New Media department as a separate profit centre, under the leadership of Group Director, Ammar Bakkar. It developed internet and mobile offerings, mainly from 2004 onwards.

In 2004, in addition to the mbc.net portal, MBC launched the Al Arabiya website. This was groundbreaking in that it allowed visitors to openly express their opinions, comment on what they read, and discuss topics generally seen as taboo. The Al Arabiya website developed into a kind of community, with some users commenting daily on the site. It was followed, in 2006, with the Al Arabiya Business website, launched as an up-to-date provider of financial and business information, and by mobile services in 2007.

Bakkar explained that in the New Media department: "We 'recycle' revenue to invest in new projects." The revenue driver was interactive TV competitions, where people could win large prizes if they—based on certain TV shows—sent an SMS to the channel. The department proved to be innovative in launching new types of competition—for example, one was based on the concept that MBC would fulfil "your dream" no matter whether the dream was a car, a house or starting a business. MBC partnered with telecom operators to create these competitions and the revenue was shared between MBC and the operator.

Overall, there was a significant push to develop new media initiatives from at least 2004, including mobile services, VoD services and social networking.

Increasing Procedures and Systems

While MBC rapidly expanded its portfolio, undertaking one entrepreneurial initiative after another, the first steps were also made to strengthen structure and procedures. MBC was being professionalized.

In 2002, Sheikh Waleed brought in Sam Barnett as Director of Operations. He was made Chief Operating Officer and General Manager of MBC Group in 2005. He had a background in consulting, an MBA from INSEAD, and was 32 at the time. He was hired to build the structure and systems needed for an international media company that was growing at high speed.

In the early years, decision making at MBC was characterised by the fact that managers did not have all the tools they needed to manage their units commercially. People worked in departmental silos, which sometimes resulted in isolated decisions by departments. Barnett introduced new processes such as budgeting and performance management, and middle management were increasingly engaged in decision making and encouraged to provide input. People no longer worked in isolation and decision making became more rational. Throughout the company, people credited Barnett with the changes—he imposed order throughout the organization by being fair, firm and leading by example.

However, the introduction of systems, policies and procedures did not always go down well. Many thought that they slowed work down, especially some of the creative minds who liked to move fast and resisted structure. However, over time most people agreed that the increase in systems was constructive and 'a must,' as long as the company was not over-regulated. As Marketing Director, Mazen Hayek, acknowledged: "It will never be a law firm and over-institutionalised, but it needed order."

In some ways, MBC changed from being very colourful to more commercial. In 2004, MBC started to demonstrate commercial success and this has grown significantly since then,

The Consolidation Years (2008-2009)

Stepping on the Brakes

The expansion was still ongoing in 2007, when Klaus Felsinger (Felsinger) was appointed as CFO. Klaus Felsinger, an Austrian by birth, had an MBA from IESE, and had worked as a banker in Asia before relocating to Dubai. Klaus Felsinger felt the energy and creativity that characterised MBC, but realised that despite the company's fast revenue growth there was a risk of expense increases becoming unsustainable, and the company losing its financial viability. Klaus Felsinger decided to step on the brakes in the 2007/2008 budgeting cycle and slow down spending growth significantly. Barnett had already institutionalised a number of processes but during the consolidation years the focus on a more disciplined budget approach intensified.

While MBC's growth activities were slowing down and the market was becoming increasingly saturated, competitors had launched similar channels and, as a result, the cost of content increased. MBC focused on improving its existing offerings and strengthening the FTA brands. During the consolidation years, it launched MBC Persia (2008) to reach the Farsi-speaking market, and the pay-channel MBC Plus (2009) to exploit a pay window on the content that had been acquired. New Media initiatives were a priority and this was one of MBC's largest year-on-year investments during the consolidation phase. MBC renewed the advertising sales contract for the next five years (2009–2014) with the Choueiri Group. The combined result, according to many observers, was that MBC was considered the most professionally run media company in the Middle East.

In late 2008, the global financial crisis began to bite, eating into media advertising revenues. Economies in the Middle East were less vulnerable to the crisis than other developing regions, but the impact of the global recession was still significant, although the countries in the region were affected differently. In some countries, households and workers were directly impacted. For example, Egypt's quarterly growth fell to 4.1% in December 2008 from 7.7% in the same quarter of 2007. Job creation fell by 30% and unemployment rose. In Dubai, many construction projects were cancelled or put on hold indefinitely. The resulting job losses meant that thousands of migrant workers left the emirate in early 2009. Overall, oil exporters with large financial capacity and relatively small populations seemed to be in the best position to absorb the economic shock.[12]

When the financial crisis hit the region in 2008/2009, MBC was already prepared because, as Klaus Felsinger said, "we had already been turning the ship for 12 months." Various efficiency efforts launched earlier, such as detailed business planning, a thorough budgeting process, and a system of management targets and incentives, were already showing results. In the event, 2008 and 2009 turned out to be the two most profitable years in MBC's history, despite the financial crisis.

Organisational Changes

It came as a natural extension of the increase in systems when Barnett introduced a new team of corporate planners in 2008. The corporate planners, most with an MBA background, worked within the individual departments but were also closely connected across the company to ensure a high level of consistency and communication.

A second important organisational change in 2008 was the fact that a Group Directorate for Content was formed. Its purpose was to oversee content across the Group to ensure that cross-media synergies were exploited and to keep track of the different opportunities on the various platforms.

Another key priority was to build a stronger strategy team. As a result, Stephanie Holden, a Harvard graduate who had worked at McKinsey, was brought in as Head of Strategy (in 2006). Her main tasks were to build and lead the new Strategy and Business Development department, introduce systematic strategy development processes and workshops, and screen new business opportunities.

The Group Director of Human Resources, Najwa Safwat, who had been at MBC since the London era and whom some called "the mother of MBC," also worked to professionalise the HR function. It was mainly her accomplishment that MBC established the systematic use of assessment centres to get an objective view on peoples' potential, internal succession planning and training programmes.

The Green Light Committee

Although MBC had been an entrepreneurial company since its inception, it was during the expansion years that many new innovations were initiated. During the consolidation years—and as a part of the overall effort to professionalise the company—a new initiative was taken to test and discuss new ideas in an institutionalised way: the Green Light Committee. The Committee also aimed to tackle some of the new challenges that MBC faced, such as how to develop cross-media initiatives and cross-functional teams that better met and understood the needs of consumers.

The Green Light Committee consisted of 10 people who represented different functions at MBC, such as Radio, TV, Acquisition, Production, Strategy and Sales. If, for example, someone in the company had an

---

12 The World Bank, http://web.worldbank.org

idea for a new programme, the first step was to fill out a form and then pitch the idea to the Committee. The Committee held monthly meetings to assess incoming ideas, and if they liked an idea they would recommend further development. They functioned as a kind of advisory board; if they supported an idea, the person who had originated it could pitch it to the chairman, Sheikh Waleed, who would make the final decision.

The Turkish Soaps

In 2008, MBC had yet another big hit. The introduction of Turkish soaps on MBC4 was a major milestone for the company. O3 Productions was behind this massive success. "I found the idea by accident when I was in Antalya for a film festival," said Ismail. At the time, dubbing in Arabic was not considered a serious business in terms of drama series. The Arabic TV dramas had increasingly become repetitive in their stories, and so the Turkish series came as a way of reviving drama in the region. As he explained: "They look like us, eat like us, have furniture like ours; we just had to make them speak like us." The series pushed some cultural boundaries as people had extra-marital affairs and dealt with modern issues, but the culture was clearly Middle Eastern: they observed Ramadan and some of the same traditions as in MBC's pan Arab market.

The Turkish soaps were immensely popular in the Middle East. The best-loved series, *Noor*, attracted over 90 million viewers for its last episode. However, they were not well received by all segments of society as they dealt with taboos and topics that were considered daring. This prompted criticism from some quarters, and even the issuing of a fatwa[13] in Saudi Arabia.

For MBC it was a balancing act between openness to discuss taboo subjects on the one hand and doing so in a gentle, respectful way, on the other, so as not to insult or antagonise their key market—Saudi viewers.

Mobile Services

Mobile services were one of the priorities for MBC during the consolidation years. This was part of the overall New Media focus it had developed. In the Middle East, mobile technology and mobile phones were rapidly emerging as a rival to broadband access to internet content. With new developments in technology, mobile phones were also developing as an alternative to watching television. Amongst Middle Eastern consumers, mobile downloads (especially music) were already widespread. The penetration rate of mobile phones was particularly high in the higher-income GCC countries. In 2007, penetration levels exceeded 100% in some countries, including the UAE (169%), Bahrain (146%), Qatar (118%), and Saudi Arabia (116%).[14] The roll-out of the mobile internet also enabled so-called smart phones.

In comparison to the high mobile penetration rate amongst Middle Eastern consumers, broadband penetration varied significantly across the region. Although fibre-optic access networks capable of very high broadband speeds were being rolled out in the higher-income markets, broadband penetration was still very low in many countries (often less than 10%). Part of the explanation was the high retail pricing of broadband when compared to per capita GDP, low PC penetration, and poor telecommunications access network infrastructure outside high-income countries and urban areas. Qatar had the highest reported broadband penetration, with 70% of households.[15]

---

13 A 'fatwa' is an Islamic religious ruling, a scholarly opinion on a matter of Islamic law. (Source: http://islam.about.com/od/law/g/ fatwa.htm)
14 Source: Arab Media Outlook, 2008-2012 (PricewaterhouseCoopers, 2009) 15 *Ibid*.
15 *Ibid*

At MBC, various new mobile services initiatives were launched. For example, *Tash Ma Tash*, an MBC-produced Saudi comedy series that had been on air for the last 16 years, was turned into "mobisodes" (mobile episodes). MBC found that there was even some content—especially comedy—that was initially developed for mobile that ended up being put on TV. It also experimented with other new initiatives—building a social network called *Nas*, and launching a VoD portal, *Shahid Online*, in 2008. Overall, it focused on developing cross-media initiatives and cross-functional teams that better met the needs of consumers in terms of both mobile services and new media overall.

2010—The Beginning of a New Era?

An Innovative Culture

By early 2010, when the management team assembled to discuss the company's future strategy, MBC employed 1,800 people worldwide, representing 62 different nationalities. In its growth years, MBC had developed a unique culture of creativity that stimulated risk-taking, openness and fast action. As Group Director of Creative Services, Fadel Zahreddine, explained, "A large part of innovation consists of taking risks and at the same time taking into account the complexity of our cultural-bound thinking audience."

People were encouraged to question things, to think "out of the box", and build awareness of trends and developments in the industry. The culture was central to fostering new ideas. Across the company it was felt that Chairman Sheikh Waleed played an essential role in developing this unique culture by encouraging and pushing the employees, and by being always accessible. Ismail described Sheikh Waleed as "pioneering with an avant-garde mindset and refreshing boldness."

In addition to the work of the Green Light Committee and the market research conducted by the company, there were regular informal discussions amongst the senior management and Sheikh Waleed. Combined with a mix of brainstorming and gut feeling, these regularly led to new initiatives. There seemed to be an instinct for innovation in parts of the company, leading one commentator to note, "One has to have the wisdom to say yes, even though the focus groups say no." The question was whether this culture of creativity could co-exist with the more rigid structure and procedures that were gradually being imposed.

Advertising Still a Key Revenue Driver

MBC depended heavily on advertising revenues and the company relied to a large degree on international advertisers such as Proctor & Gamble. However, it sought to diversify and become less dependent on traditional spot advertising by developing new advertising concepts such as branded content and advertorials. Although the revenue from these sources was growing fast, it was still below 10% of total revenue.

The second most important revenue driver (after advertising) was competitions via SMS. MBC also developed other revenue streams, such as merchandising, licensing, events and TV-shopping. While these were not yet significant, they offered longer term revenue potential.

One of the priorities for further development was online advertising. To encourage sales, MBC offered online advertising to those who already used TV advertising and tried to sell online competitions to large advertisers. It offered free graphic design for advertising banners as an encouragement to join MBC's platform. Although these initiatives stimulated some growth, online advertising was still low in total, starting, as it did, from a very low base.

For management, the pressing question was how to develop new revenue streams for the company. The goal was not only to grow overall revenue as the Middle Eastern advertising market grew but also to raise the share of revenue from non-traditional advertising and sponsorship sources from less than 10% in 2010 to 25% in the coming years.

Increased Competition from New Entrants

In 2010, there were approximately 450 free-to-air stations in the region. The top 10 channels in the region represented approximately 70% of both the audience share and the commercial revenue share, and the top 50 channels represented 90–95% of the audience and revenue share. Although, at first glance, the marketplace seemed very crowded, there were actually many stations that practically no one watched, and which only survived because they were subsidised. Overall there were few commercial players and it was difficult to 'compete' against players that were not commercial.

In 2010, Rupert Murdoch's News Corp entered the Arab TV market by acquiring a 9% share in Rotana, with an option to purchase a further 9% within 18 months of the original deal for approximately US$70 million, giving the company an estimated market value of US$770 million. Murdoch had followed similar strategies before in other countries, including Germany and Italy, where he would first acquire minority stakes in the leading pay-TV provider, and then increase his stake to become the majority owner. Once in control, Murdoch would fundamentally reorganize the companies, bringing in new management, transferring best management practices from his best performing pay-TV companies such as BSkyB, and realizing scale effects with the other pay-TV stations he owned.

For the Middle East, this meant that competition would increase significantly, and the bar for running a successful TV group would be raised. The question for MBC was how to deal with both the players that were not commercial and a powerful new competitor.

Content Innovation Strategy

MBC developed new programmes in three different ways. First, they could be based on licensing Western formats (e.g., *"Who Wants to be a Millionaire?"* and *"Deal or No Deal"*). Alternatively, they could be based on home-grown ideas (e.g., "The Godfather" where local celebrities shed light on their main mentors or sources of inspiration). Lastly, they could result from collaboration with regional players who came to MBC with ideas for co-productions.

Slowly Pushing Boundaries

> *"With our heart in the Arab world, we are forging a global media company that enriches people's lives through information, interaction and entertainment."*

This was MBC's vision. Sheikh Waleed wanted to open the world to the Middle East, and believed that in principle there were no boundaries to what could be talked about. He thought that the key thing was *how* one dealt with issues; treating the audience with respect was crucial.

MBC was conscious of the fact that the Middle Eastern market had many internal variations, and some topics were considered significantly more delicate in certain countries than others. It was careful not to overstep cultural boundaries and although it did introduce taboo subjects on screen, it did so in a sensitive manner. Samar Akrouk, Director of Productions, claimed, "We produce content to reach a Pan-Arab market but we do so conscientiously as to not antagonise the Arab and particularly the Saudi viewer." She continued, "We want slow change. We are not out to do a revolution."

Getting Market Knowledge

Developing a detailed knowledge of the market and consumers was difficult to achieve given the quality of available market research. MBC faced the same challenge as many other companies in the region: market research practices were very weak, there was scant measurement of media habits and little consumer research. This was partly due to the fact that people were concerned to protect their privacy and did not want to be measured, and partly because there were few research companies operating in the region. Moreover, different market research efforts produced conflicting results.

To overcome the challenge of getting market knowledge, MBC set up its own focus groups, and facilitated discussions with its Saudi employees to better understand the Saudi culture. When in doubt, Sheikh Waleed would sometimes show new shows to his extended family to get their opinions. Going forward, the question was how MBC could continue to develop innovative content in an industry where content was king, but where broadcasters needed to be especially careful dealing with taboo subjects.

Dilemmas for MBC

Focusing on Future Growth Opportunities

By 2010, MBC had identified several growth opportunities, but there were still ongoing discussions on where to focus the company's efforts.

Growth in other Arab countries was still possible. However, this meant that there was a need for local content, both in terms of production and distribution by satellite, which was still technically difficult and expensive. Also, there was a need for local advertising sales networks.

Another option was to continue to *produce more of their own local content*. MBC had recently acquired a leading production house in Saudi Arabia, which produced 10–15 drama and comedy series per year. Creating Pan-Arab offerings was very difficult due to the heterogeneous nature of the region. The most popular content was often national content; although several soaps, such as *Noor*, were very popular throughout the region.

If content was king in the industry, MBC was aware that developing *innovative content* was absolutely key for the company's future growth. For example it began investing in Indian soaps. Moreover, the sale of MBC-produced content abroad was seen as an opportunity. Should the company strengthen its base in producing even more local content as the economic significance of individual countries grew, or should it focus on developing Pan-Arab blockbusters?

New media was also on MBC's agenda. The company needed to develop attractive revenue models for new media. There was still a long way to go and many at MBC wondered, "How do we do to new media what we did to TV?"

Moving into *pay-TV* was also a potential way forward for MBC, but so far it had not proved to be successful in the Middle East due to the piracy issue and the fact that the FTA offerings were so strong.

New sources of income were also seen as potential opportunities for MBC. The marketing department was working on several initiatives, including the licensing of children programmes and developing branded content or advertorials. However, whilst growing fast, revenues were still modest. Nevertheless, the aim was to generate at least 25% of total revenues from these activities in the medium term.

Staying Innovative

The Strengths

Historically, one of MBC's strengths was that it had been a market shaper. It had entrepreneurial energy, an eagerness to think "out of the box," and an ability to act before others. It had always aimed to surprise the viewer, its implementation times were short, and it was known to move fast.

Internally, MBC still had a strong family feel despite its fast growth. Many employees were very loyal to the company, and it was not unusual for people to return to the company after having left for a while.

There was no doubt that the main driver of the company's fast growth and unique spirit had been Sheikh Waleed. He was passionate about the continuous development of the company, and he encouraged an open culture with room for questioning and discussion, and was accessible by phone 24/7 if somebody wanted to discuss a new idea. He had the confidence to try new things and experiment, and urged his trusted employees to take bold steps, even if this went against majority opinion, or if they were unsure how the consumer or the political establishment would react. He believed in giving people space and pushed them to go in new directions, whilst affirming his support. Risk-taking was not only related to investments, but also to people. Testimony to this was Sheikh Waleed's decision to hire Barnett, who—although he had five years of experience after his MBA—was only 32 at the time. Across the company there was consensus that Sheikh Waleed was innovative, had a pioneering mindset, and his finger on the pulse of the industry.

The Challenges

Although MBC was successful, there were a number of challenges ahead. Implementation times were starting to grow longer, which was unusual for MBC. The increased diversity and number of employees called for standardised policies. The growing number of processes was generally accepted, but many of the creative people in the company were frustrated because they were used to moving fast. Sometimes, people tried to avoid processes and established committees in order to get things done quickly. When ideas worked, this made them happen more quickly; when they didn't, it meant there was not much in the way to stop them.

Furthermore, for MBC to grow its activities it was not only innovations within the company that were needed, but also across the entire regional media eco-system in terms of media measurement, distribution, TV production infrastructure, and TV production skills.

The main challenge for MBC seemed to be how to stay innovative. How could it retain the family feeling and unique entrepreneurial culture while introducing more sophisticated systems and professionalizing the company? Critical voices raised concerns about "management killing innovation," claiming that, "If you inject system, you kill creativity."

Some feared that too much organization would slow down idea generation and implementation.

Conclusion: Setting Strategies for the Future

The 12 group directors who assembled to discuss MBC's future strategy knew the company was entering a new era. To develop a plan for MBC's future, they specifically had to answer the following questions:

How could MBC continue to be a market shaper, one step ahead of its competitors, and keep creating innovative content and new media?

How could MBC find the right balance between creativity and structure?

How should MBC develop new revenue streams so that its dependence on advertising decreased? How could MBC push and further develop the brand, both locally, regionally and potentially also globally?

Exhibit 1
Overview of MBC's Offerings

Name	Year	Description
TV		
MBC1	1991	The flagship channel of MBC, with over 45 million viewers per day, targets Arab families as a safe choice for family entertainment.
MBC2	2003	The world's first free-to-air 24-hour movie channel with international blockbusters.
Al Arabiya	2003	Al Arabiya, a news channel with political, business and sports news for Arab audiences, is not part of the MBC group, but uses MBC's assets and shared resources.
MBC 3	2004	A children's entertainment channel with emphasis on interactive elements.
MBC 4	2005	Offers global entertainment and a range of drama, comedy, reality TV and magazine shows, targeting the modern Arab woman. Only MBC1 has greater market penetration among 15–24 year-old women. Peak ratings have reached 85 million viewers.
MBC Action	2007	A high-octane channel with fast-paced drama (for example *Lost* and *Prison Break*), excitement and reality shows, targeting a young male audience.
MBC Persia	2008	The first free-to-air 24-hour entertainment channel with blockbuster movies subtitled in Farsi. MBC Persia became one of the most watched channels amongst the Farsi speaking audience.
MBC MAX	2008	A free-to-air 24-hour movie channel that complements MBC2 as a 'darker, tougher and edgier' choice.
Radio		
MBC FM	1994	A radio channel providing music, poetry and entertainment to the Saudi market. MBC FM reaches 47% of the Saudi population.
Panorama FM	2004	A radio channel that broadcasts classical music, news, talk shows and contemporary Arab hit music. It targets the region's youth market.
Online services		
Mbc.net		MBC's main web portal with interactive Arabic content.

Alarabiya.net	2004	Arabic news portal that covers politics, economics, social and sports news. The most visited Arabic website.
AlAswaq.net	2006	Business information website with stock market news and financial updates. It targets GCC companies and personal investors as well as the Arab world in general.

Mobile services

MoBC	MBC Mobile Services (MoBC) includes services for mobile users, for example SMS and MMS content, mobile TV and video on demand.

Magazine

Haya MBC	A weekly lifestyle magazine with social and entertainment news, for example, interviews with celebrities. It includes weekly programme listings for MBC's TV and radio channels as well as updates on latest initiatives launched by MBC.

Exhibit 2

Overview of Management Team 2009

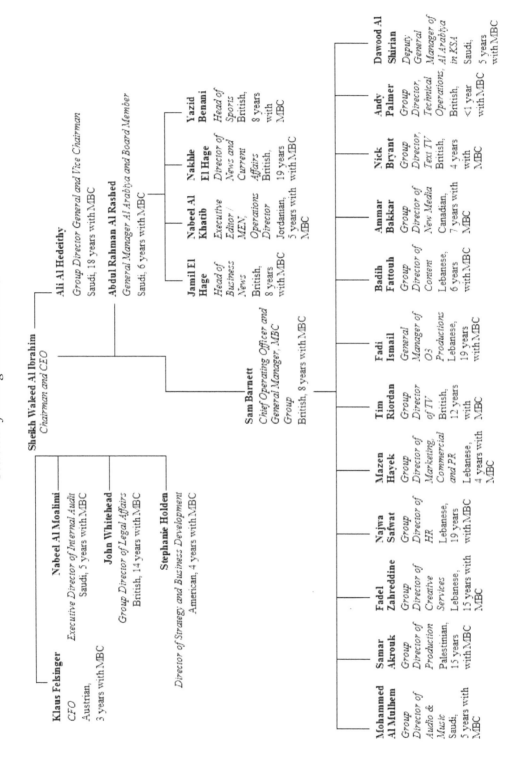

Sheikh Waleed Al Ibrahim
Chairman and CEO

Klaus Felsinger
CFO
Austrian,
3 years with MBC

Nabeel Al Moalimi
Executive Director of Internal Audit
Saudi, 5 years with MBC

John Whitehead
Group Director of Legal Affairs
British, 14 years with MBC

Stephanie Holden
Director of Strategy and Business Development
American, 4 years with MBC

Ali Al Hedeithy
Group Director General and Vice Chairman
Saudi, 18 years with MBC

Abdul Rahman Al Rashed
General Manager Al Arabiya and Board Member
Saudi, 6 years with MBC

Jamil El Hage
Head of Business News
British, 8 years with MBC

Nabeel Al Khatib
Executive Editor / MEN, Operations Director
Jordanian, 5 years with MBC

Nakhle El Hage
Director of News and Current Affairs
British, 19 years with MBC

Yazid Benani
Head of Sports
British, 8 years with MBC

Sam Barnett
Chief Operating Officer and General Manager, MBC Group
British, 8 years with MBC

Mohammed Al Mulhem
Group Director of Audio & Music
Saudi, 5 years with MBC

Samar Akrouk
Group Director of Production
Palestinian, 15 years with MBC

Fadel Zahreddine
Group Director of Creative Services
Lebanese, 15 years with MBC

Najwa Safwat
Group Director of HR
Lebanese, 19 years with MBC

Mazen Hayek
Group Director of Marketing, Commercial and PR
Lebanese, 4 years with MBC

Tim Riordan
Group Director of TV
British, 12 years with MBC

Fadi Ismail
General Manager of O3 Productions
Lebanese, 19 years with MBC

Badih Fattouh
Group Director of Content
Lebanese, 6 years with MBC

Ammar Bakkar
Group Director of New Media
Canadian, 7 years with MBC

Nick Bryant
Group Director, Text TV
British, 4 years with MBC

Andy Palmer
Group Director, Technical Operations
British, <1 year with MBC

Dawood Al Shirian
Deputy General Manager of Al Arabiya in KSA
Saudi, 5 years with MBC

Exhibit 3
Overview of Competition

Rotana, based in Saudi Arabia. Initially launched in 1987 as a record company, and has since successfully extended the brand to different businesses, such as TV and film production, magazines, cafés, cinemas, etc. Owned by Waleed bin Talal.

Al Jazeera, based in Qatar. Launched in 1996 as the first editorially independent news channel in the region, and has attracted international attention for its frank style. Owned by the Emir of Qatar.

SMRD (Saudi Research & Marketing Group), based in Saudi Arabia. It focuses on print (newspapers, magazines).

LBC Group (Lebanese Broadcasting Corporation), based in Lebanon. Satellite television channel owned by Waleed bin Talal.

Dubai Media Incorporated (DMI), based in Dubai. Broadcasts the TV channel Dubai One. Acquired Dubai EDTV in 2004.

Abu Dhabi Media Company, based in Abu Dhabi. Focuses on TV and print (newspapers, magazines).

Saudi TV, based in Saudi Arabia. Owned by the government of KSA, provides local Saudi content (terrestrial and satellite), and has recently made major investments in HD.

Exhibit 4
Number of Pan-Arab Satellite TV Channels, 2004–2009

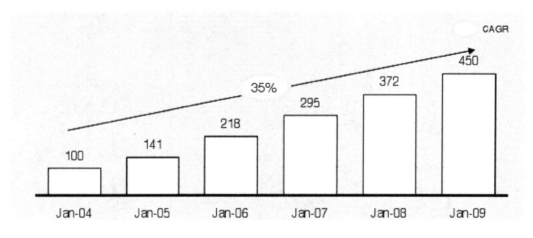

15

Islamaphobia and Sexism

Muslim Women in the Western Mass Media

by Laura Navarro

Introduction

By claiming to champion objectivity and report "real" news, the informative discourse of the mass media conceals their important role as "builders of realities[1]" and, consequently, their key role in the processes of imagination—and social construction—of the communities to which they belong (either national[2] or transnational[3]). This article analyses knowledge of these processes, the discursive strategies that reveal ethnic differences and, in particular, the different representations of Muslims in the Western mass media.

While depending on the ideological color of the government in power it is possible to observe changes in the way the media construct certain events related with Islam and the Arab world[4], there exist a continuum

---

1 For a more in-depth examination of the theoretical perspective according to which the *mass media* participate in the construction and reproduction of social images of reality, see Patrick Champagne (1993).

2 See Benedict Anderson (1983).

3 See Roger Silverstone and Myria Georgiou (2003).

4 For example, the change of perception in information presented on TVE's newscasts about the Iraq war that took place soon after the PSOE came to power after their victory at the 2004 General Elections.

Laura Navarro, "Islamophobia and Sexism: Muslim Women in the Western Mass Media," *Human Architecture, vol. 1, no. 1*, pp. 95-114. Copyright © 2002 by Ahead Publishing House Okcir Press. Reprinted with permission. Provided by ProQuest LLC. All rights reserved.

in the media representations about "what is taking place in the world" that transcend the interests of any political party in power. This situation may be defined—to quote Deputy Commander Marcos—as "a monologue with various voices." This paper analyses this dominant monologue, without addressing other minority or "minoritorised" discourses that undoubtedly exist, and that constitute a less distorted and stereotyped vision than that examined in this article.

Different authors have studied the media discourse in news on Arabs and Muslims[5], including most notably Saddek Rabah (1998), Vincent Geisser (2003) and Thomas Deltombe (2005) in France. In Spain, pioneering studies have been carried out on this subject, such as *El Mundo Árabe y su Imagen en los Medios* ("The Arab World and its Image in the Media"[6]), and more recently the work by Eloy Martín Corrales (2002), Laura Navarro (2007, 2008b) and Pablo López et al. (2010), the articles by Gema Martín Muñoz (1994, 2000) and Teun A. Dijk (2008) and, finally, doctoral theses such as the one by Mohamed El Maataoui (2005). However, the most studies on this subject have been published in English. Noteworthy examples include the work by Edward W. Said (1997), Mohammad A. Siddiqi (1997), Karim H. Karim (2000), Elisabeth Poole (2002) and John E. Richardson (2004).

Practically all these studies highlight the "otherisation" caused by establishing "us and them" oppositions, assigning positive elements to "us" and negative elements to "them," as well as treatment in the media that instead of facilitating better knowledge of "others," exacerbates feelings of rejection and incomprehension. Many of the above mentioned authors have also studied in depth the relationship between discourse and power. For example, Edward W. Said examined how and why the mass media (especially in the US, Great Britain and Israel) constantly reduce Islam and Muslims to a series of stereotypes and generalisations that merely portray this religion as monolithic, as a threat and danger to the West, as a violent and irrational religion. Gema Martín Muñoz has highlighted the persistence of an "agreed cultural paradigm" that western societies have forged on the Arab and Muslim "Orient" "based on a culturalist interpretation of Islamic societies explained from an essentialist and ethnocentric perspective, thus preventing the comprehension of much more plural and changing political and social realities than what normally seems to be the case" (2005: 206). In two of my studies (2007, 2008b), I have also underlined the important role played by this Orientalist discourse in the legitimisation of hegemonic military policies (applied for many years in the Middle East), as well as in the legitimisation of police and military immigration policies, which have largely been responsible for the deaths of thousands of people on geostrategic borders, such as the southern US border and the southern European border.

Nevertheless, although these studies have contributed to research on the social reproduction of racism, most of these studies also have the same shortcoming: the space dedicated to the image of the "other woman." Virtually all these studies focus on the image of Muslim *men* and ignore the specific representations of Muslim *women*. This paper examines in detail these images which have been studied less. To this end, I

---

5 Authors who have studied the media discourse in fiction (especially in film) include, most notably, Eloy Martín Corrales (2000), "Árabes y musulmanes en el cine español de la democracia (1979–2000)", *Mugak*, April–June 2000, nº 11; Bernabé López García (1999), "El cine y las relaciones hispano-marroquíes: de la imagen del protegido al del inmigrado", *Cuadernos Africanos de la Asociación de Africanistas*, nº 4, pp. 43–52; Isabel Santaolalla (2005), *Los "Otros". Etnicidad y "raza" en el cine español contemporáneo*, Zaragoza and Madrid, Prensas Universitarias de Zaragoza and Ocho y Medio. In terms of the English media, noteworthy studies include those carried out by Jack G. Shaheen (2003), "Reel Bad Arabs: How Hollywood Vilifies a People", *The Annals of the American Academy of Political and Social Science*, nº 588, pp. 171–193; and in French media, Pascal Bauchard, "Les représentations de l'Arabe dans le cinéma français: des 'salopards' aux beurs," available at: http://educine.chez-alice.fr/analyses/esquivearabe.htm (consulted on 8–6–2009).

6 A collective work published by José Bodas and Adriana Dragoevich (1994).

will first focus on the dominant representations of "Muslim woman"[7] in the western media in general in order to highlight the specific characteristics of the image of the female Muslim "other" and analyse, from a gender perspective, the symbolic mechanisms legitimising certain Islamophobic thoughts and practices. To conclude, I will look specifically at the treatment of *l'affaire du voile* ("the veil affair") by the French media in order to introduce an analytical perspective adopted in the latest *Gender Studies* and which consists in not losing sight of the "overlapping" or "interlinking" of sexism, racism and classism.[8]

These analyses are also based on two premises: the notion that audiences are able to actively appropriate media texts (D. Morley and K. H Chen, 1996); and that the media do not construct representations on their own but instead belong to the mechanisms that maintain the existing hegemony[9], i.e., institutions that participate in the economy, culture, public opinion and social mobilisation and that, according to Antonio Gramsci's thesis, allow to intellectually, morally and politically manage society without having to resort to physical violence to obtain the consensus of the majority. This complex system of building social consensus—through which dominant images are also constructed of "other men" and "other women"—is a fundamental explanatory factor for understanding the social and cognitive processes that allow us to unconsciously absorb racist, classist and/or sexist representations (and even thoughts and practices). These collective images are neither the same in all geographical contexts nor fixed or immutable because they change over time as a result of specific historical and social experiences, education, institutional policies, as well as the cultural industry and public discourses (including the media discourse).

In Spanish society, for example, historical conflicts with Muslims, especially Moroccans, have been decisive in the social reproduction of racist stereotypes and prejudices regarding Islam and the Arab world (E. Martín Corrales, 2002). Likewise, fears (J. Delumeau, 2002), the disproportionate need for security and lack of communication (M. A. Vázquez, 2004) can exacerbate such distorted visions of the "other," as do culturalist visions of history and the politics of Arab and Muslim societies, mainly transmitted through the education system (G. Martín Muñoz *et al.*, 1998) and also, as will be discussed later, through the dominant mass media discourse. Thus, today different converging factors imbue the dominant Spanish collective image of Islam and the Arab world with essentially negative characteristics, many of which are not new, e.g., the laziness, cruelty, lechery, male chauvinism and fanaticism of Muslim men.

Muslim Women: Victims of Their Own Culture and a Threat to Ours

Are the characteristics historically used to describe Muslim women the same as those applied to Muslim men? Eloy Martín Corrales (2002), despite not focusing specifically on this aspect, mentions some characteristics that have been historically attributed to Moroccan women in particular and to Muslim women in general.

---

7 I have indicated this in inverted commas because I am referring to the social categorisation of the "Muslim woman," and not to its real sociological meaning. In other words, I am referring to the category-object of "Muslim woman" (within the scope of collective representations) and not to its sociological concept.

8 Perspective analyzed in the Chapter 6 "Intersections" by Laure Bereni *et al.*, 2008, pp. 191–222.

9 According to Antonio Gramsci, for whom constructing hegemony was equivalent "to creating a social process of persuasion and generation of active consensus allowing social groups to join a cultural and/or political project [...]. Compared with systems of domination through coercion and force, hegemony entails creating social power through proposals that generate the active establishment of population masses, since it is based on the premise that all directionless domination reveals a profound weakness that will sooner or later produce a crisis." Definition quoted from the *Dccionario de Sociología* (2004) by Salvador Giner, Emilio Lamo de Espinosa and Cristóbal Torres (Madrid, Alianza Editorial, p. 349).

These include ignorance and submission, but also—albeit with different levels of intensity according to the historical period—sensuality.

This sensual image of Muslim women is, to a certain extent, a continuation of the thesis put forward by Mary Nash (1984). Since the first mass media institutions appeared in the late 19th century, women of other cultures have been represented, according to Nash, as exotic and sexually active women (in postcards, labels on alcoholic beverages, etc.), in contrast to the bourgeois model of the *domestic angel*. Later, this conception was transferred to the 20th century, since, as described by Catherine A. Lutz and Jane L. Collins[10] in their analysis of numerous articles published in the middle of last century in the magazine *National Geographic*, women of other cultures were almost absent from politics and were only portrayed as mothers and nice consumable objects, a perception accentuated by nude images of women (since, at that time, this was the only way to see naked women because pornographic magazines were still uncommon). Later, in the nineteen-eighties and nineties, Lutz and Collins observed that these women were still shown as the refuge of the cultural tradition of the country through images in which they wore traditional clothing while men copied the Western model. Thus, progress was identified as something masculine and tradition as something feminine.

As regards the stereotypes of ignorance and submission associated with Muslim women and prevalent in the Spanish social imaginary, if we take into account the dominant representations transmitted in the hegemonic media discourse, today these stereotypes seem to have been reinforced. The main characteristics of these representations are presented based on the results of the analysis of the sample studied in my doctoral thesis (Navarro, 2007), on the representation of this collective on the television news programmes on the national public channel TVE1, broadcast at 3 p.m. and 9 p.m. during the week from August 9 to August 16, 2004[11], as well as on the results of an in-depth study on the subject, the conclusions of which were presented in an article by Gema Martín Muñoz (2005). This second study is one of the first carried out in this country to research the image of Muslim women in the Spanish media[12]. Although this study was written in 1997—before important events such as the terrorist attacks on September 11, 2001, and March 11, 2004—its main conclusions are particularly relevant, not only due to the rigour and strength of many of these conclusions, but because this is one of the few research studies currently available on this subject.

Predominance of Culturalist Perceptions

Firstly, according to Gema Martín Muñoz, news on Muslim women "is dominated by the culturalist presentation and interpretation of Islam" (2005: 208). In fact, the discrimination of these women (an issue that attracts special media attention) tends to be explained almost exclusively according to theories on Islamic culture. For example, when referring to "the rights of Muslim women," the news discourse tends to focus on symbolic and religious issues such as the veil or Islam, thus eluding more important matters relating to the equality of these women, such as rights to education or public freedoms.

---

10 Catherine A. Lutz and Jane L. Collins (2002), "The color of sex: postwar photographic histories of race and gender". Reference mentioned in Estela Rodríguez García (2005).

11 Of the 269 news stories that were broadcast in that period on that channel, 45 referred—more or less explicitly—to Islam and the Arab world. The analysis of the representations was based on the study of different semiotic aspects of the discourse, such as the following: 1) thematic selection; 2) the actors in the news stories; 3) the language used; 4) the selection of the information sources; and 5) the visual aspect of the news.

12 Supervised by Gema Martín Muñoz, Julia Hernández Juberías and Mª Ángeles López Plaza, carried out in 1997 within the framework of the Institute of University Studies on Women's Affairs of the Autonomous University of Madrid, on *The image of Muslim women in the Spanish media*, and based on a sample of 417 articles published in the Spanish press between 1995 and 1997.

This dominant culturalist perception of Islam also leads to "ethnocentric perceptions that make it very difficult to under stand dynamics that do not reproduce our construction of modernity and our feminist secular model" (2005: 209). These are biased visions also hindered by the fact that many experiences of women in non-Muslim countries during long periods are considered to be exclusive to Arab countries. In fact, until the 1960s in Spain, if a father or husband murdered his daughter or wife for reasons of adultery or for having sexual relations before marriage, this was considered an attenuating circumstance in the penal code. Moreover, the *Sección Femenina* (Women's Section) of the Spanish Falange was not suppressed until 1977[13]. In short, and as in the case of the dominant media representations of "Muslim man," the situations and processes reported in the news are largely explained as a consequence of Islam itself, rather than the result of specific political or socio-economic situations.

Martín Muñoz also considers that these visions are far removed from reality because they fail to take into account the conscious and deliberate adhesion of millions of women to their Islamic identity. In fact, they are not differentiated according to the criterion of Islamic women (with veil) = traditional and mentally retarded women vs. Westernised women = modern women, which is the image the mass media appear to transmit. On the contrary, the sociological reality shows that although a distinction is made between traditional and modern women, "the latter are distributed between Islamist and non-Islamist women. And the factor distinguishing traditional women from modern women is not the veil […], but whether or not they have had access to education (2005: 210[14]). Nevertheless, these modern Islamist women are largely absent from the mass media.

Bearing in mind that much of the textual strategy in ideological production is not dictated by what is really said but by what it is not said, it is important to highlight the type of information and images that tend to be omitted. The mass media not only exclude modern Islamist women but also, in general, the socially and culturally diverse communities of Muslim women living in Spain. These women are not only housewives, mothers and Muslims (the simplified image transmitted by the media) but also students, researchers, entrepreneurs, domestic workers, artists, politicians, volunteers, activists, etc. In this respect, it is also not accidental that the media do not report on the evolution of pro-human rights movements (including women's rights and freedoms movements) that exist in some Arab countries, such as Egypt and Morocco. Although the concept of the sexual emancipation of women has not reached these countries in the same way that in Europe, changes are taking place, fuelled mainly by women's associations and NGOs[15].

Dominant Representations: Passivity, Victimisation and the Veil

Continuing with the research carried out by Martín Muñoz (2005), the newspaper articles studied mainly present Muslims women in three ways: as passive women, as victims and as veiled women. Their passivity stems from the fact that they are not portrayed as individuals who work or seek media attention but as "victims, in family relations or illustrating a specific cultural landscape" (often linked to Islam), "instead

---

13 Created in 1934 as the Women's Section of the Spanish "Falange". Their slogan was "the essential purpose of women, in their human function, is to provide a perfect complement to men, forming with them, individually or collectively, a perfect social unit." See the *Women in Blue* exhibition organised by the Documentary Centre on Historical Memory of the Ministry of Culture, from 28 April to 28 June 2009: http://gl.www.mcu.es/novedades/2009/novedades_Mujer es_de_Azul.html.

14 See Gema Martín Muñoz, 1996 (pp. 45–59) and 1997 (pp. 75–90).

15 Social changes that, as Martín Muñoz (1997) explains, often appeared within Islam itself, especially within reformist Islamist movements, due largely to new generations' disappointment with previous experiences inspired by European models—the liberal and socialist models—that had ended in failure.

of as a source of information on important events in their communities." In short, they are portrayed as "observers rather than as active participants in their community" (2005: 210).

Their role as victims is basically reflected through the recurrence of news stories describing conflicts (e.g., the Afghan or Algerian conflicts in which women are clearly victims), and through news stories on the veil, the imprisonment or exclusion of these women, all symbols of "the relations and limitations of women in the lands of Islam" (2005: 211).

In my research (2008b: 231), I also observed that most news stories mentioning Muslim women tend to refer to violence against women (outside and inside our borders), focusing mainly on issues such as stoning, ablation of the clitoris or polygamy. The repetition of, and the way of informing about, these themes exacerbates victimisation and associates the practice of Islam with the discrimination of and physical violence against women. In fact, most television news and reports on these issues do not usually explain the political, economic and educational factors that fuel intolerable practices, such as stoning or ablation, consequently fostering—as mentioned before—the perception that Islam is ultimately responsible for this situation, as well as the perception of Muslim countries as uniformly intolerant and anti-democratic.

Another strategy that accentuated the stereotype of Muslim women as passive and submissive women is that whenever the issue of "women in Islam" is discussed or reported, women are hardly ever given the chance to express their opinions; hence, they are deprived of preferential access to this discourse, a source of power comparable to social resources as important as wealth, knowledge and education. Sometimes, as highlighted by Gema Martín Muñoz, when Muslim women appear as active sources of information, they are normally "Westernised" women (who do no wear veils) and they almost never belong to Islamist movements. Interestingly, this practice contrasts with the general tendency to choose photographs of "anonymous and passive veiled women interpreted from a culturalist and traditionalist perspective" to accompany information on Muslim women (2005: 213).

As regards the third dominant representation—veiled women—the monolithic interpretation of this garment is striking: "as a sign of mystery (Orientalist historical interpretations), of submission and oppression (traditionalist interpretations)" (2005: 211). In fact, women who wear veils are normally portrayed as "lacking individual or personal attributes." In contrast, whenever "Westernised" Muslim women are represented, "similarities with Western culture are emphasized and their individual professional status is mentioned," suggesting that women who wear veils have no responsibilities or professional filiations (2005: 211).

Thus, the dominant informative discourse tends to represent the veil as the ultimate symbol of the exclusion of women but also not normally reflect its multidimensional character. It should be remembered that there are different types of veil—ranging from veils that cover the whole body to small headscarves—and that they are used for different reasons; some are imposed by national law or by the family while others are used simply due to the inertia of tradition. Veils are also actively used both consciously and politically as a symbol of identity and/or political vindication[16]. They can even be used by women to optimise their scarce resources and thus achieve a certain level of prestige or a better marriage, or as a means of social mobility. Or simply because they believe in God[17]. Alima Boumedienne (2007) describes an interesting example of how

16 As indicated by Aïcha Touati (2006), after studying the emergence of Muslim feminists in Arab countries and in the countries of immigrants from the North, feminist struggles were determined by the socio-political context and the veil or headscarf does not have the same meaning for women who wear it (or refuse to wear it) in different contexts.

17 As described by Gema Martín Muñoz (2005), different sociological studies and surveys carried out with women who wear veils or headscarves voluntarily have shown that, among the various arguments used by these women in favour of the use of the *hijab*

the French mass media tend to present the veil as an absolute "scarecrow" in terms of ghosts and stereotypes of Islam:

> In August 2006, when the British authorities decided to keep aeroplanes grounded at Heathrow airport in order to dismantle a series of terrorist attempts. […] liberación.fr [the web page of the French newspaper "Libération"] announced "attempted attacks" which it described as Islamist […] and could not find anything better to illustrate its article than the photograph of a veiled woman with one hand pushing her baby's pram and the other carrying a small child in the corridors of Heathrow airport.

The fact that many educated and working Muslim women have started wearing veils voluntarily in recent years "is not only difficult for the West to accept, but even irritates it because it undermines the traditional interpretation that it clings to so acrimoniously" and, therefore, the mass media conceal this fact or simply ignore it (Martín Muñoz, 2005: 211). Thus, women associated with having a Muslim identity or directly involved in Islamist militancy are largely absent from news on "women in Islam."

Invisibilization and Stereotyped Representation of "Immigrant Woman"

Since many Spaniard citizens associate "Moroccans" with "immigrants,"[18] it is also important to analyse the way immigration is collectively represented. According to a CIRES report (1997: 264–291), the Spaniards interviewed considered the presence of immigrants to be "advantageous" for "our" culture, but qualified their opinion in the case of "Arab" and "black" immigrants, considering that their sociocultural integration was more "problematic" than that of "Latin Americans" and "East Europeans." In 2002, a CIS barometer prepared a type of "sympathy" list, in which "North African immigrants" were ranked last[19]. However, if these surveys had also asked the interviewees about "women"—i.e. "Arab women," "black women," "Latin American women" and "European women,"—would the answers have been similar? When most participants identified "Moroccans" with "immigrants," were they also referring to "immigrant women"?

The CIS (Sociological Research Centre) surveys on " the social perception of immigrants" do not normally take into account the gender variable in these questions. It is therefore difficult to determine whether Moroccan immigrant women enjoy the same "sympathy" as their male compatriots in Spanish society. The general failure of these surveys to take into account the gender perspective is encompassed within a context characterised by a lack of interest on the part of social scientists in the study of immigrant women in our country. The same occurs in the field of information and communication sciences and although many studies have been published in recent years on the image of "immigrants" in the media (particularly in

---

(professionals, feminists, nationalists or anti-imperialists), "religious reasons *stricto sensu* are almost never mentioned alone nor are they the main reasons in the discourse of these women" (2005: 212). Noteworthy studies include those by Hinde Taarji (1991), Nilüfer Göle (1993) and F. Adelkhah (1996).

18 According to a research study carried out by the *Fundación de las Cajas de Ahorros* (FUNCAS—Savings Banks Foundation), 77% of the Spaniards interviewed thought of "Moroccan" when "immigrants" were mentioned. Percentage published in *El País* on 22-1-04.

19 At the top of the list were Western Europeans (6.7 out of 10), followed by Latin Americans (6.5), North Americans (5.4), Sub-Saharan Africans (5.5) and, finally, North Africans (4.9).

journalistic discourse), it is striking that very few have examined the specific representations of immigrant women in the media in our country.[20]

One of these studies is the research carried out by Estela Rodríguez (2005[21]), which confirmed that today news stories do not integrate a gender perspective when addressing immigration issues. On the one hand, she describes the "insufficient visibilization of migrant women, who are often seen as victims, and associated with tradition and cultural underdevelopment". On the other, she observes that "initiatives carried out by these women, self-management, political action, research or education, have not been covered in daily news reports and articles in the last seven years" (2005: 177). Rodríguez offers two very representative examples of this: the lack of coverage of the different ways of life of Moroccan women and the different conceptions of Islam; and the "almost non-existent" coverage of the sit-in by immigrant women at the Sant Pau del Camp Church in Barcelona in 2001 at a time when there were many sit-ins in churches. As the above-mentioned author explains:

> their analysis in the media was completely biased because no explanations were given of the specific demands of immigrant women, thus an opportunity was lost to demonstrate many differences in the plans of immigrant women and highlight their importance given the number of immigrant women in our country. (2005: 182).

This lack of visibilization contrasts with their actual demographic presence. In fact, immigrant women in Spain represent 47% of the total foreign population, according to data in the 2004 municipal census carried out by the INE (National Statistics Institute). Ecuadorian women account for 17% of the total, followed by Moroccan and Colombian women (9.9% of the total), and Rumanian women (6.5%). However, as indicated by Mary Nash, this is not the collective perception, which is dominated by the prevailing traditional model, i.e., dependent women excluded from society. This image distorts the real sociological profile of immigrant women as dynamic individuals with a high level of education and who seek employment.

Other studies, such as those by Faviola Calvo (2001) and Clara Perez (2003) which both analyse the press, also conclude that newspapers provide insufficient information in this respect and highlight the distorted and inaccurate manner in which the social reality of migrant women is portrayed. The most recent study on this subject, carried out by Erika Masanet Ripoll and Carolina Ripoll Arcacia (2008[22]), also emphasizes the invisibility of immigrant women in the press (where immigrant men are more present) and the fact that the media only reflect the reality of a specific group of women: the most marginalized.

The only research to examine the media representation of immigrant women on television is the study carried out by Asunción Bernárdez Rodal (2007[23]). One conclusion drawn by this author—beyond variations according to the socio-political context at each moment in time and the specific characteristics of the nationality or place of origin of immigrant women—was that whenever "immigrants" are mentioned in

---

20 Publications on the fictional discourse are equally scarce. Noteworthy examples include those by Rosabel Argote (2003, 2006), Jo Labanyi (1999) and Isabel Santaolalla (2006).

21 A study carried out within the framework of the R&D project subsidized by the Women's Institute (Ministry of Social Affairs) called *Rethinking the images of Others: immigrants and other cultures in the Spanish press*, incorporating a gender perspective in the analysis of newspaper articles, after it was detected that no stories were published on immigrant women.

22 Within the scope of the "Representation of immigrant woman in the national press" project, financed by the Center for Women's Studies (CEM) of the University of Alicante in 2005. Based on the qualitative analysis of articles appearing during 2004 in *El País*, *El Mundo* and *ABC*.

23 The body of work of this research consisted of three samples of television news programmes during a period of one month each in 2004, on the national channels TVE-1, La-2, Antena 3 and Tele 5.

television newscasts "they are normally reports on and with men, as if immigration was a purely "masculine" phenomenon, when official data and the latest research show that this is not the case"[24] (2007: 106).

Furthermore, the latter study also corroborates the failure to recognise immigrant women as social individuals. This lack of recognition is evident if we analyse leading stories in which immigrant women are the protagonists. According to Bernárdez Rodal, there are four possible types of news reports: 1) stories that report violence against women in which only their first name or nickname is mentioned, with special emphasis on their nationality and attributing less importance to their lives (their past or present, the factors that have caused them to be abused or/and murdered by their partners or ex-partners, etc.); 2) stories that describe the daily lives and customs of immigrant women, in which they are responsible for describing or illustrating the different characteristics of "immigrants," without speaking as immigrant women but instead as part of the cultural or religious group to which they belong; 3) stories about prostitution which are normally the ones that present a more consistent representation, among other reasons because immigrant women are almost the only protagonists of these news stories (this exclusivity is not shared with immigrant men or, in most cases, non-immigrant women); 4) stories on the arrival of small duck boats (*pateras*) which only focus on women who are mothers or if they are the exception among a majority of men.

Finally, although immigrant women of all origins portrayed in the media that were analysed are collectively represented as poor, Bernárdez Rodal highlights a series of specific stereotypes depending on their origin. It is important to distinguish that "Muslim immigrant women" do not appear in the four stories described above, as the analysis shows. Specifically, they do not appear in reports on prostitution or the arrival of duck boats, or in news stories on Muslims congregating in public acts in the street. In most cases, these women are "recognised" by their veils and gowns and normally appear walking along a street in their neighbourhood with a shopping bag or trolley, "simply to illustrate news stories on any subject relating to immigration or terrorism" or "to explain customs, in their homes":

> In both spaces, they are represented as traditional women associated with religion and family life
> [...] They are classified according to the stereotype of "traditional" women due to their education,
> culture and religion, more inclined to be submissive and more exposed to male violence (they share
> this feature with Latin-American women and low-working classes women). (2007: 137–138)

In contrast, "Latin American women" are mainly associated with certain places (discotheques, queues at police stations, markets) and certain jobs (looking after elderly people, domestic work, prostitution). Although they are also poor and appear as mothers or victims of abuse from their partners (men), they are also characterised as exuberant and do not appear in news stories on religion. They also speak more (compared with Muslim or Sub-Saharan women) (2007: 137). "Sub-Saharan women" normally appear in news stories on arrivals of small duck boats:

> ... [a]ssociated with the stereotype of poor and unfortunate mothers, emphasizing their poverty
> and vulnerability, as well as their irresponsible character by deciding to risk their lives and those
> of their innocent children on such ventures. Although the women are characterized as mothers or
> future mothers, the stories never mention that fathers also travel or arrive on duck boats. Nor is
> there ever any mention of the presence of couples or families. (2007: 138[25])

---

24 See C. Gregorio (1997) and L. Oso (1998).

25 The sample selected by Bernárdez Rodal does not include the recognizable stereotype of East European women. This is probably because the sharp increases in the number of immigrants from these countries had not yet started in 2004, or perhaps also because

The "Integrated Immigrant"

These dominant images are accompanied by another less visible image that sometimes appears in the media, namely the image of the "successful immigrant." Although this type of image is normally very present in most printed media targeted specifically at immigrants[26], this is not true in the case of the mass media in which the aforementioned image prevails. Mathieu Rigouste has studied media representations of "successful immigrants" in the French press and carried out a revealing analysis of the transversal economic and political interests inherent in these apparently positive images. In his article entitled "Immigrant, but successful" (2005), Rigouste described several representative examples of a discourse that, since the first case concerning the use of the Islamic veil in 1989, is becoming increasingly common in all the main French daily newspapers. This discourse consists of associating successful integration with the socio-economic status achieved by immigrants and presenting this success, first and foremost, as the result of essentially personal motivations. Here are two examples of articles "reporting" on "two successful immigrants":

> Article 1: "Karim, wearing a Lead grey suit, blue-striped shirt with matching yellow tie, hair combed back, born 24 years ago in Mantes-la-Jolie, has just left his well-paid job as a sales technician to set up his own business."[27] Article 2: "The owner of the premises [an Arab restaurant], Najia el-Mouna Cifi, aged 46, looks like she's come straight out of an Afflelou advert. Short hair, black rectangular glasses, dark sweater and perfect makeup, this social worker who looks after elderly people contrasts dramatically with the image portrayed in *A thousand and one nights*."[28]

This discursive technique, based on the idea that the exception confirms the rule, would by opposition define a person who has failed to integrate, i.e., the poor or excluded. According to Rigouste (2005), the inferred message would be as follows: "a person who really wants to integrate can do so, while others choose or accept failure." However, in addition to the media figure of the entrepreneurial immigrant, "successful immigrants" also include teachers, prefects, technicians or bureaucrats. All these images of "integrated immigrants" are "manipulated by the mass media like so many other anti-racist guarantees and compensatory measures against a rhetoric of threat."

Since 1995, Rigouste has also observed an increase in the media presence of images of singers, comedians (e.g. Djamel Debouze) or sportspersons (e.g. Zinedine Zidane). These consolidate "the image of immigrants valued for their spectacular performances, often as self-sacrificing, courageous, servile and especially competitive individuals." According to Rigouste, this "positive" representation of integrated immigrants has been imposed "as the most common way of portraying immigration in a favourable light, prompting the general relegation of the group." In short:

> The figures perceived as a threat are based on the generation of a desire for security and successful figures on a mimetic desire that operates like a compelling force toward likeness. The images of successful immigrants are not a sign of progress in the representation of visible minorities: they are used to justify and promote a message of security. (2005)

---

the distinctness of these women (but not men) may be more blurred in dominant perceptions of these groups.

26 See Laura Navarro (2008a) and Jéssica Retis (2008).

27 Quote taken from the article "Grâce aux injustices, je me suis forgé un caractère," 28–1–2004, p. 13, published in the newspaper *Le Parisien* as part of a series of 6 articles entitled *Muslims who managed to integrate*.

28 Quote taken from the article "Je n'ai jamais été montré du doigt … ," 29–1–2004, p. 11, published in the newspaper *Le Parisien* as part of a series of 6 articles entitled *Muslims who managed to integrate*.

These "positive" images of "integrated immigrant men and women" may be accompanied by a more specific image of women that is particularly visible in the French media: the image of "liberated and rebellious Muslim women." According to Alina Boumediene (2007), "the mass media, and the French media in particular, are full of surveys, articles and reports that portray the archetypal woman of Muslim faith or culture who has managed to escape from the *carcan* (straightjacket) of religion, customs and parents and older brothers." According to Boumediene, in France these women, often classified as *beurettes* (female Muslim immigrants), are normally presented in a positive and favourable light. They are presented as "fighters," as "women who have been successful" *in spite of*. And once more, every positive description of these women that appears in the media is accompanied by other negative references to Islam, the mother of all evil, and to Muslim men in particular. In summary, according to Nacira Guénif-Souilamas (2004), the stereotype of the liberated *beurette* is the counterpoint to the stereotype of Arab youths of *voleur, violeur et maintenant voileur* ("thieves, rapists and now veilers"), who thus also end up as victims of an imaginary construction. We will now look more closely at this counterpoint referred to by Guénif-Souilamas.

The Anti-Veil Law: Sexism and Islamophobia Interlinked

After France approved the law prohibiting the use of "ostensive" religious signs in state schools (better known as the "anti-veil law"), French feminists, anti-racist militants, as well as the political parties and civil society actors take a stance and two points of view quickly emerged: on the one hand, the defence of women's rights and gender equality was used to justify the law (an argument supported first by political groups and later by associations and feminists); and on the other hand, the denunciation of discriminatory aspects of the law and opposition to the exclusion of girls from schools prompted opposition of the law (from anti-racist militants and also feminists).

According to the analysis presented in the issue of *Nouvelles Questions Féministes* entitled "Sexism and racism: the French case" (2006), the dominant point of view in the public debate and media in France was the first point of view described above, which justified the law based on the defence of "women's rights," ignoring claims identifying the racist aspects of the law and in spite of the fact that, as indicated by the author (2006: 4), this law affected—and continues to affect—mainly the Muslim community (comprising principally immigrant men and women from Maghreb countries and Sub-Saharan Africa, former French colonies, as well as their children born in France), with clear racial implications fuelling division and discrimination. I will later examine the origin and social implications of this law, in order to analyse in greater depth the mechanics behind the "interlinking"[29] of sexism and racism, from both a material standpoint and, above all, in terms of its discursive and symbolic dimension by analysing the political and media treatment of this law.

Genesis of the Law

As shown by the authors of the above-mentioned issue of *Nouvelles Questions Féministes* (2006: 5–6), the promulgation of the French anti-veil law (in March 2004) was the result of a long and complex process that

---

29 This term refers to the idea that persons may belong to various disadvantaged groups (for example, women belonging to ethnic minorities). This situation may entail more serious and specific forms of discrimination. This idea was acknowledged and initially defined as "intersectional" discrimination in the late 1980s by some feminist Afro-American teachers in the US. One of the most representative was Kimberly Creenshaw (1989). For more information on this theory, also known as *interseccionalité* or *consubstancialité*, see Laure Bereni *et al.* (2008: 191–222) and Danièle Kergoat (2008).

started in France in 1989, when the use of headscarves by secondary school girls was starting to become a "problem":

1. September 1989: three girls were temporarily expelled from a school in Creil (Oise) after it was considered that their headscarves represented an alleged "attack on secularism." The French Minister of Education at the time, Lionel Jospin, closed the debate by reminding the French Council of State of legislation in force at the time. The Council responded as follows: "female students enjoy 'freedom of conscience' and therefore the 'right to carry religious signs,'" "only proselytism and the interruption of school activities are grounds for expulsion," and headmasters are invited to "evaluate the situation on a case-by-case basis."

2. September 1994: controversy reared its head following a circular by François Bayrou—the new French Minister of Education—aimed at school headmasters, defining the headscarf as an "conspicuous sign in itself" that reveals a "proselytist attitude" (unlike the Christian cross or the Jewish kipa). The circular invited headmasters to prohibit the use of headscarves in state schools.

3. July 1995: after being asked to declare on the exclusion of 18 pupils in Strasbourg, the French Council of State concluded that girls wearing Islamic veils or headscarves cannot be prohibited from doing so or automatically expelled. Once again, the Council ruled that no sign can be considered "conspicuous" by nature and that, pursuant to the 1905 law on the separation of Church and State (popularly known as the "Law on secularism"), no religious sign may in itself be in opposition to secularism.[30]

4. However, the position adopted by the French Council of State was harshly criticised by the defenders of secularism, which they considered to be under threat; they did not so much oppose the proselytism of certain girls as the presence of any girl wearing a headscarf in state schools, regardless of their attitude. The only way the opponents of headscarves could avoid the Council of State's interpretation was to pass another law through Parliament. To do so, in 2003 they reminded the Union of Islamic Organisations of France (UOIF) that headscarves could not be worn in identity card photographs. Consequently, the pro-law (or "secular") lobby rekindled the debate, launching a campaign mainly advocating women's rights. The new law was eventually approved in 2004, restricting the freedoms guaranteed by the 1905 Law.[31]

The Discourse Legitimising the Law

While the law was being drafted, a public discourses began in favour of the law and gradually became the dominant discourse (Natalie Benelli *et al.* (Eds.), 2006: 6). In this process, male politicians suddenly discovered that they were staunch feminists and that the arguments postulated by militants who already supported the new law were accompanied by criticism of the oppression suffered by young women in the

---

30 At this point, it is worthwhile mentioning, in line with the authors, that the arguments put forward by the French Council of State coincided with those guiding the doctrine of the majority of international conventions and tribunals on this subject: Article 18 of the Universal Declaration on the Rights of Man (1948), Article 9 of the European Convention on the Protection of the Rights of Man and Fundamental Freedoms, Article 18 of the International Pact on Civil and Political Rights (1966) and in education, Article 2 of the First Additional Protocol to the European Convention and Article 14 of the Convention on Children's Rights (1989). See Fabienne Brion, "L'inscription du débat français en Belgique: pudeurs laïques et monnaie de singe," pp. 121–147, in F. Lorcerie (dir.) (2005).

31 See Françoise Lorcerie, "À l'assaut de l'agenda public. La politisation du voile islamique en 2003–2004," pp. 11–36, in F. Lorcerie (dir.) (2005).

quartiers[32] (neighbourhoods). I will now examine how the use of headscarves by female secondary school students gradually became a problem.

Firstly, as from January 2001 media coverage of collective transgressions (referred to as *tournantes*) committed in these neighbourhoods intensified. In 2002, after the so-called "March by women from the *quartiers*" (organised by *Ni Putes Ni Soumises* to denounce violence in these neighbourhoods), the spokeswomen of this association began to receive coverage in the media and greater political support. At the same time, other instruments were launched to prepare this law. On the one hand, *Ni Putes Ni Soumises* joined the pro-law lobby (prohibition of headscarves) of the Socialist Party and the government (which financed them). On the other hand, Jacques Chirac set up a commission "to apply the principle of secularism," presided by Bernard Stasi. In September 2003, the Stasi Commission began its public hearings and soon declared that:

> "Equality between men and women [...] is an important element of the republican pact" and "the State cannot remain impassive if this principle is attacked."[33] The commission also declared that young women living in the *quartiers* suffer "harassment from political-religious groups" that would incite them to wear clothes in accordance with their religious principles, and that they suffer "verbal, psychological or physical violence" from young men who force them to "lower their eyes on seeing a man" and wear "clothes that are concealing and asexual," adding "forced marriages, polygamy, female genital mutilation."[34]

In short, although the Stasi Commission recognized the exclusion, unemployment and racial discrimination suffered by French descendants of migrants originally from Maghreb countries, it considered that the main problem was the visibility of Islam. According to Natalie Benelli *et al.* (2006: 7), "the denunciation of the place of women in Islam and in the *quartiers* will hereinafter be at the core of arguments in favour of the law." Rémy Schwartz, one of the main authors of the Stasi Commission, even criticised "actions *against* secularism [...], which are increasingly numerous, especially in the public sphere," referring to women who wear headscarves in public (Lorcerie, 2005). Thus, women wearing headscarves become gradually, in the French social imaginary, like the evils that threatened the Republic and its values. Moreover, the public discourse has gradually legitimised the need for a law to reduce the visibility of this "sexist" Islam, in the only place in which international conventions permit such restrictions: state schools.

As regards media coverage of this process, the arguments of opponents of the law did not receive the same amount of coverage in the mass media. Firstly, the opinions of girls wearing headscarves were largely ignored. Little attention was given to the voice of political, trade union and associative representatives, secular organisations and associations that opposed the law, or feminists who emphasized the need to support young women who wore headscarves at state schools *at all cost*. The media gave much more coverage to men and women who invoked the dignity of women to justify the exclusion of such women. In contrast, while the few conflicts in schools received excessive media coverage, situations of "peaceful coexistence" among teachers and female students wearing headscarves went unreported by the main media (press, TV and radio[35]).

---

32 Term used to refer to generally marginal neighbourhoods in the suburbs of large French cities.

33 Bernard Stasi (dir.) (2004), Rapport de la Comission de réflexion sur l'application de laïcité dans la République, Paris, La Documentation française, p. 35.

34 Stasi (2004: 101–105).

35 At this point, it is important to indicate that this law was not a feminist initiative (feminists had other priorities, although many let themselves be influenced in that sense) nor an initiative of male or female students or teachers who, in the immense majority of cases, did not consider the veil to be a problem before the campaign to promote the law (P. Tévanian, 2005).

In short, most media focused on the civilization problem (through debates on "religion vs. secularism" or "Islam vs. West"), without addressing the real challenges of the debate, such as the specific problem caused by the presence of female students wearing headscarves in class and the consequences for students expelled from school.

The Instrumentalisation of Women's Rights

Many academic studies have been written about this controversial issue. Some authors, like Emmanuel Terray (2004) and Saïd Bouamama (2004), have interpreted it as the result of a specifically French form of Islamophobia. Feminists have expressed their fear that social mobilisation would focus on racism rather than on male chauvinism, thus conferring the oppression of women , once again,[36] secondary importance.

I would especially draw attention to the theory presented by the female authors of the article in *Nouvelles Questions Féministes* because they try to overcome these fears (which are, nevertheless, very legitimate) by analysing the "interlinking" of both forms of oppression: sexist oppression; and racist oppression. Christine Delphy (2006) examined this interlinking, claiming that the feminist discourse on "women's rights" was instrumentalised by the supporters of the law for racist purposes because although the law refers to "conspicuous religious signs in general," in practice it affects a specific sector of the population: the Muslim community resident in France, formed mainly by immigrant men and women from Maghreb countries and Sub-Saharan Africa, former French colonies, as well as their children born in France.

Also, the strategy of addressing sexism present in the homes of "others"—in this case, Arabs, Muslims— has two implications: a clearly Islamophobic implication because this strategy helps consolidate belief in the existence of racial differences (as demonstrated by Nacira Guénif-Souilamas since 2000) and, more specifically, plays a key role in the construction of the violent and abusive "essence" of Muslims; and a sexist implication because it relativises and even conceals masculine domination in "our" home, as well as elements present in the entire patriarchal system.

The above-mentioned authors concluded that the (re)emergence of the social figure of "Islamic women" (silent, manipulated victims) in the debate on the use of headscarves in state schools is neither the product of chance nor the reflection of a particular obsession of France. The social figure of "Muslim women" (rooted deeply in the history of power struggles between neighbouring civilizations) underpins a dual system of oppression: the system that classifies persons as inferior due to their "race"; and the system that condemns them as inferior for reasons of gender. These authors asked the following question: "Which elements would underpin one or several forms of feminism that refuse to choose between anti-sexism and anti-racism and oppose one more justifiably than the other?" (Natalie Benelli *et al.* (Eds.), 2006: 9).

Houria Bouteldja, a member of the feminist collective *Blédardes* and the mouvement of the *Indigènes de la République*, provides certain clues to answer this question. In an interview with Christelle Hamel and Christine Delphy in the same issue of the magazine *Nouvelles Questions Feministes* (2006: 122–135), she describes her career as a politically active feminist and anti-racist, emphasizing her experience of both sexism and racism, as well as the way in which this experience had influenced her feminism. She describes her feminism as "paradoxical" because she has to protect "Arab women" from real sexism in her community (and sexism on the part of French society) and, at the same time, defend "Arab men" from racism when they

---

36 In reference to the marginalisation of feminist issues by left-wing movements that, during the sixties and seventies, eventually prioritised mobilisation against "class" oppression.

are accused of being sexist by nature. She supports a type of feminism encompassed within the emancipation movements that fought for independence and decolonisation.

Conclusions

The Western mass media tend to construct an image of Muslim women using a discourse dominated by the notions of passiveness and victimisation. The same media, albeit in a minority of cases, also portray a seemingly positive image of "liberated Muslim women", closely linked to their "Western-style clothes" and/or their economic success. This reductionist construction on the part of the mass media tends to erode the social, cultural and economic diversity of Muslim women. Many women of Muslim culture or faith, like Alima Boumedienne (2007), emphatically reject this:

> I, a woman of Muslim culture and/or faith, and many people like me refuse to be prisoners of either of these stereotypes. We are who we decide to be and not what the mass media want to us to be!

Islamophobia and Market Journalism

The media representations studied promote a reductionist perception of Muslim women as victims of "the male chauvinistic violence of Islam" or Islamic fundamentalism. This vision—which is very widespread in Western societies—tends to hinder the acceptance of other more complex perceptions than would help us understand, for example, that refusal of the right to voluntarily wear headscarves may also be a manifestation of intolerance. These Orientalist representations also fuel prejudices such as considering that women are submissive simply because they wear an Islamic veil (when this really depends on their use of this garment because, as we have seen, this can be very diverse) or only recognising Muslim women who copy our culture or dress codes as valid intermediaries (thus hindering comprehension of this extremely complex cultural reality).

Journalists' responsibility not to exacerbate these simplistic perceptions that hinder comprehension and intercultural coexistence acquires greater importance if we acknowledge that stereotypes regarding the discrimination of Arab-Muslim women is today one of the most effective instrument for demonising their societies and also an extremely forceful instrument for legitimising culturalist theories such as those that claim that Islam and modernity are incompatible, or those that argue that Muslim immigrants, due to their religion, cannot "join" European societies. In order not to favour culturalist explanations of the discrimination of Muslim women, journalists should give more consideration to other (legal, educational, political and economic) aspects when reporting on the situation of these women. As Martin Muñoz concludes:

> Why is it not reasonable to think that in Muslim societies, as has occurred in most European countries, social change and the deterioration of patriarchal structures is due more to democratisation, development and the possibility that these societies have to define themselves without having to be defined by the West? (2005: 214–215).

In spite of the foregoing, I am not suggesting that we should ignore these intolerable situations of tremendous injustice that exist in many of these countries. However, it is important to highlight the pernicious effect of only emphasizing, dramatising, almost always generalizing and failing to contextualise the catastrophic and negative aspects of the situation of these women, because the reality is multiple and diverse.

So many converging factors influence the construction of essentialist representations of Muslim women that this Islamophobic discourse cannot only be changed by ensuring journalists are responsible when reporting. In fact, these factors include not only interests and the journalistic ethics of news professionals, their ideology and their training on subjects such as Islam, the Arab world and immigration, but also dominant journalistic practices such as available time, the news agenda, the prevalence of emotion over explanation, the preference for institutional sources of information, the political and economic interests of media companies, etc.[37] Structural factors closely linked to the globalisation of communications and its subsequent effects on information and on informative procedures are also extremely important.[38]

In short, structural factors are so complex that, as reported by Chiara Saez (2008: 4), the wide variety of discourses on the media system in general is less dependant on changes in traditional media discourse than on identifying the necessary conditions to ensure that the discourses of other social collectives have an equivalent presence in the public arena. Hence, the importance of supporting the access of immigrant women (and especially Muslim women) not only to the mass media but also to so-called Third Sector[39] media, and also of somehow counteracting the US monopoly on film distribution circuits and news agencies.

Islamophobia and Sexism

Finally, I would like to highlight that the media discourse analysed in this study is inextricably linked to one of the most important forms of Islamophobia in Spain and France today, a discourse that is based on the imagination and construction of the social figure of the "Muslim woman." In other words, to quote Ángeles Ramírez (2006), "neocolonial sexism" is the "best resource" available to fuel Islamophobia. This sexism is similar to what was known as "colonial feminism" in the colonial period (19th century and early 20th century) when the condition of colonised women was used to make colonised men primitive and, in short, confirm the basic idea that Muslim women were submissive and weak and that Muslim men were authoritarian and aggressive. Islamophobia today appears to still be based largely on the perception of the women of "other men" and is especially visible in the criticism of the situation of Muslim women who wear headscarves and who seem to be in need of salvation.

However, this particular racist discourse does not occur only in the West. According to a comparative analysis of Western and Eastern political and media discourses carried out by Laura Nader (2006: 9), the assessment of the intentionally favourable treatment reserved for women in the group to which they belong, is accompanied by a devalued interpretation of the way in which "other men" treat "their women." Thus, while headscarves are seen in the West as a sign of the submissive nature of Muslim women, in Muslim countries, pornography, prostitution and lack of respect for women in the mass media are used by the heads of Muslim States to systematically criticise Western countries and their citizens. In both discourses, there is not a real concern for "the condition of women" but rather the will to defend a geopolitical space in which the West seeks to maintain its "position of superiority" and the Orient strives to challenge that position.

---

37 Each of these factors is examined in more detail in the paragraph "Hegemonic media: the (re)production of Orientalism," pp. 338–367 of my doctoral thesis (see Navarro, 2007).
38 See Pierre Bourdieu (2000) and Manuel Castells (1997).
39 These media, also referred to as community, free or alternative media, do not belong to either the commercial media sector or the public media sector.

Bibliography

ADELKHAH, Fariba (1996), *La revolución bajo el velo. Mujer iraní y régimen islamista*, Barcelona, Bellaterra.

ANDERSON, Benedict (1983), *Imagined Communities*, Londres, Verso.

ARGOTE, Rosabel (2003), "La mujer inmigrante en el cine español del inaugurado siglo XXI," *Feminismo/s* (Revista del Centro de Estudios sobre la Mujer de la Universidad de Alicante), nº 2, pp. 121–138.

ARGOTE, Rosabel (2006), "Princesas … de la calle alejadas de sus reinos," *Mugak*, Centro de Estudios y Documentación sobre racismo y xenofobia, San Sebastián, marzo 2006, nº 34, pp. 17–22.

BENELLI, Natalie; HERTZ, Ellen; DELPHY, Christine; HAMEL, Christelle; ROUX, Patricia and FALQUET, Jules (eds.) (2006), "Édito: De l'affaire du voile à l'imbrication du sexisme et du racisme," *Sexisme et racisme: le cas français* (*Nouvelles Questions Féministes),* vol. 25, nº 1, pp. 4–11.

BERENI, Laure; CHAUVIN, Sébastien; JAUNAIT, Alexandre and REVILLARD, Anne (2008), *Introduction aux Gender Studies. Manuel des études sur le genre*, Bruxelles, De Boeck.

BERNÁRDEZ RODAL, Asunción (dir.) (2007), *Mujeres inmigrantes en España. Representaciones en la información y percepción social*, Madrid, Editorial Fragua.

BODAS, José and DRAGOEVICH, Adriana (eds.) (1994), *El Mundo Árabe y su Imagen en los Medios*, Madrid, Comunica.

BOUAMAMA, Saïd (2004), *L'affaire du foulard islamique. La production d'un racisme respectable*, Paris, Geai Bleu.

BOUMEDIENE-THIERY, Alima (2007), "Femmes musulmanes dans les médias", 12 juillet. Disponible in: http://alima-boumediene.or g/spip.php?article318 (30–4–2009).

BOURDIEU, Pierre (2000), *Sobre la televisión*, Barcelona, Anagrama.

CALVO, Faviola (2001), "Apuntes para un análisis de prensa," in E. Bonelli and M. Ulloa, *Tráfico e inmigración de mujeres en España. Colombianas y ecuatorianas en los servicios domésticos y sexuales*, Madrid, ACSUR-Las Segovias, pp. 51–64.

CASTELLS, Manuel, *La era de la información. Economía, sociedad y cultura* (vol. 2: El poder de la identidad), Madrid, Alianza.

CREENSHAW, Creenshaw (1989), *Demargenalizing the Intersenction of Race and Sex: A Black Feminist Critique of Antidiscrimination Doctrine, Feminist Theory and Antiracist Politics*, University of Chicago Legal Forum.

CHAMPAGNE, Patrick (1993), "La construcción mediática de malestares sociales," *Voces y culturas. Revista de comunicación*, nº 5, pp. 60–82.

DELPHY, Christine (2006), "Antisexisme ou antiracisme Un faux dilemme," in N. Benelli *et al.* (eds.) (2006), *Sexisme et racisme: le cas français* (*Nouvelles Questions Féministes)*, vol. 25, nº 1, pp. 59–83.

DELTOMBE, Thomas (2005), *L'islam imaginaire. La construction médiatique de l'islamophobie en France, 1975–2005*, Paris, La Découverte.

DELUMEAU, Jean (2002), *El miedo en Occidente: (siglos XIV–XVIII): una ciudad sitiada*, Taurus Ediciones.

EL-MADKOURI MAATAOUI, Mohammed (2005), doctoral thesis *La imagen del Otro. Lo Árabe en la prensa española*, Complutense University of Madrid, Departamento de Estudios Árabes e Islámicos.

EMMANUEL, Terray (2004), "La question du voile: une hystérie politique," in Ch. Nordmann (dir.), *Le foulard islamique en questions*, Paris, Éditions Ámsterdam, pp. 103–117.

GEISSER, Vincent (2003), *La nouvelle islamophobie*, Paris, La Découverte.

GRAMSCI Antonio (1975), *Quaderni del carcere*, Torino, Einaudi.

GREGORIO, C. (1997), "Las relaciones de género dentro de los procesos migratorios: ¿reproducción o cambio?," in V. Maquieira and M. J. Vara, *Género, clase y etnia en los nuevos procesos de globalización*, Madrid, UAM.

GÖLE, Nilüfer (1993), *Musulmanes et modernes. Voile et civilisation en Turquie*, Paris, La Découverte**.**

GUENIF-SOUILAMAS, Nacira and MACÉ, Eric (2004), *Les féministes et le garçon arabe*, Edition l'Aube.

KARIM, Karim H. (2000), *Islamic Peril, Media and Global Violence*, Montreal, Black Rose Books.

KERGOAT, Danièle (2008), « Dynamique et consubstantialité des rapports sociaux », in E. Dorlin (dir.), *Sexe, classe, race. Pour une épistémologie de la domination*, Paris, PUF.

LABANYI, Jo (1999), "Raza, género y denegación en el cine español del primer franquismo: el cine de misioneros y las películas folclóricas," *Archivos de la Filmoteca. Revista de Estudios Históricos sobre la imagen*, nº 32, pp. 22–42.

LÓPEZ, Pablo; OTERO, Miguel; PARDO, Miguel and VICENTE, Miguel (2010), *La imagen del Mundo Árabe y Musulmán en la Prensa Española*, Sevilla, Fundación Tres Culturas del Mediterráneo.

LORCERIE, Françoise (dir.) (2005), *La politisation du voile. L'affaire en France, en Europe et dans le monde arabe*, Paris, L'Harmattan.

MARTÍN CORRALES, Eloy (2002), *La imagen del magrebí en España. Una perspectiva histórica siglos XVI–XX*, Barcelona, Bellaterra.

MARTÍN MUÑOZ, Gema (1994), "El imaginario español sobre el Islam y el Mundo Árabe y su influencia en los medios de comunicación," in J. Bodas and A. Dragoevich, *El Mundo Árabe y su imagen en los medios*, Madrid, Comunica, pp. 279–283.

MARTÍN MUÑOZ, Gema (1995), *Mujeres, desarrollo y democracia en el Magreb*, Madrid, Ediciones Pablo Iglesias.

MARTÍN MUÑOZ, Gema (1996), "Fundamentalismo islámico y violencia contra las mujeres. Las razones de un falso debate," in Mª D. Renau (coord.), *Integrismos, violencia y mujer*, Madrid, Ediciones Pablo Iglesias, pp. 45–58.

MARTÍN MUÑOZ, Gema (1997), "Mujeres islamistas y sin embargo modernas," en *El imaginario, la referencia y la diferencia. Siete estudios a cerca de la mujer árabe*, Granada, Universidad de Granada, pp. 75–90.

MARTÍN MUÑOZ, Gema (2000), "Imágenes e Imaginarios. La representación de la Mujer musulmana a través de los medios de comunicación en Occidente," in A. Valcárcel and D. Renal (eds.), *Los desafíos del feminismo ante el siglo XXI*, Sevilla, Instituto Andaluz de la Mujer.

MARTÍN MUÑOZ, Gema (2005), "Mujeres musulmanas: entre el mito y la realidad," in F. Checa y Olmos (ed.), *Mujeres en el camino: el fenómeno de la migración femenina en España*, Barcelona, Icaria, pp. 193–220.

MARTÍN MUÑOZ, Gema; VALLE, Begoña and LÓPEZ, Mª. Ángeles (1998), *El islam y el mundo árabe. Guía didáctica para profesores y formadores*, Madrid, AECI.

MASANET RIPOLL, Erika and RIPOLL ARCACIA, Carolina (2008), "La representación de la mujer inmigrante en la prensa nacional," *Papers*, nº 89, pp. 169–185.

MORLEY, David and CHEN, Kuan–Hsing (eds.) (1996), *Stuart Hall. Critical dialogues in cultural studies*, Londres, Routledge.

MUNRO, Mara (2006), "Les voiles du sensationnalisme : portrait des musulmanes dans les médias d'information occidentaux", *Magazine Interculture*, Institut Canadien du Service Extérieur, juillet 2006. Disponible in : http://www.international.gc.ca/cfsi-icse/cil-cai/magazine/v02n03/1-4-fra.asp (consulted the 30th April 2009).

NADER, Laura (2005), "Orientalisme, occidentalisme et contrôle des femmes," in N. Benelli *et al.* (eds.) (2006), *Sexisme et racisme: le cas français (Nouvelles Questions Féministes)*, vol. 25, nº 1, pp. 12–24.

NAVARRO, Laura (2007), European doctoral thesis *Interculturalidad y comunicación. La representación mediática del mundo árabemusulmán*, University of Valencia.

NAVARRO, Laura (2008a), "Los medios de comunicación de las nuevas migraciones," *III Anuario de la Comunicación del Inmigrante*, Madrid, Etnia Comunicación.

NAVARRO, Laura (2008b), *Contra el Islam. La visión deformada del mundo árabe en Occidente*, Córdoba, Editorial Almuzara.

NASH, Mary (ed.) (1984), *Presencia y protagonismo. Aspectos de la historia de la mujer*, Barcelona, Serbal.

OSO, Laura (1998), *La migración hacia España de mujeres jefas de hogar*, Madrid, Instituto de la Mujer.

PÉREZ, Clara (2003), "Las inmigrantes en la prensa: víctimas sin proyecto migratorio," *Mugak*, nº 24, tercer trimestre 2003.

POOLE, Elisabeth (2002), *Reporting Islam. Media Representations of British Muslims*, London, I. B. Tauris.

RABAH, Saddek (1998), *L'Islam dans le discours médiatique. Comment les médias se représentent l'Islam en France*, Beirut, Al-Bouraq.

RAMÍREZ, Ángeles (2006), "Sexismo neocolonial," *El País*, 08/10/2006.

RETIS, Jéssica (2008), *Espacios Mediáticos de la Inmigración en Madrid: Génesis y Evolución*, Observatorio de las Migraciones y de la Convivencia Intercultural de la Ciudad de Madrid, UAM, Madrid.

RICHARDSON, John. E. (2004), *(Mis)representing Islam. The racism and rhetoric of British broadsheet newspapers*, Philadelphia PA, John Benjamins Pub.

RIGOUSTE Mathieu (2005), "Inmigrante, pero exitoso," *Le Monde diplomatique*, Jun 2005, p. 14. Disponible in http://www.mondediplomatique.fr/2005/07/RIGOUSTE/ 12454 (consulted the 1st May 2009).

RODRÍGUEZ GARCÍA, Estela (2005), "Mujeres inmigradas y medios de comunicación. Movimientos sociales en búsqueda de una representación propia," in F. Checa y Olmos (ed.), *Mujeres en el camino: el fenómeno de la migración femenina en España*, Barcelona, Icaria.

ROQUE, Mª Ángeles (dir.) (2000), *Mujer y migración en el Mediterráneo Occidental. Tradiciones culturales y ciudadanía*, Barcelona, Icaria.

SAEZ BAEZA, Chiara (2008), doctoral thesis *Tercer Sector de la Comunicación. Teoría y praxis de la televisión alternativa. Una mirada a los casos de España, Estados Unidos y Venezuela*, Autonomous University of Barcelona.

SAID, Edward W. (1997), *Covering Islam. How the media and the experts determine how we see the rest of the world*, Londres, Vintage.

SANTAOLALLA, Isabel (2006), "Inmigración, 'raza' y género en el cine español actual," *Mugak*, Centro de Estudios y Documentación sobre racismo y xenofobia, San Sebastián, March 2006, nº 34, pp. 9–16.

SIDDIQI, Mohammad A. (1997), *Islam, Muslims and media, Myths and realities*, Chicago, NAAMPS Publications.

SILVERSTONE, Roger and GEORGIOU, Myria (2003), *Mapping Diasporic Minorities and Their* Media in Europe. *Studying the Media. Investigating Inclusion and Participation in European Societies, European and Transnational Communities, European Media Technology and Everyday Life Network* (EMTEL 2). www.lse.ac.uk/Depts/Media/ EMTEL/Minorities

TAARJI, Hinde (1991), *Les voiles de l'Islam*, Casablanca, Edif.

TÉVANIAN, Pierre (2005), *Le voile médiatique. Un faux débat: "l'affaire du foulard islamique,"* Paris, Éditions Raisons d'Agir.

TOUATI, Aïcha (2006), "Féministes d'hier et d'aujourd'hui, ou le féminisme à l'épreuve de l'universel," in N. Benelli *et al.* (eds.), *Sexisme et racisme: le cas français (Nouvelles Questions Féministes),* vol. 25, nº 1, pp. 108–121.

TOUATI, Aïcha (2008), *Racismo, Prensa e Islam*, University Pompeu Fabra. Disponible in the Centro de Documentación y Datos del Observatorio Español del Racismo y la Xenofobia: http://www.oberaxe.es

VÁZQUEZ, Manuel Ángel (2004), "Los signos de la violencia/ la violencia de los signos. Una reflexión contra el racismo, la xenofobia y la intolerancia," in F. R. Contreras and F. Sierra (eds.), *Culturas de guerra. Medios de información y violencia simbólica*, Madrid, Cátedra, pp. 101–122.

16

Muslim Women in the Middle East

by Allen Webb

One of the topics of greatest interest to our students about the Middle East is the status and life experience of women. If there is anything that our students know from the mass media about contemporary culture in the Middle East it is that, in the Middle East women are oppressed. Islam condemns women to a subordinate role. Women must wear veils, headscarves (hijab), and full coverings (chador). They are forced to marry against their will. They are dominated by men, who are allowed to marry more than one wife. In some countries women can't drive cars or even leave their homes. Some are subject to barbarous acts of female circumcision and others, still worse, to "honor killings" by their own family members.

When it comes to teaching about women in the Middle East, I think our most important job as teachers is to complicate this simplistic and distorted picture of female oppression and domination. This is not to deny that women in the Middle East are oppressed—as women the world over are oppressed. Of course, there is domestic violence and spousal abuse in the U.S. A woman dies as the result of spousal abuse every six hours in the U.S. ("Most Recent"). Students need to learn about the oppression of women in the Middle East—and draw on that knowledge to consider how women are oppressed in their own country and culture. In this way we help our students go beyond the polarized, binary thinking fostered by the one-sided

Allen Webb, "Muslim Women in the Middle East," *Teaching the Literature of Today's Middle East*, pp. 49-66. Copyright © 2012 by Taylor & Francis Group LLC. Reprinted with permission.

stereotypes proffered by the mass media and popular culture. But teaching in a thoughtful and balanced way about women in the Middle East is complicated.

First, there is no one common woman's experience in the Middle East. Instead, as in the rest of the world, there is an enormous diversity of experiences that depend on country, social class, geographical location (rural vs. urban), religious practice, social group, and individual families. Throughout the Middle East, as in other parts of the world, there are struggles between liberal and conservative factions over women's rights and freedoms. In Saudi Arabia, women are required to wear an abaya (full black cloak), but in Turkey it is illegal for public school or college students, government employees, or doctors to wear even a headscarf. Afghanistan under the Taliban—where women were excluded from school—is completely different from Iran, also an officially Muslim nation, where 70 percent of the college students in the country are women. Although abortion is illegal in most Arab countries (it is legal in Turkey and Tunisia) women in the Middle East often find ways to obtain abortions. While most Muslims view the Quran as allowing a man up to four wives, if all can be financially supported and equally treated, polygamy is actually uncommon in the Middle East. It is illegal in Turkey, Tunisia, Israel, and the former socialist countries of Tajikistan, Turkmenistan, Kazakhstan, and Kyrgystan. Even in countries where polygamy is legal, it is typically practiced by only 2–5 percent of the population. (And remember that polygamy is not unknown in the United States, as the popular television program *Big Love*, about renegade Mormons, demonstrates! Not to mention issues in the West of frequent divorce, women with children in poverty, marital infidelity, and so on.)

FIGURE 16.1 Hijab

Copyright © 2009 by Zharif Hussein / Flickr / CC BY 2.0

There is no one yardstick by which to measure oppression, and many of the cultural practices that might at first seem to symbolize oppression, may, in fact, provide women with increased freedom. In Islam, women pray separately from men, either in separated parts of the mosque or at home. Since Muslim prayers involve kneeling and bending over in an open room without pews, women feel more comfortable praying in separate spaces rather than in front of men. Depending on the country, many Muslim women do not wear veils or head-scarves. Some Islamic feminists reject the veil, and their protests go back at least as far as Egypt in the 1920s where there was an organized feminist movement whose leaders threw their veils into the sea. Muslim women who do choose to wear headscarves do so not only as a sign of piety and modesty, but so they will be judged by their personality, character, and morality—not how they look. There are a great variety of types, styles, and ways to wear veils and hijab, such that, perhaps ironically, in many contexts the headscarf itself becomes a fashion statement. On the other side, the headscarf may reduce the costs of clothing for working women. During the period of direct European colonial domination of the Middle East, the veil was, at times, a symbol of anti-colonial resistance. Today, the veil in certain contexts continues to be a statement of Islamic self-assertion in the face of invasive Western culture. Recently in some European countries the veil has been banned in schools or public places, leading to claims of discrimination against Muslims and protest by Muslim women. Obviously, the veil has become the center of a complex discourse, and an interesting topic for students to investigate. A good discussion starter is the essay "The Burka and the Bikini" by Aziz Poonawalla (available at AltMuslim. com). Poonawalla describes different types of clothing for Muslim women, distinguishes Muslim and tribal practices, and argues that both bikini and burqa, depending on how they are used, "can serve to reduce women from a person to an object."

Throughout the Middle East there are many powerful, vibrant women, and Middle Eastern people will tell you that women have an important say in family and community affairs. In the region, women often play significant roles in politics, government, business, and the arts. Women have served as government ministers in Syria, Jordan, Egypt, Iraq, and Tunisia, as vice president in Iran, and prime minister in Israel. Women are members of parliament in the Middle East in numbers roughly parallel to the U.S. and Britain (Iran 25 percent; Egypt 12 percent; Turkey 10 percent; U.S. 17 percent; England 20 percent). While in some countries a woman cannot obtain a passport without permission of a male relative or her husband—and women do not enjoy equal rights under Muslim Sharia law statutes governing divorce, inheritance, and child custody—many predominately Muslim countries do not follow these laws and there is general agreement that, at the time of Muhammad, the Quran represented a significant advance for women. Female genital mutilation and honor killings are not sanctioned by Islam, but have their origins in cultural practices in specific regions and among certain ethnic groups.

As in the English-speaking world there is an active debate among Muslims about sexism, discrimination, and the roles and rights of women. Some argue that women in the Middle East are no more oppressed than women elsewhere. Others recognize oppressions, but argue that the oppression of women is not intrinsic to Islam and the Quran but that inequality and oppression have their roots in non-Islamic cultural practices. Nawal El Saadawi, an Egyptian medical doctor, novelist and well-known feminist has argued:

> I've noticed that many people including professors of religion and Islamic studies, pick up one verse and say that in the Quran, God allowed men to beat women. They don't compare it to other

verses. They also don't compare the Quran to the Bible. If you do, you will find the Bible more oppressive to women.

(quoted in Kamguian)

Indeed, in regard to the position of women, conservative Islam has much in common with Orthodox Judaism and Eastern Orthodox Christianity, other religions with origins in the Middle East long before Islam. Interestingly, some historians believe that the seclusion and veiling of women came to the Arabic world from Christian Byzantium. Of course, certain orders of Catholic nuns still wear veils and the Virgin Mary is rarely depicted with her head uncovered. Indeed, many protestant Christian women wear veils on their wedding day: an elegant wedding dress fashion as well as a symbol of modesty and chastity.

In the first chapter we examined Edward Said's critique of Orientalism. One dimension of Orientalism is a tradition in Western thought of identifying the Orient with the oppression of women. "The colonialist logic attributed the backwardness of Muslim societies and the inferiority of their cultures particularly to two main observed practices: veiling and seclusion of women"(Kincheloe, 47).

This "backwardness" is often used as a justification for bringing "civilization" or "democracy" to the region in the name of protecting women. Indeed, there are racial and sexual dimensions to this discourse, with white men coming to the rescue of brown-skinned women, saving them from brown-skinned men. Yet, the facts relating to European and American actions in the Middle East often tell a different story. Colonial and neo-colonial interventions have been about strategic geopolitics and access to resources, not protecting women. For instance, throughout the 1970s and 1980s, U.S. foreign policy in the region was guided by a concern about the rise of Arab nationalism and socialism—movements which called for national rights to control oil exports. At the same time, those Arab movements took large strides in obtaining rights for women in education, the family, and the workplace. As a counter force to Arab nationalism, groups that opposed women's rights—conservative religious elements in Islam—were supported by the American government. The same story was true in Afghanistan, where a socialist government created more rights for women than at any point in the history of the country. When the Russians intervened to support that government, the U.S.' "secret" arming of the Mujahidin brought to power the Taliban and drastically curtailed rights for women. As'ad AbuKhalil writes,

> Ever since the 1950s, successive American governments have supported Saudi Arabian Islam and have funded and armed Islamic fundamentalist groups, which have tormented Middle Eastern women and frustrated their efforts at emancipation.

A polarizing discourse between East and West, talk of crusades, of "Evil Empires" or an "Axis of Evil," military interventions, support for Israeli domination of Palestine—all of these play into the hands of the conservatives in the Middle East who use American and European involvement in the region as their justification for a narrow interpretation of the Quran and curtailment of women's rights.

> Strict policing of women' bodies and lives and a retraditionalization of the Muslim family, both taken as major features of religious ethical and moral law, are considered by virtually all fundamentalists among the viable strategies for countering Western imperialism and curbing the impact of its powers.

(Kincheloe, 44)

The desire to signal rejection of Western imperialism may well be part of a woman's decision to wear a veil or headscarf, not necessarily something imposed by the men around her. My point is that teachers of literature from the contem -porary Middle East need to recognize the complexity of the issue of women's rights in the region, the problematic history of American and European involvement in regard to women's rights, and the pitfalls of prescribing, from America or Europe, solutions to women's issues in the Middle East.

Teaching in a thoughtful way about the Middle East, it is vital for teachers and students to learn more about Middle Eastern women, to identify authentic, realistic, and balanced literature from the Middle East that features women, and to examine stereotypes prevalent in the West. While there are many books published about Middle Eastern women, identifying the best and appropriate materials is surprisingly difficult. Be alert that there are groups, including certain fundamentalist Christians, who go out of their way to attack Islam and present, on the Internet and in published books, inflammatory and distorted stories and images; our students often encounter these materials and it may be important as a class to examine and critique them. Even more responsible sources should be treated with care. American and British publishing houses have found that writing by women from the Middle East that provides images of oppression can generate sales, appealing to women's reading groups, teachers and students, and others eager to learn about women in the region. This literature is important, but needs to be understood in a balanced way.

The Iranian scholar Fatemeh Keshavarz, now a professor at Washington University in St. Louis, has published a book combining scholarship and personal narrative that I recommend to teachers interested in the topic of women in the Middle East. *Jasmine and Stars: Reading More than* Lolita *in Tehran* addresses this outpouring of recent publications about the oppression of women in the Middle East, books such as *Reading Lolita in Tehran, Lipstick Jihad, Nine Parts of Desire, The Bookseller of Kabul, The Kite Runner, Persepolis*, and so on. Written as non-specialized, autobiographical narratives, first person novels, or eyewitness accounts for non-expert Western readers, these recent books are effectively marketed yet can, while they point to important issues, also, like any representation, reproduce stereotypes. Keshavarz calls this literature "the New Orientalist narrative" and describes it in this way,

> The emerging Orientalist narrative has many similarities to and a few differences from this earlier incarnation. It equally simplifies its subject. For example, it explains almost all undesirable Middle Eastern incidents in terms of Muslim men's submission to God and Muslim women's submission to men. The old narrative was imbued with the authority of an all-knowing foreign expert. The emerging narrative varies somewhat in that it might have a native—or semi-native—insider tone. Furthermore, as the product of a self-questioning era, it shows a relative awareness of its own possible shortcomings. Yet it replicates the earlier narrative's strong under current of superiority and of impatience with the locals, who are often portrayed as uncomplicated. The new narrative does not necessarily support overt colonial ambitions. But it does not hide its clear preference for a western political and cultural takeover. More importantly, it replicates the totalizing—and silencing—tendencies of the old Orientalists by virtue of erasing, though unnuanced narration, the complexity and richness in the local culture.
>
> *(3)*

Keshavarz is not the only one making this observation. Mitra Rastegar, for example, makes a similar argument in her essay "Reading Nafisi in the West: Authenticity, Orientalism, and 'Liberating' Iranian Women."

> While Nafisi [author of *Reading* Lolita *in Tehran*] challenges a wholly monolithic understanding of contemporary Iran, she ultimately reframes the predominant Orientalist binary—of the

"West" as modern, rational, and dynamic and opposed to an "East" that is static, irrational, and antimodern—into one of promodern Iranians versus antimodern Iranians. Nafisi's representation of women as victims of state violence in Iran becomes a key component of asserting this binary, opposing a monolithic and barbaric Iranian state to the democratic ethos that she argues is implicit in the (Western) novel and appreciated by her female students.

(*108*)

So images of oppression need to be complicated, and literary and autobiographical narratives need to be read carefully and with balance. Saba Mahmood describes the contribution of feminist scholarship: "Feminist scholarship performed the worthy task of restoring the absent voice of women to analyses of Middle Eastern societies, portraying women as active agents whose lives are far richer and more complex than past narratives had suggested" (6).

One of the most popular books from the Middle East, focused on the experience of women, and rapidly become known to secondary and college teachers and students, is Marjane Satrapi's graphic novel *Persepolis*. Written in French (2000–2001) and translated to English (2003, a portion was first published in *Ms. Magazine*) *Persepolis: A Story of a Childhood* (2001, 153 pages, middle school–college), it has a sequel volume (French 2002/03, English 2004) *Persepolis 2: The Story of a Return* (2003, 192 pages, age 17–college) and was made into a fascinating black and white animated film (2007). This autobiographical narrative in the first volume apparently traces the author's life from her girlhood in an intellectual, privileged family in Tehran during the Islamic Revolution in 1979, and in *Persepolis 2*, her teenage years studying abroad in Switzerland, and her return to Tehran as a young woman in 1991.

Original, engaging, and appealing, *Persepolis* facilitates American students' connection with the main character who likes American music (Iron Maiden and Michael Jackson), dancing, and rebels against the oppressive efforts of the Iranian revolutionary government to enforce "Islamic" behavior and wearing the veil. My students are passionate about the work—and quick to view it as *the* story of contemporary Iran and Iranian women.

As a young girl, Marjane is a good student who only begins to rebel when her formerly secular school becomes strictly religious. She can't help but point out the irony of religious rules and punishments. Her parents, who share and encourage her liberal political views, are very proud of the strong woman their daughter has become. But Marjane's strength under Iran's new fundamentalist regime, where women are discouraged from having a voice, becomes her weakness, and her parents begin to fear for her safety.

Marjane Satrapi's graphic novel, *Persepolis*, is not only a story of a childhood, but the story of a people and a nation. Her consistent wit and humor in the face of traumatic violence drew me in as a reader, opening my mind to more dry political subjects.

(*Ashley Hillyard*)

Her story gives tons of perspective on the history of Iran, it's relationship with Islam, the struggle between the ideals of the West and East, exile, and repression in her own country. The story is very accessible through vivid images. I was completely moved by this book. I don't think one can read this book and not feel a sort of compassion for the Iranian people and their struggles. For anyone who wants to begin to understand Iranian people, I believe this graphic novel is a fantastic first step.

(*Marie Tietgen*)

Persepolis is such an engaging text that it is a valuable resource for classroom teaching, for learning about the Iranian revolution, and for considering the diversity of women's perspectives. Students are drawn to *Persepolis* first by the intriguing graphic format. Teachers will want to help students learn to read graphic texts and examine how panels use detail, proportion, angle of view, visual clues, sequence, language bubbles, etc. to convey meaning, and how the "gutters" between the panels allow the reader's imagination to fill in action. Because of their appeal and interesting working together of images and texts, graphic novels, autobiographies and other forms are increasingly popular for instruction. Resources for teachers working with the medium include *Understanding Comics* by Scott McCloud, *Graphic Novels* by Paul Gravett, and *Building Literacy Connections with Graphic Novels* edited by Bucky Carter (to which I contribute a chapter on the subject of teaching about anti-Semitism in *Oliver Twist* using the graphic novel *Fagin the Jew* by Will Eisner).

Readers of *Persepolis* will be attracted to a loving family with wise, caring parents who do their best to support each other and their daughter through times of change and even violence. Students should note that this is an extremely privileged family. The great grandfather was apparently the Iranian Emperor; the grandfather was the Prime Minister to the Shah; they have a maid; drive a Cadillac; take vacations in Europe; and the daughter—the narrator—is enrolled in an elite French language school in Tehran. Highly educated intellectuals, the parents are not religious, but sympathetic to Marxism and critical of the Islamic revolution. The centrality of the family to national events does add interest to the story and provides readers with information about Iranian politics. It is difficult for English-speaking young people to put these events into perspective. Unless teachers provide students with additional background information or encourage them to do more research, young people are likely to find more memorable the scene where women from the Guardians of the Revolution stop Marjane because she is wearing a Michael Jackson pin, rather than other more historically significant scenes exploring the 1979 revolution, friends of the family tortured by CIA trained secret police, the coming to power of the Islamic fundamentalists, and the devastating war between Iran and Iraq.

Persepolis portrays a variety of women characters and clearly demonstrates that Iranian women, and by extension women of the Middle East, are by no means a demure or submissive group. Examining the diversity of portrayals of women in this text creates important possibilities for student writing and learning. At the center is the narrator Marjane, an independent and flamboyant girl who challenges the authority of her teachers, loves American heavy metal music, mocks and resists wearing the veil—and is enormously appealing to Western students. Marjane's mother is a loving wife and parent, a protestor who takes to the street to defend women's rights, and a thoughtful person who carefully weighs the risks and dangers of opposing the regime. Marjane's grandmother is perhaps the most free-thinking, liberated character in *Persepolis* with a bawdy sense of humor and a commitment to honesty and fairness. We see other independent, yet tragic, young women including Niloufar, a communist girl who helps make fake passports and is killed by the secret police, and a Jewish girl, Neda, who lives next door to Marjane and is killed in an Iraqi bomb attack.

Persepolis 2 focuses in the first half on Marjane's stay in Austria and in the second half on her return to Tehran. In Europe Marjane develops a number of rebellious friendships, continuing struggles with teachers and authority figures, and experiences a period of homelessness. Back in Iran she is depressed and makes an unsuccessful suicide attempt. She finds that in her group in Tehran in the 1990s the young people lead defiant social lives, privately ignoring narrow religious authority, to party and drink behind walls. Marjane starts an unhappy marriage at twenty-one, divorces, and, at the conclusion of the story, leaves Iran to live in France because, as she explains, she "can't take" the restrictions on women any longer. While continuing the interesting narrative, *Persepolis 2* may not be as useful to students as the first text. (It does include drugs and sexual experimentation and some secondary teachers may be uncomfortable assigning it to all students.) There is also a third volume, *Embroideries*, set entirely in one scene in the Satrapi home sometime after *Persepolis 2*. After dinner with friends, the men go off into one room and the women into another. Since Marjane is an "experienced" divorcee the other, older women freely discuss past marriages and sexual experiences. An interesting and explicit read for college students, the text once again breaks stereotypes about Middle Eastern women as modest, reserved, or demure.

While *Persepolis I* does not center the viewpoint of the "average" working-class or rural Iranian citizen, it does include an important side story about the family's maid, Mehri, who apparently at the age of ten was "given" to the narrator's parents because her parents couldn't afford to feed her. Mehri lives in the family home, takes care of Marjane, and has no chance of an education. Even the ten-years-younger Marjane thinks she is "not very talented." After developing a crush on the boy neighbor, Mehri is told by Marjane's (supposedly Marxist-leaning) father that she can't marry the neighbor because "in this country you must stay within your own class" (37).

There are also any number of conservative, apparently conformist, female figures, including women protestors who support wearing the veil; the frightening female guardians who enforce dress codes in the streets; and women teachers who repeat the various orthodoxies of the regime. Written from Marjane's point of view, the autobiography has little or no sympathy with these women, likely of poor or working-class backgrounds. We learn from *Persepolis* about how boys from poor families are given "keys to paradise" and taken as cannon fodder in the war with Iraq. There are clearly many teachers, soldiers, and citizens who support the measures that appear repressive to Marjane, but the reader doesn't get a sense for much of anything potentially positive about the Islamic revolution, about the benefits it may have had for sectors of the population. The hints in the graphic novel about working-class people and those with other perspectives are intriguing, and could be used by teachers to open the door for students to explore a fuller range of Iranian and women's perspectives.

Two additional and wonderful resources for the classroom that enrich the picture of women in Iran after the revolution, and that would make a good match with *Persepolis*, are the film *Two Women* and the collection of ethnographic stories by Erica Friedl, *Women of Deh Koh: Lives in an Iranian Village*. *Two Women* (1999, 96 mins., age 16–college), by the leading Iranian female film director Tahimine Milani, was filmed entirely in Iran and addresses the experience of two architecture students during the early years of the Islamic Republic. Niki Karimi is the most famous and internationally acclaimed actress and filmmaker in Iran. She plays the role of Fereshteh, a brilliant student from a working-class family in Isfahan, a provincial city. Marila Zare'i plays Roya, a girl from a wealthy, urban family in the capital Tehran and Fereshteh's best friend. The contrast of their experiences is dramatic, as Fereshtah is stalked, pushed into marriage with a controlling husband, kept from finishing school, and trapped in her home, while Roya is able to pursue a career as an architect directing teams of men in the construction of major office buildings. The film is unsparing in its criticism of the treatment of women, of their inequality in the home and before the law. At the same time it shows the women as self-reflective, making careful choices, and working together to support each other.

> It was really interesting to see the relationship of Roya and Fereshteh develop and how the two women coped with different aspects of their culture … Fereshteh's marriage was anything but a fairytale. Her husband was controlling and manipulative. Fereshteh lost all respect for herself and found herself stuck at home with no means of communication. Her only hidden pleasure was her books that she had to keep from her husband … The movie ended with Fereshteh contemplating different scenarios for her life. But how was she going to manage? How was she going to live for

herself and for her children after being confined for so long? The movie left you wondering and that's what a truly liked about it.

(Chelsea Leatherman)

The film doesn't paint a simplistic portrait of Iranian men either. As another of my students Saralynn Bush notes,

> What I thought was most interesting was the different types of men portrayed in this film. There were … men who stop and stare at women in the middle of the road. Men who are stalkers. Men who stick up and defend women. Men who are traditional fathers. Men who are controlling husbands. Men who are distracted doctors who won't give women the time of day. Finally, there are quality, caring men such as Roya's husband who want the women in their lives to succeed.

While *Two Women* is a well-made film, students might be forewarned that it doesn't have production values or special effects of a Hollywood blockbuster and that it is in a foreign language (Farsi) with English subtitles. (I was surprised to learn that some of my small-town, Midwestern college students had never seen a film with subtitles before; they needed some help learning to read subtitles and watch the film at the same time.)

Erika Friedl's *Women of Deh Koh: Lives in an Iranian Village* (1991, 256 pages, age 16–college) offers a rich way to further extend the understanding of women in Iran after the revolution. Friedl is a German anthropologist and a former colleague of mine who spent 20 years off and on living in a small town in the mountains of Iran. The *New York Times Book Review* describes the book as "enthralling" convincing" and "remarkable,"

> A single brilliant description of a visit to "the city," seen as it were through the veil of a village woman, serves to emphasize the centrality of the community of families whose members, and whose mud houses and courtyards, are so intricately related to one another among the poplar-lined watercourses of the village.

(Glazebrook)

Teachers can chose to use these stories either individually or as a set. Taken together they remind us that most woman of the Middle East are undertaking the tasks of everyday life, providing for themselves and their families, often under the difficult conditions of developing nations. We see jealousies and rivalry between families, an intense social life among the women, as well as evolving social practices.

Examining together this graphic novel, film, and ethnographic short stories, we have discovered an enormous range in the representation of women's experience in one country at a particular historical moment, illustrating the importance of considering women in the context of the diversity of historical periods, cultures, societies, and nations of the region. The Iran of the 1980s depicted in these works is not the same as the Iran of the present day. While the country has achieved substantial economic and educational development and passed through several liberalizing movements and repressive backlashes, teachers and students will need to find ways to continually update their assessment.

Another text that would be interesting for students to complexify their understanding of women in the Middle East would be *Girls of Riyadh* by Rajaa Alsanea (2007, 304 pages, age 16–college). Tracing the life of four wealthy college-age women in conservative Saudi Arabia over six years, the book might be called an epistolary novel, since it is made up of a collection of email letters sent anonymously to a large circle of Saudi Arabian readers. The use of email, the informality of style, and the inside perspective on the hidden lives of these young women navigating school, college, and marriage will interest young people. Reviewers frequently describe the book as "Sex in the City" for Saudi Arabia. One element the work chronicles is how the changing technology and economy is rapidly evolving life, even in this most conservative country. Although women are not allowed to date, be alone with men, or be seen in public without full burqa covering them from head to toe, the young women in this book all visit modern shopping malls, access the Internet, use Instant Messenger, carry cell phones, and spend extensive time talking with prospective boy friends. This book caused a sensation when it was first published in Arabic in Saudi Arabia, and was initially banned, but now has led to an outpouring of literature by women from that country.

While the women have similar backgrounds and social situations, they take different approaches to trying to negotiate their strict society and the power of family obligations. The young men portrayed in the novel are disappointing. The men submit to family pressures and enter into arranged marriages that they have no interest in. Although they pressure girls for sex, if the young women succumb they lose interest. They are more attracted to younger, weaker, less educated women than strong, independent ones. In short, while the upper-class world of Saudi women is unique, readers will likely find elements they may identify with or find familiar from their own society.

The other end of the spectrum of literature addressing the experience of Middle Eastern women is the best-known feminist work from the region, the short novel *Woman at Point Zero* (1975, 108 pages, age 16–college). The novel was written by Nawal El Saadawi and translated into English in 1983. My student Kendra Matko describes the novel this way,

> The book opens with a confident, concerned woman psychologist and author trying to learn the story behind quiet, death row inmate Firdaus, a mysterious, ex-prostitute who killed her pimp and refuses to speak with anyone in or out of the prison. She at last agrees to speak to the woman psychologist/author, and slowly unravels her tragic life history . . . her turbulent childhood, abused and witnessing the abuse of her mother by her father, her female circumcision as a young woman, twisted molestation by her uncle, betrayal by lovers, and on to bitter exploitation by pimps, and last and possibly most ruthless—the persistent taunting of men, women, and law enforcement—as she struggles to live an adult life she has no tools for.

Firdaus' father is a *fellah*, a poor peasant farmer and the lowest social class in Egypt. Although Firdaus manages to obtain a secondary certificate and thus middle-class status, she finds herself in a cruel arranged marriage to an older man and is often beaten both by her husband and uncle. The author, Nawal El Saadawi, is a medical doctor who served as director of public health in Egypt and has written nine novels. In Egypt Saadawi is a controversial figure, and she and her husband were imprisoned for their political views by Anwar Sadat (Sadat is remembered more fondly in America than Egypt). *Woman at Point Zero* traces the darkest underside of women's oppression. My student Heather Winowiki describes it in this way,

> From a female perspective, there are a lot of things that hit close to home for me. In no way am I comparing my life and situations to Fidaus', but her pain and suffering at the hands of men is still something that can be seen splashed across the headlines of newspapers today. Women abused, battered, raped and prostituting themselves out as a profession is still common today in our own country. It made me angry, the further into the book that I went, not only at the men who abused

FIGURE 16.2 Turkish Basketball Player Nilay Yiğit

Copyright © 2010 by User:Jaripk / Wikimedia Commons / CC BY-SA 3.0

Firdaus, but at Firdaus herself for not fighting harder for respect and self dignity. The book was very powerful and I would recommend it to anyone looking for a book that shows the struggles of a woman in modern Middle East culture.

Linda Cross responds,

> I agree with you that Firdaus is so abused and used she can only see the bad in men. But in a situation where women are abused many don't understand that what is happening to them is abuse. The abusers make their victims feel they deserve what is happening and it's a very hard cycle to break free from. Many fear for their lives if they leave their abuser and for good reason too.

Woman at Point Zero is an important narrative but far from the only perspective on women from Egypt or Islam. I caution teachers to not use this as the *only* text their students read from the region. (For a dramatic contrast on perspectives on Egyptian women, *Woman of Egypt* (1987, 466 pages, age 16–college) by Jehan Sadat, Anwar Sadat's widow.)

Reading Middle Eastern texts carefully reveals complexities in the role of women that may alter the stereotypes students bring to the works. A case in point occurred when I was teaching the short and wonderful Egyptian novel, *Aunt Safiyya and the Monastary* (1996, 115 pages, age 13–college) by the male writer Bahaa' Taher. (So popular in Egypt that it was made into a TV soap opera!) The full text is available free online from the publisher University of California Press. Reading this novel my students were quick to see the oppression of women, and blame them for their situation. Many initially viewed the mother of the family as oppressing her daughters. Before class discussion Ashley Auberman wrote,

> The mother's relationship with her son, her daughters, Safiyya [an adopted daughter], and her husband was quite shocking. The fact that she openly favored her son over her daughters, and was even slightly abusive to her daughters when they did anything wrong, took me by surprise! I expected that the mother would have had sympathy toward her daughters, I guess like my own mother has toward me. Also, she favored Safiyya over her own daughters, because of her beauty and prospect of advancing the family's honor by a prosperous marriage.

During discussion, still wrestling with the role of the mother, Ashley herself brought up an interesting point. Was the mother's harshness toward her daughters part of ensuring that they will be successful in the village in which they live? Ashley wondered. There were other elements of the story that emerged during discussion. After one student pointed out that education was not encouraged in the village for the girls, another pointed to the father's insistence on his daughter's education—and argued that this broke his own stereotype of Arab fathers. At first students noticed that the mother submitted to the father's wishes regarding the daughter's education, then other students pointed out that the mother got her way in the case of Safiyya, so that the decision making in the family was actually more balanced than it at first appeared. Students were disturbed that Safiyya marries a much older man, but as they examined the text more closely they noticed that her parents, though they may have had objections, allowed Safiyya to make her own choice and supported what she wanted—especially after they learned that the man they thought she was going to marry endorsed the union. John Ebbing wrote, "An arranged marriage may seem unfair to me and you, but Egyptian fathers do not do this because they like to be cruel and torture their daughters; they do it out of love and because they want what is best for their families."

Students were also surprised to see that Safiyya, even as a young woman in her twenties, ends up having enormous power once her wealthy husband dies. As we further discussed the novel, and they wrote papers about it, my students began to see that the roles for women were not as limited as they initially thought, and they came to recognize how those roles are rapidly evolving in Egypt as new forms of communication and transportation link village and urban life. At the same time there is something attractive about even the traditional village.

> While reading *Aunt Safiyya and the Monastery*, you begin to realize that the customs of the Middle East are greatly valued and respected by the villagers. Everyone has a purpose in the village and everyone works together to achieve harmony. Their religion and their beliefs are their motivators. Everything they do is done with respect for their fellow neighbors and relatives. They treat each other like they would treat a close family member.
>
> *(Chelsea Leatherman)*

Aunt Safiyya also offers an interesting introduction to many other important themes, such as father–son relationships; respect and hospitality in Arabic society; class distinctions between villagers and land owners; relations between Egyptian Muslims and Coptic Christians; distinctions between Upper and Lower Egypt; issues of honorable brigandage and "outlaws" somewhat in the mold of Robin Hood; the vendetta system as a form of justice in a region without legitimate authority; the mobilization of Egyptians in the 1967 war with Israel; and so on.

The changes in women's experience in the Middle East are also a central theme in the novel *The Bastard of Istanbul* (2008, 368 pages, age 16–college), Elif Shafak's second novel in English. The best-selling female author in Turkey, Shafak has an MA and PhD in women's studies and international relations from Middle East Technical University in Ankara, one of the most prestigious universities in the region. *The Bastard of Istanbul* is told from the point of view of an American girl, Armanoush Tchakhmakhchian, with Armenian parents and a Turkish stepfather. She travels to Turkey to live with her stepfather's family in an effort to better understand her roots. The novel examines the intimate relations between Turks and Armenians before, during, and after the Armenian genocide. (Because the word "genocide" appears in the text, Shafak was charged in Turkey with "public denigration of Turkishness"—the charges were later dropped.) My students were fascinated with this story.

> I haven't read a book that was so difficult to set aside when my evil demon told me to get back into reality and the duties of everyday life, in a long time. Elif Shafak does beautiful work in telling an exciting story, providing cultural insight, making bold statements, and creating a need to learn more about two cultures that seem so distant, but in actuality aren't.
>
> (*Maria Benson*)

> *The Bastard of Istanbul* by Elif Shafak resonated deeply on many different levels. I found myself unable to put it down! The text weaves a scintillating tale, alternating between past and present narratives in order to ultimately divulge a horrific family secret.
>
> (*Megan Carlson*)

In addition to addressing the important topic of Armenian–Turkish relations, the novel presents a wonderful variety of women living in contemporary Turkey. There is: Banu, a devout head-scarf-wearing mystic with powerful abilities; Cevriye, an atheistic high school history teacher; Feride, who changes her hair color and style "at each stage of her journey to insanity," and is variously diagnosed as "depressive," "borderline," and "schizophrenic;" Zeliha who has a string of lovers, uses foul language, and runs a tattoo parlor for the *avant garde*, urban and secular Turks; and her daughter, Asya, a cigarette-smoking rebel, obsessed with Johnny Cash, who hangs out in a cafe with a group of alienated philosophy types. What's striking is that all these women are in the same family, live together under the same roof, and share their meals—so much for stereotypes of Turkish or Middle Eastern women!

One of the most memorable and helpful things I have done as I have taught Middle Eastern literature and addressed the experience of women, has been to invite women from the region to speak in my class. Students welcome visitors who can talk about their cultural background and answer questions. Of course, since there is no one experience, I have found it valuable to have panels of speakers when possible. My student Jennifer Wiley commented,

> I really enjoyed hearing from our guest speakers on Tuesday. To get a firsthand account from women who practice Islam and can understand the way that Islam is applied to woman and Middle Eastern society is a treat, and I particularly enjoyed hearing from two different women of varying ages, from different regions and with different methods of practicing Islam. I though that the presentation that was given to us was very useful in helping us to understand the place that women have in Islam and that, much like our ideals in Christianity, women are to be treated with respect and it is acknowledged that woman are created from men and are to be considered equals with them. I like how she made the distinction between what Islam says about female treatment

and what is actually practiced. There is a discrepancy there, but this is the kind of pattern that one would find in any society, under any religion. We tend to associate violence against women with a problem concerning Islam, but she made it clear to us that this was not the case; rather it is caused by a problem with society not obeying the laws of Islam. I found this presentation very helpful in understanding divisions between religious and societal standards in the Middle East.

Teachers should not feel awkward reaching out to invite speakers from the Middle East to their classes—my experience is that people welcome the opportunity.

The experience of women in the Middle East is an enormous topic and the focus of a corpus of teachable works translated into English. While I have addressed works from Iran, Egypt, and Turkey, there is no shortage of additional materials that may come to hand. As we teach about women in the Middle East, just as with the theme of justice, I believe it is important for students to break down categories of "us" and "them" and begin to see that while there is progress, there are also women the world over, including in Europe and America, who face challenges, discrimination, abuse, and even violence because of their gender. Women in the Middle East, like people everywhere, are focused on critical issues of obtaining education, employment, quality food and housing, and so on. There are progressive women working for change and equality and there are conservative movements seeking to restrict women's rights and freedoms. The recognition of this kind of commonality is important to help our students make personal connections with the experience of women in the Middle East that they encounter in literature and face-to-face.

Further Reading

The Last Chapter by Leila Abouzeid (1989) tells the story of a young woman high school student in Morocco who wonders if it is OK to be single.

Salwa Bakr's *The Wiles of Men and Other Stories* (1993)—Powerful short stories from Egypt focusing on the experience of women.

West of the Jordon by Laila Halaby (2003) portrays the coming to age of four young Arabic women in Jordan, Palestine, and the United States.

A Thousand Splendid Suns by Khaled Hosseini (2003), a powerful and disturbing novel that examines the experience of women in Afghanistan before and under the Taliban.

Zaat by Son'allah Ibrahim (2004). Zaat is the name of a typical middle-class Egyptian woman. The chapters alternate between her everyday life and the headlines of the Egyptian newspaper that she works for in the late 1980s and early 1990s.

Dreams of Trespass by Fatima Mernissi (1994), a well-known sociologist and feminist in Morocco. Her memoir of a childhood during the 1940s explores women growing up in a traditional Muslim household, crossing boundaries, and developing solidarity.

Daughter of Damascus by Siham Tergeman (1994) is a collection of nostalgic related stories about a young woman growing up in Syria.

17

Political Change in the Middle East

by Helen M. Rizzo

Democratization in the Middle East

There is a body of theory and research that examines impediments to the global trend of democratization, particularly in Islamic nations (Addi 1992; Butterworth 1992; Hadar 1994; Huntington 1991, 1993a, b; Kolakowski 1993; Lewis 1988, 2003; Miller 1994; Ooman 1994; Zartman 1992). Scholars disagree about whether or not Islam is compatible with democracy, and part of the controversy stems from their examination of different aspects of the issue. There are at least three components of the controversy that have been considered at the macro level: 1) principles and beliefs within Islam which influence the structure of political regimes (Gellner 1989; Huntington 1993; Kolakowski 1993; Lewis 1988, 2003; Lipset 1993), 2) the actual stability and instability of democratic systems in Islamic countries (Hadar 1994; Huntington 1993a, b; and Ooman 1994), and 3) the opposition of Islamists to both dictatorial and democratic regimes (Plattner 1993). Each of these elements—important parts of the more general controversy—focuses on the content of Islamic belief systems and the characteristics of regime structures, especially democratic ones.

A fourth important component of the controversy is phrased at the micro level. Briefly stated, it is: to what extent are the behaviors, attitudes and beliefs of citizens in Islamic countries compatible with a

Helen M. Rizzo, "Political Change in the Middle East," *Islam, Democracy, and the Status of Women*, pp. 1–24. Copyright © 2005 by Taylor & Francis Group LLC. Reprinted with permission.

democratic system of government or with elements of democracy? This issue reflects the importance of civic culture to processes of democratization. In particular, it calls attention to the fact that citizens' beliefs and behaviors are ingredients in the institution and/or the preservation of forms of government. Regarding democracy, citizen participation is a central component and how it is influenced by the civic culture is important.

On one side of the debate, Huntington (1991; 1993a, b), Kolakowski (1993), Lipset (1993; 1994) and Lewis (1988; 2003) argue for the incompatibility of Islam with democracy at both the macro and micro levels. Because Islam does not separate the secular (especially politics) from religion, it emphasizes obedience to authority and sacrificing individual desires for the good of the community, and it can lead to intolerance of other viewpoints. Thus the Muslim world lacks the core political values that facilitated democracy in the Western world—the rule of law and social pluralism, institutions of representative government such as elected parliaments, and protection of individual rights and civil liberties that prevent the state from abusing its power. This thesis, described as the "Clash of Civilizations" by Huntington in 1993, has become even more salient after the events of 9/11 with the debate intensifying over whether or not the Muslim world can be become democratic.

However on the other side of the debate, Esposito and Voll (1996), Inglehart and Norris (2003a, b), Norris and Inglehart (2002), Moaddel and Azadarmaki (2002), Tessler and Corstange (2002), Meyer, Ali and Locklear (1998), Meyer, Rizzo and Ali (2004; 2001; 1998) and Rizzo, Meyer and Ali (2002) question the incompatibility of Islam and democracy at both the macro and micro levels. Esposito and Voll (1996) point out that there are aspects of Islam doctrine that are very compatible with democratization. Islamic doctrine emphasizes both consultation and consensus in political leadership which is also part of the democratization and participation process (Nagel 1987). Furthermore, even though the Western model emphasizes competition, there are instances in Western democracies when consensus is used in the decision-making process and can allow for everyone to have a voice as long as voicing disagreement is part of the process, making democratization compatible with Islamic doctrine. Moreover, even with the absence of democratic regimes in much of the Muslim world, scholars using the World Values Survey (i.e. Inglehart, Norris, Tessler and Corstange, Moaddel and Azadarmaki for example) and those using a national survey of the Kuwaiti citizen population (Meyer, Rizzo and Ali 2004) have consistently found high support for both the ideals of democracy as the best form of government and high agreement that it can perform as a stable and effective political system among citizens who are highly religious in Muslim countries (i.e. Egypt, Jordan, Algeria, Morocco, Pakistan, Turkey, Bangladesh, Iran and Kuwait). Furthermore, Meyer, Ali and Locklear (1998) demonstrate the compatibility of some aspects of Islam with micro-level components of democratization, political participation, in their work on Kuwaiti citizens' political behaviors and attitudes. They found that Kuwaiti citizens who held orthodox Islamic beliefs tended to have high levels of political participation regardless of sect membership (Sunni versus Shia). Thus at the individual level of religious identity and culture, Islam does not seem to be a barrier to the democratization process.

However, another important aspect of democratization at the micro-level is support for extending citizenship rights to currently disenfranchised groups in society, particularly women. As the United Nations Human Development Programme's Arab Human Development Report (2002) observed, "no society can achieve the desired state of well-being and human development, or compete in a globalizing world, if half of its people remain marginalized and disempowered (as quoted in Inglehart and Norris 2003b: 65)." In the Middle East then, debates rage over whether or not women's empowerment and public participation are also compatible with Islamic values. Recently Ronald Inglehart and Pippa Norris (2003 a,b; 2002) revised Huntington's "clash of civilizations" thesis. They argue that the core clash between the Islamic world and the West is not over whether or not democracy is the best political system, but rather over issues concerning gender equality and sexual liberalization. Again using the World Values Survey, Norris and Inglehart found that citizens of Muslim societies are significantly less supportive of equal rights and opportunities for women and have significantly less permissive attitudes towards homosexuality, abortion and divorce than those living in Western, democratic countries. They argue that these issues are indicators of tolerance, trust, political activism, and support for individual autonomy, which are strongly correlated with democratic societies. They argue that support for gender equality and acceptance of homosexuality are key indicators of tolerance and personal freedom, which are closely associated with stable democratic regimes. Moreover, Inglehart, Norris and Welzel (2002) found that the positive correlation between support for gender equality and democracy was overwhelming (r=.82) for 55 of the countries in the World Values Survey. They conclude that since historically,

> … democratic institutions, by themselves, do not guarantee gender equality. But does it work the other way around: does rising emphasis on gender equality improve the chances that democratic institutions will emerge and flourish? The answer seems to be yes. In virtually every authoritarian society, a majority of the public believes that men make better political leaders than women; in virtually every stable democracy a clear majority of the public rejects this belief … (Inglehart, Norris and Welzel 2002: 329–330).

Therefore, the implication of their research is that until Muslim populations under authoritarian rule, especially women, believe that women and men are equal in all aspects of life, this will be the main cultural barrier (besides political, economic and social ones) to sustaining democratization in the Muslim world (Inglehart and Norris 2003 a, b; Norris and Inglehart 2002).

But there is also growing evidence that Islamic values can be very compatible with women's empowerment and participation in society. Among a general Muslim population, Rizzo, Meyer and Ali (2002) and Meyer, Rizzo and Ali (1998) found that Kuwaiti citizens who held orthodox Islamic beliefs tended to be very supportive of extending rights of citizenship to women. More importantly, women themselves in Iran, Egypt, Kuwait (secular, religious and Islamist) are using Islamic principles to justify women's equality, access to resources and participation in the public sphere in order to increase democratization (Afshar 1996; Hafez 2001; al-Mughni 2000; Tohidi 1994; Tohidi and Baynes 2001). The research here will build upon this previous work at the micro-level by investigating the effect of women's organizations and their interpretations of Islam on the political participation and attitudes toward extending citizenship rights of their members.

Another challenge to democratization in the Middle East was the Gulf War in 1990–1991. Kuwait, along with Iraq, Jordan, Saudi Arabia, Yemen and Egypt, was among the most affected by the changes brought on by the Gulf War. Despite variation from country to country, the whole Arab world was affected both economically and demographically by the war. Using conservative estimates, over five million were displaced intra or internationally and much of this mobility was involuntary. Among these, over 350,000 Palestinians moved from Kuwait mainly to Jordan, about 2 million Iraqi Kurds were displaced within Iraq, and about 1 million Yemenis were expelled from Saudi Arabia. These involuntary population movements did not expedite friendly relations between and within Arab nations. Further, national economies were also devastated. The rich Gulf countries of the Arab world were no longer as rich as before the war and the poor countries of this region (except Egypt) were even poorer. Therefore, both rich and poor nations' economies suffered; however, the gap between them remained (Faour 1993). All of this demographic and economic upheaval throughout the Arab world produced complicated social and political fallout.

Thus, the Gulf War brought issues surrounding democratization to the forefront. Some Western scholars, journalists and policy makers expected the Allies' victory to reinforce the international trend toward political liberalization and democratization in the Gulf region. Others predicted the opposite trend because of heightened security fears. The evidence regarding democratic transitions was mixed (Faour 1993). On the one hand, at the macro-level or regime level, there was little evidence of a significant movement towards polyarchy as defined by Dahl (1982); however, many Arab states implemented additional democratic measures and expanded constitutional rights. At the micro level, citizens appealed to their rulers for increased political representation and renewed their pre-war demands for liberalization, particularly in the Gulf. Western media also reinforced these demands for increased democratization, especially in the Gulf Coast countries-countries with universal media access. Whether or not citizens had an interest in democratization, the salience of democratization was increased for everyone after the Gulf War.

Thus in the years since the 1991 Gulf War, signs of increased democratization in the Middle East, such as holding competitive elections for national legislatures, have appeared in fifteen countries, (e.g., Tunisia, the Palestinian Authority). Yet other political rights, particularly for women, are limited. Although countries' constitutions were written using universal, gender neutral language guaranteeing all citizens certain rights, in practice this has not been the case. None of the fifteen countries gave women the right to vote at the same time as men, and in some countries women still do not have voting and other political rights of citizenship. In this research, I focused on Kuwait, a democratizing country representative of how citizenship rights, including political rights, have been gendered in the Middle East. Although Kuwait's constitution grants rights to all citizens, the law that spells out who can vote and seek political office in Kuwait begins with the phrase, "Each Kuwaiti man … "

Women's liberation and equality are intertwined with the democratization process in the Middle East and around the world (Inglehart and Norris 2003a,b, 2002; Norris and Inglehart 2002; Inglehart, Norris and Welzel 2002). "Both have in common a concern with emancipation, freedom (personal and civic), human rights, integrity, dignity, equality, autonomy, power-sharing, liberation [and] pluralism (Suryakusuma 1993)." In Kuwait, women lack certain formal political rights as stated above. This barrier to the democratization process has been recognized both inside and outside Kuwait. Kuwaiti voters writing to their local newspapers and outsiders, such as the U.S. State Department in a human rights report on Kuwait, see this lack of enfranchisement for women as a significant problem *(New York Times International,* Sept. 24, 1996: p. A3).

Gendered Citizenship

The notion of citizenship has been gendered from the beginning in the development of the modern nation-state in the Middle East. Often governmental institutions and political processes work under the assumption that the citizen is a man and women are dependent, second class members of the society. Citizenship rights and benefits for women are often tied to being the wife or daughter of a male citizen. For example, social welfare benefits are distributed to citizens based on labor force participation, thus making unemployed women dependent on employed men. Political benefits are often tied to family membership instead of to individuals as in Western, liberal democracies. Joseph (1996) argues that this situation exists because patriarchy integrates civil society, state, market and the family. Women's relationship to the state is negotiated through family membership; and their status as citizens, like children's, is dependent on their relationship to men.

However, there is variation in the rights and status of women across the Middle East, and the arena of the nation-state is key to these differential outcomes. It is here where women win or lose key legal and political protection from other political interest groups, patriarchies, and religious and nonreligious non-democratic groups. Furthermore, Kandiyoti (1991) argues that the state building process and the relationship between Islam and the state affects women's rights and political status through three avenues:

> 1) links between Islam and cultural nationalism; 2) processes of state consolidation and the modes of control states establish over local kin-based, religious and ethnic communities; and 3) international pressures that influence priorities and policies (10).

In terms of cultural nationalism, the process of developing modern nation states in the Middle East has forced these countries to deal with issues of citizenship and women's rights. Women were often given citizenship rights in order to consolidate and legitimate the state's power. However, even with equal citizenship rights guaranteed in constitutions (including Kuwait's), in practice men are given advantages in the areas of marriage, divorce, maintenance and inheritance laws, and political participation.

In terms of state consolidation, Middle Eastern governments have had to balance local interests (i.e. kinship and ethnic groups) with national interests, such as developing a civic society and consciousness, and enabling more sectors of the population to become involved in the economic development process (i.e. women). The attempts of states to gain control over and change local communities have had various outcomes in terms of government policies toward women and the family. In Tunisia, Morocco and Algeria, for example, Charrad (1990) argues that power differentials between the national governments and local groups during the struggles for independence resulted in significant differences in family law, with Tunisia embracing the most reform, Morocco keeping in line with established Islamic legislation until very recently and Algeria vacillating over the past thirty years since independence.

In terms of international pressures, several trends have influenced the rights and status of women in the Middle East. First, the division between the oil-rich and resource-poor countries has resulted in migration from poorer countries to the oil-rich Gulf, while outflows of cash and political influence from the Gulf to resource-poor nations strengthen Islamist movements in the latter. There have been varied responses within countries to these pressures, but often the response, in terms of women, has been greater control over their behavior and limitations of their rights. Second, international involvement in local economies increased dramatically as a result of privatization of economies and export-oriented development through structural adjustment packages implemented by the International Monetary Fund and investment in development projects by Western donor agencies. For women, these trends have resulted in a dramatic increase in labor force participation, especially in low-paid, informal and non-unionized sectors of the labor market. In addition, the Women-and-Development lobby of the United Nations has also put pressure on national governments to integrate women into development projects, to recognize women's role in the struggle against poverty, illiteracy, and high birth rates, and to end all forms of discrimination based on sex. Thus, as Kandiyoti (1991) has argued, the interplay between the state and various interests in the region has had diverse outcomes in terms of women's rights and status.

The Struggle for Women's Rights in the Middle East

As noted earlier, the scholarly literature on women's rights and participation in the Middle East has focused mainly on case studies of women activists in the following countries: Algeria, Egypt, Iran, Morocco, Tunisia, Turkey and the Palestinian Authority. Across the region, women are symbolic of national and cultural identity for both modernizing forces and anti-West, anti-imperialistic forces (Joseph 1996). Women activists have worked with and responded to multiple forces in their struggle for rights. The cases of the Palestinian Authority and Iran serve as examples of that struggle.

In the Palestinian Authority, women's political opportunities are shaped by a society that is trying to build a state that aims to show the world that it is a "modern" society. The state showcases women in leadership positions who were active participants in the first *Intifada* (Hasso 1998). The *Intifada,* (1987–1990), was an unarmed liberation movement that had to mobilize all sectors of society, including women, in order for it to be successful. Women were mobilized to participate in education and literacy classes, health care, vocational training, growing and canning food, running child care centers and the like. The experience empowered them, gave them the opportunity to network, and taught them skills that would be useful in the struggle for women's liberation.

In the early 1990s, an autonomous Palestinian women's movement appeared at the end of the *Intifada,* a low point of the national struggle. This movement, reflecting a diversity of experience and voices among Palestinian women, emerged out of the *Intifada* and favorable international conditions, such as the international women's movement. It was sustained through the 1990s by the large number of women's organizations, study centers, libraries, clinics, skills training centers and other organizations that direct their activities toward women. At the same time, the women's movement's struggle for women's rights and emancipation has been challenged by Islamic movements, such as Hamas, and by the PLO with its lack of recognition as yet for women's rights. The movement is caught between modernizing and traditional forces in the Palestinian Authority (Abdulhadi 1998).

In the Islamic state of Iran, women also challenge the state for their rights in a society that is forming an identity in opposition to Western imperialism. Moghadam (1995) classified the Iranian revolution as a "woman-in-the-family" model of revolution, which

> … excludes or marginalizes women from definitions and constructions of independence, liberation and liberty. It frequently constructs an ideological linkage between patriarchal values, nationalism, and the religious order. It assigns women the role of wife and mother, and associates women not only with family but with tradition, culture and religion (336).

More specifically, the revolutionary government stressed that men's and women's roles were separate and complementary. It emphasized the importance of women returning to the private sphere (even though they were never required to by law) and of sex segregation in public and the need for women (and men) to behave and dress modestly.

However, the revolution had the unexpected outcome of raising the nation's gender consciousness (Mir-Hosseini 1996) and increasing the politicization and empowerment of women who were involved in the revolutionary movement (Gerami 1994, 1996; Riesebrodt 1993). Moreover, the most successful group of women in countering the patriarchal nature of the Islamic Republic were those who participated in the movement, devout Muslim women from the elite and middle classes (Afshar 1996). According to Tohidi (1994: 139), women confronted the government using their status as "bearers and maintainers of cultural heritage and religious values", over its failure to deliver on its Islamic state obligations, which consequently marginalized women politically, legally and economically. Justifying their claims by using the teachings of Islam, Qu'ranic laws and the traditions and practices of the Prophet Muhammad, Islamic reformist women have made some changes in the areas of education, the labor market, child care, divorce and political participation (Mir-Hosseini 1993, 1996; Nakanishi 1998). As in the Palestinian Authority, the Iranian women's movement operates in a contested cultural and social context.

Women have also been involved on their own behalf in liberation and nationalist movements in Algeria and Tunisia, Islamic and feminist movements in Egypt, and in formal and informal organizations throughout the Middle East and North Africa. These groups, along with the international women's movement, have been successful in bringing gender to the center of the struggle for citizenship rights. In the research presented here, I examine the role of women's organizations in Kuwait in the struggle for women's political rights in the Gulf. The struggle became particularly salient when the nation's top political leader, the emir, through an edict in May 1999, granted women the right to vote and run for Parliament in 2003. But the directive was twice rejected by close votes in Parliament in November 1999. In addition, in July 2000 the Constitutional Court rejected four cases that challenged the constitutionality of the election law's ban on women's participation (Human Rights Watch 2001). As of 2004, the parliament is once again considering draft legislation that would give women the rights to vote and stand as candidates for Parliament. In the meantime, Kuwaiti women continue to lobby, oganize demonstrations, and they held mock parliamentary elections in 2003 to obtain formal political rights. The results of Kuwait's July 5, 2003 parliamentary elections potentially indicate further difficulties for the women's rights campaign. The liberals lost almost all of their seats in parliament to the Islamist revivalists. The *Associated Press* reported on July 6, 2003 that the liberals won only three seats, down from 14 seats in the previous parliament, while the Islamists gained for a total of 21 seats in the 50 member parliament. Both the *Associated Press* story and John Kifner's report for the *New York Times* on July 7, 2003 expressed pessimism for women obtaining political rights from the new parliament, since it was the losing liberals who had actively advocated women's voting rights as part of their parliamentary campaigns. However, the BBC reported on July 6, 2003 that its correspondent in Dubai, Julia Wheeler, believed that "despite the liberals' poor showing, their campaign for greater women's rights has more chance of success in the new parliament." She also reported that "many of the new Islamist MPs are predicted to be less opposed to women having political rights than outgoing colleagues." In order to understand the role of women's organizations in the battle for citizenship rights and increased democratization, I first discuss Kuwait's political and economic development and how that has affected civil society and women's status in Kuwait.

Political and Economic Development in Kuwait

As stated earlier, Kuwait has gone the furthest among the Gulf states in terms of democratization and the development of an extensive civil society. This occurred in spite of the fact that, as Crystal (1990; 1996) has argued, rentier states often have very weak democracies and civil societies. In the Gulf, oil revenues have allowed states and ruling families to weaken the power of existing social groups to attract citizen loyalty and prevent the creation of new opposition groups. In essence, oil wealth gave regimes the opportunity to buy citizen acquiescence through providing services, such as housing and health care, which other institutions may have once supplied or would have supplied if the oil wealth did not exist. Moreover, oil revenues have allowed states to weaken other social groups by either co-opting them as a whole or using the wealth to divide them by buying off key members. Thus, the Gulf States have used oil wealth to weaken civil society by co-opting avenues to citizens' political participation.

However, despite strong attempts by states to limit or eliminate organized groups and civil society, Islamist, human rights, tribal, technocratic and other independent groups are active in the Gulf and are making demands on governments. These groups have the greatest opportunity for political expression in the

Kuwait, considered among the freest of the Gulf States. The Kuwaiti government has come closest to the playing the role of referee, rule-maker and regulator of civil society that states in democratic societies play (Crystal 1996). Therefore, in order to understand Kuwait's present situation and the potential opportunities for women to open up the political process even more, the history of Kuwait's political and economic development will be examined.

Pre-Oil Political and Economic Development

Kuwait was founded in the early eighteenth century as a city-state. Legends about the creation of Kuwait emphasized the relative equality among the original elite families. Most Kuwaiti historians agree that the state and ruler-ship was formally established in the 1750s and that the Al-Sabah family became the ruling family through a voluntary consensus by the leading families about the division of economic and political responsibilities (Al-Ebraheem 1975; Rush 1987). While the Al-Sabah family achieved political preeminence through this compromise, the elite merchant families gained economic power through their control of Kuwait's economy, which was based on trade, ship-building, pearling, and fishing before the discovery of oil in the 1930s (Crystal 1990; al-Mughni 1993). Thus from the beginning governance in Kuwait was based on compromise and coalition-building, not extreme authoritarianism or brute force.

However, British involvement in Kuwait during the late nineteenth century shifted the balance of power between the merchants and the ruling family in favor of the ruling family, leading to subsequent protests by the merchant class. Because Kuwait's position in the Gulf was crucial for Britain's economic interests, Kuwait's emir established friendly ties in return for protection from the Ottoman Turks, who had attempted to invade Kuwait several times during this period. In 1904 Kuwait agreed to a treaty which promised British defense against foreign invasions, and Kuwait remained under this British protection until 1961.

This alliance with Britain weakened the merchants' political power. The emir rarely consulted the merchants and moved toward controlling a greater part of the wealth that Kuwait's trade and pearling industry had created. Because his military ambitions required significant funding, he implemented a series of taxes and price controls. In 1909, the merchants organized opposition to the emir's policies with the leading pearl buyers and traders by leaving Kuwait for Bahrain in protest. Realizing that the merchants' revenues were crucial to his rule, the emir retreated and made concessions to ensure their return.

This protest marked the beginning of a new era for the merchants. It represented both the last time they would use secession as a political strategy and the first of several instances in the twentieth century in which they would organize politically to oppose the leader of the ruling family. This was the first experiment in new political tactics for the merchant class. It was also the first time that the merchants gave an unambiguous statement of loyalty to Kuwait—they returned because they considered themselves Kuwaitis by birth and family tradition. The enduring legacy of this rebellion was a politically mobilized merchant class (Crystal 1990).

In the period between the two World Wars, the merchant class had become an increasingly powerful political force. It had become a homogeneous and united social and economic elite: urban, coming from prestigious Sunni families, linked by marriage, and achieving its wealth from trade, pearling and shipbuilding. Its political power, which stemmed from its economic and social power, was institutionalized in informal and semiformal access to the ruling family through marriage and the majlis (tribal councils). However, the interwar period was characterized by severe economic setbacks for the merchant class, such as the decline of the pearl industry due to the introduction of cultured pearls, the Saudi blockade of Kuwaiti exports, and the worldwide depression in the 1920s. When the ruler responded to this economic depression by implementing new taxes in the 1930s, the merchants felt even more strapped.

The Dawn of Oil

Then in 1938, oil was discovered in Kuwait. The revenues from oil sharpened divisions within the Sabah ruling family and between the emir and the merchant class. The members of the Sabah family wanted higher living allowances because of the oil revenue, and the emir gave into their demands. The merchants also demanded a voice in the distribution of the new revenue, but the ruler did not appease them. Instead he raised custom taxes.

The merchants' response was angry but politically organized. The merchants felt an historical entitlement to political power because of the ruling family's previous financial dependence on them, which led them to believe that they had a voice in how the new wealth would be distributed. Thus, they sought allies both within Kuwait (disgruntled members of the ruling family) and outside of the country (Britain and Iraq). Their political organization culminated in the Majlis Movement of 1938. This campaign began when a group of leading merchants secretly met and produced a list of demands announced by way of leaflets and through anti-government wall-writing. They also pressed for popular demands, such as improvements in basic social services—education, health care and development—and limits on corruption.

The movement achieved brief success with the emir's consent to an elected Legislative Assembly. However, the Assembly lasted only six months because 1) the merchants could not sustain the initial support of Iraq and Britain and 2) the merchants could not maintain a unified domestic opposition coalition, one that went beyond the urban, merchant elite. Even though the merchants' movement did not result in a lasting and formal access to political decision-making, it did leave two important legacies—one coalitional and the other institutional.

The coalitional legacy of the movement left the merchant class as a cohesive and politically organized community at a time when the historical economic base of its political power was about to be replaced by a new outside source of revenue for the ruling family: oil. It was crucial for the merchants to fight back politically, because after oil the rulers no longer depended on the merchants economically. It was the ruling family's memory of the merchants' opposition that convinced the emir to buy them out of politics rather than force them out. In the first years of oil, the merchants were the one group capable of sustained, organized and possibly successful opposition, as the ruling family soon realized.

The institutional legacy of this period was that the popular demands from the movement and the need for the ruler to expand his support, given the merchant opposition, led to a small growth in basic social services. By the early 1940s, 25 percent of customs duties were set aside for education, health and other programs.

Because of World War II, oil drilling was temporarily suspended until 1945. In 1946, Kuwait exported its first commercial shipment of crude oil, and by the 1950s oil revenues provided the ruling family with a steady income. During this period, the new wealth was used to modernize the country. The social infrastructure was developed by the building of schools, hospitals, and housing, and the establishment of water supply projects. A more comprehensive welfare state was also established with part of the oil revenues being redistributed to the Kuwaiti population through free social services such as health, education and other social allowances.

The Development of the Welfare State and Kuwaiti Citizenship

The emergence of the welfare state in Kuwait is crucial to understanding its current economic development and democratization, as well as women's status and rights. Crystal (1990) argues that the welfare state was the end result of the shifting alliances among the elite in Kuwaiti society. The revenues from oil made the ruling family financially independent from the merchant class, but the ruling family still feared their potential organized, political opposition. Thus the ruling family, instead of trying to force the merchant class out of the political arena, opted to buy them out. The merchant class withdrew from politics in exchange for guarantees of its economic position and promises of more wealth from the oil revenues. These guarantees from the ruling family included direct aid and de facto redistribution of wealth to the merchant class through land sale programs, protective economic legislation and merchant elite control of the private sector, especially the real estate market, construction and services. The merchant class was only interested in political power for its economic advantages, and since it could have economic benefits without direct political power, its members left politics without a fight. Oil revenues gave the ruling class the strength to force the merchants to choose between economic and political power. The merchants chose economic power.

The ruling family also sought new allies in order to secure its political independence from the merchant class. The ruling family created the welfare state largely to get support from the less affluent majority of the Kuwaiti population by providing comprehensive and free social programs and public employment for Kuwaiti citizens. For these services, the Kuwaitis were initially grateful, but it was unknown how long their appreciation and support for the ruling family (the state) would last. As early as 1955 the British Political Resident observed that "amongst all classes of Kuwaitis the idea is growing that while paying no taxes they are entitled to free or State-subsidized education, health, water, electricity, telephones and other services" (Crystal 1990: 79). In order to maintain support for the ruling family, the government perpetuated an aura of privilege around welfare state benefits by institutionalizing preferential treatment based on nationality through a series of citizenship laws in the 1950s. These gave Kuwaiti citizens exclusive or preferential access to state benefits and services. Other programs also strengthened this national awareness. At the government's urging, new housing areas segregated Kuwaitis and non-Kuwaitis in 1951. Public housing also segregated non-Kuwaitis. Because of the growing number of foreigners in Kuwait, preferential treatment based on nationality was becoming a privilege. By 1957, Kuwait's first census revealed that non-Kuwaitis made up almost forty-five percent of the population.

Large numbers of immigrants were coming to Kuwait due to the rapid growth of the economy after the discovery of oil. Kuwait's economic expansion led to labor shortages because the Kuwaiti population itself could not meet employment needs. There were several reasons for the shortage of labor among the Kuwaiti nationals. First, the small size and young age structure of the Kuwaiti population (the median age was fourteen in 1957) meant that only a limited number of Kuwaitis was available and old enough to work. This was exacerbated by the low labor force participation of women at that time, because of traditional norms. Second, the low educational and skill level of the Kuwaiti population meant that there were many new jobs in the growing economy for which Kuwaiti nationals were not qualified. Thus, Kuwait needed foreign workers for its economic development.

As the numbers of immigrants grew, the government enacted stricter nationality laws to perpetuate the preferential treatment of Kuwaitis. In 1948, two laws established the first legal basis for citizenship. Citizens of Kuwait now included only the ruling family members, those who had been permanently living in Kuwait since 1899, children of Kuwaiti men and children of Arab and/or Muslim fathers born in

Kuwait. Naturalization was possible after living ten years in Kuwait and by meeting work, Arabic language proficiency and "valuable services" requirements. The Nationality Law of 1959 changed some of the citizenship requirements, expanding the definition of "original" Kuwaiti to descendents of those who had lived in Kuwait since 1920 but restricting naturalization possibilities. A 1960 amendment allowed some naturalization after a long residency period (ten years for Arabs, fifteen years for non-Arabs starting with the year 1960) and limited naturalizations to only fifty per year. When in 1965 Kuwait nationals for the first time became a minority in their own country, subsequent amendments to this law passed in that year and in 1966 stated that Kuwaiti nationality could be given to Arabs who had lived in Kuwait since 1945 and to non-Arabs who had lived in Kuwait since 1930, in order to increase the size of the Kuwaiti citizenry (Alessa 1981; Crystal 1990; Ismael 1982; Russell 1989). Furthermore, the 1959 Labor Law also gave Kuwaiti citizens preferential treatment in hiring practices and the Civil Service Law of 1960 granted higher posts and pensions exclusively for Kuwaitis. Nationality now had some real economic benefits and gave the ruling family a way to co-opt any potential opposition among the Kuwaiti citizenry.

The end of British protection in 1961 spurred Kuwait's ruler, Sheikh Abdullah al-Salim, to appoint a Constituent Assembly to draft a national constitution, which was ratified on November 11, 1962. The constitution declared Kuwait a hereditary emirate and limited succession to the descendants of the late emir, Mubarak Al Sabah. The emir was also designated the head of state and commander of the armed forces. Legislative powers were to be shared by the emir and the National Assembly, which was to be elected every four years. However, the emir also had the power to adjourn the National Assembly (for no more than a month), or to dissolve it by decree. The constitution further institutionalized the welfare state by guaranteeing the right to education and employment (provided by the state) for all Kuwaiti citizens. It also guaranteed personal liberty, freedom of religion, and freedom of the press and association, but did not allow for political parties.

The Institutionalization of Voluntary Associations

Because the constitution banned political parties, voluntary associations filled the vacuum by providing an avenue for political expression and participation for Kuwaiti citizens. Ironically, these associations emerged in the 1950s during the period of rapid development and social change after the discovery of oil, and at the same time that the emir was trying to buy citizen loyalty through the services provided by the welfare state. The most important of these organizations—the Teachers' Club, the National Cultural Club and the Islamic Guidance Society—wanted Arab unity, national independence and a constitutional government. The Teachers' Club had been founded by young, educated merchant class men, who had a liberal but not radical nationalist ideology. The members sought a constitutional government, a more controlled national economy and they supported women's rights and liberation. The National Cultural Club, with a more diverse membership consisting of Arab expatriates and educated, young middle class Kuwaiti men, was more radical and socialist. Its members wanted the Kuwaiti government to give equal rights to Arab expatriates and a just redistribution of national wealth. Finally, the Islamic Guidance Society was heavily influenced by the Egyptian Muslim Brotherhood movement. In 1956, when the Brotherhood was suppressed in Egypt, many members came to Kuwait and joined the Islamic Guidance Society. The organization saw Arab nationalism and Islamic unity as very compatible, with the former as a necessary precondition for the latter. It called for Middle Eastern governments to work together to promote Islam, which it felt had been weakened by Western colonialism.

During the 1950s, these nationalist organizations led a series of demonstrations that eventually resulted in the emir banning both voluntary organizations and the press in 1959. In 1956, these organizations held protests against British involvement in the Suez crisis. The government had the police break up the crowds and arrest protesters, which led to public indignation. An explosion near the oil refineries at this time, which caused severe damage, resulted in the deportation of many Arab expatriates by the Kuwaiti government. Despite government threats of a crackdown on these organizations, Kuwaiti nationalists and Arab expatriates led a demonstration in 1959 in support of the first anniversary of the establishment of the United Arab Republic. The speeches called for Arab unity and criticized the authoritarian government of the ruling family, leading to harsh actions against the associations and press by the emir.

Upon Kuwait achieving independence from British protection in 1961, the government allowed voluntary associations to be reinstated. At the request of the government, the associations that were founded in the 1950s picked new names to distinguish themselves from the societies that had been banned before independence. The Islamic Guidance Society changed its name to the Social Reform Society, the National Cultural Club to the Independence Club and the Teachers' Club to the Society of Kuwaiti Teachers. The government instituted changes that placed the associations further under its direct control and attempted to depoliticize them, due to the political demonstrations these associations had organized and the growing political power of the Arab expatriates in the 1950s. In 1962, the government passed legislation that limited the activities of associations to 'social welfare purposes' and forbade non-Kuwaitis from holding leadership positions in these organizations. Thereafter, voluntary associations were not allowed to engage in any kind of political or religious activity that could 'endanger the stability of the state.' In addition, the Ministry of Social Affairs and Labour took control of the voluntary associations. Associations could only be established by Kuwaiti nationals and had to be registered with the Ministry. The Ministry gained the power to deny an association a license, to disband an association if it was not providing benefits to society as a whole, or not following its constitution, and the Ministry became the main source of funding for these organizations.

Despite increasing government regulation, voluntary associations continued to play an active role in Kuwaiti politics, especially with the establishment of the Parliament. The 1960s and 1970s saw the Kuwaiti nationalists use voluntary associations to gain popular support and act in opposition to the government both inside and outside of Parliament. Between 1963 and 1976, the Kuwaiti nationalists established many associations including the National Union of Kuwaiti Students, the Graduates Society, the Teachers Society, the Lawyers Society and the General Union of Kuwaiti workers, in addition to the Independence Club. The nationalists' demands included: political unity with other Arab governments, independence from foreign rule, the liberation of Palestine, nationalization of the oil industry, better employment, women's suffrage, the right to unionize and establish political parties, freedom of the press and more rights for Arab expatriates. Their political opposition challenged and thus threatened the stability of the Kuwaiti government.

In response to this growing and vocal opposition, the government passed legislation in 1965 (with the help of 16 appointed government ministers who had voting rights in Parliament) that further restricted the freedom of association and the right of organizations to be involved in politics. As a result eight of the 50 members of Parliament resigned in protest. After the second election for Parliament in 1967, many of the associations charged that the government had manipulated voting results, and several of the successful candidates for Parliament resigned in protest. The government was able to counteract the opposition of the associations and members of Parliament through the social welfare policies and political and bureaucratic appointments that co-opted large proportions of Kuwaiti society.

The Decline of Arab Nationalist Associations and the Rise of Islamist Groups

Arab nationalism and its associated associations in Kuwait also suffered setbacks with the 1967 Arab-Israeli war. The loss hurt the legitimacy of the Arab nationalist ideology and it divided the movement in Kuwait and throughout the Arab world until 1981. In Kuwait, the nationalist associations were significantly weakened as a voice of opposition. However, the oil boom of the 1970s and the perceived Arab victory in the 1973 Arab-Israeli war strengthened both the confidence of the Arab states and the nationalist opposition in Kuwait. During this time, the nationalists gained new allies in Parliament and again opposed the government on many issues. With the increasing criticism by the Parliament and the outbreak of civil war in Lebanon in 1975 the government dissolved the Parliament for the first time since independence in response to this instability both at home and throughout the region. The government also suspended several articles of the constitution and limited freedom of the press. In response to protests by students, teachers and workers angered over the dissolution of Parliament, the government took over their organizations' elected boards and replaced them with state-approved appointees. Union members were arrested and the Independence Club, which was the center of political opposition and debate at that time, was banned. Ghabra (1991) argues that the associations' role of public opposition to the regime was dramatically weakened when Parliament was dissolved.

In order to suppress the Arab nationalists and to defend itself against the critics of its decision to disband the Parliament in 1976, the government sought allies within the passive, nonradical, nonpolitical Islamic forces in Kuwait. Because the Social Reform Society (heavily influenced by the Muslim Brotherhood) had not criticized the government for disbanding Parliament, the government rewarded the Society by appointing its chairperson as minister of religious endowments. With its new relationship with the government, the Social Reform Society was well positioned to fill in the political vacuum left by the weak and divided nationalist and secular associations (Ghabra 1991). As a result, the Social Reform Society and the Muslim Brotherhood grew in membership and popularity during the 1970s. By 1977 Islamists controlled student activity at Kuwait University and in 1979 the Brotherhood defeated the nationalist groups in the election for the Student Union.

The Islamic revivalists became increasingly politicized and powerful in Kuwait after the 1979 Iranian Revolution. They were no longer passive organizations. The Social Reform Society joined the secular nationalist opposition in protesting a rewriting of the Kuwaiti constitution which would have restricted the Parliament's power. Their campaign was a success, and the government gave in to public demands and decided not to change the constitution in 1980. Moreover, the Islamists and the Social Reform Society were very successful in the 1981 parliamentary elections, the first one to be held after Parliament was dissolved in 1976. The secularists lost key seats to the Muslim Brotherhood, and other Islamist groups also gained strength in Parliament. As a result, the Social Reform Society became the most important Islamic organization in the Gulf.

Also during this Islamic revival of the 1970s and 1980s, a more extreme and less tolerant ideology emerged that rejected any conduct that did not follow strict Islamic principles. The Salafiya movement sought to return to the roots of Islam by emulating the Prophet Muhammad's behavior as spelled out in the hadith and codified in the Shari'a, and interpreted the Qu'ran literally without any regard for modern contexts. In 1981, followers of this movement established the Islamic Heritage Society. Though always more marginal than the Social Reform Society, this association grew in popularity during the 1980s and became increasingly involved in politics. Conflict developed between the more conservative and traditional

Islamic Heritage Society, which tended to support government policies, and the more flexible and critical Social Reform Society.

The Cultural and Social Society, whose membership included a large proportion of the Shia community (who make up 20 to 30 percent of Kuwait's citizens), also became politicized during the 1980s as a result of the pan-Islamic ideology emerging from the Iranian Revolution. Shia Muslims established this society in 1968 and over time it became more Islamic and more important to the Shia community, especially after the Iranian Revolution. It provided many religious, educational and social activities as well as serving as an instrument for political mobilization. For example, it supported Shia candidates for Parliament and voiced concern over the discrimination they faced as a minority group in Kuwaiti society and politics.

During the period of the late 1970s to the mid 1980s, the Islamists, led by the Social Reform Society, also overtook the secular and nationalist forces by dominating Kuwaiti social and political institutions, including labors unions, food cooperatives (supermarkets), and some voluntary associations. By 1979, their power seemed almost invincible, while the nationalist secular forces lost their traditional power bases. In many of the associations, every election after 1979 saw the Islamists attempt to take control. The Social Reform Society, the Islamic Heritage Society and the (Shia) Cultural and Social Society often worked together to take control of the country's social and political institutions.

Suspension of Democracy and the Iraqi Invasion

The popularity of the Islamic movement waned by the mid 1980s because it organized itself ineffectively and failed to provide solutions to many of the social and political problems that Kuwaiti citizens faced. The secular nationalists themselves took stock of their strategies and decided to emphasize Islamic political and cultural values in order to survive. As a result, they were able to maintain leadership in several key associations, like the Graduates Society (which represented the democratic, secular and pan-Arab nationalist middle class) and regain positions of power, especially in the labor unions. Moreover, the government grew leery of the Islamists' growing power and sought to gain control of these groups throughout the 1980s. In the 1985 parliamentary elections the government supported the secular progressives in an attempt to counteract the popularity of the Islamists. The success of the secular nationalists in these elections demonstrated that these groups were still strong among voters and their resurgence surprised both the political elite and Islamic groups.

The government dissolved the Parliament again in 1986 because of growing instability caused by the Iraq-Iran War, the stalemate between the government and parliament over almost all government policy, and the increasing militancy of some Kuwaiti Shias. Unlike 1976, the government did not dissolve the associations' boards, but appointed a censor to monitor every newspaper and publication for the first time since independence.

The new crisis resulted in cooperation and tolerance between the Islamic and nationalist groups (Hicks and al-Najjar 1995; Ghabra 1991). Both sides recognized that restrictions on democracy hindered the process of nation building and development. To rectify this situation, these groups worked together to spur public debate and demand the restoration of the constitution and Parliament. The groups gathered 30,000 signatures on a petition supporting democracy and a return to the 1962 constitution in the fall of 1988. Beginning in December 1989, a series of public meetings (diwaniyya) was held every Monday with several thousand citizens demanding that the Parliament be restored. The government made several arrests in order to discourage the meetings, but they continued to draw thousands of people and some became silent sit-ins.

As a result, the government became willing to make some concessions, though it did not restore Parliament. Instead, the government proposed that an interim national assembly (Majlis al-Watani) with limited powers review the previous parliamentary experience. In June 1990, a divided Kuwaiti citizenry elected members to the Majlis al-Watani.

This crisis represented one of the most severe Kuwait had faced in its short history, because it shook the foundations of Kuwaiti society and politics. The commercial class, which normally sided with the government, supported the democratic movement and opposed the interim assembly. In addition, the ruling Sabah family alienated the opposition, intellectuals, and merchants by relying on the rural Bedouin population to support the Majlis al-Watani. Finally, the government antagonized the Shia community by banning the Cultural and Social Society in the fall of 1989 after some of its members were implicated in the planting of bombs in Saudi Arabia during the hajj.

Thus before the Iraqi invasion on August 2, 1990, the nationalist and religious groups provided a forum for open and popular political dissent and debate. Recognizing that their survival depended on their successful cooperation and use of appropriate tactics, the opposition discarded the ideological disagreements that divided them in order to form more pragmatic coalitions. As a result, a new political consciousness emerged among Kuwaitis which included a belief in pluralism and the equal rights of all groups to exist and campaign through nonviolent methods of participation.

Without the parliament and a free press to express debate, dissent and/or support for government policies, Hicks and al-Najjar (1995) and Ghabra (1991) argue that the absence of the parliament and a free press to express dissent or support for government policies led Saddam Hussein to make the huge miscalculation that the Iraqi invasion would be welcomed by Kuwaiti citizens. Ghabra (1991) suspected that Saddam Hussein thought he could use the apparent divisions among Kuwaiti people to his advantage, while Hicks and al-Najjar (1995) argue that without reliable information coming out of Kuwait about the will of the people, Saddam Hussein underestimated the popularity of the ruling family and the strength of Kuwaiti identity among its citizens. The leaders of the resistance movement during the Iraqi occupation were the very groups that comprised the opposition to the Kuwaiti government and had demanded democratic reform: members of the Islamic and nationalist movements in Parliament and their voluntary associations. Furthermore, the citizens that had been the most politically marginalized since the dissolution of Parliament in 1986—the opposition, the Shias and the commercial class—ended up being the most loyal supporters of Kuwait's sovereignty and the emir as its legitimate ruler, even willing to fight and die for it during this time of crisis.

At the Jidda Conference held in Saudi Arabia on October 13–15, 1990, members of the ruling family and the Kuwaiti political elite recognized the need for a freely elected National Assembly (Parliament) and a well-developed civil society. The conference was attended by all sectors of Kuwaiti political groups including the opposition, former parliamentarians and government leaders. The government conceded that constitutional government would have aided in the prevention of the Iraqi invasion and was necessary for the continued legitimacy of its regime. Therefore, both Emir Jabir al-Ahmad and Crown Prince Saad al-Abdallah committed the government to holding elections once the occupation ended, and to restoring the democratic process, the Kuwaiti constitution, and the National Assembly. Thus the opposition, former parliamentarians, and its associations were able to use the crisis to gain more political rights and democratization in Kuwait once the Iraqis withdrew.

Democracy in Post-War Kuwait

In post-war Kuwait, the Parliament has been restored and elections have been held regularly since 1992. The 1992 election was marked by strong campaigning and open critiques of the government. As a result, 35 candidates who had run against government-supported candidates won, and six out of sixteen ministers were appointed from the elected members of Parliament. As predicted by Ghabra in 1991, the ruling family has to govern with the parliament taking a more dominant role and with government supporters in the minority. However, since the crisis the Parliament and the ruling family have been more willing to work together. After the 1992 elections, the speaker of the Parliament regularly met with the emir, whereas in 1985 this same speaker rarely did so. Also, for the first time in Kuwaiti history, there was an official joint committee consisting of both members of Parliament and the Council of Ministers to promote coopera-tion between the two bodies of government. Thus, it seems that the spirit of pluralism continued with different political groups recognizing that all of their demands could not be met immediately and that the constitutionally established branches of government, such as the National Assembly and the office of Emir, were necessary. Moreover, it seemed that Kuwait was moving towards a real parliamentary system where all parties agree to the rules of the democratic game; it had moved beyond the zero-sum politics of the late 1980s (Hicks and al-Najjar 1995).

Challenges to Democratization in Post-War Kuwait

There are still challenges to the democratic process in post-war Kuwait. The government wields a great deal of power due to its control over oil revenues, social welfare programs and political appointments, as well as its ability to rule by exploiting the divisions within the opposition: competing clan and family loyalties, secularists versus Islamists, Sunnis versus Shias, and even between different factions of the Sunni Islamists. For example, two contentious issues at the heart of the democratization process in Kuwait—expanding rights of citizenship to women and the stateless—have divided the opposition and citizen population alike. More specifically, there are divisions among Sunni and Shia citizens over women's political rights, with Sunnis who follow the Egyptian school of thought and Shias who follow the Iranian school of thought supporting women's rights, while Sunnis who follow the Saudi Arabian school of thought and Shias who follow the Iraqi school of thought opposing women obtaining political rights (Meyer, Rizzo and Ali 1998). Other divisions among Sunnis and Shias include the following: 1) Shia Islamists are in favor of women's political rights, while Sunni Islamists are opposed, 2) Sunni members of voluntary organizations support women's rights, while Shia members do not, and 3) Shias who supported Kuwait's Gulf War allies favor women's rights, while Sunnis who supported Kuwait's allies do not (Rizzo, Meyer and Ali 2002). Finally, the plight and security of the stateless population in Kuwait has brought the Shias, second class citizens, nonurban residents and Arab nationalists together in favor of the stateless gaining a more secure position in Kuwait, while the more privileged first class citizens, urban residents and Sunnis are against the state-less gaining citizenship rights (Rizzo, Meyer and Ali 2004). Thus, as the democratization and economic development processes continue in Kuwait, the issue of who should have access to the welfare state and rights of citizenship is being contested.

Since the focus of this research is the role of women in the democratization process and their lack of formal access to the political system, I need to elaborate on women's status in Kuwait. Social and economic development has been a contradictory process that both enhances and diminishes women's status. The result of this process is a disjuncture in women's status, which is especially acute in Kuwait. "Kuwaiti women occupy a contested space in the Kuwaiti political economy" (Tetreault 1995: 38). While many Kuwaiti women have university degrees and have demonstrated their abilities, women are still denied political rights and full citizenship status and have an uncertain position in the labor force. The importance of examining women's status multi-dimensionally in order to capture this contradictory effect of development was demonstrated in my previous work, *The Distribution of Wealth, Investment in Social Programs and the Status of Women in the World System* (1995).

I found that at the cross-national level, modernization has positive effects on women's health and education but economic development has negative effects on women's access to employment. Therefore, I expect on the national level modernization should have positive effects on women's education and health. However, I would argue that it is not only modernization through industrialization which improves women's status through increased access to education, modern medicine and decreased fertility, as modernization theorists, such as Alonso (1980), Deane (1979), Kerr et al. (1960) and Rostow (1960) would argue, but also it is modernization through the redistribution of Kuwait's oil and overseas investment wealth by means of the welfare state which has resulted in mass education and a modern health care system, free to all citizens, that has improved women's education and health.

Since women's employment is still a contested area in Kuwaiti society, I would also argue that there are contradictory processes that are affecting women's employment. First, since Kuwait has been incorporated into the world capitalist system as a supplier of a much valued commodity to industrialized nations, oil, it has not fit neatly into the predictions of both traditional modernization and dependency theories—it is a very wealthy and modernized nation in terms of consumption and its welfare state, but with an extreme dependency on oil wealth from the international market for this development. Using the New International Division of Labor perspective, Moghadam (1993) has found that the type of development in oil-rich Arab nations does not facilitate increased female labor force participation because oil-extraction is a capital-intensive process. Arab countries that have developed using export-led, labor intensive industrialization have seen the fastest rates of increased female labor force participation in the developing world. Thus Kuwait's type of economic development does not seem to facilitate women's labor force participation.

However, about thirty percent of Kuwait's working age women do participate in the labor force. Most women are employed by the public sector, in female-dominated occupations such as nursing and teaching. I argue Kuwait's welfare state that guarantees jobs for all citizens that has facilitated this.

In Kuwait, women face a severe disjuncture in status that they do not face in Western nations. They do have access to education, health, and employment, but Kuwait's modernization has not resulted in women having formal rights to participate in politics, such as the right to vote and run for public office, in contrast to industrialized nations where women possess political rights. Thus the inconsistency in status, as will be discussed in the next chapter, has been an impetus for some women to become involved in organizations of civil society. It has implications for women's political participation and attitudes toward gaining rights.

CPSIA information can be obtained
at www.ICGtesting.com
Printed in the USA
LVHW101947110821
695097LV00004B/22